The United States
and the
Second World War

The United States and the Second World War

New Perspectives on Diplomacy, War, and the Home Front

. . . .

Edited by

G. KURT PIEHLER AND SIDNEY PASH

FORDHAM UNIVERSITY PRESS

New York   2010

Copyright © 2010 Fordham University Press

Library of Congress Cataloging-in-Publication Data
The United States and the Second World War : new perspectives
on diplomacy, war, and the home front / edited by G. Kurt
Piehler and Sidney Pash.—1st ed.
    p.   cm.—(World War II : the global, human, and ethical
dimension)
Includes bibliographical references and index.
ISBN 978–0-8232–3120–1 (cloth : alk. paper)
1. World War, 1939–1945—United States.   2. World War,
1939–1945—Participation, American.   3. World War,
1939–1945—Diplomatic history.   4. World War,
1939–1945—Social aspects—United States.   5. United
States—Foreign relations—1933–1945.   6. United
States—Social conditions—1933–1945.   I. Piehler, G.
Kurt.   II. Pash, Sidney.
    D769.U495 2010
    940.53'73—dc22
    2009014588

Printed in the United States of America
12 11 10   5 4 3 2 1
First edition

For John Whiteclay Chambers II
Scholar, Teacher, Mentor, Colleague, and Friend

CONTENTS

PREFACE

This anthology honors John Whiteclay Chambers II—my dissertation advisor, mentor, colleague, and friend. In conceiving this volume as series editor, I sought to pay tribute to John's distinguished record of scholarship and teaching, as well as his support in launching Fordham University Press's "World War II: The Global, Human, and Ethical Dimension" series. John has served on the advisory board since the series was formally announced in 2000, and over the past several years, has offered wise counsel and guidance.

This volume bears the imprint of John's ideas and his impact on the writing and teaching of history. Although this volume is not conceived as a narrow *festschrift*, all the contributors who participated in the volume have some relationship or connection with John; some were his students, and others have been longstanding colleagues. These essays cover a diverse range of themes related to the Second World War and are characteristic of John's intellectual interests. No easy labels apply to John's scholarship: He is a historian of war but also of peace. John has served as both president of the Peace History Society as well as nominee for the presidency of the Society for Military History. He has written on a diverse range of subjects, including conscription during World War I, the role of the peace movement in American foreign policy, conscientious objection to military service, the Progressive era, the ex-presidency, the Office of Strategic Services, and war and film. A prolific scholar, he has contributed works in multiple genres, authoring monographs, official histories, scholarly articles, edited anthologies, a textbook, and a major reference work, *The Oxford Companion to American Military History*. He has received several distinguished scholarly awards, including the Distinguished Book Award in 1988 from the Society of Military History for *To Raise an Army: The Draft Comes to Modern America*.

John is a proponent of peace, but he also understands the military mind. Although no scholar can be completely bias free, John brings both great passion as well as vitally important scholarly detachment when writing about issues of war and peace. The present volume reflects this interest, with essays examining such diverse topics as conscientious objection in World War II, commemoration of the atomic bombing of Hiroshima, the operational history of D-Day from the perspective of the U.S. Navy and U.S. Coast Guard, and wartime planning for the postwar reconstruction of Japan. This volume speaks to scholars interested in traditional guns-and-bugles military history, in peace history, and in understanding the impact of the war on American society.

As director of the Rutgers Center for Historical Analysis (1993–1995), John brought together scholars from diverse disciplines to consider the themes of war, peace, and society. During his tenure, John not only attracted such talented scholars as Stephen Ambrose, Ronald Spector, and J. M. Winter to take up residence as senior postdoctoral fellows, but he also organized several international conferences, including one on war and film that evolved into his anthology *World War II, Film, and History*. While directing the Center, John was instrumental in creating the Rutgers Oral History Archives of World War II in the fall of 1993. He organized a pivotal meeting between Ambrose (at the time in residence at the Rutgers Center for Historical Analysis), Rudolph Bell (History Department chair at the time), and Tom Kindre of the Rutgers College class of 1942. Out of this meeting emerged the idea of creating an oral history archive to document the Second World War. I became the founding director, and I easily enlisted John to serve on the scholarly advisory committee for this endeavor. Throughout my time as archives director, I could always count on John's wise advice and support. The Rutgers Oral History Archives has thrived under the leadership of my successor, Sandra Stewart Holyoak, and this continuing success is due in no small measure to John's continued involvement.

My relationship with John dates back many years. I first met him when I was a young graduate student in spring 1984 and he taught an entry-level historiography course on modern U.S. history at Rutgers. In fall 1986, I became John's teaching assistant for his trademark course, "War, Peace and the Military in U.S. History." Immediately, I was struck by John's incredible enthusiasm and skill as an undergraduate lecturer, especially by the emphasis he placed on fairness to students. Despite his other responsibilities, he always reviewed my grading. Even in that first year of assisting him, our relationship quickly blossomed; I was a graduate student who gained a trusted and supportive advisor. We often walked back from the classroom and chatted about a range of topics. I still vividly remember John's disappointment the day I decided to go to the library instead of following him to his office.

When I first worked as his teaching assistant, I had no idea that he was a Quaker. In retrospect, the only hint was his enthusiasm for the career of the lapsed Quaker, General Nathanael Greene of the American Revolution. One day years later, over dinner, John talked about his own early life and especially his youthful rebellion. How does a Quaker rebel? He asks to go to military school, whereupon John found himself at Valley Forge Military Academy, where he quickly realized he had made a big mistake and drifted to the school newspaper for sanctuary. This experience of working at the school newspaper at military college proved crucial. Before becoming a historian, he earned his stripes as a print—and later, television—journalist in the San Francisco Bay Area. John fondly recalls his experience as a television writer/producer for KRON (the local NBC affiliate) covering the Free Speech movement at Berkeley, as well as the tense atmosphere during the Cuban Missile Crisis.

This anthology also exemplifies John's involvement in promoting scholarly dialogue and exchanges between American historians in the United States and Japan. In 1997, John was selected by the Organization of American Historians (OAH) and the Japanese Association of American Studies (JAAS) to lecture for two weeks at the University of Tokyo as part of the "Short Term Residency Program." This visit to Tokyo led to John's networking with a host of Japanese historians and graduate students, many of whom came to Rutgers either to visit or to attend graduate school. John also became chair for three years of the joint OAH/JAAS Historians' Collaborative Committee that sought funding to continue to promote scholarly exchanges between American scholars and their Japanese counterparts. In 2004, I had the good fortune to lecture at Kobe University in this program, and my doing so sparked an interest in Japanese culture and society that led me to become a Fulbright Lecturer in American Studies at Kobe and Kyoto universities.

John has received numerous awards and honors for teaching as well as for scholarship. He received outstanding teacher awards from both Barnard College, where he began his academic career, and from Rutgers. As a professional scholar, John has stressed the need for historians to communicate their knowledge not only to the academy but also to policymakers and to the general public. Accordingly, John has undertaken such diverse tasks as overseeing the research for a major Public Broadcasting Service (PBS) documentary, served as a historical consultant to the House of Representatives Judiciary Committee during the hearings into the impeachment of President Richard M. Nixon, participated in countless seminars for high school teachers, and organized a statewide program of public lectures on the theme of war, peace, and society funded by the National Endowment for the Humanities. Collaborating with Arlene Gardner, John developed an innovative program to integrate peace education into the high school curriculum.

Finally, anyone who knows John would be remiss in failing to acknowledge his generosity of spirit in both large and small ways. To graduate students, John can be counted on not only to offer critical and careful readings of their dissertations, but also to send them supportive notes and e-mail messages as they make their way in the academic world. Few friends have been as thoughtful and dependable as John. It is with great pleasure that I dedicate this volume to "Docktorvater" John Whiteclay Chambers II.

G. Kurt Piehler
Series Editor
World War II: The Global, Ethical, and Human Dimension
Kobe, Japan
July 30, 2008

The United States
and the
Second World War

INTRODUCTION

Sidney Pash

John Chambers' wide-ranging scholarship, which includes studies of the Progressive era, the peace movement, United States foreign relations, conscientious objectors, the Army Corps of Engineers, the draft—and, most recently, the Office of Strategic Services—has attracted a diverse set of students and admirers. This volume, focusing on the Second World War, brings together essays from many of those whom John has mentored and befriended over the years. To varying degrees, each contributor's interests—and, therefore, the work that follows—have been shaped by our relationship with John Chambers and by our study of his eclectic, approachable, and penetrating scholarship.

Just as John's interests have shaped the content of this work, this anthology reflects, in another far more important way, his imprint on the authors. I hope that we have brought some of John's passion for history to this collection. I hope that John's interest in the mighty and the meek, in the warrior and the peacemaker, is also apparent in our work. I hope that our study sheds additional light on the story of World War II, while telling the equally important stories of how America became a part of the global struggle, how the country shaped its outcome, and in turn how the war reshaped the nation. Finally, I hope that we have done what John so often did and continues to do. I hope that we have, to paraphrase William Appleman Williams, written history that allows us to see our nation as it was and how we wish it could have been.

The first two essays in this volume examine the origins of the Second World War, a topic that John has taught to a generation of Rutgers students. Although many know John primarily for his work in military history, both *The Eagle and the Dove*[1] and *Tyranny of Change*[2] offer detailed studies of United States foreign relations during the Progressive era. In "Roosevelt at the Rubicon: The Great Convoy Debate of 1941," J. Garry

Clifford and Robert H. Ferrell capture John's long-standing interest in American foreign relations, taking readers back to the dark days of 1941 when the fates of England—and, by extension, of the United States—hung in the balance. Combining the personal insights on President Franklin D. Roosevelt's diplomacy, found in works such as Warren Kimball's *The Juggler*[3] and in the compelling narrative on the approach of war best seen in Waldo Heinrichs' *Threshold of War*,[4] "Roosevelt at the Rubicon" focuses on the critical issue of the U.S. Navy's convoying of merchant ships across the Atlantic during 1941. Clifford and Ferrell examine how lukewarm public opinion, Congressional opposition, incomplete rearmament, and the pressing needs of other theaters led Roosevelt to dissemble and delay rather than address the convoy question. Their study offers a particularly penetrating re-examination of Roosevelt's legacy of bipartisanship, his mishandling of isolationists in 1941, and his lack of candor toward Congress and the public.

Sidney Pash's "Containment, Rollback, and the Onset of the Pacific War, 1933–1941" traces the evolution and eventual failure of the Roosevelt administration's strategy for containing Japanese expansion. Begun in 1933 and accelerated soon after the start of the Second Sino–Japanese War in 1937, the United States, Pash contends, sought to contain Japan by sustaining Chinese resistance and weakening the Japanese economy. Pash demonstrates that American containment sustained Chinese resistance but in the process accelerated Japan's embrace of the Axis Alliance and its advance into French Indochina. Containment was, Pash contends, a patient, cautious, and largely successful American program that changed radically only after the German invasion of the Soviet Union in June 1941. Convinced that Tokyo would not strike against Western targets prior to a Soviet collapse and certain that England was safe from invasion until the summer of 1942, the Roosevelt administration abandoned containment in an ill-fated effort to roll back Japanese expansion and break up the Axis. While Pash charts a middle course in his study, tacking well away from works such as Robert Stinnett's *Day of Deceit: The Truth About FDR and Pearl Harbor*,[5] the latest in a string of works dating to the 1940s that explain the Pearl Harbor tragedy as the result of a conspiracy, he nonetheless recognizes that senior American officials inadvertently, and in a genuine effort to avoid war, fatally undermined Japanese–American efforts to keep peace in the Pacific.

The second part of this study features two essays that consider the home front during World War II. Justin Hart's "'In Terms of Peoples Rather Than Nations': World War II Propaganda and the Conceptions of U.S. Foreign Policy" reflects John's interest in war and propaganda, most clearly evident in his *World War II, Film, and History*,[6] as well as in his wildly popular Rutgers course History on Film. Hart's research into the Office of War Information (OWI) highlights this often overlooked organization's crucial role in the formulation of postwar foreign policy and provides the most thorough examination of the agency since the publication of Allan Winkler's *The Politics of Propaganda: The Office of War Information, 1942–1945*.[7] Hart's study focuses on the OWI during 1942 and 1943 and highlights in particular the OWI's critical role in popularizing the concept of a postwar United Nations and in trying unsuccessfully to bridge the chasm separating America's wartime idealism with its all-too-obvious racism. Hart traces how profound differences over wartime propaganda, combined with political backbiting and policy disagreements, crippled the agency. In the end, although Hart and Winkler often concur on the course of OWI's downfall, Hart recognizes how the agency's wartime role profoundly influenced the conduct of the nation's Cold War propaganda campaign.

Ann Pfau's "Allotment Annies and Other Wayward Wives: Wartime Concerns About Female Disloyalty and the Problem of the Returned Veteran" examines wartime concern with sexual morality in general and with the fidelity of military wives in particular, reflecting John's long-term interest in how war has affected American society. Pfau analyses how popular culture, public officials, the Red Cross, and fighting men themselves reflected and produced ever wider anxiety over the fidelity of servicemen's wives. Drawing on wide-ranging secondary sources and an extraordinary number of contemporaneous sources, Pfau offers a thorough exploration into wartime America's concerns over how returning GIs would adjust to civilian life, as well as the vital role that wives and sweethearts would play in a smooth transition to peacetime. Making extensive use of the University of Chicago's pioneering study of the war's domestic impacts, Pfau describes soldiers' wives as realistic and more often than not ready to take on the burdens of leading their husbands' adjustment. "Allotment Annies and Other Wayward Wives" highlights how single servicemen saw marriage as a source of stability and as a bridge easing the transition from military service to a productive and purposeful civilian life. Her work provides an extraordinary insight into a part of the home front's history heretofore overlooked in comprehensive studies such as Richard Lingeman's commanding *Don't You Know There's a War On?*[8] and Emily Yellin's *Our Mother's War.*[9]

The theme at the heart of this volume—the American military at war—clearly bears the imprint of John's decades-long and continuing study of American military history. Nicholas Molnar's "General George S. Patton and the War-Winning Sherman Tank Myth" analyzes Patton's defense of the Sherman in the face of scathing criticism following the Battle of the Bulge and concludes that the general's advocacy on behalf of the tank salvaged its reputation both at the time and for generations to come. In the course of his study, Molnar shatters Patton's defense of the Sherman, and unhesitatingly demonstrates that all too often the men assigned to America's premier tank "were slaughtered because of the use of such an inferior" weapon. Patton, who understood all too well the Sherman's myriad flaws, rushed to defend the tank because he knew that it would remain the armored division's workhorse and that public criticism would only hurt the morale of his tankers and in turn the war effort. Molnar concludes that Patton's defense of the Sherman inadvertently contributed to a host of postwar studies that championed the tragically flawed weapon and that played a role in fostering contemporary popular culture's depictions of the Sherman as a war-winning weapon. "General George S. Patton and the War-Winning Sherman Tank Myth" offers rare insights into the Patton legacy, which remains underexamined in leading studies of the great general, including Martin Blumenson's *Patton: The Man Behind the Legend, 1885–1945*[10] and Carlo D'Este's *Patton: A Genius for War.*[11]

Barbara Brooks Tomblin's "Naval Gunfire Support in Operation Neptune: A Reexamination" delivers a captivating narrative that takes readers from the choppy and cold waters of the French coast to the shores of North Africa, to Sicily, and to the deadly beaches of Salerno, and then back again to Normandy on June 6, 1944. Tomblin's meticulous research, which includes all major published sources, relevant records from the National Archives as well as diaries, interviews, and letters from participants, demonstrates that the U.S. Navy's successes on June 6 were largely the result of putting into practice the lessons learned from previous amphibious assaults launched in the Mediterranean during 1942 and 1943. In part, because none of the major Mediterranean landings included pre-invasion bombardments of the landing zones, Allied planners recognized the need to wear down German defenses at Normandy with a pre-landing shelling, even at the sacrifice of surprise. The landings in North Africa and Italy not only highlighted the need for close-in fire support for the troops assaulting the beaches, but also revealed the effectiveness of air spot gunfire support and the need for more effective minesweeping operations. Amphibious operations prior to June 6, 1944, also uncovered the need for better defenses against German U-boat, E-boat, and air attacks. Tomblin also notes that even by the time of the Normandy landings, war planners failed to recognize, despite a wealth of information, the inherent limitations that Allied warships and landing craft would have in silencing enemy shore batteries. This oversight, Tomblin concludes, contributed much to the bloodshed on June 6.

For more than a decade, John has served on the Scholarly Advisory Committee of the Rutgers University Oral History Archives of World War II, and his interest in the individual experiences of the American soldier is on display in both G. Kurt Piehler's "Veterans Tell Their Stories and Why Historians and Others Listened" and Mark A. Snell's "*Semper Paratus*: The U.S. Coast Guard's Flotilla 10 at Omaha Beach." Piehler's groundbreaking study examines how the support of influential Americans, including President Roosevelt and Army Chief of Staff George C. Marshall, combined with the pioneering work of combat historian S.L.A. Marshall to produce richly detailed histories that contributed to the U.S. Army's unprecedented drive to document the services' wartime history, a practice that the Army had not followed either during or after other major conflicts. Piehler demonstrates that in addition to its use in official histories, others put oral history to use to serve the war effort. Samuel Stouffer and the U.S. Army's Research Branch often used oral histories to improve survey questions that went out to hundreds of thousands of soldiers. The Research Branch's work proved invaluable in many instances, and perhaps nowhere was it more worthwhile, Piehler argues, than in reshaping treatments for battle fatigue. The extensive use of oral histories during the war led to its widespread acceptance by the U.S. Army after 1945, and, Piehler notes, because of the active campaigning of wartime practitioners such as historian Forest Pogue, the wider community of academic historians, who often disparaged the value of oral history after the war, came increasingly to embrace the practice during the 1960s and the 1970s.

Snell's richly detailed and vibrant work offers both a valuable overview of the United States Coast Guard's role in World War II as well as an in-depth examination of this often forgotten service in the major amphibious operations of the war. Making extensive use of oral histories and memoirs, Snell takes the reader from the coast guardsman's early training to operations in Sicily and the Italian mainland, to raucous liberty in Gibraltar, and on to the deadly serious preparation in the months leading up to Normandy. The heart of Snell's study focuses on the heretofore unexamined history of Flotilla 10, each of whose 36 LCIs (landing craft, infantry) carried a crew of 24 and as many as 188 troops in the assault on Omaha Beach, amid an ocean of lethal anti-tank mines, treacherous tides and currents, and German defensive fire. "The U.S. Coast Guard's Flotilla 10" is an especially important work given that the leading studies of the Second World War often carry no mention of the United States Coast Guard, and the grand narratives of the Coast Guard, including Robert E. Johnson's *Guardians of the Sea*[12] and Tom Beard's *Coast Guard*,[13] can by their very nature offer only a cursory look at this unsung service's role on June 6, 1944.

Scott H. Bennett's "American Pacifism, The 'Greatest Generation,' and World War II" clearly mirrors John's interest in the American peace movement and the history of conscientious objectors. Bennett, a leading authority on both fields, presents a sweeping study that examines both secular and religious pacifists, the movement's reaction to prewar preparedness, the Japanese attack on Pearl Harbor, the vital role that peace activists and conscientious objectors played in supporting civil liberties during the ensuing war, and the latter's heroic role in serving the mentally handicapped in often dangerous and appalling conditions. Bennett also traces how peace activists, especially the Fellowship on Reconciliation, fought Jim Crow by helping to create the Congress of Racial Equality. As the title of the study suggests, many in the so-called "greatest generation" nobly served the republic without taking up arms, and Bennett explores the histories of those pacifists who served as medics in some of the most brutal war zones. Just as military service provided veterans with newfound skills and abilities, so too, Bennett concludes, did conscientious objectors emerge from prison and Civilian Public Service camps with valuable skills that shaped a generation of postwar activism.

The final section of this volume, which examines the end of World War II, reflects John's interests in peace studies, conflict resolution, and the impact of wars on the societies that wage them. Yutaka Sasaki's article, "Foreign Policy Experts as Service Intellectuals: The American Institute of Pacific Relations, the Council on Foreign Relations, and Planning the Occupation of Japan During World War II," is a timely and compelling study of the origins of the phenomenally successful postwar occupation of Japan. Sasaki focuses on the role of the Institute of Pacific Relations (IPR) and the Council on Foreign Relations (CFR), and he highlights the complexity of planning for the postwar occupation as well as the competing visions that went into the making of the U.S. occupation of Japan. Making use of both Japanese and American archival material, "Foreign Policy Experts as Service Intellectuals" closely studies the heretofore underexamined 1945 Hot Springs Conference, at which 150 delegates from 12 IPR member states met to compare ideas for the postwar occupation and details the very limited occupation that many British members of the IPR envisioned as compared with the extensive program that American members called for. Although Sasaki concludes that it is impossible to determine the exact influence of the conference on the occupation, key State Department officials attended the meetings, and the final conference report reached President Roosevelt's desk. Sasaki also makes extensive use of the records of the Council on Foreign Relations' *Studies of American Interests in the War and Peace*. Begun in 1939 and carried out in conjunction with the State Department, *War and Peace Studies* began to focus on the postwar occupation of Japan not long after Pearl Harbor. Key Council members rose to policy-making positions at the State Department by war's end, and the research that *War and Peace Studies* undertook on postwar Japan clearly "established the framework of analysis" for such critical issues as the future of the emperor and the demilitarization of Japan. Sasaki's study fills a valuable niche in the historiography of the occupation thus far overlooked in more sweeping works, such as Michael Schaller's *The American Occupation of Japan*[14] or John Dower's *Embracing Defeat*.[15]

Rieko Asai's groundbreaking work, "Hiroshima and the U.S. Peace Movement—Commemoration of August 6, 1948–1960," explores the role that anti-nuclear activists have played in shaping public memory of the war's cataclysmic end. Asai explores how, soon after the war's end, a diverse network of nuclear activists, led by atomic scientists, world federalists, and pacifists, challenged the then-dominant view supporting the atomic attacks on Hiroshima and Nagasaki. The major force that struck out against the orthodox view of the atomic bombings, the World Peace

Day movement, began in 1948 owing to the work of Hiroshima survivor Kiyoshi Tanimoto and Austrian émigré Alfred Parker. Asai demonstrates that Cold War tension and virulent anticommunism delivered setbacks to World Peace Day, from which the movement would never recover. Asai explains, however, that even as the efforts of Parker and Tanimoto began to founder, Christian pacifists in the United States, anchored by the Fellowship for Reconciliation (FOR), injected new life into the movement to commemorate August 6. In turn, this revived movement galvanized anti-nuclear activists to push for successful limits on nuclear testing during the 1960s while simultaneously dehistoricizing the bombings of Hiroshima and Nagasaki.

The essays before you provide a fresh examination of familiar topics and take you into new fields of inquiry in the ever expanding history of the Second World War. For all the contributors, this work was a pleasure to produce, owing to our abiding interest in the subject matter, and most of all, to our profound admiration and respect for our dear friend John Whiteclay Chambers II.

NOTES

1. John Whiteclay Chambers II, *The Eagle and the Dove: The American Peace Movement and United States Foreign Policy, 1900–1922* (New York: Garland, 1976).

2. John Whiteclay Chambers II, *The Tyranny of Change: America in the Progressive Era, 1890–1920* (Piscataway, N.J.: Rutgers University Press, 2000).

3. Warren F. Kimball, *The Juggler* (Princeton, N.J.: Princeton University Press, 1994).

4. Waldo Heinrichs, *Threshold of War: Franklin D. Roosevelt and American Entry into World War II* (New York: Oxford University Press, 1990).

5. Robert Stinnett, *Day of Deceit: The Truth About FDR and Pearl Harbor* (New York: Free Press, 2001).

6. John Whiteclay Chambers II, *World War II, Film, and History* (New York: Oxford University Press, 1996).

7. Allan Winkler, *The Politics of Propaganda: The Office of War Information, 1942–1945* (New Haven, Conn.: Yale University Press, 1978).

8. Richard Lingeman, *Don't You Know There's a War On? The American Home Front, 1941–1945* (New York: Putnam, 1970–2006).

9. Emily Yellin, *Our Mother's War: American Women at Home and at the Front During World War II* (New York: Free Press, 2004).

10. Martin Blumenson, *Patton: The Man Behind the Legend, 1885–1945* (New York: Harper Perennial, 1994).

11. Carlo D'Este, *Patton: A Genius for War* (New York: Harper Perennial, 1996).

12. Robert E. Johnson, *Guardians of the Sea: History of the United States Coast Guard, 1915 to the Present* (Annapolis, Md.: Naval Institute Press, 1987).

13. Tom Beard, *Coast Guard* (Westport, Conn.: Hugh Lauter Levin Associates, 2004).

14. Michael Schaller, *The American Occupation of Japan* (New York: Oxford University Press, 1987).

15. John W. Dower, *Embracing Defeat: Japan in the Aftermath of World War II* (New York: Penguin, 2000).

chapter one

ROOSEVELT AT THE RUBICON: THE GREAT CONVOY DEBATE OF 1941

J. Garry Clifford and Robert H. Ferrell

In early June 1941, the former Republican presidential candidate and ex-governor of Kansas Alfred M. ("Alf") Landon received a confidential communication from his erstwhile running mate, Frank M. Knox. At that time Secretary of the Navy in the administration of President Franklin D. Roosevelt, Knox wrote of his recent meeting with John G. Winant, the U.S. ambassador to England, "who gave me the very latest news of the situation in London. Frankly and confidentially, the situation is that we must get in or see England go down with Hitler dominating the world." Knox pleaded with his old friend to "subordinate everything else to national unity" and fully support the Roosevelt administration's policy of all-out aid to Britain even if it led to war with Nazi Germany.[1]

Landon replied politely but negatively. He had been willing to close ranks after the president's announcement of an unlimited national emergency on May 27, but FDR had seemingly reversed himself at his press conference the following day by saying there were no plans to have the U.S. Navy convoy Lend-Lease supplies to Britain. Only the incumbent in the White House, according to Landon, could bring about national unity by furnishing "the kind and degree of information to the Congress and to the people that [Prime Minister Winston S.] Churchill furnishes the English." Such candor was simply not FDR's style. "When the President really crosses the Rubicon [a reference to Julius Caesar's decision to march on Rome in 49 B.C.]," Landon promised, "I will of course rally around him. But I won't break any ice for him to cross the Rubicon."[2] Much to Knox's disappointment, Alf Landon continued to oppose formal American participation in the war until Japan's attack on Pearl Harbor.[3]

The Landon–Knox exchange occurred just two weeks before the German invasion of the Soviet Union, by most accounts the key turning point of World War II. Adolf Hitler's attack crystallized plans in Tokyo to occupy all of Indochina, a move that prompted the American freezing of Japanese assets (including a de facto embargo of oil) in retaliation, and the clock began to tick in the Pacific. This private colloquy about crossing the Rubicon also came near the end of a great public debate in the United States during the spring of 1941. The issue—U.S. naval convoys—had potentially crucial consequences. Knox himself had publicly urged convoys in a speech that *The New York Times* had labeled "This Is Our Fight."[4] Advocates of U.S. intervention saw convoying as essential for getting Lend-Lease materials to Britain at a time when German U-boats and surface raiders were winning the Battle of the Atlantic against the Royal Navy. "What should history think," recorded Secretary of War Henry L. Stimson, if "we should let the British Government go down just for a lack of willingness to have convoys by our Navy."[5] Isolationist opponents feared that England was already beaten and that only Roosevelt's promises of further aid kept the Churchill government from seeking a separate peace. Convoys would inevitably lead to clashes with German U-boats and to another foreign war that might destroy American democracy at home, or so they believed.[6] Nearly everyone—except probably President Roosevelt—saw convoys as the fatal, irrevocable step. Shooting, they agreed, meant war.

Even though the president had already in January 1941 instructed that "the Navy should be prepared to convoy shipping in the Atlantic to England," he "flipflopped, dodged, waffled, and dissembled" during the ensuing months, as the historian David M. Kennedy has written.[7] FDR was in no hurry to cross the Rubicon. He did not order actual U.S. naval escort of convoys until September—and then only as far as Iceland. Rather, he stretched patrols, as he described the tactic by which the U.S. Navy sought out German submarines and then radioed their positions to waiting British planes and destroyers. He quietly ordered the occupation of Greenland by U.S. forces in April. He declared the Red Sea open to American merchant ships by pretending that it was not a war zone, thus enabling military supplies to flow to British forces in North Africa. Only in June did he transfer units from the Pacific fleet to the Atlantic—three battleships, an aircraft carrier, and supporting vessels, hardly a major redeployment. Basically, he waited. He told the British and his own impatient advisers that public opinion was not ready for convoys.[8]

There were additional reasons for caution. The president needed to gauge what would happen with Japan. Conversations between the State Department and Japanese Ambassador Kichisaburo Nomura had begun in mid-April, just after the unexpected Soviet–Japanese neutrality agreement. FDR and Secretary of State Cordell Hull always worried that naval clashes between German and American warships in the Atlantic might provoke Japanese countermoves in Asia under the Tripartite Pact. In May, Japanese Foreign Minister Yosuke Matsuoka privately challenged the United States to do the "manly, decent, and reasonable" thing by openly declaring war on Germany "instead of engaging in acts of war under the cover of neutrality."[9] Only by mid-summer did it become clear that Tokyo would not regard an undeclared naval conflict in the Atlantic as a *casus belli* on behalf of Germany. As for Europe, even though U.S. spies had obtained German plans for the invasion of Russia (Operation Barbarossa), no one could be sure when and if it would come off; indeed, the seemingly invincible Germans might move first against Britain or Spain or North Africa, or else the Soviets might also capitulate in a new Brest–Litovsk surrender rather than fight. Thus, the international prospects in the Pacific, but especially in Europe, were murky. Moreover, the U.S. Atlantic Fleet needed time to refit, reorganize, coordinate intelligence with the British, and prepare for the actual escort of convoys.[10]

That spring and early summer, inaction became the order of the day. As the historian Waldo Heinrichs has argued, the president did not know what he could or should do as the rampaging *Wehrmacht* smashed Yugoslavia, Greece, and Crete during April and May. With General Erwin Rommel's *Afrika Korps* approaching Egypt, pro-Nazis staging a coup in Iraq, the British barely hanging on in the Mediterranean, and "tremendous" shipping losses in the Atlantic three times the rate of replacement, the president thought first and foremost in terms of the physical security of the Americas.[11] Just after the giant German battleship *Bismarck* broke out into the North Atlantic in late May, he told friends of an ominous dream: "He was at Hyde Park; that there had been a light bombing of New York; that the secret service had provided him with a bomb-proof cave 200 feet under a cliff near a little cottage he has up on the hill there; that he and several of his people had gone down in it to stay until a squadron of German planes had passed over Hyde Park."[12] Until FDR knew for sure where Hitler would strike next, he hedged his bets. "When I don't know how to move I stay put," he once said.[13]

Physical and emotional pressures may also have contributed to the president's penchant for "making haste slowly."[14] Throughout the spring, Roosevelt suffered from severe sinus and upper-respiratory infections that spawned rumors and caused him to postpone his national emergency speech until May 27.[15] Shortly thereafter, with Eleanor Roosevelt often absent from the White House, he secretly renewed contacts with Lucy Mercer Rutherfurd, the woman who had nearly broken up his marriage some 20 years earlier.[16] At almost the same time, FDR's longtime companion and personal secretary Marguerite ("Missy") LeHand, who knew of Rutherfurd's reappearance, fell victim to two debilitating strokes followed by a nervous breakdown.[17] Then the president's 86-year-old mother, Sara, died in September. If this personal turmoil had any effect on presidential statecraft, it probably reinforced caution.

Nonetheless, as Roosevelt monitored events in Europe and Asia, he continually sought to take the pulses of the American people and Congress. Heinrichs has written that the public debate over war and peace had essentially ended with the passage of the Lend-Lease Act in early March, and yet this stark conclusion seems improbable.[18] Certainly, the president did not think that the debate had ended. Long before, FDR had learned that no policy could make its way without objections; someone would always object. He tried to remain sensitive to ripples of public opinion but not so sensitive that he stopped moving forward. "It's a terrible thing when you're trying to lead," he famously said, "to look over your shoulder and find no one there."[19] As for Congress, although he never mastered the national legislature in the way that his successor Lyndon B. Johnson did in the 1960s, he always tried to keep the beasts in their cages. Badly mauled in the Supreme Court fight of 1937 and not wanting another donnybrook if he could avoid it, the president tiptoed warily around Capitol Hill.

How to gauge public opinion? To Roosevelt, despite all his concern, this was no easy task. Compounding the problem was the fact that he occupied the White House at a time when the academic study of public opinion was in its infancy. He did not trust the leading pollster, George Gallup, believing him to be a Republican, which was true enough, but he also thought that Gallup skewed his polls according to his politics. He had more respect for the work of Hadley Cantril, who began polling for him secretly; Cantril sent his findings to FDR through their mutual friend Anna Rosenberg.

Instead of trusting polls, however, the president preferred to rely on old-fashioned surveys of editorial opinion, which actually reflected the views of conservative publishers more than they did readers, and he paid particular attention to the White House letter count.[20] In this latter regard, FDR did not understand what later became a truism: Adverse letters are more likely to dominate favorable ones for the simple reason that irritability tends to pass into letters more easily. On one occasion in late April, just after Secretary Hull made a speech about expanding naval patrols, the secretary received 1,700 telegrams, of which 600 were favorable and 1,100 opposed. He reported the tally to Roosevelt, who agreed that the American public was not yet ready for convoys.[21] When an overwhelming majority of letters and telegrams following his May 27 speech seemed to favor further naval activities in the Atlantic, FDR seemed pleasantly surprised.[22] Indeed, national polls that had showed only 41 percent in favor of convoys in April jumped to 55 percent in late May and climbed to 60 percent by September.[23] In addition to these varied indices of *vox populi*, the president also heeded an aphorism from Abraham Lincoln, passed along by Cantril prior to the May 27 speech: "What I want is to get done what the people desire to get done, and the question for me is how to find that out exactly."[24]

Despite such measurements—letter counts, editorial surveys, Cantril's polls, and Lincoln's commentaries about a much different war—Roosevelt seemed inclined to rely on international events, not on his own forceful explanation of those events, to move public opinion. The British ambassador, Lord Halifax, reported that the president was "ultra respectful of public opinion. He has got to respect it, of course, and cannot move without it, but I have the feeling that it is sometimes ahead of him . . . and that he could move it a bit faster than he does by being too ready for it to move independently."[25] Chief of Naval Operations Admiral Harold R. Stark, a strong advocate of convoys, reported his own puzzlement about Roosevelt's thinking to his colleague at Pearl Harbor, Admiral Husband E. Kimmel: "What will be done about convoys and many other things, and just how much a part of our Democratic way of life will be handled by Mr. Gallup, is a pure guess."[26]

The testimonies to Rooseveltian caution in confronting public opinion were so ubiquitous that they must have been accurate. Lowell Mellett, a former newspaper reporter who served as a White House assistant in charge of public relations, urged his boss to remain "wryly amused by the present clamor for 'leadership' on your part." The most successful approach, according to Mellett, "has been in part due to the recognition of conditions as they are and of public opinion as it is, from month to month, and to the patience you have shown in not getting out ahead of these two things."[27] Even Roosevelt's closest adviser, Harry Hopkins, remarked that the president "would rather follow public opinion than to lead it."[28] *Time* magazine, whose anonymous writers sometimes exaggerated for effect, depicted FDR as "tiptoeing around, listening at keyholes of public opinion, studying polls," while national support allegedly "slipped through his fingers."[29] Perhaps the most unflattering assessment of his dilatory methods came from that singular actress-politician Clare Boothe Luce, who liked to draw the president's essence for her audiences. She would say that that famous leaders employed famous gestures. For Churchill, it was the V for victory sign. For Hitler, it was the upraised arm in the *Sieg Heil* salute. For FDR, she would then wet her finger and hold it aloft to test the breezes.[30]

Almost certainly a key motive for Roosevelt's querulous drawings of public opinion was his vivid memory of what had happened to his most recent predecessor as a war president, Woodrow Wilson. The fate of the president whom FDR had served in his younger days reminded him of what he should *not* do. Much later during the war, he watched a private screening of the Hollywood film *Wilson*, and when the movie came to the point of Wilson's stroke during which the Treaty of Versailles had failed in the Senate, Roosevelt raised himself in his wheelchair and said aloud: "By God, that's not going to happen to me."[31] He was not going to make Wilson's mistake of getting too far ahead of public opinion. A former adviser, Raymond Moley, thought that the president was "in a hole, as a result of his previous promises [to stay out of war]. Surely he realizes that if a second Democratic president in a generation fails the American people on keeping us out of war, it will be a long time before they ever elect another."[32] FDR's courting of Republican internationalists, especially his appointment of Stimson and Knox to the cabinet, suggests that he did not consider his moves in such a purely partisan way; rather, he wanted to avoid Wilson's mistakes by getting too far ahead of public opinion and Congress.

And so, uncertain of what he was up against, but knowing that it was something he must face and calculate, however gingerly the calculation, he sought a clever ploy to get Lend-Lease materials across the Atlantic, and he conveniently found a careful word: "patrol." Assistant Secretary of State

Breckinridge Long learned about it through a zoological metaphor. Talking to Secretary Hull, Long was asked by his Tennessee boss: "Did you ever see a tadpole turn into a frog?" That, Hull explained, described the state of the president's convoy policy. "We have got a tadpole that someday may be a frog," Long concluded in his diary.[33] Wall Street banker Thomas W. Lamont cited another animal to make the same point. "The word 'convoy,'" he wrote the president, who surely appreciated the letter, "is like a red rag to a bull. But 'patrol'—expanded and strengthened to make a safe sea lane across the Atlantic—strikes a popular note. It will appeal."[34] Roosevelt himself in a famous explanation just three weeks later, again resorting to a barnyard simile, insisted at his press conference that the difference between a patrol and a convoy was akin to the difference between a cow and a horse and that "you can call a cow a horse" but that did not make it so. Any accusation that the Navy was convoying rather than patrolling, he said, was a "deliberate lie."[35] Having found the correct word, the president moved logically to extend its geographic meaning; and during much of the spring and early summer of 1941; he sought to justify wider naval patrols in the Atlantic as a defense of the Monroe Doctrine. Many doubted his defensive motives. "You are not going to report the presence of the German fleet to the Americans," Stimson admonished the president. "You are going to report it to the British fleet. I wanted him to be honest with himself."[36] Roosevelt told his cabinet on April 25 that "he could avoid convoying by pushing the patrolled area farther out into the Atlantic."[37] He had actually ordered extended zones two weeks earlier by placing Greenland and all waters west of 25 degree west latitude under naval patrol, but he had been careful not to say so in cabinet meetings. On April 10–11, according to Director of the Budget Harold Smith, also a diarist, FDR drew up the necessary orders but told only four cabinet members because the others "could not keep their mouths shut."[38] Some weeks later, the president instructed Secretary of Agriculture Claude Wickard (probably one of the talkers) always to use the passive voice and say that farm products "would be delivered" to England—not "we were going to deliver" them—when making public speeches.[39] Early in May, Roosevelt spoke expansively to Lord Halifax, another diarist, and subtly suggested that "if we [the British] ever had to occupy the Canaries and Cape Verde Islands, we should not give them back after the war. They were dangerous things in unsafe hands." The president "looked forward to the possibility, if we did collar the Azores, of our asking the Americans to take them over for us."[40] Later in May, he discussed with the War Cabinet (Stimson, Knox, Hull, Treasury Secretary Henry Morgenthau, Army Chief of Staff General George C. Marshall, Hopkins, Stark, and assorted staff officers) a possible operation to occupy the Azores and the Cape Verdes. Stark argued that any such deployment would require three months' preparation, but FDR gave him only a month.[41] "I am so tired of *words*," an impatient Marshall told the Argentine ambassador. "Words, and nothing but words. Our navy . . . could win the Battle of the Atlantic."[42] All the while, there were false rumors about the West African port city of Dakar, Senegal, which Vichy French authorities had allegedly turned over to the Germans for offensive operations in the Atlantic.

Fearful that the commander in chief would commit the country to naval hostilities, the isolationists tried to stymie him with public opinion. Republican Congresswoman Jeannette Rankin of Montana reminded her constituents that "Congress still has the power to declare war, that we still have a Neutrality Act and that public opinion can [still] control if it will take the pains to express itself."[43] Anti-convoy rallies and petitions, communist youths picketing the White House, antiwar speeches by Charles Lindbergh and other celebrities over national radio hookups, peace parades, letter-writing campaigns, referendums on war and convoys in individual Congressional districts, speaking tours for congressional representatives and senators under the auspices of the America First Committee—all would presumably restrain the president from crossing the Rubicon. The public relations expert Chester Bowles assured R. Douglas Stuart of America First that "Roosevelt won't take a chance until he's sure he has public opinion behind him."[44] Stuart in turn told retired Brigadier General Robert E. Wood that their organization was using "Roosevelt's old trick of making it appear that public opinion is powerfully with us."[45] Stuart and Wood both professed to believe that their agitation would hold the president back from the fatal step, the ordering of naval convoys. An isolationist member of Congress from Missouri agreed, telling a constituent that the "president talks peace but his Cabinet talks war. You and I know that Cabinet members do not talk contrary to their Cabinet chief. The President is hesitating because he feels public opinion against him."[46] Their only recourse was to invoke Roosevelt's tactic of appealing to public opinion, the fickle force that he so feared.

Those on the other side of the national debate, the interventionists, also tried to arouse public opinion in *favor* of convoys, but they were quickly warned off by the president, who quietly but firmly told them "not to wave the red flag of immediate convoy."[47] Thus admonished, the Committee to Defend America by Aiding the Allies and the more militant Fight for Freedom Committee played down convoys until mid-summer, although the indefatigable New York lawyer Grenville Clark, working primarily through Secretary Stimson and New York Republican Congressman James Wadsworth, tried to push for a "test vote" on convoys, either by calling the Tobey Anti-Convoy Resolution to the floor or by sponsoring separate legislation specifically authorizing convoys.[48] As Clark saw it, such private activities would repeat the tactics of the previous summer when they aroused public opinion in favor of both conscription and the Destroyers-Bases Deal and thus "forced" the president to do what he wanted to do anyway.[49] FDR would have none of it, however, and when the Tobey Resolution came before the Senate Foreign Relations Committee on April 30, the Democratic majority obediently tabled it by a vote of 13 to 9. Despite continued public agitation and debate in Congress, the convoy issue never did come up for a floor vote.

In a curious episode prior to FDR's national emergency speech on May 27, a group of war hawks inside the cabinet tried to gang up on the president, forcing him to confront the urgent need for greater aid to Britain—in particular, the transfer of fleet units from the Pacific to Atlantic to escort convoys—and even pushing for a formal declaration of war if necessary. Stimson and Knox tried to collaborate with Attorney General Robert H. Jackson and Secretary of the Interior Harold Ickes in circulating a round-robin petition that would show united administration support for stronger measures, convoying, and more, so that the president would have to move. Nonetheless, the Roosevelt administration on this and other matters proved so disorderly, so comprised of competing egos and institutional crosscurrents, that it was impossible to get a clear consensus on exactly what to do. By bringing Ickes into the equation, the hawks had enlisted a rancorous ally who could not work with the indispensable Harry Hopkins, whom Ickes loathed. Cordell Hull in particular held firm against moving the Pacific fleet, whose deployment at Pearl Harbor he regarded as a necessary deterrent against Japanese aggression.[50] Nothing came of the effort. Master juggler that he was, Roosevelt probably sensed what was afoot and could make further calculations of support by seeing which cabinet members came down where.[51]

FDR was also nettled by supporters who called for openness and telling hard truths. These voices urged the consummate politician in the White House that he should be more candid about England's needs for supplies and ships; more candid about the number of ships, the routes, and the risks of naval patrols; and more candid about contingency plans and the real possibilities for war. The situation, at least from Roosevelt's perspective, really did not permit such transparent management. It was impossible for him to be open, partly because of the crosscurrents of public opinion, probably more because the international situation remained opaque until Hitler actually invaded Russia. Nonetheless, as Landon complained to Knox, conducting foreign policy "behind a smokescreen . . . doesn't tend to promote national unity."[52] According to Raymond L. Buell, a thoughtful interventionist and former head of the Foreign Policy Association, Roosevelt's clever decision to extend patrols had given "new fuel" to those who charge presidential "trickery." Instead of justifying "secretiveness on grounds of military necessity," noted Buell, the president should make "fundamental decisions of this sort . . . openly and with the consent of the country, if democracy is to be respected and a subsequent isolationist reaction averted."[53] When FDR failed to follow up on his national emergency declaration, Buell stated his critique even more bluntly. "The issue at stake here," he wrote, "is not only the defeat of Hitler but the re-adaptation of our democratic institutions to meet an emergency problem. If we cannot find a device to overcome the veto of the minority then our democratic system was doomed." He saw Roosevelt as "a paradoxical figure" who exercised "the most extreme personal power" but who failed "to take decisive action on the main issue—namely, convoying, because of an unwillingness to face the Congressional problem."[54]

Notwithstanding the sincerity of its advocates, the desire for a pure solution probably seemed childish to Roosevelt. One of his wife's Republican cousins, Kermit Roosevelt, had pleased the president by volunteering for the British army, and FDR cultivated Kermit's wife, Belle, who was active in the Committee to Defend America by Aiding the Allies. Belle talked often with FDR, who told her that it might be possible to convoy "quietly" to Greenland and thence to Africa, but he could not do more because the public was not quite ready for the escort of convoys. She was full of respect for his guile: "He has the most incredible sense of timing and amazing acumen and has done a most superb job in educating the people and getting them behind him." Yet even Belle grew impatient, believing that "the Country is ready to accept . . . that we must convoy to Great Britain. Our position does seem false—unnatural—and anything that is unnatural is unhealthy."[55]

In this regard, Roosevelt's predilection for doing things in a manner verging on untidiness, sometimes turning policy making into a Rube Goldberg machine, the British ambassador saw much more clearly than did many of the president's ardent fellow citizens. "Things do happen," Halifax confessed to a colleague, "but not in a way that you would expect . . . [and] it is rather like a disorderly line of beaters out shooting; they do put the rabbits out of the bracken but they don't come out where you would expect."[56]

In dealing so warily with public opinion, the president may in fact—as his accusers would say after the war and after the revelation that the highest American officials were reading the Japanese Purple Cipher—have been hoping for an incident to galvanize support for war. There was much talk of such a tactic in the spring of 1941 when patrols were not yet convoys. The idea coursed through the conversations and diary notes and letters by isolationists and interventionists alike. Halifax wrote to a London friend: "His [FDR's] general attitude is one of trailing his coat all he can for the Germans, and praying for an incident that will make them shoot first."[57] Buell observed in mid-May that "I think FDR hopes that during the next two weeks the Axis will 'attack' U.S. interests in the Red Sea or Dakar. Under such circumstances FDR could tell the American people that he was respecting the pledge in the 1940 Democratic platform."[58] Following the cabinet meeting on May 1, Wickard jotted in his diary: "The President plainly intimated that he expected a clash sooner or later but that the Germans would have to fire the first shots."[59] William R. Castle, Jr., former Under Secretary of State in the Hoover administration, resident in Washington, and very well connected, heard from several sources that the administration wanted a ship sunk.[60] The irony of FDR's waiting for an incident during this period is particularly acute because when a U-boat sank the American freighter *Robin Moor* in the South Atlantic on May 21, news of the sinking did not reach Washington until after the president's May 27 speech, and he made no effort to portray the incident as another *Lusitania*. Nonetheless, one Republican isolationist called FDR's speech "a declaration of undeclared war."[61]

When Roosevelt looked to the Congress, he found himself in the same quandary that afflicted him in attempting to move public opinion. Unwilling to put matters to a vote until he was sure of the outcome, the president preferred to procrastinate. The labyrinthine procedures of Congress often tempted FDR to despise his adversaries on the Hill, for some of them were hardly worthy of reverence. As it happened, Republican Senator Charles Tobey of New Hampshire, the principal advocate of smoking out the administration on patrols and convoys, did not seem much of an opponent. For one thing, he came from a state hardly noted for contributing great national legislators.[62] For another, Tobey himself was a worthy Baptist who must have aroused all of Roosevelt's Episcopalian prejudices. Nor was the Granite State Republican much of an orator. Years later, Senator John A. Danaher of Connecticut told one of the authors of this essay that whenever his fellow New Englander grew excited, he talked twice as fast as a normal person and sounded very much like Daffy Duck in the Warner Bros. cartoons.[63]

Tobey's idea of a showdown was to go up to Dartmouth College and make a speech. One such self-appointed mission on behalf an anti-convoy resolution met with what seemed to be mixed results. The senator was booed, hissed, and presented with a yellow umbrella. "There was a very angry crowd of professors there," he reported to his son. "Several of the students were against me, and pretty caustic." The small-bore nature of the meeting should have warned him, but Tobey deemed it a great occasion. "They thought they had me when they said why do you want to give Britain money, say $2 billion, if it isn't our war, and why should you stop then with money, half way, as it were." Logic did not deter him. Tobey said "the Congress had decided to aid Britain and I was willing to go along." At that point "three professors walked out with feeling."[64]

Aroused in his crusade for clarity, Tobey wrote the president, asking a series of questions. Had the president used the Navy to convoy in recent weeks? Were any vessels currently convoying? Did the administration contemplate convoying? What orders had been issued to officers in case any merchant ships carrying cargoes to belligerents were attacked? FDR carefully passed these hot potatoes to Secretary Knox, who replied under the date of April 22. Knox gave a flat no to the first two questions and refused to answer the third. As to the fourth, "they would, without orders, defend any vessel, foreign or United States, if our neutrality were violated by an attack on them in our Territorial waters. This is as true today," Knox added resoundingly, "as it was 100 years ago."[65]

Unable to pin down the administration, Tobey opened floor debate in the Senate by displaying his sources of information, and perhaps the president himself had been waiting for this show-and-tell, which turned out to be pathetic. The senator cited three sources. First, a government investigator had word from within the Maritime Commission that convoys were being secretly employed. The second came in a letter from a woman whose relative in the Navy on shore leave told her that the Navy had been convoying for about a month. Finally a Navy ensign had given Tobey the same information.[66]

The senator had fired his popgun, so to speak, and the isolationists were hardly proud of him. Ruth Sarles, a first-rate staffer of the America First Committee, shuddered as she watched the antics of the man who was leading her side of the great debate. Tobey, she believed, had little stature among the Senate isolationists but had fervently seized on the convoy issue when others hesitated.[67] Tobey relished his new status. "The Administration hate[s] me more than any other member of the Senate," he wrote a constituent proudly, "and if they could get me in a concentration camp they would do it with glee."[68]

With reason, Roosevelt found Tobey irksome, even though he had no wish to turn the senator into a martyr. The president likewise evinced little respect for other opponents in the upper house who were hardly major figures in American politics. Sarles also recognized the limits of some of the senators. Whenever she visited the office of Senator Robert R. ("Buncombe Bob") Reynolds of North Carolina, she always made it a point to take along another woman staffer because it was unsafe to talk to the lascivious legislator by herself.[69] Because Sarles was quite fond of Senator Bennett C. Clark of Missouri (whose wife, Miriam, was active in the Washington chapter of America First), she would sometimes go by his office in late afternoon, call for a taxi, and drive the bibulous senator to his home instead of a bar. Her favorite senators—Republicans Robert A. Taft of Ohio (a "sweet man" but "private, distant"), Robert M. Lafollette, Jr. ("did his homework"), and George D. Aiken of Vermont ("decent, kindly")—were better at tactical planning than stump speaking, and Senator D. Worth Clark of Idaho also imbibed too much.[70] In addition, the most effective Senate orators, Gerald P. Nye of North Dakota and Burton K. Wheeler of Montana, both of whom had infuriated Roosevelt with their charges of presidential warmongering, often absented themselves from Capitol Hill to speak around the country against convoys and war.

Apart from his personal feelings toward opponents, the president faced other obstacles in managing both houses of Congress. The Democratic Congressional leadership was lax and inefficient. Representative Jerry Voorhis of California contrasted the lack of discipline with that shown by the Republicans. The Democratic whip would come around and say: "Well, Jerry, I hope you can vote with the President on this issue." "I'm sorry, I just can't," Voorhis would reply. "Well," the whip would say, "please don't take any offense. I just wanted to hope that you might see it that way."[71] The president himself, despite his reputation for twisting arms in Congress, actually twisted very few. He seldom singled out individual members. According to one former congressman, FDR was "hardly a Ronald Reagan who called you on the phone and asked for your vote on all sorts of measures. He was sometimes so subtle we were not sure what he wanted."[72]

Cohesion in Congress was especially poor in the spring of 1941. In a somnolent system where seniority (and even senility) still ruled, the former vaudeville composer Sol Bloom had proved incompetent as chair of the House Foreign Affairs Committee.[73] The chair of the Senate Foreign Relations Committee, Walter George of Georgia, actually opposed naval convoys even though he loyally voted to table the Tobey Resolution.[74] Moreover, the president had no one on the tiny White House staff working full-time as a liaison or watchdog for Congress although Marvin McIntyre eventually did a creditable job when called on later that autumn. Nor did the State, War, and Navy departments have regular representatives who went around the House and Senate office buildings, door to door, explaining their positions and inferentially asking support. Assistant Secretary John J. McCloy had done this successfully for the War Department during the Lend-Lease debate but did little thereafter. Later that summer, after the near-debacle over draft extension—the cliff-hanging 203–202 vote by which the 18-month extension of service barely passed—Secretary Stimson called on his New York friend Grenville Clark to serve as an unpaid assistant to watch Congress. General Marshall proved to be the most persuasive witness for the administration on Capitol Hill, but it was hardly the chief of staff's principal duty.

Even worse, a series of deaths on the Supreme Court and in the Senate resulted in a reshuffling that left FDR with little confidence that he could count and control votes. James F. Byrnes of South Carolina, the administration's principal lieutenant in the Senate, was elevated to the Supreme Court. Senator Reynolds of North Carolina, an erratic isolationist who gave Roosevelt no help in either the convoy or draft extension debates, became chair of the Military Affairs Committee. The interventionist Tom Connally of Texas replaced George as head of the Foreign Relations Committee but only after the convoy issue had died down. In the critical June days prior to the German attack on Soviet Russia, Senate proceedings became so confused that FDR had to rely on the friendly Republican leader, Charles McNary of Oregon, to maintain an orderly agenda.[75]

To all this, Roosevelt then added an act of omission: his utter failure to court the opposition in Congress. Except for his old friend Senator George Norris of Nebraska, FDR had written off all isolationists as hopeless by 1941. This attitude doubtless derived from the president's self-righteous credo, whereby anyone (administration officials or members of Congress) who deserted the team had great trouble returning to the fold. Always judgmental, FDR became dogmatic as he saw the European war increasingly in black-and-white terms. He too easily labeled his opponents on international issues as pro-fascists even though perhaps a few were. Indeed, the president's orders to the FBI to investigate America First and his encouragement of others to smear Charles Lindbergh and other isolationists as pro-Nazi showed him at his worst.[76] Some opponents, however, were capable of being co-opted, and a few almost desperately wanted the president to reach out to them. Arthur H. Vandenberg of Michigan was one of the latter, and throughout 1941, he put out occasional feelers to the White House, inquiring of the possibility of consultation. A friendly gesture might have brought Vandenberg around, but the president did nothing. Indeed, when Vandenberg's old friend from his publishing days, Lord Beaverbrook, came to Washington later that summer, the British cabinet minister was flabbergasted when "Van" told him he'd had little or no contact with the White House for years.[77]

Historians have tended to portray FDR as bipartisan (to use one of Vandenberg's words, admittedly fuzzy, as was its inventor) because of his willingness to include Republicans in his administration and for subsequently cultivating his 1940 electoral opponent, Wendell Willkie. The portrayal was true enough, but virtually all the president's contacts in this regard were fairly outspoken internationalist Republicans: Senator Warren

Austin of Vermont, Congressman James Wadsworth of New York, Secretaries Stimson and Knox, Under Secretary of War Robert P. Patterson, Coordinator of Information William J. Donovan, and Ambassadors John G. Winant and Patrick Hurley. With others, he could be quite vindictive. In the famous mock refrain of "Martin, Barton, and Fish," only New York Congressman Hamilton ("Ham") Fish irrevocably opposed Roosevelt's "aid short of war," and even Ham Fish (that "old Pooh-bah," as FDR called him) was a supporter of military preparedness.[78] The president might have salvaged such people as Vandenberg, Taft, Aiken, and Representative Henry Jackson of Washington, all prewar opponents who became internationalists during and after World War II. Far from being "illustrious dunderheads," the Yale University students who founded the America First Committee included a future ambassador to England (Kingman Brewster, Jr.), a future ambassador to Norway (R. Douglas Stuart, Jr.), a future Supreme Court justice (Potter Stewart), and a future president of the United States (Gerald R. Ford).[79] In the crucial year of 1941, Roosevelt did little—surprisingly, stubbornly, even stupidly little—to bring them around.

It is possible, even likely, that FDR would have obtained a favorable tally if he had permitted a floor vote on convoys. The isolationist leadership thought so and dissuaded Senator Tobey from pushing the matter after the Foreign Relations Committee tabled his resolution on April 30. Stimson and Congressman Wadsworth expressed confidence that victory would come easily and that the "isolationists are more noisy than they are numerous."[80] But what if such a vote were close? Roosevelt feared that a close vote, even if favorable, would be dangerous on such a momentous issue as convoys. It would send the wrong message—both to Hitler and to the British. Here, he was quite similar to the cautious Hull. The latter, perhaps out of long service in the House of Representatives, was always looking for complexities. A critic once allowed that Hull had vision. Yes, he said, Hull had vision. He could see a mare's nest at a thousand paces. In what must have been a rare similarity between FDR and Hull, so did the president when it came to Congress. When Congress then obliged with a close 203–202 vote over Selective Service extension and did it while the president was ceremoniously conferring with Prime Minister Churchill at Argentia Bay in August, it looked as if the legislators were doing their best to humiliate the president, or so Roosevelt believed. Actually, the close vote did not mean too much because even if the 18-month extension of service had failed, there doubtless would have followed some arrangement whereby the men in the Army would have been kept in for another 6 or 12 months. It would not have meant the instant collapse of the U.S. Army on the order of the "one-hoss shay," nor would it have been riot time in October when the one-year terms of some inductees came to an end and presumably the men could "take off" or, using the phrase of the moment, resort to "OHIO" ("going over the hill in October"). Moreover, the one-vote margin for extension bore the maneuver mark of all such close votes, whereby everybody kept tally as the vote proceeded and individuals in delicately balanced districts were able to vote nay and yet see a measure that they fundamentally supported obtain enough votes to pass.[81]

The president also had to pay attention to know-it-alls in the Senate, such as James F. Byrnes (D–S.C.), who offered worst-case analysis on what might happen on almost any issue. Byrnes once gave the following analysis, albeit on the question of whether to repeal the Neutrality Act:

I would not sponsor such a proposal. If such a bill were to be seriously considered, it should be introduced in the Senate by the Chairman of the Foreign Relations Committee and have the active support of the Secretary of State and the President. My opinion is that if it passed the Senate at all, it could not be passed for months. There were thirty votes cast against the Lend-Lease Bill. These thirty Senators would be bitterly opposed to repealing the Neutrality Act. In addition, there would be a number of Senators who voted for the Neutrality Act two years ago and made many speeches favoring it. I think there would be a majority for the Bill provided the President and the Secretary of State threw the support of the administration behind it. However, it certainly would be filibustered in the Senate and there would [not] be sufficient votes to prevent cloture even if that were possible. If the President and the Secretary of State appealed to the people for its repeal and such sentiment was aroused in favor of it as it is not today, it might be repealed provided there could be cloture in the Senate. Any proposal introduced by individual Senators without the wholehearted cooperating of the administration would not have a chance of enactment, and would possibly only serve to muddy the water and prevent the adoption of a measure which can secure a majority votes.[82]

Faced with such advice, the president might be excused for thinking of a course other than a grand debate over convoys in the Congress, led by the likes of Senator Tobey in the upper house. It was more convenient to extend naval patrols until international events and public opinion, not to mention combat readiness, made it possible to use the Navy to escort convoys. As in his approach to the equally thorny issue of public opinion, so in dealing with Congress, he seems to have sought the path of least resistance. As in the case of public opinion, he may well have thought of a possible incident; so with Congress, he thought of fighting a quasi-war, which he could manage without going to Congress.

And there is no doubt that Roosevelt anticipated undeclared war. The lessons of the 1790s, which he regarded as the "most crucial period in American history," would support him.[83] In cabinet on April 18, in the middle of the patrols-versus-convoys debate, he "took some time," as Secretary Wickard noted, to describe "the founding of the U.S. Navy as a guard for our commerce. He told of the naval engagements in the West Indies with the French Navy during the presidency of John Adams. He pointed out there was no declaration of war."[84] FDR also told Canadian Prime Minister W. L. Mackenzie King of his plans to use Bermuda as a base to "send planes . . . out as far as the Mid-Atlantic, to watch for German vessels" such as the battle cruisers *Scharnhorst* and *Gneisenau*, whereupon the planes "could immediately send out a signal [which] would enable the convoys to scatter. . . . He told me to say nothing of this to anyone."[85] The historian David Reynolds has described these sinuous contingencies as "war in masquerade."[86] The historian Michael Sherry has gone so far as to argue that the air buildup in the Philippines prior to Pearl Harbor was aimed at using the B-17 bombers offensively against Japan's "paper cities" in a twilight war scenario: that is, if Japan moved north or south but not directly against U.S. territory. It would be another quasi-war: not with frigates, but with flying fortresses.[87] Admiral Stark, by pushing for convoys in April and May, was doing the same thing; according to Waldo Heinrichs, Stark "urged battle, if not war."[88]

In this hidden agenda, if such it was, the president did not need to consult Congress in his capacity as commander in chief. Of that fact, the isolationists were well aware, and the suspicious Vandenberg saw a dark possibility that was more likely than the senator realized. "In any event," wrote Vandenberg, "I think we may take it for granted that the President will give himself the benefit of the doubt (if there be any) and the convoy decision will be made in the White House."[89]

And so the days and weeks lengthened into months. Through the spring and summer of the crucial year, the president watched and waited, awed by the volatile nature of public opinion and equally deterred by the indefinable complexities, so he thought, of a Congress mortgaged to stupidity and quixotic behavior and antediluvian rules. Not until the German invasion of the Soviet Union on June 22, 1941, did FDR move with new decision, sending American forces to occupy Iceland in July; meeting with Churchill off Newfoundland in August; freezing Japanese assets; and making further commitments to supply Britain, China, and Soviet Russia as proxies against the Axis powers. Churchill also passed along signals intelligence indicating that Hitler, "so long as he was fighting his war of conquest against the Soviet Union . . . wanted at all costs to avoid incidents which might bring the U.S. into the war." Thus emboldened, Roosevelt ordered the Atlantic fleet to "chase German raiders" as long as the Royal Navy could render assistance.[90] Not until the notorious U-boat attack on U.S.S. *Greer* in early September did FDR announce that the Navy, now escorting convoys as far as the new base in Iceland, would henceforth shoot at U-boats as part of an undeclared war in the Atlantic. Congress was informed, not consulted. With reason, by his own measure, Roosevelt had finessed the great debate over convoys.

It is impossible to be certain, after almost 70 years, whether this was a good or bad decision, but it does seem clear, as Heinrichs has argued, that FDR avoided decisive action in the spring of 1941 because he was primarily thinking defensively. Getting the goods to England was imperative, to be sure, but achieving that goal did not necessarily entail the naval escort of convoys. Extended patrols would suffice. His talk of incidents and of Germany's firing first referred less to the sinking of a ship such as the *Robin Moor* than to a major German move into Dakar or the Azores, at which point Roosevelt might have led the United States across the Rubicon because he regarded such German action as a direct threat to the hemisphere. Until the Nazi assault on Russia, he could not risk moving prematurely with his Navy so thin and his Army so unprepared. FDR's secret decision to occupy Iceland, made at the end of May, required six weeks to prepare, during which time Hitler took the fateful plunge to the east. Had the Germans moved into Iberia or the Atlantic islands, FDR could have shifted the Iceland expeditionary forces accordingly.[91] Keeping much of the fleet at Pearl Harbor may have been an inadequate deterrent (eventually making it a target), but it seemed the only viable option as the Hull-Nomura talks probed Japan's intentions. Half steps in the Atlantic also kept the British reasonably content, if anxious and often puzzled. What

Roosevelt could not know was that his belated shoot-on-sight order very likely precipitated Hitler's decision in September to begin transporting German Jews to the east, a "massive step" in his genocidal Final Solution.[92] Nonetheless, the president acted carefully and wisely, not precipitously, in light of the perilous international situation.

Where FDR proved inadequate was on the home front. The U.S. Constitution mandates conclusive debates prior to war, notwithstanding many subsequent experiences to the contrary. In this sense, the president did not lead. He wanted to be "pushed into the war, rather than to lead into it," he confessed to Morgenthau.[93] Although he leveled with the public on the essence of his policy—namely, the goal of defending the hemisphere by keeping the Atlantic sea lanes open—he was not at all candid with respect to Anglo-American naval agreements, promises made, and probable future steps. He did not lie about patrols being different than convoys, but neither did he dwell on the hostile actions of American vessels patrolling the Atlantic on behalf of one belligerent against another. Similarly, while he encouraged a national debate over convoys by his coyness, he did what he could to render that debate harmless and inconclusive, and he did more than necessary to imply that his opponents were akin to fifth columnists and traitors. Senator J. William Fulbright's famous remark about Roosevelt's deception in a good cause making it possible for Lyndon Johnson to do the same in a bad cause comes easily to mind. He did communicate with interventionists not to push ahead on convoys, but he did not inform allies, either inside or outside the administration, of his full motives. He confided in no one. He allowed convoys to become a litmus test on war and peace when, in fact, he was determined to avoid convoying for the near future. He did speak of the importance of Dakar and "the island outposts of the New World" in his May 27 speech, but their significance seemed buried amid speculation that he would immediately order the Navy to convoy under the new national emergency powers.[94] Nor did he say anything in this most important address about the Soviet Union, except in an indirect and misleading way by eliminating Finland from a list of countries invaded since the beginning of the war.

Inasmuch as the president led and educated the public in this period, he did so in behalf of his basic formula of aiding the allies and defending the Americas in steps short of war. It was a formula for drift and muddle. It avoided conclusive debate on clear issues. "Haranguing the country doesn't help," he told a friend. "It will take a 'shock' like 1932" to change isolationist attitudes.[95] As late as October 1941, he warned the British ambassador that "if he asked for a declaration of war, he wouldn't get it, and opinion would swing against him."[96] The country thus inched ahead through executive action. Congress spun its wheels. Opponents grew paranoid. Militant interventionists became frustrated.[97] Confusion prevailed. Only the German attack on the Soviet Union extricated FDR by extending his options, gaining him time, adding another proxy to arm and deploy against the Axis, and offering further opportunities (all of which he finessed) to lead boldly.

Roosevelt did what he did in part because it was convenient to do so without consulting Congress. When he finally instituted the naval escort of convoys in September (again without consulting Congress), he proceeded at a time when Hitler, bogged down in the Russian campaign, was unlikely to retaliate immediately with full-scale war. That step, in combination with mounting economic pressure against Japan, nonetheless made the war that came in December all the more probable. Did FDR intend that fateful result? Not necessarily. He knew the direction he was heading in, but not his final destination. Always the optimist, the president ignored counsel that "we can't count on the good Lord and just plain dumb luck forever."[98] Instead, he hoped to avoid war by deciding not to decide, much like the amiable sailor gliding with wind and tide and occasionally tacking to avoid shoals. Yet both captain and crew in reality were caught up in strong international currents pulling them toward war in the ocean where he least expected it. No wonder the confused electorate did not follow enthusiastically. No wonder historians still debate. The great irony, of course, is that the final decision for war, made so compelling by Japan's attack on Pearl Harbor and by Hitler's declaration four days later, actually produced a much broader consensus than Roosevelt could ever have achieved through more candid and conclusive tactics with respect to convoys.

NOTES

1. Frank Knox to Alfred M. Landon, June 11, 1941, Alfred M. Landon MSS, Kansas Historical Society, Topeka, Kan.

2. Landon to Knox, June 16, 1941, Alfred M. Landon MSS, Kansas Historical Society, Topeka, Kan.

3. See Donald R. McCoy, *Landon of Kansas* (Lincoln: University of Nebraska Press, 1966).

4. Quoted in James C. Schneider, *Should America Go to War: The Debate over Foreign Policy in Chicago, 1939–1941* (Chapel Hill: University of North Carolina Press, 1989), 133.

5. Diary of Henry L. Stimson, April 8, 1941, Henry L. Stimson MSS, Sterling Library, Yale University, New Haven, Conn.

6. For the isolationists, see Wayne S. Cole, *America First: The Battle Against Isolation, 1940–1941* (Madison: University of Wisconsin Press, 1953), chap. 9; Wayne S. Cole, *Roosevelt and the Isolationists, 1932–1935* (Lincoln: University of Nebraska Press, 1983), chap. 29; and Justus D. Doenecke, *Storm on the Horizon: The Challenge to American Intervention, 1939–1941* (Lanham, Md: Rowman & Littlefield, 2000), chap. 12.

7. FDR quoted in Mark W. Watson, *Chief of Staff: Prewar Plans and Preparations* (Washington, D.C.: Department of the Army, 1950), 124; David M. Kennedy, *Freedom from Fear* (New York: Oxford University Press, 1999), 491. At the same time FDR was ordering the Navy to prepare for convoys, he told a press conference in mid-January that convoys "were the last thing we have in our minds." Quoted in Justus D. Doenecke and Mark A. Stoler, *Debating Roosevelt's Foreign Policies, 1933–1945* (Lanham, Md: Rowman & Littlefield, 2005), 37.

8. See David Reynolds, *The Creation of the Anglo-American Alliance: A Study in Competitive Cooperation* (Chapel Hill: University of North Carolina Press, 1982), 195–204.

9. Quoted in Herbert Feis, *The Road to Pearl Harbor* (New York: Atheneum, 1967), 203.

10. Waldo H. Heinrichs, "President Franklin D. Roosevelt's Intervention in the Battle of the Atlantic, 1941," *Diplomatic History* 10 (Fall 1986): 332; and Alan Harris Bath, *Tracking the Axis Enemy: The Triumph of Anglo-American Naval Intelligence* (Lawrence: University Press of Kansas, 1998), 53–55.

11. Quoted from the Hap Arnold diary, April 22, 1941, in *American Air Power Comes of Age*, ed. John W. Huston (Maxwell Air Force Base, Ala: Air University Press, 2002), vol. I, 158.

12. Diary of Adolf A. Berle, May 26, 1941, Adolf A. Berle MSS, Franklin D. Roosevelt Library (hereafter FDRL), Hyde Park, N.Y.

13. Quoted in William L. Langer and S. Everett Gleason, *The Challenge to Isolation, 1937–1940* (New York: Harper and Brothers, 1951), 597.

14. Quoted in Ian Kershaw, *Fateful Choices: Ten Decisions That Changed the World, 1940–1941* (New York: Penguin, 2007), 304.

15. Diary of Courtney Letts de Espil, May 22, 1941, Box 3, De Espil MSS, Library of Congress: "I heard the following in New York—from my hairdresser,

who does the hair of New York's wealthiest. 'Have you heard,' he said, 'that the four most important heart specialists of New York were called to Washington yesterday to see the President?'" Mrs. Espil was the American-born wife of Don Felipe de Espil, Argentina's ambassador to the United States.

16. Helen Essary, quoted in the diary of Courtney Letts de Espil, April 16, 1941: "'When I dined there [the White House] one night in the family dining room, . . . I saw an army of cock roaches making themselves completely at home.' . . . 'Where was Mrs. Roosevelt?' 'Away. So was the President. She asked me to be hostess in her place.'"

17. According to White House usher's logs, FDR saw Lucy Mercer Rutherfurd (code-named Mrs. Paul Johnson) at the White House on June 5, August 1, and August 2, 1941 for visits that averaged more than two hours. Missy LeHand suffered strokes on June 5 and June 22. See Frank Costigliola, "Broken Circle: The Isolation of Franklin D. Roosevelt in World War II," *Diplomatic History* 33 (November 2008): 690–93.

18. Waldo Heinrichs, *Threshold of War* (New York: Oxford University Press, 1988), 11.

19. Quoted in John E. Wilze, *From Isolation to War* (Arlington Heights, Ill: Harlan-Davidson, 1968), 27.

20. See Richard W. Steele, "The Pulse of the People: Franklin D. Roosevelt and the Gauging of Public Opinion," *Journal of Contemporary History* 9 (October, 1974): 195–216.

21. Cordell Hull, *The Memoirs of Cordell Hull*, 2 vols. (New York: Macmillan, 1948), vol. II, 943.

22. Robert E. Sherwood, *Roosevelt and Hopkins* (New York: Grosset & Dunlap, 1946), 298. Sherwood notes that FDR had expected no more than "an even break" on his speech. On the eve of the president's speech, one perceptive noninterventionist noted: "In this country intervention has moved merely from talk of convoys to more talk of Convoys. The President [is] expected to shoot the works. . . . My own emotions are still mixed. Hopefully I scan the news for a scrap that will lend hope for Britain's chances; but in the company of most 'interventionists' I am overcome with a loathing almost as great as I experience when in the presence of a Nazi." Journal of Selden Rodman, May 26, 1941, Selden Rodman MSS, Sterling Library, Yale University, New Haven, Conn. Rodman was the co-editor of the liberal magazine *Common Sense*.

23. For the actual polls on convoys, see Hadley Cantril, ed., *Public Opinion 1935–1946* (Princeton, N.J.: Princeton University Press, 1951), 1127–28.

24. Cantril to Anna Rosenberg, May 20, 1941, PSF, Box 75, Franklin D. Roosevelt MSS, FDRL.

25. Halifax to Winston Churchill, April 10, 1941, PREM 4/27/9, Prime Minister's Files, Public Record Office, Kew, England.

26. Quoted in Patrick Abbazia, *Mr. Roosevelt's Navy: The Private War of the U.S. Atlantic Fleet, 1939–1942* (Annapolis, Md.: Naval Institute Press, 1975), 154.

27. Mellett memo for FDR, May 5, 1941, Lowell Mellett MSS, FDRL.

28. Henry Morgenthau Presidential Diary, May 14, 1941, Morgenthau MSS, FDRL.

29. *Time*, May 19, 1941.

30. James L. Baughman, *Henry R. Luce and the Rise of the American News Media* (Baltimore, Md.: The Johns Hopkins University Press, 2001), chaps. 7–8.

31. Howard G. Bruenn interview in J. K. Herman, "The President's Cardiologist," *Navy Medicine* 81 (March–April 1990), 12.

32. Raymond Moley to Kenneth Hogate, April 28, 1941, Raymond Moley MSS, Hoover Institute, Stanford University, Stanford, Calif.

33. Diary of Breckinridge Long, May 12, 1941, Breckinridge Long MSS, Manuscript Division, Library of Congress, Washington, D.C.

34. Thomas W. Lamont to FDR, May 7, 1941, PPF 1820, Roosevelt MSS, FDRL.

35. Quoted in Richard W. Steele, *Propaganda in an Open Society: The Roosevelt Administration and the Media, 1933–1941* (Westport, Conn.: Greenwood, 1985), 116.

36. Diary of Henry L. Stimson, April 22, 1941.

37. Diary of Claude Wickard, April 22, 1941, Claude Wickard MSS, FDRL.

38. Diary of Harold Smith, April 11, 1941, Harold Smith MSS, FDRL.

39. Diary of Claude Wickard, May 17, 1941.

40. Lord Halifax "Secret Diary," May 3, 1941, Borthwick Historical Institute, York, England.

41. Henry Morgenthau Presidential Diary, May 22, 1941.

42. Quoted in Diary of Courtney Letts de Espil, entry of May 29, 1941.

43. Jeanette Rankin to Patrick Timmons, June 2, 1941, Jeannette Rankin MSS, Schlesinger Library, Harvard University, Cambridge, Mass.

44. Bowles to Stuart, April 22, 1941, America First Committee MSS, Hoover Institute, Stanford, Calif.

45. Stuart to Wood, April 26, 1941, America First Committee MSS, Hoover Institute, Stanford, Calif.

46. Congressman Wallace Bennett to C. W. Driver, April 30, 1941, Marion Bennett MSS, Western Historical Collections, University of Missouri, Columbia, Mo.

47. Quoted in William L. Langer and S. Everett Gleason, *The Undeclared War, 1940–1941* (New York: Harper and Brothers, 1954), 444.

48. Grenville Clark memorandum for Henry L. Stimson, April 19, 1941, Grenville Clark MSS, Baker Library, Dartmouth College, Hanover, N.H.

49. See J. Garry Clifford and Samuel R. Spencer, Jr., *The First Peacetime Draft* (Lawrence: University Press of Kansas, 1986). Manfred Landecker identifies this dynamic as the "concept of anticipatory reaction" in *Franklin D. Roosevelt and the Formation of the Modern World*, ed. Thomas C. Howard and William D. Pederson, (Armonk, N.Y.: M. E. Sharpe, 2003), 24–44.

50. See especially Mark W. Lowenthal, *Leadership and Indecision: American War Planning and Policy Process, 1937–1942*, 2 vols. (New York: Garland, 1988), vol. II, chap. 8.

51. Mark Chadwin has argued that "by counterbalancing the outpourings of the isolationist organizations, they [the interventionists] helped the Roosevelt administration to decide foreign policies on their merits rather than because of external pressure." Mark L. Chadwin, *The Hawks of World War II* (Chapel Hill: University of North Carolina Press, 1968), v.

52. Landon to Knox, June 16, 1941, Alfred M. Landon MSS.

53. Raymond L. Buell to Henry Luce, May 1, 1941, Raymond L. Buell MSS, Library of Congress.

54. Buell to Luce, June 12, 1941, Raymond L. Buell MSS, Library of Congress.

55. Belle Willard Roosevelt to Kermit Roosevelt, March 18, 1941, Belle Willard Roosevelt MSS, Library of Congress.

56. Halifax to Sir John Simon, March 21, 1941, Hickleton MSS, Churchill College Library, Cambridge, England.

57. Halifax to Hankey, June 10, 1941, Lord Hankey MSS, Churchill College.

58. Buell to Luce, May 14, 1941, Buell MSS.

59. Diary of Claude Wickard, May 2, 1941.

60. Diary of William R. Castle, Jr., April 27, 1941, Houghton Library, Harvard University.

61. Congressman Roy Woodruff of Michigan, quoted in Doenecke, *Storm on the Horizon*, 141.

62. See Marjory Z. Bankson, "The Isolationism of Charles Tobey" (MA thesis, University of Alaska, 1971).

63. J. G. Clifford interview with John A. Danaher, Hartford, Conn., May 10, 1982.

64. Charles Tobey to Charles Tobey, Jr., April 24, 1941, Charles Tobey MSS, Baker Library, Dartmouth College.

65. Frank Knox to Tobey, April 22, 1941, OF 4193, Roosevelt MSS.

66. *Congressional Record* (15 April 1941): 3113–14.

67. J. G. Clifford interview with Ruth Sarles Benedict, Washington, D.C., August 12, 1985; see also Ruth Sarles, *A Story of America First* (Westport, Conn.: Praeger, 2003).

68. Charles Tobey to Harriet Newell, May 5, 1941, Tobey MSS.

69. See Julian M. Pleasants, *Buncombe Bob: The Life and Times of Robert Rice Reynolds* (Chapel Hill: University of North Carolina Press, 2000), chap. 10. Ruth Sarles also "kept her distance" from Arthur Capper of Kansas, another isolationist senator who "liked the ladies too much." Wayne Cole's notes of interview with Ruth Sarles Benedict, April 19, 1984, Wayne S. Cole MSS, Herbert Hoover Presidential Library, West Branch, Iowa.

70. Clifford interview with Ruth Sarles Benedict, August 12, 1985; see also Wayne Cole's notes of an interview with Ruth Sarles Benedict, September 28, 1976, Cole MSS.

71. Interview with Jerry Voorhis, Box 10, Former Members of Congress Oral History Project, Library of Congress.

72. J. G. Clifford interview with Thomas H. Eliot, Cambridge, Mass., February 10, 1983.

73. On Bloom's inadequacies, see Warren F. Kimball, *The Most Unsordid Act: Lend-Lease, 1939–1941* (Baltimore, Md.: The Johns Hopkins University Press, 1969), 145–46, 160–61.

74. Breckinridge Long memorandum of conversation with Senator Walter George, May 13, 1941, Box 204, Long MSS.

75. Charles McNary to Mrs. Walter Stolz (sister), June 20, 1941, Box 2, Charles McNary MSS, Library of Congress: "Strange as it may seem the Democratic situation in the Senate has thrown more work on me there. Senator [Alben] Barkley has been in the hospital for three weeks. Senator Byrnes, his first-string assistant, has been appointed to the Supreme Court. Senator [Pat] Harrison, my old friend and one of the best Senate manipulators that ever lived, is passing his last days in a local hospital. I am familiar with the rules and procedures and, naturally, it falls on me to guide the destiny of the organization in these times."

76. See Cole, *Roosevelt and the Isolationists*, chap. 30.

77. Arthur H. Vandenberg, Jr., ed., *The Private Papers of Senator Vandenberg* (Boston: Houghton Mifflin, 1952), 13–15.

78. Congressmen Bruce Barton and Joseph Martin, both moderate internationalists, resented their pairing with Fish, whom FDR detested. Bruce Barton to Joseph Martin, September 20, 1960, Bruce Barton MSS, Wisconsin Historical Society, Madison, Wis. See also Richard M. Fried, *The Man Everybody Knew: Bruce Barton and the Making of Modern America* (Chicago: Ivan R. Dee, 2005), 189–92. For Roosevelt's description of Fish as "Pooh-bah," see Clifford and Spencer, *First Peacetime Draft*, 215.

79. Rex Stout, *The Illustrious Dunderheads* (New York: Alfred A. Knopf, 1942).

80. James W. Wadsworth to Mrs. R. W. Bliss, May 28, 1941, Wadsworth Family MSS, Library of Congress.

81. See J. Garry Clifford and Theodore A. Wilson, "Blundering on the Brink, 1941," in *Presidents, Diplomats, and Other Mortals*, ed. J. Garry Clifford and Theodore A. Wilson (Columbia, Mo.: University of Missouri Press, 2007), 99–115.

82. Byrnes to E. Willoughby Middleton, June 9, 1941, James F. Byrnes MSS, Clemson University Library, Clemson University, Clemson, S.C. See also Scott Lucas to Alvin Boon, May 15, 1941, Box 26, Scott Lucas MSS, Illinois State Historical Society, Springfield, Ill. This Democratic Senate leader also counseled caution: "You ask me if I favor war; today, no; tomorrow, I do not know. We live from day to day in this turmoil. The man who makes his mind definitely as to what he will do three months from now is doing his country a disservice."

83. For Roosevelt's utilitarian approach to American history, see Philip Abbot, *The Exemplary Presidency: Franklin D. Roosevelt and the American Political Tradition* (Amherst, Mass.: University of Massachusetts Press, 1990), p. 4.

84. Diary of Claude Wickard, April 18, 1941.

85. Diary of W. L. Mackenzie King, April 16, 1941, Canadian Public Record Office, Ottawa.

86. Reynolds, *Creation of the Anglo-American Alliance*, chap. 8.

87. Michael S. Sherry, *The Rise of American Air Power* (New Haven, Conn.: Yale University Press, 1987), 100–15.

88. Heinrichs, *Threshold of War*, 43.

89. Vandenberg to Leland Sumner, March 21, 1941, Arthur H. Vandenberg MSS, Bentley Library, University of Michigan, Ann Arbor, Mich.

90. Quoted in Jurgen Rohwer, "The Wireless War," in *The Battle of the Atlantic, 1939–1945*, ed. Stephen Howarth and Derek Law (Annapolis, Md.: Naval Institute Press, 1994), 411–12. See also Jerome M. O'Connor, "FDR's Undeclared War," *Naval History* 18 (February 2004): 27; and Lisle A. Rose, *Power at Sea: The*

Breaking Storm, 1919–1945 (Columbia, Mo.: University of Missouri Press, 2007), 244–50.

91. Henry Morgenthau Presidential Diary, May 22, 1941: "The President's idea is that there's a very good likelihood that Germany will move into Spain and Portugal at any moment, and when they do, then he wants to take over these islands [Azores, Canaries, Cape Verdes] and wants to be ready."

92. David Reynolds, "The Origins of the Two 'World Wars,'" *Journal of Contemporary History* 38 (January 2003): 40. When Hitler declared war on the United States after Pearl Harbor, he blamed the so-called Jewish clique surrounding FDR for American intervention: "It was the Jew, in his full Satanic vileness, who rallied around this man [Roosevelt], but to whom this man also reached out." Quoted in Saul Friedlander, *The Years of Extermination: Nazi Germany and the Jews, 1939–1945* (New York: HarperCollins, 2007), 279.

93. Quoted in George McJimsey, *The Presidency of Franklin Delano Roosevelt* (Lawrence, Kan.: University Press of Kansas, 2000), 206.

94. Quoted in David Reynolds, *From Munich to Pearl Harbor* (Chicago: Ivan R. Dee, 2001), 130.

95. FDR quoted in Joseph Lash Diary, February 5, 1940, Joseph Lash MSS, FDRL.

96. Quoted in Steven Cascy, *Cautious Crusade* (New York: Oxford University Press, 2001), 44.

97. Raymond Gram Swing in *London Sunday Express*, May 11, 1941, quoted in Landecker, "FDR's Leadership," 36: "The more his friends are in anguish about his inscrutable delay, the better they serve him. The more vocative the protests in newspapers and at public meetings, the safer the future and the sounder is the President's leadership when it comes. That is not to say that he is egging his associates on to create a demand, which is not an accurate way to describe the situation. He feels that the public is not yet aware enough of the dangers and the gravity of the hour for him to move now. That being his view, he still does not undertake to instruct the public himself. That is for others to do, and do with all eloquence and alacrity. They are doing it. Hull, Knox, Stimson, and [Wendell] Willkie, the four most authentic secondary leaders in the country, are hammering and teaching."

98. Henry Morgenthau, Jr., quoted in Stephen E. Ambrose, "'Just Plain Dumb Luck': American Entry into World War II," in *Pearl Harbor Revisited*, ed. Robert W. Love, Jr. (New York: St. Martin's Press: 1995), 99.

chapter two

CONTAINMENT, ROLLBACK, AND THE ONSET OF THE PACIFIC WAR, 1933–1941

Sidney Pash

Admiral Yamamoto knew that the Empire's future rested on the opening battle of the war. His task force had to sail undetected over a vast sea and destroy the enemy fleet in port. If his ships were detected or if the enemy set a trap, all would be lost. A smashing victory in the war's early hours could lead to a negotiated settlement but not victory because the enemy possessed a true two-ocean navy and Japan's European ally had not proven that it could prevent the redeployment of this second mighty armada. Compared with its opponent, whose people numbered more than 100 million and whose territory spanned a continent, Japan was a second-rate power. But Yamamoto had to set these considerations aside. Convinced that negotiations had failed and alarmed by the enemy's continued military buildup, the Japanese cabinet voted for war.[1]

In the months leading up to war, Japan's rival celebrated the success of its Far Eastern strategy because desultory negotiations bought time for the deployment of tens of thousands of soldiers and scores of warships to Asia. But in the end, the strategy for containing Japanese continental expansion may have been too successful. In the final months of peace, the conviction that Japan would never fight had spread to friend and foe alike, thus obviating the need for compromise and fatally undermining any chance of achieving the kind of diplomatic breakthrough that could have averted war. In Japan, meanwhile, the specter of continued diplomatic failures, combined with a deteriorating strategic position, led the government to cast the die for war. Japan's last pre-war prime minister, a diehard opponent of the coming conflict, saw that the Empire had little choice. "There is no question," he argued, "but that [our opponent's] aim was from the start to increase her military and naval forces and then reject Japan's demands." Given this policy, he noted, "if Japan does not now go to war and defend her threatened interests, she will eventually have to kowtow." The decision to wage war, however, could not mask fatalism akin to desperation. Another former prime minister and onetime general—hardly a rarity for interwar Japan—neatly summed up the Empire's position: "Although we cannot foretell victory or defeat, we must enter the battle confident of victory. If we should by any chance fail, it would be an immeasurable catastrophe."[2]

Given these considerations, Japan's senior leaders opted to gamble all on a war that the Empire likely would not survive. One day after the Imperial Conference endorsed the cabinet's decision for war, Admiral Gonnohoye Yamamoto ordered Admiral Heihachiro Togo to attack the Pacific fleet at Port Arthur. Russian containment had failed. It was 1904, and the Russo-Japanese War had just begun.

A generation later, another Japanese rival adopted a strategy startlingly similar to the failed Russian program of the early 1900s. Longer in duration and grander in scope, America's containment strategy also helped to bring about the war that it was designed to avert. Following the start of the Second Sino–Japanese War in July 1937, the Roosevelt administration developed a remarkably cautious and generally successful strategy to stave off a Chinese defeat, contain Japanese expansion, and after September 1940, negate Tokyo's contribution to the Axis. This successful American containment strategy rested on four firm, apparently proven pillars. First, the United States sought to avoid any diplomatic agreements that might strengthen Japan and weaken China. Second, senior officials increased American economic and military aid to China in an attempt to even the odds on the battlefield and bolster Chinese morale. Third, the United States vastly increased its martial power and later its military presence in Asia in an attempt to deter further Japanese expansion. Finally, American policymakers set about weakening the Japanese economy through a multifaceted program of sanctions.

This policy, although often unpopular at home among supporters of China, isolationists, interventionists, and competing government agencies, was generally successful. By spring 1941, Chinese armies had managed to tie down the vast Japanese war machine for almost four years. This was no mean feat given that although the 1894–1895 Sino–Japanese War dragged on for nine months, the issue was decided in four. As late as 1931,

Japanese forces drove China from Manchuria in a matter of months and set up the puppet state of Manchukuo the following year. To be sure, American policy had contributed to Japan's decision to join the Axis and absorb northern French Indochina in 1940, but the overall benefits of containment far outweighed these drawbacks. During the summer of 1941, however, American officials began to abandon their cautious containment policy in favor of a strategy that sought to roll back Japanese gains in Asia and drive Tokyo from the Axis. This shift in policy began soon after the German invasion of the Soviet Union and accelerated in the final months before Pearl Harbor as an increasing number of policymakers grew convinced that as long as the Nazi-Soviet conflict continued, the United States could drastically increase sanctions with little risk that Tokyo would lash out. As the war in Russia dragged on into autumn without a decision and the Anglo-American strategic position improved worldwide, senior officials, lured by rollback's siren song, abandoned containment and helped bring on the Pacific War.

Throughout the summer and fall of 1941, U.S. officials, like their Russian counterparts some 40 years earlier, conducted elaborate negotiations designed to buy time but never bear fruit. In Japan, meanwhile, Hideki Tojo's government grew convinced that additional negotiations were useless and that they were only further playing into American hands. Mirroring the fatalism of an earlier generation, Japan for the second time chose to wage a war that most senior statesmen did not believe the Empire would survive.

AMERICAN CONTAINMENT

By early 1933, the men who would become the architects of the American containment of Japan believed three things unequivocally. First, they believed that Japan sought hegemony in China and quite possibly in all Asia. Even after the adjournment of the 1921–1922 Washington Conference, which among other things produced a naval disarmament treaty favorable to the United States, ended the Anglo-Japanese Alliance, and provided for the Japanese return of Shantung province to China, future Secretary of State Cordell Hull remained certain that Tokyo "will agree on paper and then proceed with her fixed policy of economic penetration of China, Siberia, Manchuria, and other portions of the Far East." His views had not changed a decade later when he entered the Roosevelt cabinet. Second, officials believed that traditional diplomacy could not halt Japanese expansion. Following Japan's seizure of Manchuria, America's new ambassador to Japan, Joseph Grew, glumly concluded that the "Japanese are fundamentally incapable of comprehending the sanctity of contractual obligations when such obligations conflict with what they conceive to be their own interests." Finally, American policymakers believed, as they had for a generation, that economic and/or military deterrence could slow and even halt predatory Japanese expansion. Since 1908, when the Great White Fleet paid a courtesy call in Japan to impress Tokyo with American naval power at a time of heightened Japanese-American tension, far too many Americans believed that military deterrence could bend Japan to America's will. When Pacific hostility subsided with the fleet's arrival in 1908, President Theodore Roosevelt determined that naval deterrence "stopped the Japanese talk of war." Later, during World War I, American economic power in the guise of threatened steel, cotton, and loan embargoes seemed to restrain Japanese policy in China and Siberia. When Japanese and American interests again clashed on the Asian mainland during the 1931–1932 Manchurian crisis, Henry Stimson (Herbert Hoover's secretary of state and William Howard Taft's former and Franklin Roosevelt's future secretary of war) noted that the decision to leave the Pacific fleet in Hawaii after its spring 1932 cruise "undoubtedly exercised a steadying effect" on the Japanese. Even career diplomat Joseph Grew believed that military preparedness represented the best possible deterrent to Japanese expansion. In the generation leading up to the Pacific War then, deterrence, either military or economic, seemed to have a salutary effect on Japan.[3]

The administration of President Franklin D. Roosevelt broke ground for the first pillar of America's containment of Japan in March of 1933 soon after China's minister to the United States, Alfred Sze, met with Stanley Hornbeck, head of the State Department's Division of Far Eastern Affairs. Sze sought a meeting with Hornbeck to sound out the latter as to the new administration's willingness to improve Sino-Japanese relations. Rather than support Sino-Japanese talks, which he believed would lead to Nanking's recognition of Manchukuo, Hornbeck urged his superiors to make no effort to improve Sino-Japanese relations. Hornbeck informed Cordell Hull that any American initiative "would re-invigorate Japanese animus against this country" and that successful negotiations were bound to create a lasting bitterness "on the part both of the Japanese and of the

Chinese (in general) towards us." He predicted that negotiations would likely fail but argued, quite significantly, that the United States had far more to fear from successful talks. Japan, Hornbeck noted, had long demanded negotiations with China, and their success could only mean "a capitulation on the part of China in terms of recognition of the new *status quo* in Manchuria and a pledge to refrain from any further efforts to upset that *status quo*." The Far Eastern chief argued that China's capitulation would mean a defeat for the policies that the League of Nations and Washington had developed in response to the Far Eastern crisis and would allow "the Japanese to consolidate their position on the Continent and prepare for their next move (either further coercion of China or conflict with Russia or conflict with the United States)." In effect, Hornbeck began to enunciate the theme in early 1933, which eight years later still governed the ill-fated Hull–Nomura discussions of August–November 1941. To wit, a Sino-Japanese peace would serve neither Chinese nor American interests but rather would act as a springboard to further Japanese aggression and conquest.[4]

Within a year of the Hornbeck–Sze meeting, Secretary Hull had come around to embrace Hornbeck's conclusions. In 1934, he built on Hornbeck's theme and rejected Tokyo's proposal for a joint Japanese-American declaration on trade and mutual respect for Pacific territory. Rather than engage in serious or even lengthy negotiations to improve Japanese-American relations, Hull rejected the entire Japanese proposal within 72 hours and then pressured FDR to reject any further Japanese entreaties. Clearly reflecting the dominant view that traditional diplomacy would not contain Japan, he informed the president that Woodrow Wilson's approval, over Secretary of State Robert Lansing's objection, of a bilateral agreement with Tokyo "resulted in no end of confusion and embarrassment." Hull's message was clear: Do not repeat Wilson's mistake. Heed State's advice. Do not conclude any new political agreements with Japan.[5]

Rather than help Tokyo repair its strained relations with Nanking and Washington, senior American policymakers instead set about building the second pillar of American containment and strengthened China's ability to contain Japanese expansion. In spring 1933, the Roosevelt administration approved a $50 million commodity credit for China as well as the sale of some $6 million in new military hardware. Two years later, Hornbeck and State gained a valuable ally in their effort to bolster Chinese resistance when Secretary of the Treasury Henry Morgenthau engineered the first of many American purchases of Chinese silver. After convincing the Chinese government to abandon its silver coinage in favor of a paper currency, the secretary embarked on a policy that in time led Washington to purchase virtually all of China's considerable silver stock by late 1938.[6]

The Roosevelt administration began to construct the third pillar of containment in 1933 when it embarked on a major naval building program designed to combat the Great Depression and contain Japan. Three months after taking office, the president reversed Hoover's policy of beating swords into plowshares and earmarked nearly $250 million in relief money for naval expansion. The following year the president's pro-Navy views and the active campaigning of influential legislators, including Georgia's Carl Vinson, chairman of the House Naval Affairs Committee, secured congressional authorization to fund fleet construction up to treaty limits by 1942. That this building program was designed largely to deter Japan is clear. The president's friend, Ambassador Grew, concluded that Japan could not afford a naval arms race and that the United States had no choice but to "build up our Navy and our air force to the limit or withdraw from the Far East." An expanded military capacity, Grew noted, remained "the best possible restraining influence on further Japanese imperialist aggression."[7]

With the outbreak of renewed Sino-Japanese hostilities in July 1937, the architects of American containment continued existing polices in expanded form while undertaking new efforts to strengthen China and contain Japan. Henry Morgenthau and the Treasury Department took the lead in aiding the Chinese war effort during 1937 and 1938 through expanded purchases of Chinese silver as well as $45 million in credits for Chinese tung oil and tin. Morgenthau even helped China secure tanker trucks to haul imported oil and personally dispatched public health officials and transportation experts to help build the Burma Road. By the summer of 1940, as isolationist sentiment began to abate, the State Department stepped up efforts to bolster Chinese coffers. In the autumn, State arranged for a $50 million package of loans and credits and in December successfully worked to secure a mammoth $100 million loan.[8]

Although economic aid proved critical in keeping Chinese resistance alive, gradual American economic sanctions proved equally crucial in containing Japan's military in an endless Chinese morass. Sanctions evolved slowly owing largely to legal niceties, including the 1911 Treaty of Commerce and Navigation, and the fear that Congress would not approve a wide-ranging program of economic warfare. Despite these impediments, Washington moved forward with the final pillar of its containment program beginning in July 1938 when the State Department began its program of so-called "moral embargoes." Starting with the aircraft industry, these embargoes soon expanded to such interests as finance, oil, and steel. In each case, State and Commerce Department officials pressured various businesses to refrain from doing business with Japan. Aircraft manufacturers, for example, all but ceased doing business with Tokyo, and, under intense pressure, J&W Seligman and Company abandoned a $20 million credit deal with Japan's Manchurian Industrial Development Corporation. In December 1939, the department's Division of Controls added processing equipment for aviation gasoline—a critical component of Japan's expanding war machine—to the moral embargo list. Controls informed major oil exporters "that the national interest suggests that for the time being there should be no further delivery to interests of certain countries of plans, plants, manufacturing rights, or technical information required for the production of high quality aviation gasoline." Just as the moral embargo reached its high-water mark, the State Department, in conjunction with the Treasury, began a far more lethal form of economic warfare when it unveiled its program of preclusive purchasing.[9]

The advocates of preclusive purchasing convinced Congress that their program was a simple preparedness measure designed to stockpile critical raw materials that might become unavailable with the spread of war in Europe and Asia. In reality, preclusive purchasing sought to deny Germany, Italy—and in particular, Japan—the opportunity to buy raw materials on the world market by financing massive, preemptive American purchases; that is, the United States would purchase a given commodity before Japan could or alternatively just outbid the Japanese. Herbert Feis, a leading State Department officer and point man on preclusive purchasing, confirmed in late 1940 "that purchase was suggested almost purely as a means of preventing . . . commodities from going to Japan." By the summer of 1941, the United States had effectively preempted Japanese purchases of raw materials from around the world, including Bolivian tin and tungsten, Chilean copper, Brazilian rubber, Turkish chrome, and Spanish zinc.[10]

Washington added to its policy of economic warfare in the summer of 1940 when Congress approved a new National Defense Act, which gave the administration authority to restrict exports considered vital to national defense. Beginning with aviation fuel, the United States soon denied Japan licenses for iron and steel scrap, iron ore, ferro alloys, bronze, copper, and petroleum refinery equipment. By the summer of 1941, Japan could essentially purchase only cotton and crude oil.[11]

In addition to stepped-up aid to China and new multipronged economic sanctions, Washington also redoubled its existing program of old-fashioned military deterrence. In 1938 and again in 1940, Congress approved massive naval expansion programs. The May 1938 Vinson Act authorized building 69 additional warships, and twin 1940 bills authorized some 160,000 tons of new construction, half of which went to build new aircraft carriers. In 1940, the Roosevelt administration also transferred elements of the Pacific fleet from the West Coast to Hawaii and strengthened U.S. forces in the Philippines.[12]

To be sure, American containment had its fair share of drawbacks. In an effort to end the fighting in China, for example, Japan occupied northern French Indochina in September 1940. This move seemed crucial to ending the war given that almost half of Chiang Kai-shek's overseas aid came through northern Vietnam. Northern Indochina also provided valuable bases from which to attack the southern Chinese interior. In September 1940, again in part to help end the war in China, Japan also joined the Axis Alliance. Finance Minister Kawada Isao and Chief of the Cabinet Planning Board Hoshino Naoki supported the controversial alliance owing to their hope that with "this pact, we may be able to settle the China Incident." Nearly a year later, however, with Chiang still resisting Japanese forces, Tokyo occupied the remainder of French Indochina, once again with an eye to bringing China to its knees. Army Chief of Staff Sugiyama Gen argued "[the] move southward . . . [would] sever the links between the Chunking regime and the British and American powers, which support it from behind and strengthen its will to resist."[13]

These notable shortcomings notwithstanding, by the summer of 1941, containment had fulfilled its creators' grandest expectations. Japan still remained tied down in China, a fact that many believed explained Japan's decision neither to join the German attack on the Soviet Union nor to follow up the absorption of French Indochina with an attack on the Philippines, Malaya, Singapore, Burma, or Thailand. But just as containment was proving its worth, the Roosevelt administration abandoned its limited and cautious policy in favor of a strategy designed to drive Japan from China and out of the Axis Alliance. This decision resulted from a number of factors, including a fundamental misunderstanding of Japanese and U.S. power, events in Europe, and continued Japanese expansion. Taken as a whole, these factors moved senior leaders during the summer and autumn of 1941 to abandon the limited victories that containment offered—stalemate in China and a nullified Japanese contribution to the Axis—in favor of the grand, but in the end, disastrous policy of rollback that ended at Pearl Harbor. In late July 1941, following the Japanese absorption of southern French Indochina, the United States froze Japanese assets, effectively ending all trade between the two countries. After Great Britain and the Dutch East Indies followed Washington's lead, Japan faced a worldwide, American-led embargo. In early August, Prime Minister Fumimaro Konoe, with the support of key cabinet members and Emperor Hirohito, sought an extraordinary summit with President Roosevelt designed to end the embargoes and avert war with the West. The continued misreading of Japan's history and the failure to appreciate the limits of American power, however, led policymakers to once again eschew diplomacy.[14]

Even before containment fell victim to the rollback strategy, the kind of diplomatic engagement that produced détente in the midst of the Cold War and that indeed proved essential in containing the Soviet Union was nowhere to be seen in the Japanese-American relationship. Opposition to any Japanese-American accord, which dated back to 1933, remained a cornerstone of American policy after July 1941, and if past practice proved a reliable guide, Konoe had little chance of improving Japanese-American relations. In mid-1939, for example, when continued Chinese resistance and the announcement of the Nazi-Soviet Pact led Japan to explore the possibility of a negotiated settlement to the war in China, the United States refused to listen. William Bullitt, the former U.S. ambassador to the Soviet Union, informed Hull that Japan was attempting to use Poland as a conduit to arrange American help in ending the war. The U.S. embassy in China also informed Hull that Japan's new government sought an end to the war. And on September 1, as German troops streamed across the Polish border, Hull received the clearest signal possible that Japan sought an end to hostilities. Japan's new prime minister, Abe Nobuyuki, informed the press that his government would not rule out cooperating with outside powers to end the war. Given that German-Japanese relations had just sunk to a new low, Abe could only have meant that Japan would accept English or American help.[15]

However, the prospect of continued Chinese resistance (one object of American containment) undercut any reason to help end the war. The Council of the Institute of Pacific Relations had already concluded that China would continue "resistance over a long period" and "keep large bodies of Japanese troops in the field." From China, Ambassador Nelson Johnson informed President Roosevelt that with American aid—including sanctions on Japan—Chinese resistance would continue indefinitely. Hull, who by this time had long doubted the usefulness of diplomacy in dealing with Japan, understood that as long as Nanking continued to fight, he did not have to strike a deal with Japan to save China.[16]

Even after rejecting a role in ending the Sino–Japanese War, Hull and Hornbeck still had an opportunity to aid Abe Nobuyuki's moderate government. General Abe proved himself a steadfast member of the Japanese government's Anglo-American camp when he harried pro-Axis officials from their posts and replaced them with unwavering members of the Anglo-American faction. The prime minister quickly signaled to friend and foe alike his determination to improve relations with Washington when he named Admiral Kichisaburo Nomura, former naval attaché in Washington, his new foreign minister. Widely praised by the Japanese press, the American embassy also interpreted Abe's selection of the pro-American Nomura as a positive sign. Ambassador Grew meanwhile informed Hull that negotiations designed to normalize trade relations "would exert a powerful and salutary influence in Japan." When Abe's government pressed for improved trade relations, Grew warned Hull that if Washington refused to consider the request "we shall be administering a rebuff which may well bring about the fall of the present cabinet." Grew as usual was correct. After Hull refused to consider normalizing trade relations, Abe's cabinet collapsed in January 1940.[17]

Fortunately, the United States had a second opportunity to pursue improved relations when Abe's successor, Admiral Yonai Mitsumasa, took office. Ambassador Grew described Yonai as a diehard opponent of the Axis, whose elevation to power promised a moderated China policy. But neither Hornbeck nor Hull would consider improved relations. Hornbeck scoffed at the notion "that two strokes of a pen on one piece of paper by two diplomats will transform a predatory nation overnight into a contented, peace loving and peace-supporting power." When the British government suggested that Yonai might prove receptive to Anglo-American good offices in ending the Sino–Japanese war, Hull still refused to take action.[18]

Even with the collapse of the Yonai cabinet in the summer of 1940 and the subsequent Japanese decision to join the Axis in September, all was not lost. In the winter of 1941, Japan's new ambassador to the United States, Kichisaburo Nomura, arrived in Washington determined to arrest the precipitous decline in Japanese-American relations. For the better part of five months, Hull met Nomura regularly in what appeared a genuine American effort to improve relations. What Nomura failed to understand, however, was that the course of the European war, coupled with rising fears of an imminent Japanese strike against Europe's vulnerable Asian colonies, demanded that Washington do all it could to keep peace in the Pacific. With England alone resisting Germany, American policymakers, including Hull, believed that it was imperative to prevent Japan from entering the war. Hull therefore conducted elaborate negotiations while all along waiting for the pendulum of war to swing back toward the Anglo-American camp.[19]

Hull and Nomura began their desultory talks in February and terminated them, at the former's insistence, in late June. During the discussions, Washington consistently sought Japan's exit from the Axis Alliance, but this was only a blind. Neither Hull nor Secretary of War Henry Stimson evidenced much fear over Japan's membership in the Axis, and even Hornbeck conceded in April 1941 that he had little fear that "[Foreign minister Yosuke] Matsuoka and/or the real authorities in Japan will make of Japan a German tool." But in the interests of stringing out the talks, American negotiators allowed Tokyo to believe that the Axis Alliance remained a critical obstacle to a Japanese-American accord. Japan's membership in the Alliance allowed Hull and Hornbeck to drag out the talks, at the same time permitting the United States to force Prime Minister Konoe to oust his pro-German foreign minister from the cabinet. On May 28, Hull informed Nomura that Matsuoka's consistent pro-Axis stance was impeding negotiations; and on June 2, he informed Nomura "that in light of the loud statements which Matsuoka and others were daily making . . . one was forced back to the inquiry of whether Japan really" wished to conclude an agreement. On June 21, when Hull declared his talks with Nomura at an end, the secretary again singled out Japan's membership in the Axis and Matsuoka's support for the alliance with Germany. Although the Konoe cabinet sought improved relations with America, it refused to sacrifice its alliance with Berlin to curry favor with Washington. Konoe had few qualms, however, about sacking Matsuoka, who lost his job as foreign minister the following month.[20]

A second American red herring, which masqueraded as a bone of contention during the ill-fated Hull–Nomura talks, concerned ongoing Sino-Japanese hostilities. In April, Hornbeck included terms to settle the China Incident in an American draft proposal subsequently passed on to Nomura. Just days before, however, Hornbeck privately argued that Japan sought peace in China in order to free its forces for military action elsewhere. He concluded that "Japan's present involvement in China is to the advantage of the United States and Great Britain." Clearly, Hornbeck sought anything but an end to the fighting in China, but by placing terms to end the conflict on the conference agenda, he convinced Nomura that ending the war was an American concern. This, along with wrangling over the Axis pact, meant that the talks would continue until the day that Hull could safely dispense with the fiction of diplomacy. That day came on the first day of summer 1941.[21]

On June 22, 1941, the day that Hull terminated his talks with Nomura, the direction of the Second World War swung toward the Anglo-American camp in a most profound way with the German invasion of the Soviet Union. The Nazi onslaught not only allowed Hull to end his talks with Nomura, but also permitted the secretary and others to abandon containment in favor of the rollback strategy.

THE REVOLUTIONARY SUMMER AND
THE ONSET OF ROLLBACK

Even as German forces destroyed the overmatched and overextended Red Army in the opening weeks of the war, American officials recognized that the German attack freed Washington from a host of old fears. The U.S. Army's War Plans Division, for example, reckoned that the Nazi-Soviet war freed England from the threat of a cross-channel invasion as well as an intensified German assault in the Middle East. The State Department Far Eastern Division, meanwhile, concluded that owing to the German assault on the Soviet Union, Japan would likely refrain from any attack on British and Dutch possessions for the next several months. The Army War Plans Division reached the same conclusion just weeks later with the added argument that Japan would avoid action that would lead to war with either the Soviet Union or the United States.[22]

Convinced that England would not succumb to Germany and that Japan would not wage war against the West for the foreseeable future, advocates of greater sanctions gained an upper hand in decision-making circles. Alger Hiss, a chief Hornbeck aide, insisted that the time was ripe for increased economic sanctions and concluded that Tokyo would not resort to war with America until Germany defeated the Soviet Union. Hornbeck, who also pressed his superiors to step up action against Tokyo, informed Under Secretary of State Sumner Welles in late July that Japan would not choose to wage war against the United States should Washington intensify sanctions. By early summer, advocates of greater sanctions held the upper hand and needed only a new *casus belli* to prod the president into acting on their demands.[23]

In late July 1941, Tokyo provided a reason for stepped-up sanctions when its forces began occupying southern French Indochina. United States officials learned of the impending move during the first week of July but made no move to deter Japan despite Ambassador Grew's opinion that a clear, private warning might be sufficient to warn Tokyo off. Instead of a private warning, the State Department issued a blistering press release on July 24, which both castigated Japan and simultaneously garnered public support for a freeze on Japanese assets in the United States, which the president put in place on July 26. It is clear that although the president intended to allow limited trade if either the public balked at an embargo, if Germany decisively defeated Russian or British forces, or if Japan immediately set about preparing for war, he too had become intrigued by the possibility of driving Japan from China and the Axis without firing a shot.[24]

Within days of the freeze announcement, Prime Minister Konoe set about arranging a meeting with President Roosevelt in a last-ditch effort to restore trade relations and avoid war in the Pacific. While FDR initially welcomed Konoe's planned visit, his inner circle, as they had for decades, viewed Japan as untrustworthy and vulnerable, and they steadfastly opposed the idea of a Pacific summit. Secretary of War Stimson saw the proposed meeting as nothing more than "a blind to try to keep us from taking definite action," and Hull informed fellow cabinet members that "with the Japanese advancing into Indochina, any peace conference was absurd." The secretary did not, however, confide this opinion to either Konoe or Nomura. Instead, he signaled his willingness to reopen talks in preparation for a summit. Hull wished to extend negotiations for several reasons, none of which had anything to do with bringing about a leaders' conference. Initially, with Washington and Berlin fighting an undeclared naval war in the Atlantic, conversations might reveal Japan's reaction to a German-American clash. Moreover, as Hornbeck informed Hull, continued Japanese-American talks so worried Berlin that perhaps "the Germans would within three months or so 'not be speaking to the Japanese.'" Finally, as long as Konoe hoped that he could reach a diplomatic solution, Japan would not resort to war to break the Western embargo.[25]

During the rest of August and September, Hull and other opponents of the summit ensured that Roosevelt and Konoe would not meet. Hull, for example, demanded that Japanese and American negotiators agree on such issues as Japan's relation to the Axis and the settlement of the Sino–Japanese War—the very issues that the previous four months of talks had failed to resolve—prior to a summit. It is also clear that Hull set about to derail the conference by breaking elementary security precautions. On August 19, for example, Ambassador Grew warned Hull not to share with anyone at State other than Welles news of the proposed meeting. Should "the proposal become prematurely known," Grew warned, "it would in all probability lead to further attempted assassinations" in Japan. Despite Grew's warning, Hull shared the ambassador's telegram with Hornbeck; Max Hamilton, the Far Eastern Division's new chief; and possibly others. Hull also got tongues wagging on both sides of the Pacific when he told the press on August 28 that Nomura had just given FDR a personal message from Konoe. A week later, the secretary told the Chinese minister to Washington "[t]he chief points" concerning the recent Japanese-American talks. The Chinese government's reputation for secrecy was such that it once prompted a member of the British Foreign Office to observe that "anything of a confidential nature, if communicated to the Chinese Government, would reach the Japanese shortly afterwards." Hull knew this and was in all likelihood using the Chinese to pass along information to torpedo the leaders' summit. Should Chinese officials fail to pass along confidential information in time to sandbag the meeting, Hull went a step further and informed the Japanese embassy in Washington about the contents of secret information sent by Ambassador Grew and tagged for FDR's and Hull's eyes only.[26]

To succeed, containment historically has required successful diplomacy, especially in times of crisis. Since early 1933, however, neither Hull nor Hornbeck believed that Japanese-American diplomacy could protect America's Far Eastern interests, and unfortunately this opinion continued to guide their thinking in the final months before Pearl Harbor. Hull remained convinced that even a successful summit would not halt Japanese expansion, while Hornbeck decried the Japanese proposals as an effort "to weaken China, to drive a wedge between the United States and China and to strengthen Japan." Even Stimson, who had served under Presidents Taft and Hoover before joining the Roosevelt cabinet, could not shed his distrust.[27]

Hull, Hornbeck, Stimson, and others also shared the view of senior military officials that a successful summit could have disastrous consequences for America's strategic position in Asia. A negotiated end to the war in China and the prompt withdrawal of Japanese forces would be a *sine qua non* of any agreement and this, military officials argued, America must avoid. In October 1941, Hayes Kroner, chief of the British Empire Section for the War Department General Staff, informed Army Chief of Staff General George C. Marshall, as follows: "[A]t this stage in the execution of our national strategic plan, a cessation of hostilities in China . . . would be highly detrimental to our interests." Only a military government could control returning Japanese forces, Kroner reckoned, and such a government, he concluded, would have "neither the ability nor the inclination to continue diplomatic negotiations with any of the democratic powers."[28]

In the late summer of 1941, there also seemed no reason to deal with an inherently untrustworthy and expansionist Japan to avoid the possibility of war. Should Japan attempt, for example, to break the Western embargoes by taking the Netherlands East Indies, American war planners concluded that the Dutch would either beat back a Japanese assault or destroy the oil facilities. Other potential Japanese targets (Malaya and Singapore) also appeared highly defensible. As early as February 1941, Air Chief Marshal Sir Robert Brooke-Popham, British commander-in-chief, Far East, assured the Australian War Cabinet that Singapore could hold out against a Japanese assault for up to six months. Churchill also believed that should the Japanese strike at Singapore—a move he considered highly unlikely—the island fortress would resist for as long as one year. In the Philippines, meanwhile, General Douglas MacArthur assured General Marshall in early September that with the delivery of antiaircraft batteries and the new B-17 bomber, he could successfully defend the archipelago.[29]

A final impediment to peace came from a most unlikely source: the American public. Drawn to pacifism in the 1920s and riven by isolationism during the 1930s, public opinion, which had previously tied the hands of administration interventionists, now hamstrung efforts to avoid war. Growing support for Washington's get-tough policy is clearly evident from contemporary press accounts that reveal the erroneous belief that the assets freeze was a complete embargo. Proceeding from this false assumption, the national press over the next several weeks applauded Roosevelt's strong stand. When the president placed aviation-grade petroleum on the embargo list on August 1, the press continued to cheer. The *Milwaukee Journal* declared that "[w]e want no such halfway measures as were applied to Italy when economic sanctions were declared against Mussolini for moving into Ethiopia. Halfway measures are worse than none at all." The *Washington Post* proclaimed that "[t]here need be no qualms about public opinion" inasmuch as a majority of Americans "advocate that steps should be taken now to keep Japan from becoming more powerful even at the risk of war." The August 16, 1941, edition of *Liberty* magazine first asked its readers whether the United States "[s]hall [s]ell out China?" and then informed its public that Washington should never "consider the scheme of throwing China to the little yellow wolves." The *Liberty* editorial board, which recognized that Germany rather than Japan remained America's paramount security concern and that Tokyo's Far Eastern ambitions complicated "the destruction of Hitler," reminded its readers and perhaps Washington's fainthearted that "[a]ny time the United States feels it is necessary," "it can blow the liver and lights out of the Japanese Empire." *Liberty* assured its readers that its liver-and-lights claim was premised on prevailing military opinion. Polling data, which essentially mirrored editorial opinion, revealed that a majority favored a firm American stand even at the risk of war. A significant number also approved direct American action to defend Dutch and British Far Eastern possessions as well as Australia.[30]

During the Cold War, the specter of nuclear war and the futility of MAD—mutually assured destruction—helped keep the peace by making war unthinkable. But in 1941, American leaders—and indeed a growing segment of the public—contemplated a Japanese-American war with equanimity while diplomacy was seen as unnecessary or downright dangerous. America's leaders and those they led had grown tired with the stale futility of a containment policy that left the Japanese army in China and Tokyo tied to the Axis. Neither diplomacy nor halfway measures would bring victory, but the assets freeze could. Without oil, Japan would be forced to abandon its war effort and its alliance with Germany.

TOJO, AMERICA, AND THE FAILURE OF ROLLBACK

Unable to make peace with America—or even meet with President Roosevelt for that matter—and unwilling to lead Japan in a war he did not believe it could win, Konoe stepped down on October 16, 1941. Konoe's resignation did not bring an end to diplomacy, and indeed the final weeks of peace offered the United States and Japan repeated opportunities to spare Asia and the Pacific from a cataclysmic war. That these chances may well have increased with the ascension to power of a career military officer who later swung from the gallows may come as a surprise. But in the autumn of 1941, statesmen on both sides of the Pacific formulated workable plans to avoid war.

Japan's senior leaders quickly selected War Minister Hideki Tojo to replace Konoe, who himself favored the general because "he would not plunge us immediately into war." The Emperor's closest aid, the Marquis Kido Koichi, also believed that "Tojo is someone who can handle negotiations with the United States." After taking office, Tojo agreed, at the Emperor's insistence, to continue talks with America, and in a clear signal that he had not given up on diplomacy, the new prime minister selected the former ambassador to the Soviet Union, Togo Shigenori, as his new foreign minister. In the event that negotiations compelled Japan to withdraw from China or break its alliance with Germany, Tojo retained his position as war minister and also took on the portfolio of home minister to better quell a military or popular uprising. By early November, Tojo and Togo overcame substantial cabinet opposition to continued negotiations and won approval for talks based on two proposals. In Proposal A, Tokyo pledged to immediately withdraw forces from Indochina, remove troops within two years from all of China except Hainan Island and the far north, and respect the Open Door. Japan also agreed to not automatically support Berlin in the event of a German-American war. Proposal B sought only a limited agreement in which Japan pledged to refrain from further offensive operations in return for normalized trade relations and a U.S promise "not [to] take such actions as may hinder efforts for peace by both Japan and China." With Proposal A, rollback had a better than even chance of succeeding. Should talks based on Proposal A falter, then a general agreement on Proposal B would ensure Japan's continued containment in the Chinese morass. But if Washington had refused to deal with Japan since 1933, could anything prompt Hull and Hornbeck to deal now?[31]

The American reaction to Tojo undercut what little chance remained of averting war. On the one hand, military analysts greeted the news of Tojo's appointment with something approaching shrill alarm. Navy analysts, for example, concluded that "[t]he ultra nationalist element of Japan has seized control of the Japanese Government and is prepared to push collaboration with the Axis powers and the opposition to the democracies to the ultimate extent." Their Army counterparts, meanwhile, argued that the Tojo cabinet's pro-Axis tilt "make all protestations of peaceful intent a sham or objective [sic] of suspicion." On the other hand, civilian analysts maintained that Tojo would not embark on immediate hostilities, nor could the new prime minister expect victory should he lead Japan to war. State Department analysts, in fact, saw Tojo as both more benign and less threatening than their military counterparts. Leading members of the Far Eastern Division, as well as Ambassador Grew, believed that Tojo would continue diplomacy at least for the time being. In the event they were wrong, however, there seemed no reason to panic. State Department analyst William Langdon saw that Japanese manpower problems made it impossible for Tokyo to carry the war beyond China. Hornbeck believed that if war did come, "[w]ith Japan as comparatively weak as she is today and with this country as comparatively strong as it is today, we need not fear unduly the military outcome—or even the immediate consequences—of such a conflict." The United States was, Hornbeck argued, "physically capable now of waging a properly conducted war with Japan and at the same time carrying on in the Atlantic all operations which it would be advantageous for us to make." Even General Marshall concluded in mid-November that within a month, air power would secure the Philippines from a Japanese invasion. This combination of mistrust for the Tojo cabinet and an almost fatal underestimation of Japanese military capabilities undermined eleventh-hour diplomacy and reinforced the growing belief that Japan could be forced from China and the Axis with an ever decreasing risk to Western interests.[32]

The first chance to deal with Tojo came in early November when President Roosevelt approached Henry Stimson regarding a *modus vivendi* designed to give American and British forces more time to prepare for war.

Stimson, however, told FDR that such an agreement would harm Chinese morale and was frankly unnecessary. Stimson's counterpart at the Navy Department, Frank Knox, also favored a hard line with Tokyo and doubted "whether the Japs will have the guts to go through with their program of aggression when they find they are confronted with war with both the United States and Great Britain." Harold Ickes, a close Roosevelt confidant and Secretary of the Interior, told the president that war with Japan would be so short that "we would soon be in a position where a large part of our Navy as well as of the British and the Dutch East Indies Navy, could be released for service in the Atlantic." In the absence of any positive inducements and faced with the unequivocal opposition of his closest advisors, the president elected not to push forward with plans for a *modus vivendi*.[33]

A second chance to avoid war came from an extraordinarily unlikely source, Harry Dexter White. An early architect of preclusive purchasing and something of a hardliner where Japan was concerned, White presented a radical plan in mid-November, which held out the possibility of averting war in the Pacific. His 10-point plan committed Washington to a wide-ranging program, which included the withdrawal of the bulk of the fleet from Pacific waters; a nonaggression pact with Tokyo; a final settlement of the Manchurian problem; a $2 billion long-term, low-interest loan for Japan; and normalized trade relations. Although White's plan called for sweeping American concessions, he expected no less from Tokyo. For its part, Japan would withdraw completely from China and Indochina, expel the bulk of German officials, and negotiate a nonaggression pact with the United States, China, the British Empire, and the Philippines.[34]

Taken as a whole, White's plan secured Washington's fundamental aims and represented a final victory for rollback. All Allied energies, including the Soviet Siberian Army, could concentrate on the destruction of Nazi Germany. An agreement based on White's plan also rendered the Axis pact a dead letter. As for China, White's proposal protected the Open Door and restored Chinese sovereignty by removing the Japanese Army as well as eliminating Western extraterritoriality rights. For a moment, his memorandum promised to revolutionize the entire course of Japanese-American relations. Max Hamilton informed Hull that White's proposal was "the most constructive proposition he had seen." At the War Department, General Leonard Gerow, head of the War Plans Division, notified Hull that he approved using White's plan "as a basis for discussion" with

Japan. Despite the backing of senior civilian and military officials, however, Hull continued to believe that economic sanctions, coupled with a military buildup in Asia, were preferable to traditional diplomacy, which was not only unnecessary but would also prove unpopular with interventionists in and out of government as well as the with the Chinese. Consequently, he gutted White's plan within a fortnight.[35]

Hull likewise turned a deaf ear when Nomura and a second negotiator, Saburo Kurusu, broached Tokyo's Proposal B on November 20. Hull had already submitted Proposal A, put forward informally on November 7, to a cycle of drafts and redrafts from which it would never emerge. But Proposal B offered a real chance to avoid war and did not differ, in many fundamental respects, from a new *modus vivendi* plan that Roosevelt handed to Hull on the same day that Proposal B landed on the secretary's desk. Roosevelt's plan called for lifting the embargo, a freeze on Japanese troop levels in Indochina, Tokyo's pledge not invoke the Axis Pact should the United States go to war with Germany, and American good offices to end the Sino–Japanese War.[36] Japan's Proposal B likewise called for the embargo's end but pledged in return to limit its military activities in Southeast Asia to Indochina. The proposal also sought Washington's agreement not to engage in actions that might complicate an end to the war in China. After the Sino–Japanese War ended, Proposal B called for an evacuation of Japanese forces from Indochina.[37]

Hull still refused to consider any of the three proposals submitted to him in mid-November 1941, and Togo's decision to send Kurusu, whose wife was an American, backfired. Hull thought Kurusu, the Japanese ambassador to Berlin at the time that Tokyo joined the Axis, "deceitful." The promise to withdraw troops from southern French Indochina, meanwhile, only led Hull to wonder whether they would be redeployed for use elsewhere.[38]

Hull's reading of Japanese history, his understanding of Japanese-American diplomacy, his recognition that a compromise with Japan would prove wildly unpopular, his mistrust of Japan—all these issues conditioned his diplomacy. But perhaps the most important factor that shaped the secretary's actions was his belief that a deal was unnecessary. Hull knew from the MAGIC program—a top-secret Army program that broke the Japanese diplomatic code and allowed cryptographers to read Japanese diplomatic cables—that the Tojo cabinet set November 25, subsequently moved to December 1, as the deadline for concluding negotiations. For the secretary, however, the best available evidence suggested that although hostilities would commence should no Japanese-American agreement be reached before December 1, hostilities did not mean a Japanese-American war. Hornbeck concluded on November 27 that "although there may be some armed encounters similar to those to which we have been and are a party in the Atlantic, there will not be a recognized 'state of war' such as to disrupt substantially or put an end to the present program of our Army and Navy." The British, meanwhile, saw Thailand as Japan's next target. American war planners could not offer so precise an estimate of Japanese intentions, but they did note that Japan could not launch a coordinated, simultaneous attack on American, British, and Dutch targets. General Marshall and Chief of Naval Operations Admiral Harold Stark informed FDR in late November that Japan would most likely strike Thailand, the Burma Road (connecting Burma and southern China), or the Philippines. The Philippines, Marshall believed, would be ready by December 15 to repel a Japanese invasion. The War Department had already concluded that a Japanese landing on the west coast of Malaya "is considered out of the question," while "[t]he season for a landing on the east coast has passed." American analysts also predicted that British forces could easily check a limited Japanese assault against Malaya and Singapore and that only in the event of "[a]n all-out Japanese attempt, using 500–1000 aircraft, the bulk of the fleet and 10–20 divisions," would Japan take Malaya and Singapore. An all-out Japanese assault, of course, would leave little in the way of men or matériel left over for operations against the Philippines and the East Indies. At State, meanwhile, Hornbeck argued that Japan would avoid war with America and focus instead on Thailand, the Burma Road, or southern China. Thus while Hull knew of the impending deadline, there seemed no compelling reason to strike a deal with Tojo to avoid hostilities. Hull did not understand that should the deadline pass without an agreement, then war and a humiliating Western defeat in Asia would ensue.[39]

The only circumstance that could have prompted Hull to deal in order to avoid even the remote possibly of war and defeat—a debilitating British or Soviet military setback—failed to materialize. In early October, the British ambassador assured Hull that Allied forces in the Middle East "would not be taken by surprise but would be organized to a sufficient extent to meet an attack from any direction." The following month, British forces scored victories against Rommel and as Japanese-American talks approached their denouement, the American military attaché in Cairo sent word "that the British were winning a brilliant victory." In Russia, meanwhile, Stimson learned that the Red Army was "holding hard and fast at Moscow" and that German advances on the southern front were slowing down as well. Finally, in the Atlantic, while enjoying temporary success at the end of summer, U-boats no longer threatened to drive England from the war. In September, German attacks sent 210,000 tons of American, British, and neutral shipping to the bottom, but even this number represented a 40-percent decline over the preceding May; and with the introduction of American long-range patrol planes to antisubmarine operations, merchant losses fell sharply during the remainder of the autumn.[40]

With no compelling reason to reach an unpopular agreement with what most considered a completely untrustworthy Japan, Hull and his associates refused to seek an agreement based on either FDR's *modus vivendi* or Tokyo's Proposal B. On November 22, when Hull met with the British and Chinese ambassadors and the Australian and Dutch ministers, all noted their preference for an American *modus vivendi* over an attempt to reach agreement based on Japan's latest proposal. Hull, however, never submitted the American plan for a temporary peace. When he met Nomura and Kurusu later that day, he made no attempt to lay the groundwork for an American *modus vivendi* despite the wishes of America's allies. Three days later, when the secretary, Marshall, Knox, and Stimson met Roosevelt, Hull made no effort to win their approval for the *modus vivendi* that Washington's allies had asked for just days earlier.[41]

Hull, likewise, showed no interest in seeking a comprehensive settlement based on White's plan. Instead, on November 26, he submitted an American proposal that bore little relation to White's original proposition. Washington's final proposal called for Japan's withdrawal from China and Indochina but did not require Washington to withdraw the fleet from the Pacific. Hull also had shorn all of White's economic incentives from the final proposal. In his official testimony before the Pearl Harbor Congressional Committee, the secretary offered a wholly self-serving account, squarely at odds with the record, concerning his offer to Tokyo. "Well, the truth is," Hull told the Committee, that he and his associates "were most anxious, as we have said here at different times, to go forward with the conversations, and we had every motive to desire to go forward with them." The secretary explained that his note represented "an ordinary, normal plan for international relations" and that "all they had to do was to announce that they were through with conquest and aggression and that automatically they would have become the beneficiaries of these proposals." Hull might have believed that his proposal represented an honest attempt to avoid war, but others at the heart of the negotiations were less certain. Hamilton noted that the press and public "would construe the documents as something in the nature of an ultimatum," and Hull's counterpart, Foreign Minister Togo, noted that the final American proposal, as well as Hull's decision to release details to the press, "confirm[ed] our opinion that the United States had by this time become determined on war with Japan."[42]

In truth, no senior American statesman had determined to go to war with Japan in the autumn of 1941. Policymakers at the State, Treasury, War, Navy, and Interior departments who had first nurtured American containment and then embraced rollback had done so in an effort to check and then reverse the tide of Japanese expansion without resorting to war. But in the run-up to war, Washington's strategy had become too successful. The mistrust of Japan and the unfounded notion that the United States could bend Japanese diplomacy to Washington's will had shaped American containment through the summer of 1941, but after the German invasion of the Soviet Union, these beliefs warped U.S. strategy. In the American mind, Japan grew more duplicitous but also less threatening. By the autumn of 1941, the architects of American policy believed that if properly applied, U.S. military and economic power could force Japan to abandon the war in China and the Axis Alliance. To be sure, Japan might fight, but with Germany unable to bring Russia to her knees and with U-boat success declining, the chances that Japan would strike England, America, or Holland seemed unlikely. Besides, if Japan did strike, her attacks would be piecemeal blows on the Burma Road or Thailand rather than Malaya, the East Indies, or the Philippines. Therefore, senior policymakers saw no reason to resurrect the failed diplomacy of the past. Why compromise with either Konoe or Tojo, especially now that the American people, the British and Dutch Empires, and Nationalist China were united behind a policy that would in time force Japan from the Axis Alliance and roll back a decade of ill-gotten military gains? The answer, which escaped American policymakers, became painfully obvious within weeks.

By the start of summer 1941, America had contained Japanese expansion, but in the aftermath of the German invasion of the Soviet Union,

American policymakers overplayed their hand and used the tools of containment—economic warfare and a military buildup—to drive Japan from the Asian mainland. Japanese leaders perceived that this threatened the Empire's survival, and, given these circumstances, war appeared the only viable option. In December 1941, Japanese statesmen faced a crisis similar to that which their predecessors faced in the winter of 1904. They would have to either sacrifice past gains and execute a humiliating retreat from the Asian mainland or start a war that would likely end in a horrific defeat for the Empire. In 1904, Admiral Gonnohoye Yamamoto gambled on war and won an empire. Thirty-seven years later, Admiral Isoroku Yamamoto, himself something of a gambler, initiated Japan's war against a far greater adversary, which, in four years of fighting, destroyed an empire nearly a half century in the making.

NOTES

1. John Albert White, *The Diplomacy of the Russo-Japanese War* (Princeton, N.J.: Princeton University Press, 1964), 128.

2. R. M. Connaughton, *The War of the Rising Sun and the Tumbling Bear* (New York: Routledge, 1988), 22; Ian Nish, *The Origins of the Russo–Japanese War* (London: Longmans, 1985), 249; Andrew Malozemoff, *Russian Far Eastern Policy, 1881–1904* (Berkeley: University of California Press, 1958), 244.

3. Cordell Hull, *The Memoirs of Cordell Hull*, vol. I (London: Hodder and Stroughton, 1948), 117; Joseph Grew, *Ten Years in Japan* (New York: Simon & Schuster, 1944), 7; Howard K. Beale, *Theodore Roosevelt and the Rise of America to World Power* (Baltimore, Md.: The Johns Hopkins University Press, 1956), 331; Henry Stimson, *The Far Eastern Crisis: Recollections and Observations* (New York: Harper and Brothers, 1936), 138; Joseph Grew Papers, Houghton Library, Harvard University, Cambridge Mass., diary number 58, page 2150 (hereafter book/page). During this period when military and economic deterrence appeared to have a salutary effect on Japanese policy, traditional diplomacy seemed to have failed. The many incantations on behalf of the Open Door failed to gain the hallowed policy much respect in Tokyo, while agreements such as Root-Takahira and Lansing-Ishii easily did as much harm as good.

4. Franklin D. Roosevelt Papers, President's Secretary's File 26, Franklin D. Roosevelt Library, Hyde Park, N.Y., Hornbeck Memorandum, May 9, 1933.

5. Ibid., Saito to Hull, May 15, 1934; ibid., Far Eastern Division Memorandum, May 16, 1934; Hull, Memoirs, 1, 283–85; see also Roosevelt Papers, PSF 26, Hull to Roosevelt, June 9, 1934.

6. Frederick Leith-Ross, *Money Talks* (London: Hutchinson, 1968), 205–07; Henry Morgenthau Diary, Franklin D. Roosevelt Library, Hyde Park, New York, diary number 10, page 180 (hereafter book/page); Ibid., 11/17; John Morton Blum, *Roosevelt and Morgenthau* (Boston: Houghton Mifflin, 1970), 104–07; Morgenthau diary, 78/22: Everest puts the amount of silver purchased at 62,000,000 ounces; Allan Seymour Everest, *Morgenthau, the New Deal and Silver* (New York: King's Crown Press, 1950), 113–18.

7. Waldo Heinrichs, "The Role of the US Navy," in *Pearl Harbor as History*, ed. Dorothy Borg and Shumpei Okamoto (New York: Columbia University Press, 1973), 199, 207–08; Grew Papers, diary 57/2114; ibid., 54–Appendix, Notes of Frank Simonds letter; ibid., 59–Appendix, Grew to Hull, December 27, 1934.

8. Everest, 120–21; Morgenthau diary, 153/366–69, 158/223–24, 232/28, 144/306, 205/94–95, and 206/79; see also John Morton Blum, *From the Morgenthau Diaries: Years of Urgency, 1938–1941* (Boston: Houghton Mifflin, 1965), 58–63, 125; ibid., 361; Michael Schaller, *The American Crusade in China, 1938–45* (New York: Columbia University Press, 1979), 43.

9. *Roosevelt Papers*, Box 42, Folder, Diplomatic Correspondence, Japan, Green Letter, July 1, 1938; ibid., Hull to Roosevelt, December 13, 1938; Mira Wilkins, "The Role of US Business," in Borg and Okamoto, 373; *Foreign Relations of the United States* (hereafter *FRUS*), 1939, vol. 3 (Washington, D.C.: U.S. Government Printing Office), 494–95; Memorandum of Conversation, Hamilton-Breck, January 27, 1939; ibid., 503–05, Memorandum of Conversation, Hornbeck, Arensberg, et al. February 6, 1939; ibid., 549; Green Memorandum, December 10, 1939.

10. *House Report*, 76th Congress, First Session, miscellaneous, vol. 2 (Washington, D.C.: U.S. Government Printing Office, 1939); Minority View of H.R. 5191 Report 283, part 2; *Congressional Record*, 76th Congress, First Session, vol. 84, part 5 (Washington, D.C.: U.S. Government Printing Office, 1939); Morgenthau diary, 139/36; Harry Dexter White Papers, Seeley Mudd Library, Princeton University, Princeton, N.J., Box 6, Folder 15B, White to Morgenthau, April 8, 1939; Herbert Feis Papers, Library of Congress, Washington, D.C., Box 55, Memorandum of December 23, 1940 Meeting, Progress of the U.S. Government Stock Pile Program.; ibid., Box 127, File Research Material Memoirs Unpublished, Memorandum, "Recommendation on 'Protective' Buying"; ibid., Box 56, File "The Latin American Program," Feis to Sumner Welles, March 21, 1941; ibid., Box 56, File "Tin," Feis to Welles, April 30, 1941; ibid., Box 55, File "1940 Preemptive Buying Program Begins," Excerpts of Jesse Jones, March 21, 1942, Report to President and Congress; ibid., U.S. Embassy Brazil to State Department,

January 17, 1942; Morgenthau diary, 439/38; Herbert Feis, *The Road to Pearl Harbor* (New York: Atheneum, 1962), 234, fn18.

11. *FRUS*, 222–23; *Japan, 1931–1941*, 2 (Washington, D.C.: U.S. Government Printing Office, 1943), 222–23;White House Press Release, September 26, 1940; ibid., 232–33; Proclamation 2449, December 10, 1940; ibid., 233–35; Executive Order 8607, December 10, 1941; ibid., 238–60, passim.

12. Heinrichs, "The Role of the US Navy," in Borg and Okamoto 215, 218; see also *Documents on American Foreign Relations, July 1939–June 1940*, ed. Shepard Jones and Denys Myers (Boston: World Peace Association, 1940), 761; National Archives, Record Group 165, College Park, Md., War Plans Division (hereafter WPD), 4192–93, Strong to Marshall, March 2, 1940; ibid., 4192, Strong to Marshall, August 21, 1939; Henry Stimson diary, Sterling Library, Yale University, New Haven, Conn., Diary 32, 34 (hereafter diary/page).

13. Rear Admiral Sadatoshi Tomioka, Japanese Monograph #146 in *War in Asia and the Pacific*, ed. Donald S. Detwiler and Charles B. Burdick (New York: Garland, 1980), 28–29; see also Hata Ikuhiko, "Army's Move into Northern Indochina," in *The Fateful Choice: Japan's Advance into Southeast Asia, 1939–1941*, ed. William Morley (New York: Columbia University Press, 1980), 157; Hosoya Chihiro, "The Tripartite Pact," in *Deterrent Diplomacy: Japan, Germany and the USSR, 1935–1940*, ed. William Morley, (New York: Columbia University Press, 1976), 242–43; Nobutaka Ike, *Japan's Decision for War: Records of the 1941 Policy Conferences* (Stanford, Calif.: Stanford University Press, 1967), 80–81; Imperial Conference, July 2, 1941.

14. Tsunoda Jun, "Leaning Towards War," in *The Final Confrontation*, ed. William Morley (New York: Columbia University Press, 1994), 170–81; *Pearl Harbor Hearing Before the Joint Committee* (hereafter *Pearl Harbor Hearings*) (Washington, D.C.: U.S. Government Printing Office, 1946), Books 18–20, 4000 (hereafter book/page).

15. Roosevelt Papers, PSF 27, Diplomatic Correspondence China, 1939–1940, Bullitt to Roosevelt, August 28, 1939; *FRUS*, 1939, 3, 210–11, Bullitt to Hull, August 26, 1939; ibid., 214–15, Lockhart to Hull, August 28, 1939; ibid., 223–24, Dooman to Hull, September 1, 1939.

16. Brooks Emeny Papers, Seeley Mudd Library, Princeton University, Princeton, N.J., Box 19, Confidential Report, "Problems of American Far Eastern Policy," December 3–4, 1938; Roosevelt Papers, PSF 27, Diplomatic Correspondence, China, 1939–1940, Johnson to Roosevelt, February 27, 1939; *FRUS*, 1939, 3, 211–12, Hornbeck Memorandum, August 26, 1939.

17. Hosoya Chihiro, "The Tripartite Pact," in *Deterrent Diplomacy*, ed. William Morley, 191–99; *FRUS*, 1939, 3, 582–83, Dooman to Hull, September 25, 1939; ibid., 602–04, Grew to Hull, November 28, 1939; ibid., 619–20, Grew to Hull, December 18, 1939; ibid., 622, Grew to Hull, December 18, 1939.

18. Grew Papers, Letters, 1940, no. 2, vol. 99, Grew to Roosevelt, January 16, 1940; *FRUS*, 1939, 4, 449–50, Dooman to Hull, September 12, 1939; ibid., 1940, 4, 957–61, Grew to Hull, January 15, 1940; National Archives and Records Administration (College Park, Md.) Record Group 59, 711.94/1554, Hornbeck Memorandum, June 6, 1940; ibid., 711.94/1580, Memorandum of Hull–Lothian Conversation, June 27, 1940; ibid., 711.94/1581, Hull's Confidential Oral Statement, June 28, 1940.

19. Stimson Diary, 32/11; ibid., 32/32; ibid., 32/35; *FRUS*, 1941, 5, 55, Navy Department to State Department, February 4, 1941; ibid., 61, British Embassy Washington to State Department, February 7, 1941; ibid., 62–64, Grew to Hull, February 7, 1941; Robert J. C. Butow, *The John Doe Associates: Backdoor Diplomacy for Peace* (Stanford, Calif.: Stanford University Press, 1974), 18; *FRUS* 1941, 4, 22–27; Hull to Roosevelt, February 5, 1941.

20. Ibid., 55, Hornbeck to Hull, March 1, 1941; *FRUS*, 1940, 4, 159–60, Memorandum of Hull–Lothian Conversation, September 30, 1940; Stimson Diary, 30/202–03; *FRUS*, 4, 1941, 120–22, Hornbeck Memorandum, April 5 1941; *FRUS, Japan, 1931–1941*, 2, 440–43, Memorandum of Hull–Nomura Conversation, May 28, 1941; ibid., 454–55, Memorandum of Hull–Nomura Conversation, June 2, 1941; ibid., 483–84, Memorandum of Hull–Nomura Conversation, June 21, 1941; ibid., 485–86, American Oral Statement, June 21, 1941.

21. *FRUS*, 1941 4, 148–50, Hornbeck to Hull, April 15, 1941; ibid., 123–26, Hornbeck Memorandum, April 7, 1941.

22. WPD *4510*, Folder, "May–September 1941," Gerow to Marshall, July 7, 1941; *FRUS* 1941, 4, 276–77, Hamilton Memorandum, June 23, 1941; WPD 4510, Folder, "May–September 1941," Gerow to Marshall, July 16, 1941.

23. Stanley Hornbeck Papers, Hoover Institution on War, Revolution and Peace, Stanford University, Stanford, Calif., Box 463, Folder, July 1941, Hornbeck to Welles, July 23, 1941; ibid., Box 52, Folder, China Assistance, 1939–1941, Hiss Memorandum, June 25, 1941.

24. WPD 4544, Navy Department to Chief of Staff, July 5, 1941; *FRUS*, 1941, 4, 290, Hornbeck to Hamilton, July 5, 1941; Grew Papers, Personal Notes, 1941, Box 2, Folder 61, Diary 148; *FRUS*, Japan, 1931–1941, 2, 315–316, State Department Press Release, July 24, 1941.

25. Stimson Diary, 35/20; ibid., 36/37; *FRUS*, Japan, 1931–1941, 2, 553–559, Memorandum of Hull–Nomura Conversation, August 16, 1941, and Memorandum of Hull, Nomura, Roosevelt Conversation, August 17, 1941; Hornbeck Papers, Box 254, Folder Japan–US Conversations, Hornbeck to Hull, September 12, 1941.

26. Eugene Dooman Oral History, Columbia University Rare Books and Manuscripts Collection, Butler Library, New York, N.Y., 99. Dooman's draft memoirs assert that in an effort to derail the talks Hull telephoned Nomura and informed him that Konoe had accepted Hull's Four Principles. Dooman notes that the U.S. Embassy had cabled Hull that only he and the president could be privy to such information in an effort to prevent any leaks reaching Japan, 711.94/2244, 5/11. Grew to Hull, August 19, 1941. *Pearl Harbor Hearings*, 15–17/2796; ibid., 18–20/4085–87, Memorandum of Hull–Hu Shi Conversation, September 4, 1941; Christopher Thorn, *Allies of a Kind: The United States, Britain, and the War Against Japan, 1941–1945* (New York: Oxford University Press, 1978), 65.

27. William L. Langer and Everett S. Gleason, *The Undeclared War, 1940–1941* (New York: Harper and Bros., 1953), 659; Hornbeck Papers, Box 254, Folder, Japan–US Conversations. Hornbeck to Hull, September 3, 1941.

28. *Pearl Harbor Hearings*, 12–14/1357–1358, Kroner to Marshall, October 2, 1941.

29. WPD 4344, Notes on Plans for Destruction of Oil Properties in the Netherlands East Indies, May 1, 1941; ibid., Miles Memorandum, April 30, 1941; ibid., Miles to Bundy, May 22, 1941; Lionel Wigmore, *The Japanese Thrust*. Vol. 4 series 1 (Army) in Australia in the War of 1939–1945 (Adelaide: The Griffin Press, 1957), 58; David Reynolds, *The Creation of the Anglo-American Alliance 1937–1941* (Chapel Hill: University of North Carolina Press, 1982), 223–24; Larry Bland, *The Papers of George Catlett Marshall* (Baltimore, Md.: The Johns Hopkins University Press, 1986), 599; Marshall to MacArthur, September 5, 1941; ibid., 599, fn. 2; MacArthur to Marshall, September 7, 1941.

30. See Feis, 242–43, for the immediate press interpretation; Langer and Gleason, 655; see also 711.94/2248A, State Department to American Embassy, Tokyo, August 22, 1941; Hornbeck Papers, Box 52, Folder, China–Assistance, 1939–1941, August 16, 1941, *Liberty* magazine; 711.94/2047A *Data from The Commonwealth*, 17(6), February 11, 1941; Langer and Gleason, 655.

31. Koichi Kido, *The Diary of the Marquis Kido* (Frederick, Md.: University Publications of America, 1984), 314–15; Butow, *Tojo*, 292–93; *Pearl Harbor Hearings*, 18–20/4011; Konoe Memoirs, Kido quoted in Morley, *Final Confrontation*, 239;

Michael A. Barnhart, *Japan and the World Since 1868* (London: Edward Arnold, 1995), 137–38; Ike, 210–11.

32. *Pearl Harbor Hearings*, 15–17/1359, "Summary of the Far Eastern Situation," October21, 1941; ibid., 18–20/3200–3202, "G-2 Estimate of International (Japanese) Situation," October 25, 1941; *FRUS*, 1941, 4, 519, Langdon Memorandum, October 17, 1941; ibid., 522–23, Hamilton Memorandum, October 18, 1941; ibid., 541–43, Grew to Hull, October 20, 1941; ibid., 544–52, Langdon Memorandum, October 25, 1941; Cordell Hull Papers, Library of Congress, Washington, D.C., Box 75, Folder, Japan, General 1941, Hornbeck Memorandum, October 31, 1941; Forrest C. Pogue, *George C. Marshall: Ordeal and Hope* (New York: Viking Press, 1965) 201–02; Bland, 676–80.

33. Frank Knox Papers, Washington, D.C., Library of Congress, Box 4, Folder, General Correspondence, 1941, Knox to John Winant, November 10, 1941; Harold Ickes, *The Secret Diary of Harold Ickes*, 3 (New York: Simon & Schuster, 1954), 649–50.

34. White Papers, Box 6, Folder, 16 A, An Approach to the Problem of Eliminating Tension with Japan and Insuring the Defeat of Germany, November 17, 1941.

35. *Pearl Harbor Hearings*, 12–14/1097, Hamilton to Hull, November 19, 1941; ibid., 1106–07, Gerow to Hull, November 21, 1941.

36. Ibid.,1097, Roosevelt to Hull, undated.

37. *Records of the International Military Tribunal for the Far East* (hereafter IMTF) (Washington, D.C.: Library of Congress Photoduplication Service, 1974), 26,082–83.

38. Hull Memoirs, 2, 1062; ibid., 1067.

39. Ronald Spector, *The Eagle Against the Sun* (New York: Vintage, 1985), 454; Komatsu, *The Origins of the Pacific War and the Importance of "Magic"* (New York: St. Martins Press, 1999), 453; *Pearl Harbor Hearings*, 15–17/2437–43, Hornbeck Memorandum, November 27, 1941; ibid., 2141–42, Lee to War Department, November 21, 1941; ibid., 2142–2143, Summary of estimate by JIC of Japanese Intentions, November 22, 1941; WPD 4510, Folder Far East Theater, #1, November 1941; ibid., WPD 4544–13, Marshall-Stark Memorandum to Roosevelt, November 27, 1941; ibid., 4510, War Department Strategic Estimate, October 1941; Pearl Harbor Hearings 15–17/2437–33, Hornbeck Memorandum, November 27, 1941.

40. Hull Papers, 58, Folder, 214, Memorandum of Hull–Halifax Conversation, October 3, 1941; Hull Memoirs, 2, 1043; Stimson Diary, 35–/98, 36/–47, 36/ –24–25; Jun in Morley, *Final Confrontation*, 283.

41. *FRUS*, 1941, 4, 640, Hull Memorandum, November 22, 1941; ibid., Japan, 2, 1931–1941, 757–62, Memorandum of Conversation, Hull, Nomura, et. al., November 22, 1941.

42. Ibid. 709–10, Hamilton memorandum, December 2, 1941; IMTF 26, 055–56.

chapter three

"IN TERMS OF PEOPLES RATHER THAN NATIONS": WORLD WAR II PROPAGANDA AND CONCEPTIONS OF U.S. FOREIGN POLICY

Justin Hart

History has not been kind to the World War II propaganda initiatives of the U.S. government. The work of the Office of War Information (OWI)—the best known and most influential of the wartime propaganda agencies—has received very little acclaim indeed (nostalgic appreciation for the iconic images of Rosie the Riveter and The Four Freedoms notwithstanding). During the war, the OWI provoked howls of protest, mostly from conservative critics, who complained about incompetence, waste, and liberal bias. In subsequent years, historians have redirected those criticisms, but not the overall judgment, in characterizing the organization as mismanaged and ineffective.[1] Overall, the OWI story—although not exactly relegated to the dustbin of history—is certainly not regarded as central to the plotline of World War II.[2] And this is unfortunate because while the OWI may have failed on its own terms, its existence and its operations symbolized and precipitated a broader transformation in conceptions of U.S. foreign relations.

Before World War II, overseas propaganda was widely viewed as peripheral to, if not entirely separate from, the foreign policy process. When President Franklin D. Roosevelt issued Executive Order 9182, which created the OWI in June 1942, there was little expectation that it would become enmeshed in debates over U.S. foreign policy. FDR's crusty Secretary of State Cordell Hull spoke for the relentless traditionalists at the State Department when he informed the OWI that in his view, war information did "not include information relating to the foreign policy of the United States."[3] Events soon demonstrated otherwise, though. By the end of the war, the OWI experience had made it clear that propaganda did actually matter to U.S. foreign policy, and moreover, that in speaking for the United States, the OWI effectively made foreign policy.

The evidence for this proposition lies in President Harry S. Truman's decision in August 1945 to transfer the overseas propaganda functions of the OWI to the State Department. Thus, the significance of the OWI story lies less in the agency's actual accomplishments (or lack thereof) and more in its attempts to respond to rapid and dramatic changes in the global environment and to the role of the United States therein. This essay discusses some of those changes as well as the ways in which World War II propagandists grappled with them—and, in so doing, helped to lay the groundwork for the much better-known propaganda initiatives of the Cold War.

During World War II, U.S. propagandists stood at the intersection of several global historical trends that came together to redefine the nature of U.S. foreign relations. The arrival of the war in December 1941 effectively inaugurated what Time-Life publisher Henry Luce famously called the American Century.[4] Like Luce, policymakers throughout the Roosevelt administration assumed that the war offered the United States the opportunity to seize the mantle of global hegemony from the beleaguered British Empire. Just how that objective might be best achieved, though, remained the subject of some considerable debate.[5]

Roosevelt and many of his principal theorists blamed European methods of territorial colonialism for the violence and destruction that, ironically, created the void they hoped to occupy. This meant that from the earliest days of the war, American policymakers faced the rather interesting dilemma of how to fashion an imperial strategy different from the European model that they hoped to succeed. Following in the tradition of the Open Door policy that dated back to the turn of the century, U.S. officials sought a means of extending American influence *without* the baggage of a formal territorial empire. It is certainly important to remember, as Roger Louis points out, that even Americans were surprised at how rapidly decolonization progressed in the postwar period. Yet there is no question in looking at the documents of the World War II era that U.S. policymakers across a very broad spectrum were already looking ahead to decolonization and to the concomitant rise in autonomous actors in the international arena.[6]

The final thread connecting these trends was the proliferation of access to the various means of mass communications. Shaping America's image in the world thus became critical to the postwar project for attracting individual hearts and minds, in turn making propaganda attractive as a foreign-policy tool in a way that it never had been before. As the OWI story makes clear, though, the roots of this development date to the early 1940s, making the experiences of World War II propagandists more important than has previously been appreciated. Despite the many questions that they failed to answer, OWI officials identified the issues that their successors would continue to confront. Robert Sherwood, the Pulitzer Prize–winning playwright who directed the Overseas Branch of the OWI, offered perhaps the most succinct summary of the philosophy behind OWI propaganda, when he stated that "we think today in terms of peoples rather than nations."[7] And that would continue to be the central dilemma for U.S. propagandists: how to influence the opinions of individual people—not just their leaders, the traditional subjects of the diplomatic enterprise.

ANTECEDENTS

The evolution of the World War II–propaganda apparatus mirrored the nation's haphazard path toward involvement in the war itself. Between 1939 and 1941, the White House created several propaganda agencies that came close to putting the nation on a war footing with respect to information policy. Perhaps the most compelling rationale for the piecemeal approach to propaganda was to create, in effect, a moving target for potential critics of a centralized propaganda bureau. Residual hostility toward the Committee on Public Information—the propaganda bureau created by Woodrow Wilson and headed by George Creel during World War I—still ran strong, reflective of the country's general disillusionment toward the Great War itself.

Because the Roosevelt administration tried in the years leading up the war to avoid any association with Wilson's failed quest to "make the world safe for democracy" (no matter how accurate such comparisons might be), propaganda became something of a taboo issue. A comprehensive government propaganda operation would immediately have become fodder for the "Great Debate" over American involvement then raging across the country. After all, why would the U.S. government care about wartime propaganda unless it intended to enter the war? So from 1939 to 1941, the Roosevelt administration created a decentralized mishmash of information agencies—essentially the unacknowledged bureaucratic embodiment of its well-known policy of pursuing all options "short of war."

Despite their limited mandate, the work of these agencies and the officials who ran them went a long way toward shaping subsequent propaganda strategies. The two most important prewar propaganda agencies were the Office of Facts and Figures (OFF), which was run by the Pulitzer Prize–winning poet and Librarian of Congress Archibald MacLeish, and the Foreign Information Service (FIS) run by Robert Sherwood.[8] MacLeish's OFF proved especially creative on a theoretical level, constructing an entire philosophy of information and propaganda around the concepts of public opinion and morale. Although focused primarily on the domestic scene, the OFF developed ideas that applied to overseas propaganda as well. In the eight months between October 1941 and June 1942—before being incorporated into the OWI—MacLeish and company worked through countless problems of information policy. Although frustrated repeatedly by limitations on their authority and the challenges endemic to their work, OFF officials established a number of precedents through their effective use of opinion polling, their advocacy for a centralized information agency, their notion of a "strategy of truth," and their insights into navigating the boundaries between domestic and foreign information policy. Even today, these issues remain central considerations for any government information program.

MacLeish himself deserves much of the credit for the incisive analyses generated by the OFF. MacLeish was unusually perceptive—indeed, well ahead of his time—in analyzing the impact of information technology on the foreign-policy process. In fact, one might even say that he was the George Kennan of U.S. information policy, in that his thinking pervaded virtually every aspect of the emerging information programs and he continued to shape debates long after his relatively short tenure in government had ended. He moved rapidly around the bureaucratic chain during World War II—the omnipresent voice on the use of information and ideas for the pursuit of foreign policy objectives. In addition to running the OFF, he played a critical role in debates over information policy during the early months at the OWI, at the State Department, and (briefly) at Nelson Rockefeller's Office of Inter-American Affairs. He also showed a keen eye for talent, hiring whiz kids such as McGeorge Bundy and Arthur Schlesinger, Jr. Although he left government service after World War II to return to his poetry, his insights into the relationship between mass communications and civil society on a global scale continued to dominate theoretical discussions of propaganda and cultural diplomacy for years to come.[9]

During his tenure at the OFF, MacLeish grappled systematically with the challenges of formulating propaganda in a pluralistic society. MacLeish saw the purpose of the OFF as one of facilitating a "widespread and accurate understanding of the national war effort." But, as with the more general problem of leading a democracy at war, unity was hard to measure and even harder to come by. In perhaps his most crucial insight, MacLeish recognized that his office could never hope to dictate the flow of information to the public. Unlike the Axis powers, which possessed the technical means for "monopolizing the channels to the minds," U.S. propagandists had to monitor hundreds of radio stations and thousands of national, local, organizational, and foreign language newspapers. The OFF interest in public opinion derived from the fairly traditional notion of maintaining high morale at home as an essential precondition to fighting a successful war abroad. MacLeish's people worried that without domestic unity, "we will lose the war of ideas before we have even the opportunity to strike the enemy with our armed fist."[10]

Winning the word war meant more than just producing glossy government pamphlets: "It is not enough to make the full story available in Washington," warned an early policy directive from the OFF. "The issue is what actually comes to the attention of the people and various sections of the public." Government propagandists had to worry not just about disseminating information, but also about propelling it in certain directions. The American people drew their ideas from a remarkably diverse array of what OFF officials called "information channels." The complexity of those channels reflected the vast range of interest groups and identity politics in the United States. As OFF analysts recognized, "in this country we do not have a homogeneous society. We have a nation of groups." One might say, then, that American propagandists understood the problem of shaping wartime public opinion as a matter of locating Madisonian interest-group politics within a global context.[11]

In short, the task of shaping domestic public opinion was complicated immeasurably by the ever-expanding reach of global mass communications. Mass communications infinitely broadened both the sources and the reach of public opinion. Not only did the public have access to information filtered through multiple lenses (domestic, foreign, urban, rural, religion, race, class, gender—to name only the most prominent), but these channels flowed both ways, as any policymaker concerned with the politics of unity quickly came to appreciate. After all, the machinery used to promote consensus and support for the war could just as easily be turned around to record the success or failure of those efforts—a record that could be intentionally or unintentionally broadcast around the world. Although there were no easy solutions to this problem, this observation in itself shaped future approaches to information policy.

The permeability of boundaries—national and otherwise—posed the most significant dilemma that MacLeish and his staff confronted. In theory, the OFF monitored *domestic* attitudes toward the war. The nature of that work, however, often involved measuring the flow of information and the formation of ideas, both of which prodded policymakers to look overseas. They could not simply ignore the possibility that American information about the war originated in foreign sources. At this point, however, limits on the scope of OFF operations really became a problem. Responsibility for overseas propaganda lay not with the OFF, but with the other major agency that ultimately fed into the OWI: the Foreign Information Service of the Coordinator of Information. As MacLeish presciently observed a week before Pearl Harbor in a memo that he wrote to William Donovan, who ran the Office of the Coordinator of Information (COI): "Boundaries are hard to draw. Your people, in their short wave programs aimed abroad, are on the lookout for happenings at home. And happenings at home necessarily affect American opinion in the field assigned to OFF. The result is that OFF is directly concerned with attempts to 'make news' in America and that COI, though indirectly, is also affected."[12] The jurisdictional battle between MacLeish and Donovan, which only intensified after the war began, thus highlighted a broader problem endemic to the production of government propaganda: synchronizing the message disseminated at home with the message broadcast abroad.

The conflict between the agencies also stemmed from personal and philosophical differences between the two leaders, as MacLeish's idealism clashed with Donovan's cynicism. "Wild Bill," as Donovan's less ardent admirers referred to him, is primarily remembered today as the driving force behind the Office of Strategic Services (OSS)—the World War II forerunner to the Central Intelligence Agency (CIA). However, between the summer of 1941 and the summer of 1942, his office actually played a major role in the creation of an overseas propaganda program. A slick salesman, the flamboyant Donovan personally convinced FDR to augment the U.S. government's woefully inadequate resources for the collection and dissemination of information overseas. U.S. capabilities, Donovan pointed out, lagged far behind those of the major European powers. FDR agreed, and decided on the spot to create the COI.[13]

The Coordinator's Office engaged in both overt and covert activities. Donovan cared far more about the cloak-and-dagger intrigue of covert operations, which included espionage and disinformation of all sorts. (One of his more fantastic—although failed—plans proposed to pay the German ambassador $1 million to defect to the United States; another provided assistance in a plot to assassinate Hitler.) He regarded traditional overseas propaganda as fairly mundane and uninteresting, so he delegated most of those duties to Robert Sherwood, who ran the Foreign Information Service of the Coordinator's Office.[14]

Sherwood—although a shy, retiring, giant of a man (he stood 6'7")—was known for his passionate, avowedly political, morality plays. He was at that moment at the height of his fame, having just won his third Pulitzer for *There Shall Be No Night*, a heroic tale of the Finnish resistance to the Russian invasion of 1940. In addition, his speechwriting had helped FDR win an unprecedented third term as president. A true intellectual *engagé*, Sherwood signed up for government service out of a belief that intellectuals could best serve their cause through joining the fray rather than attempting to remain detached social critics. He embodied the can-do spirit of the Progressive tradition so integral to the worldview of most New Deal liberals. Norman Cousins once attributed Sherwood's commitment to public service to a "disillusion with disillusion"—an apt description not only of Sherwood's mentality but of the animating impulse behind the entire New Deal project.[15]

Temperamentally and philosophically, Sherwood had much more in common with MacLeish than with Donovan. They both disagreed with Donovan about what type of propaganda the government should produce. Today, their disagreement would be characterized as a dispute over the efficacy of what is known as "white" versus "black" propaganda. The former, which Sherwood championed, relies on public statements and official reports, in which the source of the information is clearly identified. The latter, favored by Donovan, typically involved the spread of disinformation, often misleadingly labeled to seem to originate from one government while subtly serving the objectives of another. Donovan saw black propaganda as one element of the whole covert intelligence package.

The distinction between white and black propaganda, although now generally accepted and understood, was far less theorized on the eve of World War II. In fact, World War II played a key role in clarifying for subsequent generations the issues and the stakes involved. Sherwood advocated an information policy that Archibald MacLeish would later term the "strategy of truth." As MacLeish put it, "we do not, like the propaganda bureaus of the dictators, tell one story at home and another abroad."[16] However overstated this claim may have been, MacLeish and Sherwood did believe that the truth generally favored the United States. While policymakers would, of course, arrange the facts to portray their policies and their nation in a favorable light, they would not (or should not) resort to outright falsehoods. In their view, the prevalence of "Nazi lies" had created a vacuum—even a hunger—in various parts of the world for any sort of credible information. So, telling the "truth" helped the U.S. government both because of the content of the message itself and because it threw into sharp relief the disinformation tactics of America's enemies. For Sherwood and MacLeish, the distinction between white and black propaganda represented more than a difference in tactics; it reflected a deep division over strategy.[17]

This divide also foreshadowed subsequent debates about the appropriate uses of propaganda in diplomatic and military operations. The strategy of truth insisted on the importance of credible information to perceptions of the United States around the world. Therefore, disseminating black propaganda not only jeopardized the credibility of the U.S. government's white propaganda, but it also threatened to undermine U.S. foreign policy.[18] Proponents of black propaganda or disinformation, on the other hand, viewed information as quite literally a weapon of war, to be used in the same way that one would use a tank or a bomb. (Social scientist Daniel Lerner famously referred to the use of black propaganda as "sykewar.") For the advocates of sykewar, the long-term impact on America's image did not matter as long as the disinformation accomplished its immediate goal of weakening the enemy in one way or another. Since World War II, debates about the goals and the efficacy of propaganda have frequently followed this general pattern, as various policymakers and politicians have battled over whether propaganda should focus on defeating the "enemy" or whether it should be used to explain the United States to the world. Put differently, should propaganda serve the aims of psychological warfare or the aims of what has come to be known as public diplomacy?[19]

After Pearl Harbor, criticism of the existing information programs began to crescendo. Roosevelt's casual decision to create a moving target through decentralization now came back to haunt him as politicians and the media complained about the "overlapping authority" of "Washington initialdom." One pundit blasted the OFF personnel as "several hundred ex-reporters, jobless foreign correspondents, lyric poets, dramatists, and ordinary merchants of literary mush." In reality, though, these attacks had more to do with what the propaganda agencies represented than with what they did or did not do. Ohio Senator Robert A. Taft, the noted Republican critic of American internationalism, belittled the very notion that the government needed an information program: "This nation," he said, "can neither scare its enemies nor further its own war by talk."[20] Taft's pronouncement spoke to the deep skepticism about the purpose of this new tool and how it should be utilized.

Even supporters of an active propaganda program realized that something had to change. Although nearly everyone recognized the need for greater coordination, the key question was how centralized the whole operation should be. Sherwood and MacLeish supported the creation of a new agency responsible for both domestic and foreign propaganda. MacLeish, the wordsmith, even came up with the name, when he suggested that the Office of Facts and Figures be renamed the Office of War Information and then assigned control over the other agencies. Donovan, naturally, did not care for this proposal. He could not see what domestic affairs had to do with the kind of information policy he favored, nor did he like the idea of subordinating his agenda to someone else's. Ultimately, Sherwood and MacLeish capitalized on their personal relationships with the president and convinced him to side with them. In June 1942, FDR signed Executive Order 9182, creating the Office of War Information.[21]

Suggestions for someone to head the new organization varied. MacLeish would have been a logical choice although he waffled over whether he wanted that level of bureaucratic responsibility. "I don't think I would be much good at the job of actually running the production end of a central government propaganda agency," he wrote presidential speechwriter Samuel Rosenman. He did add that "I have become intensely interested in the broad information job," indicating a greater interest in policymaking than in administration.[22] Sherwood, too, was certainly qualified, although his quiet nature made him a less than ideal choice to be the public face of the new agency. Instead, FDR turned to a relative outsider: the charismatic CBS radio personality, Elmer Davis.

A plainspoken Midwesterner from Aurora, Indiana, Davis was a journalist's journalist. He had built his career from the bottom up. At the age of 14, he joined the staff of his hometown newspaper as a printer's devil (the jack-of-all-trades in a print shop). Then, after graduating from Franklin College in Indiana (followed by a stint at Queens College, Oxford, on a Rhodes Scholarship), he reached the pinnacle of his profession when he landed a job as a foreign correspondent for *The New York Times*. Although he left journalism in 1924 to write fiction, he returned as a radio commentator on the eve of World War II. His reputation for fair and balanced reporting (ironic, for someone later excoriated for his liberal bias) made him a popular choice in many quarters. MacLeish came aboard as assistant director in charge of policy, and Sherwood brought along his staff from the Foreign Information Service to run the Overseas Branch of the OWI.[23]

The structure of the new agency mostly followed the outline that MacLeish and Sherwood had proposed. It contained both a Domestic Branch and an Overseas Branch, and it served as the central clearinghouse for all official government propaganda at home and abroad. It did not, however, have the power to dictate how other government departments and agencies released information or to create information on their behalf, making it considerably weaker than the Creel Committee during World War I. Of course, this was the point, but it did set up innumerable future conflicts over who spoke for the U.S. government. The odd man out in this configuration was Donovan, whose intelligence operations were transferred from the civilian to the military sector.

For Wild Bill, who had clashed frequently with the Joint Chiefs, this decision represented an affront. (Tellingly, FDR waited until Donovan left the country before making the announcement.)[24] Ultimately, though, the separation worked out far better than he could have imagined because it led to his assuming command of the newly formed Office of Strategic Services. In addition to its black ops, the OSS became America's first permanent intelligence-gathering operation, ultimately morphing into the Central Intelligence Agency after the war. By splitting the overseas operations of the Coordinator of Information between the OWI and the OSS, Roosevelt temporarily resolved some of the bureaucratic and jurisdictional issues that had plagued the prewar propaganda agencies. Yet the larger strategic questions about the appropriate role for propaganda and information within U.S. foreign policy remained troublesome and unresolved.

THEORIES AND PRACTICES

With MacLeish and Sherwood appointed to high positions, the OWI seemed ready to carry on most of the policies designed over the past year—but now with better coordination and clearer authority. In some cases, this happened; in others, substantial roadblocks soon emerged. Early on, though, the exuberance that accompanied the creation of the new agency allowed policymakers to articulate their philosophy in grand terms, which Elmer Davis did in his first appearance before Congress. Drawing on his expertise in three different fields of mass communications (newspapers, radio, and novels), Davis presented a broad vision of the role of ideas in modern warfare. He imagined the OWI as an "auxiliary to the armed forces," arguing that it could "pave the way for their operations and make their success easier." Alluding to the traditions established at the OFF and the FIS, Davis stressed the importance of employing "truth instead of falsehood"—an approach that he thought essential not for moral reasons, but for strategic ones. As MacLeish and Sherwood had argued before him, the suppression of freedom of speech in many countries made factually accurate information a more attractive commodity and "a more powerful weapon than ever before." After all, "many millions of people" were desperate "for any truthful account of what is going on." All the better, he implied, if that "truthful account" came from the U.S. government.[25]

Davis spun his testimony with the skill of an experienced writer. Well aware of the residual suspicion toward the propaganda efforts of the Creel Committee during World War I, Davis acknowledged that "'[p]ropaganda' is a word in bad odor in this country." But perhaps people could be made to see propaganda as a form of education. "There is no public hostility," he claimed, "to the idea of education as such, and we regard this part of our job as education." Both at home and abroad, the impact of mass communications on the permeability of national boundaries meant that keeping foreign "news out of the country would be impossible." Attempting to insulate the American public from foreign information seemed futile, as did any hope of preventing domestic affairs from reaching foreign audiences. Instead, he suggested, information should be countered with more information—falsehoods with education. Nowhere did Davis begin to define, however, the content of this education. And, as any educator can appreciate, it is the content of education and not the idea of it, as such, that tends to provoke disputes. For a short time, though, the urgency of the situation and the flourish of liberal idealism that accompanied the creation of the OWI overwhelmed the critics and naysayers. Davis walked away from his first hearings with an initial appropriation of approximately $26 million.[26]

Officials throughout the ranks of the OWI agreed that the agency's primary job would be in the field of morale and public opinion—that is, in "educating" people about the rationales for war. In a speech before the American Society of Newspaper Editors in March 1942, Archibald MacLeish provocatively claimed that "the real battlefield of this war is the field of American opinion." MacLeish did not just mean that the American people had to support the war for the United States to succeed (although he certainly meant that, too). He emphasized, instead, that *how* people responded to the war and *how* the press covered that response helped to determine the context in which the military fought its battles.[27] This mandate also applied to foreign operations. True, the organizational structure of the OWI mimicked the separation of powers between the OFF and the FIS, with the creation of separate branches for domestic and overseas operations (a decision that would come back to haunt them). But no one disputed that the central mission for both involved providing people at home and abroad with ready answers to such questions as "what we are fighting for, what we are fighting against, the nature of the enemy, our war aims, [and] the four freedoms."[28]

In disseminating these messages, OWI officials displayed an impressive familiarity with recent theories and technologies of mass communications. The Domestic Branch, for instance, created six major bureaus to deal with what it called the "channels of mass communication": News, Motion Pictures, Radio, Publications and Graphics, Intelligence, and Special Operations (which used the same liaison techniques pioneered by the OFF to engage interest group politics). Likewise, the Overseas Branch deployed "all means of communication that exist or can be devised" to convey to "the world . . . the story of America's determination to fight this war through to total victory." These means included the "international radio, the world press, publications . . . and . . . word of mouth."[29]

The emphasis on word of mouth and interest group politics signaled an awareness that the problem of public opinion had to be examined from a bottom-up as well as a top-down perspective. In other words, the OWI had to do more than preach; it had to make ordinary people the conduits of the government's message. That both branches paid equal attention to this issue also suggested an interest in exploring the transnational implications of public opinion and interest group politics. Domestic politics increasingly extended beyond the water's edge—a process only likely to intensify in the coming years.[30]

Toward this end, the *Domestic* Branch created a Foreign Sources Division, later renamed the Foreign News Bureau. Embracing the OFF theory that building morale at home required U.S. officials to know "what the enemy is trying to tell the American public," the Foreign Sources Division monitored foreign newspapers and radio broadcasts. OWI linguists took this material, translated it, edited it, packaged it, and often—especially in the case of hostile propaganda or news that they viewed as simply inaccurate or distorted—attached their own commentary. The staff of the Domestic Branch then transmitted that copy—24 hours a day, seven days a week—over a wire service to the major press associations, such as the Associated Press, *The New York Times*, Columbia Broadcasting System, and, by the end of the war, to approximately 170 others (including, in an indication of logistical complications to come, to their own colleagues in the Overseas Branch).[31]

OWI officials were especially worried that American press reports on other countries—especially enemy countries—drew too much on (allegedly biased) information from those countries. They knew that foreign broadcasts were "monitored by several radio companies and press associations," but they feared that the American press might receive from, say, Japan only the Japanese broadcasts intended for U.S. consumption. The OWI, in turn, also monitored broadcasts *within* Japan, intended strictly for the Japanese audience. The Foreign Sources Division combined all this information in putting together its wire transmissions, which often illustrated the duplicity of certain overseas broadcasts by calling attention to contradictions between the domestic and overseas statements made by those governments. OWI officials claimed that without their intervention, these messages "would be carried by American newspapers and radio stations without appropriate identification and often without the true facts." And so they sought to provide a counterweight against the information the press independently gleaned from foreign sources. Also, as they acknowledged, "experience has demonstrated . . . that much of [our] story of the story will be carried as sent, as the Axis stories now are."[32]

To learn how best to target specific audiences when projecting their message, OWI officials turned to the true pioneers in the field: American advertising executives. Although an early strategy paper expressed chagrin that "Goebbels's methods of propaganda were modeled on American methods of advertising salesmanship," U.S. policymakers had the luxury of countering Goebbels by going straight to the source. And, in fact, they established a liaison with an outfit called the War Advertising Council even before Japanese bombs rained down on Pearl Harbor. Comprising the owners and principal figures of magazines, newspapers, radio, and the major national advertising agencies, the War Advertising Council was headed by Chester J. LaRoche, the chairman of Young & Rubicam, the nation's second-largest advertising agency. Reporting to Congress on the purpose of the Council, LaRoche proclaimed that "the United States has at its command the most powerful information mechanism that exists anywhere in the world."[33] In addition to representatives from the advertising industry, the OWI also sought assistance from key figures in the booming business of public opinion polling. Hoping to incorporate "all the techniques of public opinion research which have been developed in the government, private foundations, business, and industry in the past several years," the OWI added noted pollsters George Gallup and Elmo Roper to the board of its Surveys Division during the early days of the war.[34]

The Surveys Division at the OWI canvassed opinion on a host of issues related not just to the war, but to the postwar extension of American internationalism as well. The OWI's interest in postwar planning stretched back almost to the beginning of the war. The OWI staff included a number of old Wilsonians and their intellectual descendants, who were looking for what Robert Divine has called a "second chance" to implement Wilson's agenda.[35] That opportunity arrived in November 1942, when the State Department contacted the Domestic Branch about conducting a "large scale" campaign of "public education and guidance" to ensure that the United States would "play the role indicated in the addresses of Mr. Hull, Mr. Welles, Mr. Elmer Davis, and Mr. Willkie." Even to consider such a proposition raised considerable risks. Many of the OWI's most persistent critics came from the group of conservatives opposed to the growing domestic consensus on the need for U.S. participation in a postwar international organization. On the other hand, the prospect for cooperation rather than conflict with the State Department had certain benefits as well.[36]

The latter position also happened to correspond with the sincerely held beliefs of top officials such as MacLeish and Sherwood, who saw the war as an opportunity to remake the international system. In the end, the OWI devised a large-scale propaganda campaign around the symbolic potential of the "United Nations" idea. Long before it became the moniker of choice for a potential postwar international organization, the term referred to the 26 nations who came together in Washington, D.C., on January 1, 1942, to sign the Declaration of the United Nations in opposition to the Axis powers. Beginning as early as mid-1942, the OWI used the concept of the United Nations both to spearhead its foreign mission of "projecting" certain images to the world and its domestic mission of enlisting support for Allied war aims. U.S. officials in charge of popularizing the United Nations idea initially preferred "to keep it as a symbolism rather than as a mechanism." Yet the symbol so quickly "caught public imagination throughout the United Nations world" that OWI officials could not resist expanding its meaning. Before long, the Radio Bureau explicitly instructed its employees to "drive home" the notion that the United Nations is "the nucleus—perhaps the fundamental framework—of a post-war world organization to make certain that war does not occur again." Focusing on connecting individual people to the process of preventing future conflicts, OWI officials noted that "the United Nations was called into being because . . . modern wars cannot be localized, and cannot be waged within national limits."[37]

The United Nations campaign thus became not just a domestic talking point but part of a much more ambitious, worldwide effort that Robert Sherwood labeled "the Projection of America." Reflecting the slick packaging and catchy sloganeering of the collaboration with brilliant salespeople, the Projection campaign served as a catchall directive "to govern the production of all long range media." Begun in January 1943, the program seems slightly shocking today—partly for its naked ambition and partly because it so completely predicted the message and the objectives of Cold War propaganda. Drawing on advertising methodologies, Sherwood's directive called for defining "central themes which are universal"—such as "the overwhelming power and incontestable good faith of the

U. S. A."—while still remaining sensitive to the "special treatment" required in "certain areas."[38]

Believing that "sympathy, trust and friendliness will grow only through fuller knowledge and understanding," Sherwood insisted that the projection had to follow the conventions of "strategy of truth." The so-called strategy of truth did not, however, preclude a little embellishment; indeed, it depended on such enhancements. Boasting of a "land of unlimited possibilities," Sherwood argued that America's propaganda should emphasize the strength of its institutions—its system of education, its culture, its social legislation, and its labor organizations. He also emphasized the importance of conveying the nation's credentials for leading in the postwar world: The sheer diversity of its national environment allowed the United States to "train troops to fight in the snowy mountains of Norway, the desert of Africa, or the steaming jungles of New Guinea."[39]

Gendered images figured prominently in the way that Sherwood sought to project the nation's leadership credentials. Surely, foreigners would want to know as much as possible about "what our kitchens look like" and "the place of the American woman in war and in peace." At the same time, though, he worried about widespread perceptions of a sort of "Hollywood America," replete with "glamour girls and gangsters." Axis propaganda used such images, Sherwood thought, to show "that we are effete." He argued that, in response, American propaganda should focus on the "hardiness" of the American people to make clear that although "we do not start fights . . . we have a habit of finishing them."[40]

Projecting America also led Sherwood into territory that future U.S. propagandists would cross time and again, as he contemplated ways to address the nation's embarrassing record on race relations. On this point, he actually sought to exploit the racist assumptions of Nazi propaganda. By embracing (rather than refuting) Nazi characterizations of the American people as a "hybrid race," Sherwood attempted to paper over the nation's own racist traditions and practices. "Our sympathies," he suggested, "are universal because we are ourselves composed of many racial and national strains . . . and we are proud of it." How better to convince people of "other countries that this really is a people's war and that we are not fighting merely to reestablish the old order?" To suggest that propagandists might actually capitalize on the nation's diversity certainly represented a novel strategy although it turned out to be a tough sell both at home and abroad.[41]

One of the main reasons that discussions of domestic race relations mattered to propagandists was the incredibly complicated position of the United States in a decolonizing world populated largely by people of color. Projections to the colonial world required U.S. policymakers to balance their global ambitions with their need for European alliances. These messages also required stretching the strategy of truth to tell different stories in different places. For U.S. propagandists could not, frankly, describe America's alliance with Great Britain in the same way in India or Iran as they did in Canada or the United States. An additional complicating factor was the pressure from the State Department to toe the line on official U.S. policy, without regard to what OWI officials might view as the broader long-term interests of the United States. In the British West Indies, for example, the State Department demanded that Voice of America broadcasts clearly convey that the United States was "not interested at all in any change of sovereignty." At the same time, as Elmer Davis noted to Robert Sherwood, the OWI should not miss the opportunity presented by the fact that U.S. broadcasts seemed "to be more trusted by the natives than . . . the BBC."[42]

The same general problem plagued the OWI response to the British crackdown on Mahatma Gandhi's Quit India Movement in late 1942. Although the British violated the rights of more than 100,000 protesters who were arrested along with Gandhi and future Prime Minister Jawaharlal Nehru, MacLeish acceded to the wishes of the State Department and allowed excerpts from speeches by the British ambassador, Lord Halifax, to stand as the OWI interpretation of the crisis. OWI press releases quoted Halifax to the effect that "we do not regard the Colonies as possessions." They also passed along, unchallenged, his statement that the Indian situation could *not* be reduced to the "terms of one people struggling to be free and of another people struggling to keep them down." MacLeish and his colleagues certainly grasped the bigger picture as they struggled to find ways to express "sympathy with the long-range aspirations of the Indian people." More often than not, though, short-term expediency trumped long-range aspirations. In the end, even the idealistic MacLeish grudgingly accepted the official position: Because "any real opportunity for Indian freedom" hinged on defeating the Axis, the United States had to focus "solely at this time . . . [on] measures which contribute to anti-Axis victories."[43]

The sorts of dilemmas that OWI officials encountered in trying to project America around the world would continue to challenge U.S. propagandists in future years. Standing at the juncture of transformations in U.S. foreign policy, domestic politics, colonialism, mass communications, and ideological warfare, they were often ahead of the curve in conceptualizing the nature of the postwar world and the demands that it would place on U.S. foreign policy. Beginning in 1943, though, they encountered a series of obstacles that undermined their entire operation and, for a time, threatened its existence. Some were of their own making; others developed out of the novelty of their approach and its inherent challenges. Still unsure of their own arguments and their position within the government bureaucracy, OWI officials often failed to respond effectively to their critics. Yet even their failures—maybe especially their failures—provide critical insights into the practice of government propaganda in the American Century.

DIVISIONS

The divisions that brought the OWI to its knees for a time in 1943 began from within. Although the agency ultimately faced abundant criticism from politicians, pundits, and even their own colleagues in the Roosevelt administration, it was the exodus of some of the OWI's own personnel that served as the first harbinger of trouble to come. In January 1943, Archibald MacLeish returned to full-time service at the Library of Congress after complaining to Elmer Davis that he felt marginalized in the decision-making process. His departure followed an internal debate over the very purpose of a government propaganda agency. The dispute boiled down to the perpetual question of whether propagandists should make policy or serve as nothing more than a highly sophisticated megaphone for the real policymakers.

The disagreement between MacLeish and several of his colleagues had both practical and philosophical components. MacLeish and other liberal intellectuals within the agency had strong views on many foreign and domestic policy issues, and they wanted a vehicle to convey those views, which they believed would strengthen the war effort. The problem was that if the OWI were to function in this capacity, its propagandists would encroach on the territory of other government agencies. The way that the

OWI spoke about, say, the wartime alliance with Great Britain or the Soviet Union would inevitably affect the work of the State Department. At the same time, MacLeish saw no possible way that propagandists could do their job without making judgments about what messages the public, at home and abroad, needed to hear in order to buy into the U.S. mission.

Some of the more cautious policymakers at the OWI worried that MacLeish's interpretation of their mission invited a backlash from other government agencies. In particular, Associate Director Milton Eisenhower (the General's brother) insisted that "our job is to promote an understanding of policy, not to make policy." MacLeish countered that it would be pointless to have an information agency that served as nothing more than an "issuing mechanism for the government departments." Worried about the tenuous position of his fledgling organization within the government bureaucracy, Davis abandoned his earlier support for a broad vision and sided with Eisenhower; frustrated, MacLeish left shortly thereafter.[44] But the questions he raised did not vanish with his departure. Given the massive scope of the OWI's operations and the breadth of its technological resources, how could OWI officials possibly hope to coordinate their message precisely with that of the policymakers they purported to speak for? The broader issue at stake was who got to speak for the U.S. government.

Although profoundly significant in terms of subsequent debates over propaganda strategies, MacLeish's resignation generated little attention in the press. The same cannot be said for the brouhaha that erupted over the abrupt resignation of 15 members of the OWI Writers Branch in April 1943. Led by the Pulitzer Prize–winning biographer Henry Pringle and the promising young historian Arthur Schlesinger, Jr., the writers issued a public denunciation of the OWI leadership for emphasizing fancy "advertising techniques" over solid reporting. Moreover, they complained, the OWI censored data that shed an unfavorable light on any aspect of the war effort. They condemned in particular the decision by top officials in the Domestic Branch to edit a report that the writers had produced on the food situation, after Secretary of Agriculture Claude Wickard and Director of Economic Stabilization James F. Byrnes complained that the report was insufficiently optimistic. According to the writers, the Office of War Information had become an "Office of War Ballyhoo" that prevented its employees from telling the "full truth."[45]

One could almost hear in this last criticism the suggestion that the OWI had abandoned the strategy of truth in the wake of MacLeish's departure.

In fact, MacLeish had hired most of the writers at the Office of Facts and Figures, and they then followed him to the OWI. Undoubtedly, they shared some of his frustrations with the direction the agency had taken. But the claim that American propagandists had abandoned their onetime commitment to aggressive truth telling oversimplified the situation quite a bit. Even MacLeish understood that the truth was a highly malleable concept—more of a spectrum than a fixed point. As with MacLeish's resignation, the real question raised by the writers' revolt was what role a government information agency should play within the overall bureaucratic framework.

As the OWI's internal divisions spilled out into the open, some began to worry that skeptics in Congress might use the signs of vulnerability as an invitation to pounce.[46] As it turned out, the writers were the least of the OWI's problems. In the coming months, a series of embarrassing incidents turned the agency into a virtual pariah. Some of these problems might have been ameliorated with better management, but most of them exposed deep fault lines intrinsic to the production of U.S. government propaganda. The common thread connecting all these crises was the difficulty in synchronizing the domestic with the foreign. More specifically, they stemmed from the increasingly prominent venture in projecting America. For in order to project America, one first had to define America, which was—and will always be—a highly political exercise.[47]

By the summer of 1943, complaints began to pour in about the topics covered in some of the OWI's most popular publications. In particular, critics attacked the agency for using taxpayer dollars to produce glossy leaflets extolling the virtues of the president and New Dealism. Some even accused the OWI of functioning as an unofficial re-election committee for the president's fourth term. They angrily denounced reproductions of Henry Wallace's "Century of the Common Man" speech at Madison Square Garden and the "Life of Franklin Roosevelt." OWI officials tried to defend themselves by pointing out that these pamphlets were produced by the Overseas Branch for distribution abroad. They were designed to extol the virtues of American ideologies and the leaders of the American government to overseas audiences—not to stump for FDR. But Congressman John Taber (R–NY), the most persistent critic of the OWI, was unimpressed, claiming that he had received reports of U.S. servicemen reading such material while stationed abroad.[48]

Materials targeted toward a domestic audience focused on more generic themes, such as unity, prosperity, and democracy, or on the role of individual interest groups in the war effort. Of course, the ostensibly nonpartisan nature of the materials put out by the Domestic Branch provoked just as much, if not more, outrage—never more so than with the controversy over the publication of "Negroes and the War." Concerned that the fractured state of race relations in America might undermine domestic morale, the Domestic Branch commissioned a lavish, 70-page pamphlet entitled "Negroes and the War," which appeared in early 1943. In an indication of how important the OWI considered the subject of domestic race relations, the agency spent more money distributing "Negroes and the War" than on any other wartime publication except for FDR's personal message. Well aware that enemy propaganda attacked America's notorious racial practices more frequently than any other subject, "Negroes and the War" sought to integrate the African-American story into the mainstream narrative of American history. The ostensible purpose was twofold: to show white Americans just how important black Americans were to the nation's past and future; and simultaneously to appeal to black Americans to support a fight for the sort of "democracy" that had meant subjugation, disfranchisement, and violence for them.[49]

Unsurprisingly, the OWI wound up pleasing no one. Black leaders objected to the heavy-handed introduction, in which Chicago journalist Chandler Owen tried to make the case that a victory for Hitler meant a return to slavery for African Americans. The condescension of producing a predominantly visual product (it was heavy on graphics) for African Americans also did not go unnoticed. Even so, the criticisms from African Americans can only be characterized as gentle in comparison to the vitriolic reaction of several Southern congressmen. They blasted the OWI for preaching "racial equality" and using the exigencies of war to "force upon the South a philosophy that is alien to us."[50]

The sad irony of the situation was that the OWI destroyed its credibility with Southern Congressmen (from the party of Roosevelt, at that) for no good reason. Not that racial discrimination was an unimportant issue; on the contrary, Axis propagandists constantly hammered the United States for its hypocrisy on the matter. But it was a problem that would be solved only through political and legal changes, not through the distribution of milquetoast pamphlets. Moreover, the attempt to rewrite the African-American story as one of participation and progress was far better suited to an overseas audience than to American citizens, who already knew the score. By pointing out the importance of addressing the overwhelmingly negative perceptions of American race relations throughout the world—as well as the importance of thinking more generally about how to improve the nation's image abroad—the OWI might have defused some of the criticisms directed toward "Negroes and the War" and other such publications. Of course, it is hard to imagine segregationists appreciating the distribution of even mildly integrationist material abroad any more than they did at home. But OWI officials would at least have had more ammunition to defend themselves had they been able to articulate a global mandate for producing such materials on behalf of the United States.

The third major crisis of 1943 managed to wrap all the elements of the other controversies into one explosive package: an intragovernmental squabble over who spoke for the United States; the question of whether the OWI made policy or simply reported on it; and the domestic political consequences of efforts to project America overseas. The problem erupted in July, when the Fascist party in Italy forced Benito Mussolini from power and the Italian king nominated Pietro Badoglio—a party stalwart and the infamous leader of the conquest of Ethiopia—to replace the deposed dictator. Based on previous policy directives and seeking only the sparest coordination with State Department officials, Sherwood's operatives created overseas broadcasts for the Voice of America that treated a potential Badoglio administration with skepticism. They suggested that he represented little improvement over Mussolini and quoted a *New York Post* columnist who blasted the "moronic little king who has stood behind Mussolini's shoulder for 21 years." Taking the attitude that "fascism is still in power in Italy," the OWI suggested on the air that the Allies would not rest until they eliminated all vestiges of fascism anywhere.[51]

The State Department immediately objected that the OWI had just directly contradicted official U.S. policy. FDR and Secretary of State Hull saw the Badoglio government as a potential bridge to a non-fascist future in Italy, and they were furious that an agency of the U.S. government had just exposed their policy for what it was: a marriage of convenience with antidemocratic forces. The next day, the president personally criticized the broadcast, stating that it did not represent government policy and had not been appropriately cleared with either Hull or Sherwood (although the latter had in fact given his consent). Arthur Krock, the famous columnist for *The New York Times*, who had long ago elevated criticism of FDR to near blood sport, seized the issue as another opportunity to attack the administration's foreign policy as bumbling and confused. FDR never really forgave the agency for embarrassing him and wasting his time on internal government squabbles.[52]

In many ways, the "moronic little king" episode represented the final blow to the political viability of the OWI. The previous month, the House Appropriations Committee had crippled the agency when it voted to slash the OWI's funding and to eliminate the Domestic Branch altogether. Although the Overseas Branch consumed over three-fourths of OWI's $35 million budget, Congress focused on the Domestic Branch, which from their perspective had used taxpayer dollars to sell the taxpayer on its agenda. The legislators had a point, and the principle prohibiting the production of domestic propaganda continues to this day (although it has suffered periodic challenges). The OWI, too, would have had a point had they been able to articulate what would become undeniably obvious in the postwar years: Any government propaganda program needed to pay close attention to the state of American public opinion—not just to try to shape it but because overseas broadcasts lost all credibility if they ignored reporting at home. As often as OWI officials made these arguments behind closed doors, they could not synthesize them clearly enough to defend the necessity of having a Domestic Branch. Ultimately, a less-hostile Senate stepped in to help, restoring just enough funding to keep the Domestic Branch from going under entirely. From 1943 forward, though, the OWI limped along, having avoided, as Elmer Davis later recalled, the "odium of having [Congress] put us out of business," even though it declined to authorize "enough to let us accomplish much."[53]

PRECEDENTS

In the wake of embarrassing incidents such as the public rebuke by the president over the Badoglio fiasco and repeated attacks from politicians and the media about the extravagance, incompetence, and irrelevance of U.S. propaganda, the OWI leadership significantly curtailed the number of innovative policies they pursued. In its final two years, the OWI concentrated primarily on overseas information policy, sometimes subordinating its own agenda to demands for the more aggressive use of propaganda for military purposes. At the same time, some of the earlier Wilsonian idealism remained as OWI officials engaged in extensive postwar planning.

They also extended and refined their earlier campaign for the United Nations into a comprehensive publicity vehicle for the creation of an international organization of the same name.

Historian Alan Winkler has suggested that the later years of the OWI amounted to a "vision denied." The departure of MacLeish and the scandals of 1943 marked a shift away from the idealistic propaganda vision of the OFF and the early OWI. Increasingly, the agency adopted a more cynical, if perhaps realistic, view of the true war aims of the Roosevelt administration. The strategy of truth, Winkler suggests, fell prey to the manipulative methods of advertising men, while MacLeish's ambitious policymaking agenda could not withstand the willingness of others to turn themselves into ciphers for the real decision makers.[54]

Although I agree that the OWI in its last two years was a shell of its original self, it is important not to lose sight of the many important precedents that the agency established. For example, MacLeish left the OWI only to return to address many of these same issues two years later as the first Assistant Secretary of State for Public and Cultural Relations. He and his successors also brought along a significant number of OWI officials to staff the State Department's information programs in the postwar period. More importantly, the ways in which the OFF and the OWI approached the entire propaganda enterprise would continue to inform the work of future policymakers. For all its frustrations and failures, the OWI pioneered an approach to U.S. foreign policy that could not be ignored by subsequent generations.

Near the end of World War II, as an outgrowth of their work on the postwar world, the OWI leadership prepared a memo for President Truman on the future of the federal information programs. Although most wartime agencies were beginning to pack up their tents, OWI officials "emphatically" urged Truman to expand the government's "information service . . . to the rest of the world" by transferring control of such operations to the State Department. "Never again," they declared, "should America as a nation let the telling of its official story be left to chance . . . never again should the nation . . . be satisfied with an unbalanced picture of America which must result if private telling in many media is left wholly unsupplemented." Two weeks later, the president signed the executive order that dissolved the OWI but transferred its functions to the State Department. At the beginning of World War II, a wartime information program was not seen as sufficiently integral to U.S. foreign policy to install it at the State Department; four years later, the State Department adopted that same wartime information program even though there was no longer a war.[55]

NOTES

This essay has gone through numerous permutations over many, many years. For their helpful comments and generous feedback at various stages of the work, I would like to thank Lloyd Gardner, Jennifer Pettit, Kurt Piehler, and especially my colleagues in the junior faculty reading group at Texas Tech University. Special thanks to John Chambers, who did not read this particular piece but who has helped to further my education and my career in countless ways.

1. The standard study of the OWI remains Allan M. Winkler, *The Politics of Propaganda: The Office of War Information, 1942–1945* (New Haven, Conn.: Yale University Press, 1978). Three works that devote some attention to OWI in the course of writing about the Voice of America are Holly Cowan Shulman, *The Voice of America: Propaganda and Democracy, 1941–1945* (Madison, Wis.: The University of Wisconsin Press, 1990); David Krugler, *The Voice of America and the Domestic Propaganda Battles, 1945–1953* (Columbia, Mo.: University of Missouri Press, 1953); and Robert Pirsein, *The Voice of America: A History of the International Broadcasting Activities of the United States Government, 1940–1962* (New York: Arno Press, 1979). Also containing important information on various aspects of OWI activities are Clayton D. Laurie, *The Propaganda Warriors: America's Crusade Against Nazi Germany* (Lawrence, Kan.: University Press of Kansas, 1996); Clayton R. Koppes and Gregory D. Black, *Hollywood Goes to War: How Politics, Profits and Propaganda Shaped World War II Movies* (Berkeley: University of California Press, 1987); and Barbara Dianne Savage, *Broadcasting Freedom: Radio, War, and the Politics of Race* (Chapel Hill, N.C.: The University of North Carolina Press, 1999).

2. For example, in the most recent comprehensive synthesis of U.S. foreign and domestic policy during World War II—David M. Kennedy's *Freedom from Fear: The American People in Depression and War, 1929–1945* (New York: Oxford University Press, 1999)—the OWI appears only twice in the over 400 pages he devotes to the war.

3. This quote comes from a letter Cordell Hull wrote in July 1942 to Elmer Davis, Director of the Office of War Information (OWI), shortly after the creation of the OWI. Prior to that, Hull, a relentless traditionalist, seems to have ignored the decision to establish an autonomous propaganda bureau outside his control.

However, after sensing that it encroached upon his territory, he soon went on the warpath to undermine it. See Winkler, 43–47.

4. My thinking on this matter follows closely along the lines of Bruce Cumings's analysis of the American Century in "The American Century and the Third World," *Diplomatic History*, 23 (1999), 355–70. On page 357, Cumings argues that by eliminating domestic opposition to U.S. intervention in World War II and allowing the Roosevelt administration to pursue openly its agenda of global activism, the Japanese attack on Pearl Harbor constituted, in effect, the end of the "hegemonic interregnum"—the period between 1914 and 1941 "in which England could no longer lead and the United States was not yet ready to do so."

5. To get a sense of the unanimity of this belief, examine Department of State, *Postwar Foreign Policy Preparation, 1939–1945*, by Harley A. Notter, Publication 3580 (Washington, D.C.: U.S. Government Printing Office, 1949), 67–78. Notter, a historian at Stanford University, served as the Executive Secretary of the State Department's Committee on Postwar Foreign Policy Planning and then later wrote its official history. Notter demonstrates that even at the Committee's earliest meetings, policymakers believed that Pearl Harbor had essentially eliminated "the most basic uncertainty about the outcome of the war." With the United States involved, Notter and his colleagues believed, "victory could be assumed." Policymakers also assumed that the outcome of the war would leave the United States in a position of unparalleled power in the world. But how that world would look and how the United States could wield its influence remained decidedly uncertain.

6. William Roger Louis, *Imperialism at Bay* (New York: Oxford University Press, 1978), 10.

7. Robert Sherwood, "Long-Range Directive," 1/15/43, Box 4, Entry 6B, RG 208 (Records of the Office of War Information), National Archives and Records Administration, College Park, Md. (hereafter as NARA).

8. On the predecessor agencies and their contributions to the OWI, see U.S. Congress, House, Hearings Before the Subcommittee of the Committee on Appropriations, *National War Agencies Appropriation Bill for 1944*, Pt. 1, 78th Cong., 1st sess., 1943, 912–17; and Winkler, 21–22.

9. For an in-depth examination of my thinking on MacLeish, see Justin Hart, "Rediscovering Archibald MacLeish: The Poetry of U.S. Foreign Policy," *Historically Speaking* 8 (January/February 2007): 20–22.

10. "Description of the Organizational Breakdown and Function of the Units Within the Office of Facts and Figures," 3/11/42, Box 12, Entry 6E, RG 208,

NARA; OFF Bureau of Intelligence to OFF Director, Assistant Directors and Deputy Directors, 2/25/42, Box 5, Entry 3D, RG 208, NARA.

11. OFF Bureau of Intelligence to OFF Director, Assistant Directors and Deputy Directors, 2/25/42, Box 5, Entry 3D, RG 208, NARA.

12. Archibald MacLeish to William Donovan, 12/1/41, Box 6, Papers of Archibald MacLeish, Manuscripts Division, Library of Congress, Washington, D.C.

13. Anthony Cave Brown, *The Last Hero* (New York: Times Books, 1982), 7, 55–56, 164–67. See also the more personal perspective in the biography by former Donovan assistant Corey Ford, entitled *Donovan of OSS* (Boston: Little, Brown and Company, 1970).

14. Brown, 168–215.

15. There is no outstanding biography of Robert Sherwood, partly because John Mason Brown died before completing the second volume of his two-volume study. Nevertheless, Brown's partially completed *The Ordeal of a Playwright: Robert E. Sherwood and the Challenge of War* (New York: Harper & Row Publishers, 1970) takes the story up to 1941 and includes the text of *There Shall Be No Night*. The Norman Cousins quote comes from his Introduction to this volume (p. 15). Also occasionally useful is Walter J. Meserve, *Robert E. Sherwood* (New York: Pegasus, 1970).

16. MacLeish to Davis, Eisenhower, Sherwood, and Cowles, "Basic Policy Statement on OWI Objectives," 8/19/42, Box 4, Entry 1, RG 208, NARA.

17. For one lengthy explication of the "strategy of truth" (a phrase that quickly achieved wide currency in propaganda circles), see Archibald MacLeish's address, "The Strategy of Truth," to the Annual Luncheon of the Associated Press on April, 20, 1942. This address is reprinted in MacLeish's *A Time to Act* (Boston: Houghton Mifflin Company, 1943), 21–31.

18. Freedom of the press in the United States quite obviously exacerbated the divide between "white" and "black" propaganda. The less control a government has over the information flow in its society, the greater the danger that information will emerge to contradict official accounts, making the credibility of government information more imperative.

19. In a recent revival of this debate, news reports revealed in early 2002, that the Pentagon had developed a secret information program that would potentially disseminate disinformation throughout the world. Critics claimed that in its use of black propaganda, this agency—the Office of Strategic Information (perhaps an echo of the Office of Strategic Services)—would damage the reputation of the U.S. government and discredit its distribution of legitimate information. In response, the Pentagon announced shortly thereafter that they would shut down

the project. In contrast, following the attacks of September 11, 2001, the State Department also declared that it would ramp up its use of public diplomacy, but made it clear that efforts would follow more in the tradition of the white propaganda of the OWI and its State Department successors during the Cold War. See Elizabeth Becker, "In the War on Terrorism, a Battle to Shape Public Opinion," *The New York Times*, November 11, 2001; James Dao and Eric Schmitt, "Pentagon Readies Efforts to Sway Sentiment Abroad," *The New York Times*, February 19, 2002; "Rumsfeld to Close Pentagon Office of Influence," *Associated Press*, February 26, 2002.

20. Quoted in Ford, 126.

21. Scott Donaldson, *Archibald MacLeish: An American Life* (Boston: Houghton Mifflin Company, 1992), 358–62; Winkler, 27–30.

22. Archibald MacLeish to Samuel I. Rosenman, 3/24/42, in *Letters of Archibald MacLeish*, ed. R. H. Winnick (Boston: Houghton Mifflin Company, 1983), 310–11.

23. "Profile: Davis, Elmer . . . U.S. Administration," August 1943, Box 10, Entry 6E, RG 208, NARA; and Roger Burlingame, *Don't Let Them Scare You: The Life and Times of Elmer Davis* (Philadelphia: J. B. Lippincott Company, 1961).

24. On Donovan's exile, see Brown, 235–39; Ford, 126–28; and Winkler, 25–31.

25. Davis's statement to Congress can be found in its original form in U.S. Congress, House, Hearings Before a Subcommittee of the Committee on Appropriations, *Second Supplemental National Defense Appropriation Bill for 1943*, 77th Congress, 2nd sess., 1942, 383–92; in slightly abridged form in M. S. Eisenhower to the OWI Staff, 11/20/42, Box 4, Entry 6B, RG 208, NARA; and in slightly expanded form in Elmer Davis and Byron Price, *War Information and Censorship* (Washington, D.C.: American Council on Public Affairs, 1943).

26. Ibid.

27. MacLeish, *A Time to Act*, 9.

28. MacLeish to Davis, Eisenhower, Sherwood, and Cowles, "Basic Policy Statement on OWI Objectives," 8/19/42, Box 4, Entry 1; "The Office of War Information," n.d., Box 3, Entry 1; "The Overseas Operations Branch," n.d., Box 1, Entry 6B; Sam Lubell to Archibald MacLeish, "Reorganization," 6/24/42, Box 3, Entry 1; all in RG 208, NARA.

29. "The Office of War Information," n.d., Box 3, Entry 1, RG208, NARA; "The Overseas Operations Branch," n.d., Box 1, Entry 6B, RG 208, NARA.

30. Here I am thinking especially of Akira Iriye's *Global Community: The Rise of International Organizations in the Making of the Contemporary World* (Berkeley:

University of California Press, 2002), in which Iriye describes the growth of international nongovernmental organizations from a steady stream during the early twentieth century into the absolute flood that began during the lead-up to World War II and continues to this day. Despite their many differences, the existence of these organizations represented a desire to strengthen and enrich a particular political agenda—almost always rooted in a common group interest or identity of the organization's members. One need only think of the identities and interests represented in such organizations as the Women's International League for Peace and Freedom (feminism, pacifism), the Pan-African Congress (African Diaspora), and the International Red Cross (Doctors Without Borders). To further the point about the increasing potency of transnational interest groups, one might follow the example of the African Diaspora into to the Cold War, where various people and organizations operating in this tradition exerted a profound impact upon everything from U.S. policy toward decolonization to desegregation *within* the United States. For example, see Brenda Gayle Plummer, *Rising Wind: Black Americans and U.S. Foreign Affairs* (Chapel Hill, N.C.: The University of North Carolina Press, 1996) and Mary Dudziak, *Cold War Civil Rights: Race and the Image of American Democracy* (Princeton, New Jersey: Princeton University Press, 2000). On women's internationalism, see Leila J. Rupp, *World's of Women: The Making of an International Women's Movement* (Princeton, N.J.: Princeton University Press, 1997).

31. "Final Report on Activities of the Foreign News Bureau, Office of War Information, Covering the Period from November 1942 to the Close of Operations, September 15, 1945," n.d, Box 2, Entry 6A; Matthew Gordon to John Herrick, "Questions and Answers Concerning Foreign News Bureau," 4/14/44, Box 2, Entry 6A; Matthew Gordon to John Harrick, "Budget Memo," 4/14/44, Box 2, Entry 6A; "Report from the Nation," 4/27/42, Box 12, Entry 6E; all in RG 208, NARA.

32. The Japanese example comes from Matthew Gordon to John Herrick, 4/14/44, Box 2, Entry 6A, RG 208, NARA. The notion that the American press reprinted foreign news without appropriate context was expressed many places, but this quote comes from a statement the OWI submitted to Congress, in U.S. Congress, House, Hearings Before the Subcommittee of the Committee on Appropriations, *National War Agencies Appropriation Bill for 1944*, Pt. 1, 78th Cong., 1st sess., 1943, 887. The suggestion that the OWI could also get the American press to print its material verbatim is from a letter by Charles Hulten to Milton Eisenhower, 9/1/42, Box 3, Entry 1, RG 208, NARA.

33. "The Overseas Operations Branch," n.d., Box 1, Entry 6B, RG 208, NARA. LaRoche's testimony can be found in U.S. Congress, Senate, Hearings Before a Subcommittee of the Committee on Appropriations, *National War Agencies Appropriation Bill for 1944*, 78th Cong., 1st sess., 1943, 255–70.

34. On the OWI's use of Gallup and Roper, as well as advertising techniques in general, see "Questions and Answers on Surveys Division Activities," n.d., Box 5, Entry 6A; and "Report from the Nation," 4/27/42, Box 12, Entry 6E; both in RG 208, NARA. Roper was one of the preeminent public opinion gurus of his day although he is now largely forgotten because of the hit to his reputation after his prediction in the hotly contested 1948 presidential election missed the mark by a whopping 12.3 percent. Gallup, of course, needs no introduction although it should be noted that he learned how to survey opinions while working as an ad executive at Young & Rubicam during the 1930s. For more on Gallup and Roper and the advertising industry, see Stephen Fox, *The Mirror Makers* (New York: William Morrow, 1984), 181.

35. Robert A. Divine, *Second Chance* (New York: Atheneum, 1967).

36. Charles F. Darlington to Gardner Cowles, 11/23/42, Box 12A, Entry 20, RG 208, NARA.

37. Arthur Sweetster to Archibald MacLeish, 6/19/42, Reel 2, Pt. 1, OWI Records [microfilm ed.]; "United Nations," n.d., Box 17, Entry 6E, Box 17, RG 208, NARA; and OWI Domestic Radio Bureau, "Understanding the United Nations," n.d., Box 17, Entry 6E, RG 208, NARA.

38. Robert Sherwood, "Long-Range Directive," 1/15/43, Box 4, Entry 6B, RG 208, NARA.

39. Ibid.

40. Ibid.

41. Ibid.

42. Elmer Davis to Robert Sherwood, 8/14/42, Box 6, Entry 1, RG 208, NARA.

43. Office of the Assistant Director (Archibald MacLeish) to Branch Directors, Deputies Bureau Chiefs and Administrative Assistants, "British Imperialism" (Current Issues Memorandum #3) and India (Current Issues Memorandum #2), 12/21/42, Box 2, Entry 6A; and "Minutes of the Committee on War Information Policy," 8/12/42, Box 1, Entry 1; all in RG 208, NARA.

44. Eisenhower and MacLeish quoted in Winkler, 41–42.

45. "Explanation Given on Split in OWI," *The New York Times*, April 13, 1943; "'Impossible to Tell Full Truth,' Say OWI Writers Who Quit," *Washington Post*, April 16, 1943; Lewis Wood, "Feud Within OWI Is Spreading Far," *The New York Times*, April 18, 1943.

46. Lewis Wood, "Feud within OWI Is Spreading Far," April 18, 1943, *The New York Times*.

47. I am reminded here of Benedict Anderson's point in *Imagined Communities: Reflections on the Origin and Spread of Nationalism*, rev. ed. (London: Verso, 2006) that the concept of a nation, as the partial product of a popular collective imagination, is, by definition, contested.

48. On the Publications Bureaus, see "Office of War Information, Overseas Branch, Bureau of Publications," n.d., Box 5, Entry 6A, RG 208, NARA. U.S. Congress, House, Hearings Before the Subcommittee of the Committee on Appropriations, *National War Agencies Appropriation Bill for 1944*, Pt. 1, 78th Cong., 1st sess., 1943, 760–61 and 1050–51.

49. The controversy over "Negroes and the War" receives extensive coverage in Savage, 124–35; and Winkler, 66–72. On the OWI and race, more generally, see also my "Making Democracy Safe for the World: Race, Propaganda, and the Transformation of U.S. Foreign Policy During World War II," *Pacific Historical Review* 73 (February 2004): 49–84.

50. The quotes about "racial equality" and a "philosophy that is alien to us" come from the comments of Democratic Congressman Leonard Allen of Louisiana, although Allen had plenty of company in race-baiting the OWI. See Subcommittee of the House Committee on Appropriations, *Hearings on National War Agencies Appropriation Bill for 1944*, 78th Cong., 1st sess., 1943, 1311.

51. The "moronic little king" episode receives excellent coverage in Winkler, 92–100; Shulman, 98–102; and Burlingame, 227–30.

52. Ibid.

53. Davis quoted in Winkler, 71; on the conflict with Congress in general, see Shulman, 95–98; Krugler, 29–33; Meserve, 176–82; Milton S. Eisenhower, *The President Is Calling* (Garden City, N.Y.: Doubleday & Company, Inc., 1974), chap. 7; Edward W. Barrett, *Truth Is Our Weapon* (New York: Funk & Wagnalls Company, 1953), chap. 3; and Charles A. H. Thomson, *Overseas Information Service of the United States Government* (New York: Arno Press, 1972), chaps. 2–5.

54. Winkler clearly lays out this argument in the Prologue to *The Politics of Propaganda*. The phrase "a vision denied" is the subtitle of his third chapter.

55. Edward Klauber to Harry S. Truman, 8/17/45, Reel 3, Part 1, OWI Records [microfilm edition].

chapter four

ALLOTMENT ANNIES AND OTHER WAYWARD WIVES: WARTIME CONCERNS ABOUT FEMALE DISLOYALTY AND THE PROBLEM OF THE RETURNED VETERAN

Ann Pfau

In June 1943, the Senate Committee on Military Affairs held hearings to examine several proposals to increase the allotment paid to enlisted men's families.[1] Although the legislation's intent was to soothe soldiers' worries about the welfare of dependent wives, children, siblings, and parents, Senator Edwin C. Johnson (D–Colorado) urged Army administrators present at the hearings to use this opportunity to address "the problem of immoral women marrying soldiers." General Miller G. White, Assistant Chief of Staff, Army Personnel, dodged the issue by charging that any policy designed to punish unfaithful wives might unfairly penalize innocent women, because charges of immorality were often based on hearsay.[2] However, the question of whether to punish sexual disloyalty was unavoidable; it resurfaced at House hearings on the same legislation three months later. This time, cuckolded soldiers found a more aggressive advocate in Representative John J. Sparkman (D–Alabama), who proposed to allow servicemen to terminate dependency allotments "upon showing good cause."[3]

Army administrators were well armed with arguments against such a measure. General Jay L. Benedict of the Joint Army Navy Legislative Board testified that although he had "no quarrel whatever with the principle" of punishing wayward wives, he worried that it would be "impracticable to determine the merits" of soldiers' marital complaints. In addition to the hardships that the proposed legislation might impose on loyal wives, Benedict condemned it for the harm that it would do to individual soldiers. Comparing the measure with enemy propaganda, he contended that it would demoralize servicemen by prompting them to distrust faithful wives. Similarly, General H. N. Gilbert, Director of the War Department's Office of Dependency Benefits, argued that it would be better policy to allow a few bad women to profit from deception than to investigate soldiers' often-unfounded complaints against their wives. Catering to soldiers' suspicions, Army officials insisted, would damage military morale and produce administrative chaos.[4] The Army's arguments won the day in Congress; Sparkman's proposal for moral investigations did not appear in the final version of the bill, yet widespread doubts about the sexual morality of soldiers' wives continued unabated.[5]

The groundswell of public concern about the fidelity of service wives arose, in part, out of a more generalized anxiety that wartime conditions had fostered sexual immorality and threatened to undermine family stability. Public officials and the popular press bemoaned a perceived decline in sexual morals and blamed young women for the increased incidence of sexually transmitted diseases, illegitimate pregnancies, and juvenile delinquency. So-called "victory girls," purportedly motivated by the patriotic impulse to give the soldiers "all they want," posed the greatest public health threat. In their misguided zeal to support the troops, these young women unintentionally weakened the nation's fighting forces by infecting servicemen with syphilis and gonorrhea. Female soldiers were subject to similar suspicions. Living on Army bases beyond the oversight of family and home community, members of the WAACs (Women's Army Auxiliary Corps) fit the wartime profile of feminine promiscuity. Indeed, the women who volunteered for service with the U.S. Army were commonly dismissed as government-issue whores.[6]

While victory girls and female soldiers seemed to threaten public morals and military health, wayward service wives posed an even greater threat to the nation at war. In political speeches and the popular press, these wanton women were accused of driving servicemen to suicide or draining men of the will to fight. Still, marital infidelity was not simply a problem of wartime motivation and morale; more troubling, many civilians worried that unfaithful service wives would derail the rehabilitation of veterans. For as much as they sympathized with soldiers, civilians also feared the servicemen's return, worrying that wartime traumas would translate into postwar social ills. By easing the transition from soldier to civilian, devoted wives could prevent this catastrophe and ensure postwar domestic tranquility, but many Americans—civilian and soldier alike—questioned whether the nation's women were up to the task.

Concerns about war's effect on wifely fidelity are at least as old as Homer's *Odyssey*, but during World War II, these concerns turned into an American national obsession. By the spring of 1945, news stories of disappointed soldiers and their adulterous wives had become so common that *Stars and Stripes* ran the headline "GIs' Marriage Woes Again Worrying the Nation" over an account of a debate sparked by the question "Should women whose husbands are in service go out with other men?" (The correct answer was, "It should be up to the husband," and the vast majority of soldier-husbands were emphatically opposed.)[7] A week later, the Army newspaper reported on proposed revisions to the law on adoptions in California, where state officials attributed a wartime increase in illegitimacy to soldiers' wives and sweethearts. Designed to facilitate legal adoptions and thereby combat a growing black market in babies, one measure would have allowed married women to place illegitimate children up for adoption without notifying their absent husbands, particularly husbands assigned to overseas military service. Along with the American Legion and Veterans of Foreign Wars, the editors of *Stars and Stripes* protested this policy, condemning the California legislature for attempting to authorize marital deception and for denying soldiers the right "to know the truth of [their] marriage status." This protest, which received national press coverage, forced revision of the proposed adoption policy.[8]

More sensational than adultery was bigamy by allotment brides, who married multiple soldiers in order to receive dependency allowances and life insurance payments.[9] Although rare in real life, these larcenous service wives received a great deal of press attention and even rated their own movie. Starring Kay Francis as a criminal mastermind, *Allotment Wives* exposed an imaginary syndicate of unscrupulous women who sought to cash in on the war by manipulating lonely servicemen's emotions. Nevertheless, Monogram Pictures promoted this movie as a socially relevant problem picture. The studio's press book encouraged theater owners to invite local welfare workers and judges to speak on the problem of wayward service wives: "Welfare workers will have stories of their contacts with women who have married servicemen and then left their babies at home while they went out and led a wanton life, unmindful of their duties. Judges will be able to tell of service wives who endeavored to divorce husbands while they were overseas fighting for them." The press book also suggested fostering debate in local newspapers on the appropriate penalty for contracting a bigamous marriage. The studio assured theater owners that with "properly handled" publicity, "you can get your community all wrought up over this picture with resulting big box office."[10]

By the time the film was released in the fall of 1945, many public officials were already wrought up over the problem of female misconduct. At the national level, this concern was manifest in congressional debates over the administration of dependency allotments. At the state level, the courts and judicial officials sought to ensure that undutiful service wives were punished for their transgressions. In Newark, New Jersey, for example, Judge James Pellecchia made news by threatening to jail adulterous service wives brought before him in family court. He was quoted in *Newsweek* as declaring, "If I had my way, soldiers' wives who are unfaithful would be branded with the scarlet letter and have their heads shaven" (like French women who took German lovers). In Chicago, state's attorney William Tuohy publicly vowed to prosecute unfaithful service wives on criminal adultery charges.[11] He ordered a review of recent divorce cases to identify potential perpetrators and asked judges to provide his office with any evidence that might aid in the prosecution of disloyal service wives. The hope was not only that misdeeds would be punished but also that fear of incarceration would deter infidelity.[12]

Tuohy's action was inspired by the widely reported case of wounded combat veteran Stanley Heck. From his hospital bed in Temple, Texas, Corporal Heck—a double amputee and recipient of the Silver Star and the Bronze Star—filed suit for divorce from his wife, Henrietta, on the grounds of desertion and adultery. While her husband was in the service, Henrietta commenced an extramarital affair with grocery chain executive Alvin C. Schupp. She stopped writing letters to her husband in December 1943 and later refused to visit him when he was returned to the United States for medical treatment. Stanley also sued his rival, demanding $50,000 in compensation for the loss of Henrietta's love.[13]

Stanley's case against Henrietta was clear-cut and quickly resolved,[14] but his alienation of affections suit was in litigation for almost a year. Based in the common law, such lawsuits presumed a husband's right, in the words of Stanley's lawyer, to his wife's "society, affection, assistance, comfort and consolation" and demanded pecuniary compensation for damage to those rights.[15] Yet by the early decades of the twentieth century, alienation of affections—along with criminal conversation and breach of promise to marry—suits had come to seem both obsolete and prone to fraud. In 1935, Illinois legislators outlawed alienation of affections and other heartbalm torts, branding this class of litigation "conducive to extortion and blackmail."[16] On this basis, Superior Court Judge Francis B. Alligretti dismissed Heck's claim against Schupp. "Affections . . . are an intangible, indescribable something . . . which cannot be sold, bartered, or exchanged," Alligretti asserted. "Thus they are not property in the sense that under the law the injury to which creates a right of action." But concerns about marital fidelity and family stability would soon trump prewar worries about gold-diggers and other extortionists. In May 1946, the Supreme Court of Illinois reversed Alligretti's ruling and declared the state's anti-heartbalm statute unconstitutional. Although it did not define the rights deriving from marriage, the Court asserted that the 1935 law violated the state's bill of rights by preventing injured parties from seeking legal redress for wrongs to "person, property or reputation." The justices also objected that the law "put a premium on the violation of moral law, making those who violate the law a privileged class, free to pursue a course of conduct without fear even to the extent of a suit for damages." Schupp's lawyers fruitlessly requested a rehearing, arguing that the Court acted as if it were an "ecclesiastical court," allowing moral standards, rather than constitutional provisions or legal precedents, to shape its decision. Schupp eventually settled out of court, likely fearing that sympathy for Heck would sway any jury.[17]

Concern about the fidelity of service wives was not confined to popular culture and public officials. In Morris, Illinois, for example, University of Chicago researchers discovered "an alert community-wide network of gossip and informal espionage." One young service wife described this system of surveillance:

> The wife of a veteran could do something and everybody in town would be talking about it. . . . Somebody sees you riding down a street, and they say, "uh-huh—she's out." If somebody in service comes up and talks to you they say, "Well she's going with him." The in-laws would do an awful lot of that. . . . They'd see you out with your husband when he came home and then they'd come up and give you little remarks like

"Oh, she done alright while you were in service." Or, "oh I see she's with *you* tonight."[18]

Close scrutiny, combined with the threat that any apparent misstep would be reported to absent boyfriends or husbands, caused many women to modify their behavior to conform to community standards. Mrs. G, a Chicago service wife who lived in an apartment above her in-laws, told the sociology student who interviewed her: "[T]hey watch me constantly. . . . My mother-in-law yells when I go out so I keep her from worrying by staying in. Maybe her daughters put ideas in her head. I always tell her that is silly because how could I write to him and think about him all the time if I did not care for him. She still watches me." Mrs. G reported that her days were "wrapped up" in caring for her young child, but her nights were free. Although she longed to leave the house, this young wife passed the time alone reading in her room to avoid upsetting her mother-in-law, a woman who deemed it her duty to ensure the fidelity of her son's wife.[19]

Rumors about wives and sweethearts who were running around had become so widespread by January 1945 that representatives of the American Red Cross (ARC) publicly chastised thoughtless or malicious gossips who sent "I thought you ought to know" letters to overseas soldiers. Along with real instances of infidelity, these unfounded allegations, according to Margaret Hagan, created a "serious morale problem" in overseas theaters. Unable to evaluate the situation for himself, a soldier could only worry, and his anxieties might infect his comrades. Philip Tykulsker, an ARC representative on Guadalcanal, reported such a case. According to Tykulsker, a soldier approached him with domestic problems. His wife was reported to be behaving badly. She would disappear from their house, leaving their child all alone, and had been seen in the company of "strange men." It turned out that the source of this information, the soldier's mother, was unreliable. She objected to her son's marriage as "beneath him" and so sought to destroy it. Inquiries to the ARC chapter in the soldier's hometown and correspondence with his wife cleared up the misunderstanding and preserved the soldier's marriage.[20]

Careless correspondence could be equally damaging to soldiers' morale. Two unrelated sentences in a letter from a parish priest to an overseas soldier were almost responsible for the latter's divorce. "It's amazing how some war widows behave," the priest wrote. In a separate paragraph, he mentioned that he had not seen the soldier's wife "for quite a while."

Upon receiving this letter, the soldier cabled his parents to begin divorce proceedings. Cooler heads prevailed, however, and the marriage was saved. An ARC investigation revealed that the priest had not seen the soldier's wife because she worked nights in a defense factory and cared for her children during the day. He had not intended to insinuate that she was untrue and was "horrified" to learn of the trouble his letter had caused. This story, as reported in *Stars and Stripes*, was intended to alleviate soldiers' marital anxieties, asserting that "[m]isleading letters from careless friends and relatives have caused more domestic upsets . . . than has faithlessness of wives at home."[21]

Although the ARC blamed civilians for soldiers' anxieties, friends and family often took their cues from the men themselves. One distrustful soldier, for example, requested that his mother "keep her eyes open to see whether or not his wife might be seen 'with another man.'" The officer who censored the letter commented: "I howled when I read it—it struck me as very funny, because I happen to know just how jealous this particular soldier is."[22] Army psychiatrists found such apprehensions to be common among overseas troops. Albert Mayers, who served with the 94th Infantry Division in Europe, described the case of one enlisted man whose letters home to his wife were full of bizarre and unfounded accusations. Mayers diagnosed the "presence of a delusion of infidelity" and "indications of a paranoid personality" but observed that even seemingly normal men suffered from a similar anxiety. "Most often in the 'normal,' the entire conflict is repressed," he wrote, "but if the question is ever aired, as during a 'bull session,' the conversation becomes charged with considerable feeling." Mayers blamed "projection" of soldiers' own "real or phantasized" infidelities for much of the problem.[23]

Some GIs had reason for concern about the fidelity of their wives and sweethearts. The term "Dear John letter" was coined during World War II when some servicemen received letters like this one to an enlisted man named Ahmed:

The time has come to clear things between us. You will have realized, before now, that our marriage was a mistake. I beg of you to put an end to this mistake and get a divorce. . . . As a matter of fact, I have never been yours, but now I belong to someone else, and this finishes things between us.

Another soldier's faithless fiancée was less direct than Ahmed's wife; she never formally broke off their engagement, but at the end of a long letter, she mentioned that she had recently married a "broadminded" sailor who would not "mind you writing me occasionally." After receiving a series of insulting letters from her GI boyfriend Saul Kramer, Anne Gudis's response was a brief and well deserved "Go To Hell!"[24]

Like the other letters, Gudis's brush-off message was submitted by the scorned serviceman for publication in *Yank*. A photograph of her V-Mail was printed in the Army magazine and received attention from the New Jersey press. In her hometown of Newark, Gudis wrote, "People could not have had more to say if I had murdered someone." The object of a great deal of unwanted publicity, she received approximately 100 letters from strangers, both civilians and servicemen, including Kramer's commanding officer, who accused her of damaging unit morale. Some of the men who contacted Gudis asked for dates, but most of the letters criticized her behavior, for Americans agreed, "to jilt a soldier is a serious offense."[25] Despite or perhaps because of the uproar, the couple quickly reconciled, and by December 1943, Gudis promised, "I have cast all other men aside as far as the future is concerned and am waiting only for you." They married soon after Kramer's discharge in November 1945.[26]

In the press, popular culture, and private letters, American women were bombarded with the message that it was their duty to be true to the soldiers (even though their husbands and boyfriends might not have been so faithful).[27] Most wives and sweethearts internalized this expectation of sexual fidelity to absent servicemen. One told University of Chicago researchers, "We war wives are placed on a shining altar by our husbands, and it is up to us to keep their faith." In a letter to her husband, Robert, an infantry officer stationed in Germany, Jane Easton likewise professed a strong commitment to marital fidelity. Condemning erring wives and sweethearts as "animals" motivated to cheat by biological urges or, with some compassion, as lonely women looking to love, she reminded her husband that "there are a greater number who are virtuous." "Believe me," she wrote, "there are true mates waiting over here for their soldiers." Jane included herself among them.[28]

Wifely devotion was not simply a wartime duty; marriage to a serviceman also brought postwar obligations. As the soldiers' return became imminent, service wives came under increased scrutiny and pressure. Beginning in 1944, a whole literature arose on the rehabilitation of war veterans, much of it aimed at women—mothers, fiancées, and especially wives. Accorded a key, if not the primary, role in soldiers' "readjustment" to civilian society, women were bombarded with advice from a wide range of experts.[29]

Psychiatrist Alexander Dumas and his collaborator Grace Keen described readjustment as a two-way process in which the former soldier "must do his part," but like many of this genre, their *Psychiatric Primer for the Veteran's Family and Friends* emphasized feminine—and particularly wifely—responsibility. Although the authors noted that the majority of American servicemen would be "returning to mothers instead of wives," three of the five representative women whose experiences were the basis for their chapters were wives; the fourth was a fiancée, and the fifth a mother. Not surprisingly, given popular anxiety about momism, Dumas and Keen's primary advice to mothers was to "cut those apron strings."[30] Wives, by contrast, were encouraged to organize their lives around the needs of husbands and children. Grace Sloan Overton, author of *Marriage in War and Peace*, justified this attention to GI marriages by explaining that although most servicemen might return as sons, they would soon become "the majority of husbands, lovers, and fathers among us if our American family life goes on."[31]

With the future of the American family at stake, young wives—whose questionable morals had seemed to threaten military morale and motivation—became, in historian Susan Hartmann's words, the nation's "potential redeemers." Believed to be the primary objects of wishful wartime fantasies, these women were assigned the daunting task of domesticating the returning soldiers.[32] The nation's veterans, professional advice givers asserted, were altered by wartime experiences. Military service and time away from home made them restless, aggressive, and resentful of civilians. Yet with proper guidance, a loving wife might be "the anchor" that steadied her soldier "during the stormy period of readjustment." In the pages of *Ladies Home Journal*, one combat veteran advised women to be patient with their soldiers—to forgive angry outbursts, emotional distance, and sexual indiscretions. Most important, however, a wife might help her soldier and sustain her marriage by becoming the "goddess" he imagined her to be. Similarly, Marine Corps psychiatrist Herbert Kupper called on women to mobilize their feminine wiles in the name of readjustment. Although skeptical of real women's ability to live up to soldiers' fantasies, Kupper advised wives to behave as they had during the couples' courtship. By temporarily deferring to the soldier's demands and suppressing her own desires, the wife might forestall disillusionment. But as Susan Hart-mann has noted, wives also played a more active role in Kupper's rehabili-tation plan. A dutiful wife was responsible for assessing her husband's needs and monitoring his behavior. If he failed to adjust after several months home, she should urge him to seek counseling.[33]

The goal behind much of this advice was to rebuild the veteran's ego so that he might reclaim his proper role as head of household. Overton ad-dressed this issue through the instructive story of Marybelle, who at first resisted her husband Bob's post-service educational plans by asserting her rights as wartime breadwinner. The training that Bob wished to pursue would require the couple to sell their house and move to another city; Marybelle would have to give up the job at which she excelled. Marybelle pressured her husband to return to his pre-war job, but he had no wish to resume that line of work and made no effort to find another job. It looked as though the marriage was "heading toward tragedy," but counselors "help[ed] Marybelle to see that Bob's inspiration was *her* biggest project." Conjugal peace was restored after Marybelle allowed Bob to take "the lines of the family back in hand."[34]

Despite all the coaching, most experts agreed that even the most patient and attentive wife might encounter difficulties. An epidemic of GI divorces was an anticipated side effect of the soldiers' return. Wartime separation strained most marriages, and hasty war marriages, contracted on the basis of a few weeks or months of acquaintance, were judged particularly fragile. Overton and others outlined steps to preserve such marriages, but many observers predicted their collapse.[35] Indeed, sociology professor Willard Waller, in his influential and alarmist contribution to the literature, ques-tioned whether war marriages were "really marriages" and described hasty post-war marriages as "equally hazardous." In fact, he advised the readers of *Ladies Home Journal* that "[s]ometimes the woman in a man's life may help him most by not marrying him immediately after his release from the service." Nevertheless, Waller declared "the personal side of recon-struction" to be "woman's work." Along with good jobs and an extensive system of social services, loving wives and mothers facilitated the process of rehabilitating bitter and "maladjusted" veterans who might otherwise destabilize American society and politics.[36]

Press reports from abroad seemed to confirm home-front fears and to justify the flood of advice. From a civilian perspective, the prospect of post-war domestic peace looked dim. With the relaxation of news and mail censorship following the Allied victories over Germany and Japan, Americans back home began to learn about misconduct abroad. In the summer months of 1945, fraternization between American soldiers and German women, along with the skyrocketing rate of sexually transmitted diseases among American service personnel in Europe, made the front pages of most American dailies. That fall, a new wave of articles explored the question of what to do about the anticipated "spring crop of fraternization babies."[37] Stories about GIs and geishas soon followed.[38] At around the same time, journalists began reporting from Europe that American soldiers had earned a bad reputation because of "a general increase in . . . drunkenness, petty robbery, assaults, and destruction of civilian property," not only in Germany but also in former Allied nations. Civilian concern reached such a pitch in the fall of 1945 that Edward C. Betts, Judge Advocate General for American forces in Europe, felt compelled to dispel the "unfounded" fear that the war had produced a "reservoir of potential criminals" in the returning soldiers.[39]

Reports of GI promiscuity and misconduct contributed to a picture of potential post-war disaster and fueled a popular movement to reunite soldiers with their families as quickly as possible. In the summer and fall of 1945, the families of overseas servicemen began pressuring the American government to "bring back daddy" or send wives and fiancées abroad. As early as May 29, Congresswoman Margaret Chase Smith (R–Maine) responded to press reports on fraternization by publicly urging Secretary of War Henry Stimson to permit American wives to join husbands stationed in Europe. The policy of shipping women overseas would, she argued, assist soldiers' "rehabilitation" and "prevent further disintegration of the American home and the American family life."[40] Soldiers and their families flooded the mail with pleas to expedite the discharge of sons, husbands, and fathers. In September, President Harry S. Truman estimated that he received 1,000 such letters daily.[41] By winter, service wives in major cities throughout the nation had organized local chapters of the "Bring Back Daddy Club," dedicated to convincing government officials to release fathers from their military obligations.[42] Finally, in January 1946, servicemen in all major theaters of operations took to the streets, organizing mass demonstrations to protest the seemingly slow pace of demobilization.[43]

From the fall of 1945 through the summer of 1946, World War II veterans made their way home en masse, and that spring and summer, thousands of American service wives and fiancées began heading overseas to occupied Germany and Japan. Reunited with their husbands and sweethearts at home and abroad, American women served on the frontlines of a national effort to rehabilitate war veterans. The question remained: Were they up to the task? University of Chicago researcher Anne Hurley was skeptical. In the spring of 1945, while interviewing soldiers' families in Morris, Illinois, Hurley worried about the "problem of these dangling war wives." Despite all the scrutiny, service wives seemed to receive little or no community support. In Hurley's estimation, they were "unaware of what was going on in the rest of the world" and unprepared for their soldiers' return. Most wives simply sat home and waited, "expecting everything to be just the same when their husbands come home." They had "no conception" of the challenges they would face.[44] Carol Bauman Lefevre came to a similar conclusion in her 1948 University of Chicago master's thesis based on interviews with 100 service wives. Noting the women's optimism about the stability of their marriages, Lefevre commented, "there may be wishful thinking or lack of realization of readjustment difficulties on the part of some wives." Blanche W, for example, believed that wartime separation had saved her marriage. She and Bill were "on the verge of separation" when he joined the Navy. Blanche complained that before he left, Bill preferred time with his friends to time spent at home. But, she asserted, military service had "taught him to appreciate" his wife and young son; she now hoped that Bill "would stay and be satisfied." The student who interviewed Blanche commented, "This case seemed to me to be the best case of possible un-adjustment in the post-war period, of all the cases I have interviewed."[45]

Yet University of Chicago interviews reveal that service wives were not wholly sanguine about the prospect of their husbands' return. Most of the women anticipated conflicts over finances, household management, vocational plans, marital sex, or child-rearing practices. They recognized changes in themselves and expected to find their husbands somewhat altered although not always in ways they could predict. As she awaited the return of her husband, Eli, in the summer of 1945, Chicago service wife Roselyn F seemed more concerned than most. Perhaps having read some of the literature on veterans, she commented, "[W]hen a person is away at war you get more nervous and irritable and all that." Friends observed changes in Eli when he was home on furlough, but to Roselyn's eyes, he remained unchanged. Nevertheless, she anticipated difficulties. Another service wife told sociology student Mildred Handler that although she had been married four years, the two years apart from her husband made her marriage "seem like a dream." Purportedly eager for their reunion, she also dreaded the event. She explained, "I want him to come home and yet I'm kind of scared. I'm afraid he'll seem like a stranger." Other women worried less about changes to their husbands than to themselves. One wife, for example, feared that a newfound independence would jeopardize her marriage. The problem, she told her interviewer, was that her husband "wants someone to depend on him. He wants the earth and moon to set on him. . . . And for the first time I've formed an idea of what I want—all kinds of securities, emotional and the like."[46]

War brides, who had never set up independent households with their husbands except perhaps temporarily near military bases, faced a greater challenge. In addition to helping soldier-husbands reintegrate into civilian society, these women had their own adjustments to make. Charlotte P, who married Mel soon after he enlisted, confided to her interviewer that after only three months of living together as husband and wife and more than two years of marriage by correspondence, she was "sick of writing letters" and had come to feel that she and Mel did not "know each other any longer." Differences had developed between them during their separation. Fearing the "next war," Charlotte did not wish to become a mother; Mel still wanted children. Other hurdles included setting up and learning to run her own household and helping her husband find a job. Twenty-one years old and living with her parents, Charlotte had "never bought food or cooked, or anything like that," and 25-year-old Mel had "never held down a real job." An instrument specialist aboard a cargo plane, he hoped to find work with an airline but did not have any concrete employment plans.[47]

Despite many public and parental concerns, war marriages tended to be far more permanent than anticipated. In fact, sociologists Eliza K. Pavalko and Glen H. Elder, Jr. found that servicemen who married during the war were less likely to divorce than comrades who had married before the war began, perhaps because the couple was aware of the risks before taking their vows. A comment by one service wife seems to confirm this insight. She told her interviewer that the "only difficulty" she had encountered was convincing her concerned parents that she was prepared to "cope with marriage during the war." She tried to reassure them by telling them she loved her fiancé "enough to accept him as he would be after the War, regardless of what the change might be." Although this young wife anticipated that her husband would have problems "adjusting to civilian life" and that the two of them would "have to get to know each other again," she looked forward to his return.[48]

Whether newlywed or long married, most young couples were unprepared for the difficulties that accompanied even the most successful readjustment. The oft-fantasized first moments of reunion tended to be as tentative as they were passionate. Naval officer Jerry C reported that although he and his wife, Evelyn, exchanged daily letters and many photographs during their 22-month separation, he was initially "surprised at the way she looked." Commenting that "[a]nticipation is always greater than actual reality," he described their "sexual adjustment" as slower than when they were first married. Other conflicts revolved around housekeeping and in-laws, but a year after Jerry's return to the United States, the student who interviewed the couple judged their adjustment to be almost complete. Evelyn and Jerry were expecting their first child and sought to move out of her parents' house. Evelyn, who had been employed as a social worker, was now a full-time homemaker. She had become "more domestic" since Jerry's return and had come to see "the home as a center of our life." Jerry, only recently discharged and now the family's sole breadwinner, was debating whether to resume graduate studies or to enter the civilian workforce right away.[49]

While Evelyn and Jerry seemed to affirm the strength of the traditional family, the case of Bess and Harold W exemplified civilian fears about the war's impact on marriage. Bess found Harold much changed by his experiences as a prisoner of war. She described him as argumentative, impatient, profane, and distrustful. He told her that while he was in prison, "he heard all sorts of stuff about what the wives of prisoners were doing." Some women asked for divorces "so that they could marry this year's hero rather than last year's prisoner. Others asked for money so they could have babies with other men." Harold, nevertheless, became extremely dependent on his wife, who seemed determined to make their marriage work. Initially "nervous" around other people, Harold preferred to be alone with Bess. Unsure about what he would do for a living, he allowed his wife to convince him to go back to school for accounting courses. At the time of the interview, Bess expressed some doubts about the future of her marriage but was doing her best to avoid arguments with Harold. The interviewer shared Bess's doubts but commended "the wife's desire to help her husband in any way she can," concluding that the marriage would probably survive.[50]

Bess and Harold's marriage illustrates the weight that individual Americans placed on domesticity as a balm for war wounds. Harold did not participate in the interview, but we know from Bess that like many other servicemen, he had been eager to wed before leaving for overseas service so that he would have "something to come back to." Like Jerry and Evelyn, Bess and Harold were expecting their first child and searching for a home of their own. It seems likely that the baby was planned and was intended to cement the marriage; advice givers like John Mariano characterized children as a "stabilizing force which tends to cause marriages to hold." Impending parenthood certainly seemed to focus Harold's restless energy. He read as many baby books as he could find and even planned to take charge of the baby's nighttime feeding for fear that Bess would be too tired to mix the proper formula.[51]

Although sometimes reluctant to become parents during wartime, most young couples believed that children would strengthen marriage bonds. One wife, for example, deplored childless marriages, commenting, "There's no sense in getting married if you don't have children." However, she also worried that an absent father might find it difficult to love a child he did not know.[52] Many wives sought to remedy this potential side effect of separation through correspondence. A baby or young child was typically the main topic of letters to soldier-husbands. Mothers also sent regular snapshots and other mementoes, such as baby's first shoes, overseas. They taught their children to recognize portraits of daddy and to behave in a manner that would make their fathers proud. Freda Spitzer, for example, admonished her two-year-old son, Bobby, to "eat nice so that when Daddy came home he would be pleased with the way he ate." An absent father often became part of a child's imaginative world. Once as Freda was writing to her husband, Albert, Bobby pretended to greet his father as he walked through the door. According to his mother, three-year-old Sherman P conversed with a portrait of his father "for hours at a time." Another soldier's child said her evening prayers before a photograph of her father. Like Sherman, she often spoke to the picture, asking it questions such as, "Can I go out and play?" Her fantasy father's answer was always yes.[53] But when the time for reunion came, children were not always able to connect the men standing before them with the indulgent fathers they imagined.[54]

One young boy, for example, was reportedly "bewildered" to learn that "daddy" was a person rather than a photograph.[55]

Returning servicemen, likewise, were often unprepared to become fathers to children whom they barely knew. Tom C was unable to be present at his daughter's birth; he did not meet her until he returned home from overseas service. The child greeted Tom as instructed by her mother but began crying when her father picked her up for the first time. Yet over the course of several months, the two-year-old came, in Tom's words, "to act to me like any other kid would to their fathers." Tom told University of Chicago researcher Walter Eaton that fatherhood gave him a new sense of responsibility, and Eaton noted the pride Tom took in his daughter's good manners. While parental responsibilities seemed to smooth Tom's readjustment to civilian life, for many other first-time fathers, they were complicating factors. To Rick B, for example, fatherhood was a source of frustration. He resented the demands of his young daughter's nap and feeding schedules, and he complained that the child was spoiled. His wife judged that Rick would have preferred a childless reunion. "He wants it to go on just as it was" before he left, she confided to Eaton. Other wives made similar observations. One explained, "When they want to go, that's all there is to it—they can't be bothered with children."[56]

The difficulties that Tom and Rick experienced were common to many returned soldiers who were also first-time fathers. At Stanford University, psychologist Lois Meek Stolz became aware of veterans' concerns about their war-born progeny; she found that several of the former servicemen in her class were interested in the topic for "personal rather than academic" reasons. This experience prompted Stolz to study how wartime separation affected relations between father and child, based on an experimental group of 19 veterans of overseas service and a matched control group of fathers (some of them veterans) who had been able to watch their children grow. Compared with the control group, returned fathers were particularly anxious about their ability to assert authority within the family and to establish themselves as breadwinners. One confided to Stolz, "I went through a period of wondering whether I could live up to the responsibilities of a husband."[57] Not surprisingly, all the men in the experimental group experienced some form of rejection—crying, shyness, or refusal of affection—from children who regarded them as strangers; this behavior reinforced the former servicemen's insecurities. In most cases, returned fathers responded by assuming the harsh role of disciplinarian; they thus alienated their war-born children and produced conflict within their reconstituted families. Years later, as historian William Tuttle has shown, many of these conflicts remained unresolved.[58]

The returned fathers who participated in Stolz's study viewed their war-born children through a negative lens. Compared with the control group, they were twice as likely to find fault and much less prone to praise their young sons and daughters. They described the children as unhappy, demanding, unresponsive, disrespectful, and selfish. All but one blamed the child for interfering in the reunion between husband and wife, and most worried that the mother-child bond had become too strong in the father's absence. A predictable result of such concerns, given the popular condemnation of momism, was the servicemen's fear that their sons had become sissies. Complicating the situation was many veterans' ambivalence toward their war-born children, perhaps reflecting unconscious doubts about their legitimacy (and thus their wives' fidelity). One father, for example, described his daughter as "sort of an adoption really." Another admitted that initially his son "didn't particularly seem like my child too much." Most of the men in the experimental group found it easier to love their postwar children; only two of the 16 second-time fathers claimed to love both equally. By contrast, the control group fathers were slightly more likely to report feeling closer to their first than to their second child; seven of the 16 claimed to love both equally.[59]

While married veterans adjusted or readjusted to family life, discharged bachelors pursued the bonds of matrimony with increasing ardor. Walter Eaton's fieldwork in Morris, Illinois, helps explain this phenomenon. A veteran himself, Eaton moved to Morris with his wife, Jean, in 1945. While there, he drank with his subjects at local taverns, visited veterans in their homes, and spoke with the men several times during their first months back in Morris. Eaton observed that recently returned soldiers were often restless and ill at ease in their own homes. Released from military obligation, soldiers often avoided civilian responsibilities. A recently divorced service wife complained that her former husband would "be gallivanting around all day" and "too doggone tired to make it to work at night." One former soldier described this behavior: "It's sort of a prolonged leave—that's the atmosphere prevailing." Every night and in some cases earlier in the day, veterans congregated in local taverns, such as the Seven Gables, where they could gamble in the back room, drink at the bar, and generally "blow off steam." Nevertheless, after months of renewing old acquaintances and celebrating newfound freedom, most married veterans settled into domestic routines, and many bachelors began to long for married life.[60]

Eaton's interviews reveal that some of the least-stable veterans sought marital solutions to their adjustment difficulties. Mike T, for example, had lived in his parents' home collecting GI Bill unemployment benefits ("rocking-chair money") since returning five months earlier; every night, he could be found drinking in one of Morris's taverns. After sharing a couple of beers with Eaton one afternoon, Mike complained that his "nerves" were bad and that he was drinking too much but confided that he hoped to turn his life around. His plan was to leave town, take an apprentice course at a big factory, and marry his girlfriend, Margaret. Mike believed that married life would "settle me down quite a bit," observing that it had had a similar effect on other veterans. As a married man, Mike predicted, he would stay home at night instead of going to taverns; he would drink less and become a "steady" worker. However, Mike's plan to achieve stability through employment and marriage was only half formed. Although he had selected a potential mate, he could not answer Eaton's question about where he would find the apprenticeship. Ed M, another rocking-chair veteran, shared Mike's faith in matrimony. Marriage, he asserted, "will be the best thing in the world for me. . . . Do me good in every way." He joked that it might even motivate him to hold down a steady job.[61]

To Eaton's surprise, by late summer 1946, even John N, a proud former Marine who had previously denied any interest in marriage ("No use [buying] the cow when the milk's free"), was engaged to be married. A skilled tradesman with a short temper and a weak work ethic, John had, in Eaton's words, become "troubled and worried by his present behavior." He looked to his fiancée for help and blamed her when his behavior failed to improve, as happened one night when Eaton ran into a very drunk John. The former serviceman complained about "that damn woman of mine" and, addressing Eaton, insisted, "I shouldn't be out like this, you see who I'm out with don't you." The sociologist noted, "The inference evidently was that he wouldn't have been out with these fellows and shouldn't have been out with them—but that he and his girl had an argument and that that was responsible for the trouble." Although skeptical of John's marriage plans, Eaton predicted that if married, John might "settle down and continue to live in Morris." If not, "he may find himself in six months somewhere in Texas or China, god knows where."[62]

Like Mike, Ed, and John, most Morris citizens (veteran and nonveteran alike) tended to classify married men among the best adjusted or most settled of the returned soldiers. Given a set of cards, each bearing the name of a former serviceman, unmarried veteran Tony L arranged them into three piles based on level of satisfaction since returning home. The best-adjusted men enjoyed some form of financial security, many were happily married, and all had "something to come back to." Among the second group (veterans whose adjustment Tony judged average) were men who had steady jobs or who were attending school but whose future was unclear. Tony included many of his married acquaintances among this group, explaining that these men were "forced into being halfway contented." Tony, who worked for a local manufacturer and planned to enter Springfield Junior College, placed himself among the third group of veterans, men who were dissatisfied with their civilian occupational status or unhappy in their marriages. When asked to perform the same task, Roy B, a married nonveteran who until recently had seemed a confirmed bachelor, explained that in his opinion, the best-adjusted veterans benefited from wifely encouragement and a feeling of familial obligation. Less settled veterans "[p]robably . . . didn't feel their family obligation quite as strongly."[63]

Despite wartime doubts about the fidelity of soldiers' wives and sweethearts, Americans shared a remarkable faith in matrimony. To young men and women whose lives were disrupted first by the Depression and then by the war, marriage, accompanied by parenthood and homeownership, represented the security, stability, and satisfaction they longed to attain. While the economic crises of the 1930s inhibited nuptiality and fertility, war and peace inspired high marriage and birth rates, confounding demographers' forecasts and reversing prior trends for more than a decade. No sequence of events before or since has sparked such a significant demographic turnabout.[64]

The men who served in the nation's armed forces were in the forefront of this domestic revolution. They represented three-quarters of the male population between the ages of 20 and 29 in 1947, when the median age at first marriage was 23.7 years old. Although disproportionately single when they entered military service, these men proved more prone to marry than their civilian counterparts. The federal government facilitated this marital propensity through military dependency allowances and a broad array of veterans' benefits,[65] but economic incentives alone cannot account for servicemen's and veterans' enhanced desire for domestic bliss. Along with government subsidies and economic prosperity, popular faith in the beneficial—even restorative—effects of matrimony helped propel the marriage and attendant baby booms.

Although the transition from soldier to husband, father, and breadwinner could be rocky, the anticipated epidemic of broken homes never materialized. A sharp but brief postwar upsurge in divorce was dwarfed by an even greater and longer-lasting increase in matrimony. In places like Morris, older veterans, born between the years 1916 and 1918, returned home to try to take up where they left off. Most of the bachelors married while in service or soon after discharge. Returning husbands readjusted to the families they had been forced to leave behind. As a group, these men made little use of GI Bill benefits, but four years after the war's end and roughly three years after their discharges, they had almost matched the economic and domestic achievements of peers who did not serve. Military service seemed to have temporarily disrupted but not significantly altered the course of their lives. By contrast, war was a turning point in the lives of the youngest Morris veterans, inducted in their late teens and discharged at around age 20. By 1949, 43 percent had already left town or planned to leave in pursuit of educational and employment opportunities not available in Morris. Although sociologist Robert J. Havighurst emphasized "continuity" in the behavior and accomplishments of these young men, Glen H. Elder, Jr., and his colleagues found that the majority of those who entered military service before the age of 21 believed that "their life has followed a different and more rewarding course as a result."[66]

With wife and often baby in tow, this younger cohort of veterans were pioneers of a mass migration in search of affordable and child-friendly housing. They left small towns and overcrowded cities for places like Park Forest, south of Chicago; or Island Trees, later Levittown, on Long Island. Thanks to Levitt & Sons' recruitment strategies and to government-backed home loans, by 1951, close to 90 percent of the men who rented or owned property in Levittown were white World War II veterans; their modal age was 29 years old. The developers of Park Forest—home to *Fortune* magazine editor William H. Whyte's organization man—also sought to populate the town with white veterans and their families, promising them an escape from the noise, dirt, and crime of the city.[67] "[H]arbinger[s]," in

William Whyte's words, "for the way [America] is going to be," these family-centered housing developments also satisfied the former servicemen's desire for domestic comfort and security.[68]

NOTES

1. The allowances were drawn from enlisted men's pay and supplemented by the federal government. Officers received no supplement.

2. Committee on Military Affairs, Senate, 78th Cong., 1st sess., *Hearings on S. 1131, a Bill to Amend the Servicemen's Dependents Allowance Act of 1942 . . . and S. 1279 . . ., June 28, 1943* (Washington, D.C.: U.S. Government Printing Office, 1943), 20–21.

3. Committee on Military Affairs, House of Representatives, 78th Cong., 1st sess., *Hearings on S. 1279 and Various House Bills to Amend the Act Providing Family Allowances for the Dependents of Enlisted Men. . . , September 29 and 30, October 1 and 5, 1943* (Washington, D.C.: U.S. Government Printing Office, 1943), 28.

4. Ibid., 19, 28, 115–16, 118–19. See also "Army Opposes Morals Probe," *Stars and Stripes*, London edition, October 4, 1943; "Group Debates Aid to Unfaithful Wives," *The New York Times*, October 2, 1943.

5. In fact, Senator Scott W. Lucas of Illinois would revive the issue of halting allotment payments to wayward wives soon after V-E Day; however, enlisted men would not gain this right until 1955. "Soldiers Wives Who Desert May Lose Federal Cash," *Stars and Stripes*, London edition, May 23, 1945; United Press, "Straying Wives to Pay," *The New York Times*, May 3, 1955.

6. "Schools and Mothers Are Urged to Unite to Check Rise in Juvenile Delinquency," *The New York Times*, November 19, 1942. For more on popular concerns about women's sexual misconduct during World War II, see Marilyn E. Hegarty, "Patriot or Prostitute?: Sexual Discourses, Print Media, and American Women During World War II," *Journal of Women's History* 10 (Summer 1998): 112–36; Allan M. Brandt, *No Magic Bullet: A Social History of Venereal Disease in the United States Since 1880*, expanded ed. (New York: Oxford University Press, 1987), 167–68; Leisa D. Meyer, *Creating GI Jane: Sexuality and Power in the Women's Army Corps During World War II* (New York: Columbia University Press, 1996), chap. 2; Karen Anderson, *Wartime Women Sex Roles, Family Relations, and the Status of Women During World War II* (Westport, Conn.: Greenwood Press, 1981), 103–11; D'Ann Campbell, *Women at War with America: Private Lives in a Patriotic Era* (Cambridge, Mass.: Harvard University Press, 1984), 208–11; Ann Pfau, *Miss*

Yourlovin: GIs, Gender, and Domesticity During World War II (New York: Columbia University Press, 2008), www.gutenberg-e.org/pfau, chap. 2.

7. An August 1945 Gallup poll survey on the question of whether service wives should date other men while their husbands were overseas found that 85–90 percent of American civilians disapproved of such behavior, women somewhat more than men. George H. Gallup, *The Gallup Poll: Public Opinion, 1935–1971*, vol. 1 (New York: Random House, 1972), 518; William R. Spear, "GIs' Marriage Woes Again Worrying the Nation" and William R. Spear, "Should Wives Date? GIs Reply Emphatic 'No!,'" *Stars and Stripes*, Paris edition, May 28 and June 23, 1945; see also Ruth Millett, "Wives Who Date While Husbands Are Gone to War Are Sure to Be Making Serious Trouble for Themselves," (Helena, Mont.) *Independent Record*, January 12, 1945.

8. "'Black Market' Rises in Coast Adoptions," *The New York Times*, March 8, 1945; "State Should Act to End Adoption Racket Evil," *Fresno Bee Republican*, March 11, 1945; Army News Service, "Bill Would Let Adoptions Hide Sins of Erring Wives of GIs," "Licensed Infidelity?," and International News Service, "Bill to Conceal 'Indiscretions' of GIs' Wives to Be Changed," and "'Indiscretions Bill' Amended as Result of Many Protests," all in *Stars and Stripes*, Paris edition, June 4, 5, 7, 15, 1945; International News Service, "Much Disputed Baby Adoption Bill Is Changed" and Associated Press, "Illegitimate Baby Adoption Law Loophole Is Discovered," both in *Modesto Bee and News-Herald*, June 15 and December 11, 1945. See also soldiers' letters on this topic, *Stars and Stripes* Paris edition, June 10, 1945; *Stars and Stripes*, Mediterranean edition, June 13, 1945; *Stars and Stripes*, London edition, June 19, 1945. See also E. Wayne Carp, *Family Matters: Secrecy and Disclosure in the History of Adoption* (Cambridge, Mass.: Harvard University Press, 2000), 111–13.

9. For more on bigamous wives and wartime fraud, see John Costello, *Love, Sex, & War: Changing Values, 1939–1945* (San Francisco: Collins, 1985), 269; "Marrying Woman Sentenced" and "'Georgia Belle' in Toils: Too Many Husbands, Too Many Allotments Charged," both in *The New York Times*, July 15, 1944 and January 12, 1945; "Wed 3 to Get Allotment Cash," *Stars and Stripes*, London edition, March 20, 1944; "2 Wives Says She; But She Has 6 Mates, Says He," *Stars and Stripes*, Paris edition, July 6, 1945; Mickey MacDougall, "Legions of Larceny," *American Weekly*, insert in the San Antonio (Tex.) *Light*, June 4, 1944; Jacob Fisher, *Wives and War* (New York: Exposition Press, 1949).

10. *Allotment Wives*, directed by William Nigh (Monogram Pictures, 1945); Monogram Pictures, *Allotment Wives* press book, in author's possession.

11. Conviction for a first offense brought the penalty of a $500 fine or a year in prison or both.

12. "Jail for the Faithless," *Newsweek*, August 13, 1945, 26–27; Army News Service, "Cheating Wives Begin to Pay with Loss of Allotment Checks," *Stars and Stripes*, Paris edition, August 5, 1945; International News Service, "Chicago Divorce Judges Stand Behind Servicemen," *Charleston* (W.Va.) *Gazette*, August 4, 1945.

13. "Crippled Hero Sues Executive for Alienation," *Chicago Daily Tribune*, August 1, 1945; International News Service, "Legless War Veteran Wounded Anew in Chicago Divorce Trial," *Charleston* (W.Va.) *Gazette*, August 3, 1945; Associated Press, "Maimed War Hero Charges Wife Unfaithful" and International News Service, "Parents to Sue for Allotment Accounting," *El Paso* (Tex.) *Herald Post*, August 1, 1945; Army News Service, "Erring Wife's Allotments Hit," *Stars and Stripes*, Middle Pacific edition, August 15, 1945; Army News Service, "While War Took GI's Legs, He Says Civilian Took His Wife," *Stars and Stripes*, Paris edition, August 2, 1945; "Jail for the Faithless," *Newsweek*, August 13, 1945, 26–27.

14. "Maimed Yank's Divorce Suit on Trial Today," *Chicago Tribune*, September 14, 1945.

15. Brief and Argument for Appellant, *Stanley Heck v. Alvin S. Schupp*, case 29485, March 1946, Clerk of the Supreme Court of Illinois.

16. On the history of anti-heartbalm statutes and related litigation in Illinois and elsewhere, see Jane E. Larson, "'Women Understand So Little, They Call My Good Nature Deceit': A Feminist Rethinking of Seduction," *Columbia Law Review* 93 (March 1993): 393–99; Rebecca Tushnet, "Rules of Engagement," *The Yale Law Journal* 108 (June 1998): 2586–91; Nathan P. Feinsinger, "Legislative Attack on 'Heart Balm,'" *Michigan Law Review* 33 (May 1935): 979–1009; Laura Hanft Korobkin, *Criminal Conversations: Sentimentality and Nineteenth-Century Legal Stories of Adultery* (New York: Columbia University Press, 1998), 171–77; "Alienation of Affections in Illinois: Conflict Between Judiciary and Legislature," *University of Chicago Law Review* 15 (Winter 1948): 400–04; Stanley Armstrong, "Horner Allows Anti-Balm Act to Become Law," *Chicago Daily Tribune*, May 5, 1935.

17. Opinion of the Court and Petition for Rehearing, *Stanley Heck v. Alvin S. Schupp*, case 29485, Clerk of the Supreme Court of Illinois. "Judge Dismissed Love Balm Suit of Legless Yank" and Orville Dwyer, "Supreme Court Rules Love Can Be Worth Money," *Chicago Tribune*, December 1, 1945 and May 22, 1946; Associated Press, "GI's Alienation Suit Is Dismissed," *Kokomo* (Ind.) *Tribune*, September 26, 1946; "Illinois 'Heart Balm' Act Held Unconstitutional as a Denial of Remedy," *Columbia Law Review* 47 (April 1947): 503–05; G.M.W., "Twelve

Years with the 'Heart Balm Acts,'" *Virginia Law Review* 33 (May 1947): 314, 318–20.

18. Researchers affiliated with the University of Chicago's Committee on Human Development studied the war's impact on soldiers and their families in Morris, described as a "typical small midwestern city." Robert J. Havighurst et al., *The American Veteran Back Home: A Study of Veteran Readjustment* (New York: Longmans, Green and Co., 1951), v–vi, 39–40; Walter H. Eaton, "Research on Veterans' Adjustment," *The American Journal of Sociology* 51 (March 1946): 483–85; Walter Eaton, Interview with "3 Morris Girls" (1946), File 9, Box 101, Ernest W. Burgess Papers, Special Collections, University of Chicago Library.

19. Interview 2907, File 4, Box 74, Ernest W. Burgess Papers, Special Collections, University of Chicago Library; Carol Bauman LeFevre, "The Satisfactions and Dissatisfactions of One Hundred Servicemen's Wives," (MA thesis, University of Chicago, 1948), 30–31.

20. United Press, "Some Wives Hurt Soldiers' Morale," *The New York Times*, January 8, 1945; "The American National Red Cross South and Southwest Pacific Selected Narrative Reports for Month Ending February 29, 1944," File: 900.118 FETO, Camp Service Reports, 1942–1944, Box 1548, Group 3, ARC Records, RG 200, National Archives in College Park, Md. [NACP].

21. Dudley Harmon, "Careless and Misleading Letters Cause of Most Domestic Upsets," *Stars and Stripes*, London ed. (June 1, 1944). See also Edward and Louise McDonagh, "War Anxieties of Soldiers and Their Wives," *Social Forces* 24 (December 1945): 197.

22. Comment Sheet #TC-1014 (15 March 1944), File: 726, Box T-1411, G2 Theater Censor, Southwest Pacific Area and U.S. Army Forces, Pacific, RG 496 (USAFFE), NACP.

23. Albert N. Mayers, "Dug-Out Psychiatry," *Psychiatry* 8 (November 1945): 386. See also Meyer H. Maskin and Leo L. Altman, "Military Psychodynamics: Psychological Factors in the Transition from Civilian to Soldier," *Psychiatry* 6 (August 1943): 265–66; Roy R. Grinker and John P. Spiegel, *Men Under Stress* (Philadelphia: Blakiston, 1945), 187–88; John Cuber, "Changing Courtship and Marriage Customs," *The Annals of the American Academy of Political and Social Science* 229 (September 1943): 37; Lee Kennett, *G.I.: The American Soldier in World War II* (New York: Charles Scribner's Sons, 1987), 76.

24. J. E. Lighter, ed., *Random House Historical Dictionary of American Slang* (New York: Random House, 1994), s.v. "Dear John"; Ahmed S. to *Yank*, August 18, 1944, 16; Ed Cunningham, "Jilted G.I.'s in India Organize First Brush-Off Club," *Yank*, January 13, 1943, 5; Judy Barrett Litoff and David C. Smith, eds.,

Since You Went Away: World War II Letters from American Women on the Home Front (Lawrence, Kan.: University Press of Kansas, 1991), 53–57. See also Costello, 273–74; Kennett, 75–76.

25. Ned Nordness, "Gals Back Home Insist They're Loyal to GI Heartthrobs Abroad," *Stars and Stripes*, London edition, December 17, 1943.

26. Litoff and Smith, 55–63.

27. On wartime sex and the double standard, see Campbell, 208–10.

28. "Remarks on Adjustment of Morris War Wives" (ca. 1945), File 8, Box 15, Ernest W. Burgess Papers, Special Collections, University of Chicago Library; Havighurst et al., 38–39; Robert Easton and Jane Easton, *Love and War: Pearl Harbor Through V-J Day* (Norman, Okla.: University of Oklahoma Press, 1991), 288, 293, 297–98; Susan M. Hartmann, "Prescriptions for Penelope: Literature on Women's Obligations to Returning World War II Veterans," *Women's Studies* 5: 231.

29. Hartmann, 223–39; David A. Gerber, "Heroes and Misfits: The Troubled Social Reintegration of Disabled Veterans in *The Best Years of Our Lives*," *American Quarterly* 46 (December 1994): 545–73; Robert B. Townsend, "'Home Fears Burning': Manhood, Family, and the Returning GI Problem," unpublished paper in author's possession; Robert Francis Saxe, "'Settling Down': Domesticating World War II Veterans' Challenge to Postwar Consensus," (PhD diss., University of Illinois at Urbana-Champaign, 2002), chap. 1; Rebecca Jo Plant, "The Veteran, His Wife, and Their Mothers: Prescriptions for Psychological Rehabilitation after World War II," in *Tales of the Great American Victory: World War II in Politics and Poetics*, ed. Diederik Oostdijk and Markha G. Valenta (Amsterdam: Vrije University Press, 2006), http://historyweb.ucsd.edu/pages/people/faculty%20pages/ RPlantVet eransFinal.pd f (accessed February 26, 2007). Examples of this literature on the veterans' readjustment to family life and civilian society include A. H. Edgerton, *Readjustment or Revolution?* (New York: McGraw-Hill, 1946); Herbert I. Kupper, *Back to Life: The Emotional Adjustment of Our Veterans* (New York: L. B. Fischer, 1945); Grace Sloan Overton, *Marriage in War and Peace: A Book for Parents and Counselor of Youth* (New York: Abingdon-Cokesbury Press, 1945); Howard Kitchning, *Sex Problems of the Returned Veteran* (New York: Emerson Books, 1946); John H. Mariano, *The Veteran and His Marriage* (New York: Council on Marriage Relations, 1945); George K. Pratt, *Soldier to Civilian: Problems of Readjustment* (New York: McGraw-Hill, 1944); Willard Waller, *The Veteran Comes Back* (New York: Dryden Press, 1944); Alexander G. Dumas and Grace Keen, *A Psychiatric Primer for the Veteran's Family and Friends* (Minneapolis: University of Minnesota Press, 1945); Dixon Wecter, *When Johnny Comes Marching Home* (1944; reprint, Westport, Conn.: Greenwood Press, 1970).

30. On momism and readjustment, see Plant, "The Veteran, His Wife, and Their Mothers."

31. Dumas and Keen, 12–13, 16–28; Overton, 59–60.

32. On soldiers' idealization of their wives and sweethearts, see Pfau, chap. 1.

33. Hartmann, 227–30, 232–35; Townsend, "Home Fears Burning"; Frederick Robin, "When Your Soldier Comes Home," *Ladies Home Journal* 62 (October 1945): 183, reprinted in Nancy Walker, ed., *Women's Magazines 1940–1960: Gender Roles and the Popular Press* (Boston and New York: Bedford/St. Martin's, 1998), 56–62; Kupper, 182–87, 191.

34. Overton, 44–45.

35. Jere Daniel, "The Whys of War Divorces," *New York Times Magazine*, February 3, 1946): 18, 48; Hornell Hart and Henrietta Bowne, "Divorce, Depression, and War," *Social Forces* 22 (December 1943): 191–14; Overton, 146–55; Dumas and Keen, 24–27; Pratt, 180–94; Mariano, vi–viii, 60–62. For more on popular concerns about war marriages, see Alison Lefkovitz, "The Feminine Side of the Selective Service: War Marriage and Citizenship During World War II," unpublished paper in author's possession.

36. Waller, 13–15, 132–39, 175, 183–91, 284–91; Willard Waller, "What You Can Do to Help the Returning Veteran," *Ladies Home Journal* 62 (February 1945): 26–27, 95; Townsend, "Home Fears Burning."

37. "Nothing Else to Do," *Newsweek* 26 (October 1, 1945): 58. For more on censorship and fraternization, see Pfau, chap. 3.

38. The October 22, 1945, issue of *Newsweek* featured a series of photographs entitled "Date with a Geisha," 64–65. For more on the topic of sexual relations between American soldiers and Japanese women, see John Dower, *Embracing Defeat: Japan in the Wake of World War II* (New York: W. W. Norton, 1999), 123–39.

39. David Anderson, "Belgians Reprove GI's Lax Conduct" and Drew Middleton, "Veterans Called Law-Abiding Men," *The New York Times*, September 11, October 14, 1945; "No Land of Saints," *Time* 46(September 24, 1945): 18; "The Idle GI and Liberated France Are Mighty Tired of Each Other," *Newsweek* 26 (November 19, 1945): 56, 58. For more on GI criminality and press reports from Europe, see John Willoughby, *Remaking the Conquering Heroes: The Postwar American Occupation of Germany* (New York: Palgrave, 2001), 16–19, 137–43.

40. Margaret Chase Smith to Henry L. Stimson, May 29, 1945, Statements and Speeches vol. 3, p 414, and news articles in Scrapbook vol. 32, pp. 107, 119, 121, 125, 129, all in Margaret Chase Smith Collection, Northwood University;

Associated Press, "Army to Let Families Join Troops Overseas" and "Back Soldier-Wife Plan: Many Endorse Proposal That Women Go to Europe," *The New York Times*, July 16 and 23, 1945. For more on the decision to send American wives and fiancées to join occupation soldiers, see Donna Alvah, *Unofficial Ambassadors: American Military Families Overseas and the Cold War* (New York: New York University Press, 2007), chap. 1.

41. Harry S. Truman to Hon. George B. Schwabe (September 19, 1945), File: Official 190-R, White House Central Files, Harry S. Truman Library.

42. Bring Back Daddy Club, "To Our Legislators" (ca. February 1946). In December 1945 and January and February 1946, President Harry S. Truman received daily letters, telegrams, and petitions from Bring Back Daddy Club members in Chicago, Duluth, Atlanta, Milwaukee, St. Paul-Minneapolis, Syracuse, Oklahoma City, Buffalo, Mobile, Toledo, Pittsburgh, Indianapolis, Peoria, and several smaller cities; General File, keyword "Bring," White House Central Files, Harry S. Truman Library; Associated Press, "Demand 'Daddies' Back," *The New York Times*, November 10, 1945). For more on this topic, see Pfau, conclusion.

43. For more on the demonstrations, see Pfau, conclusion.

44. Anne Hurley, "Conversation with Mr. Tope of the Methodist Church," April 10, 1945 and "Conversation with Godfrey Berg," April 20, 1945, both in File 8, Box 15, Ernest W. Burgess Papers, Special Collections, University of Chicago Library. See also Havighurst et al., 54–55.

45. The interviews analyzed by LeFevre were conducted by University of Chicago students during the final year of the war. LeFevre, 10–11, 124–25, 128–31; Interview 2350, File 3, Box 74, Ernest W. Burgess Papers, Special Collections, University of Chicago Library.

46. Interview 3306, File 5, Box 74 and Interview 43 in Mildred Handler, "Ten Cases in the Adjustments of Servicemen's Wives," File 9, Box 131, both in Ernest W. Burgess Papers, Special Collections, University of Chicago Library; LeFevre, 126, 131–34. See also Campbell, 205–07; McDonagh and McDonagh, 198–200.

47. Interview 3305, File 5, Box 74, Ernest W. Burgess Papers, Special Collections, University of Chicago Library.

48. Eliza K. Pavalko and Glen H. Elder, Jr. "World War II and Divorce: A Life-Course Perspective," *American Journal of Sociology* 95 (March 1990): 1222–24; Interview 3367 in Carolyn Barnes, "Problems of Adjustment of War Marriages" (August 1945), File 4, Box 128, Ernest W. Burgess Papers, Special Collections, University of Chicago Library.

49. Interview 4551, File 6, Box 74, Ernest W. Burgess Papers, Special Collections, University of Chicago Library. On typical patterns of adjustment to reunion, see Reuben Hill and Elise Boulding, *Families Under Stress: Adjustment to the Crises of War Separation and Reunion* (New York: Harper & Brothers, 1949), 85–97.

50. Interview 4445, File 6, Box 74, Ernest W. Burgess Papers, Department of Special Collections, University of Chicago Library.

51. Ibid.; Mariano, 54.

52. Interview 2350, File 3, Box 74, Ernest W. Burgess Papers, Special Collections, University of Chicago Library.

53. Freda Spitzer to Albert Spitzer (April 30, 1945), Albert and Freda Spitzer Correspondence, Special Collections and University Archives, Rutgers University Libraries; Interview 2906, File 4, Box 74, Ernest W. Burgess Papers, Special Collections, University of Chicago Library; Havighurst, 46–47.

54. On the father fantasies of soldiers' children, see George R. Bach, "Father-Fantasies and Father-Typing in Father-Separated Children," *Child Development* 17 (March–June 1946): 63–80; William M. Tuttle, *Daddy's Gone to War: The Second World War in the Lives of American Children* (New York: Oxford University Press, 1993), 220–21.

55. Lois Meek Stolz, *Father Relations of War-Born Children* (Stanford, Calif.: Stanford University Press, 1954), 291.

56. These and other names of persons interviewed by Walter Eaton in Morris, Illinois, are pseudonyms. Interviews with Tom C (April 17, 1946), Rick B (June 8, 1946), and "3 Morris Girls" (1946), File 9, Box 101, Ernest W. Burgess Papers, Special Collections, University of Chicago Library; Havighurst et al., 83–84.

57. On soldiers' anxieties about postwar domestic obligations, see J. J. V. Cammisa and James Clark Moloney, "Separation Anxiety," *Mental Hygiene* 31 (April 1947): 229–36.

58. Stolz, 4–12, 21–23, 30, 40–50, 291–92; Tuttle, chap. 12. A similar study by Virginia Van Meter Underwood found that veteran fathers generally "thought in terms of guidance through showing disapproval (including physical punishment) rather than through showing approval." "Student Fathers with Their Children," *Marriage and Family Living* 11 (August 1949): 101.

59. Stolz, 35–39, 65–74, 287, 290–91, 294–96; Tuttle, 222–23.

60. Havighurst et al., vi, 68–73, 77; Walter Eaton, Interviews with Ray M (May 13, 1946) and "3 Morris Girls" (1946), File 9, Box 101, Ernest W. Burgess Papers, Special Collections, University of Chicago Library.

61. Havighurst et al., 75–80, 111–18; Walter Eaton, Interviews with Mike T (May 29, 1946) and Ed M (June 5, 1946), File 9, Box 101, Ernest W. Burgess Papers, Special Collections, University of Chicago Library.

62. Walter Eaton, Interviews with John N (May 25, 1946), File 9, Box 101 and Glen H (ca. September 1946), File 1, Box 102, both in Ernest W. Burgess Papers, Special Collections, University of Chicago Library.

63. Walter Eaton, Interviews with Tony L (spring 1946) and of Roy B (June 12, 1946); both in File 1, Box 102, Ernest W. Burgess Papers, Special Collections, University of Chicago Library.

64. For historical statistics on American marriage, divorce, and birth rates, see Susan B. Carter et al., *Historical Statistics of the United States: Earliest Times to the Present* (New York: Cambridge University Press, 2006), vol. 1; Michael R. Haines, "Long-Term Marriage Patterns in the United States from Colonial Times to the Present," *The History of the Family* 1 (1996): 15–39; Michael R. Haines and Richard H. Steckel, eds., *A Population History of North America* (New York: Cambridge University Press, 2000), 149–58, 177–80, 308, 313–28, 467–73, 648–49, 655–62. On the origins of the marriage and baby booms, see Herbert S. Klein, *A Population History of the United States* (Cambridge, United Kingdom: Cambridge University Press, 2004), 156–58, 174–81; Tuttle, 18–27; James T. Patterson, *Grand Expectations: The United States, 1945–1974* (New York: Oxford University Press, 1996), 76–79; Landon Jones, *Great Expectations: America and the Baby Boom Generation* (New York: Coward, McCann, & Geoghegan, 1980), chaps. 1 and 2; Andrew Cherlin, *Marriage Divorce Remarriage* (Cambridge, Mass.: Harvard University Press, 1981), 6–12, 19–25, 31–44, 66–67.

65. Carter et al., vol. 1, 685; John Modell and Duane Steffey, "Waging War and Marriage," *Journal of Family History* 13(1) (1988): 196–203, 212–14. On the Servicemen's Readjustment Act of 1944, better known as the GI Bill of Rights, see Suzanne Mettler, *Soldiers to Citizens: The G.I. Bill and the Making of the Greatest Generation* (New York: Oxford University Press, 2005); Ira Katznelson, *When Affirmative Action Was White: An Untold History of Racial Inequality in Twentieth-Century America* (New York: W. W. Norton, 2005), chap. 5; David H. Onkst, "'First a Negro . . . Incidentally a Veteran': Black World War Two Veterans and the G.I. Bill of Rights in the Deep South, 1944–1948," *Journal of Social History* 31 (Spring 1998): 517–43; Lizabeth Cohen, *A Consumers' Republic: The Politics of Mass Consumption in Postwar America* (New York: Vintage Books, 2004), 137–46, 156–60, 166–73.

66. Havighurst et al., chaps. 10 and 11, and Appendix; Glen H. Elder, Jr., "War Mobilization and the Life Course: A Cohort of World War II Veterans," *Sociological Forum* 2 (Summer 1987): 215–31; Glen H. Elder, Jr., Cynthia Gimbel, and

Rachel Ivie, "Turning Points in Life: The Case of Military Service and War," *Military Psychology* 3 (1991): 215–31; William L. Anderson and Derek W. Little, "All's Fair; War and Other Causes of Divorce from a Beckerian Perspective," *American Journal of Economics and Sociology* 58 (October 1999): 901–22.

67. Levittown had an explicit whites-only policy, and Park Forest developers and residents quietly but effectively excluded African Americans until 1959.

68. On Park Forest, see the 69 interviews conducted under the auspices of the Park Forest Public Library, "The Oral History of Park Forest: Oh! Park Forest," many of which are available online at www.idaillinois.org (accessed 20 March 2007); William H. Whyte, Jr., *The Organization Man* (Garden City, N.Y.: Doubleday Anchor Books, 1956), part 7; Gregory C. Randall, *America's Original G.I. Town: Park Forest, Ill.* (Baltimore, Md.: The Johns Hopkins University Press, 2000); Herbert J. Gans, "Park Forest: Birth of a Jewish Community," *Commentary* 11 (1951): 330–39; Harry Henderson and Sam Shaw, "City to Order," *Colliers* (February 14, 1948), 16–17, 52–54. On Levittown, see John Thomas Liell, "Levittown: A Study in Community Planning and Development," (PhD diss., Yale University, 1952); Harold L. Wattel, "Levittown: A Suburban Community," in *The Suburban Community*, ed. William M. Dobriner (New York: G. P. Putnam's Sons, 1958), 287–313; William M. Dobriner, *Class in Suburbia* (1963; reprint, Westport, Conn.: Greenwood Press, 1981), chap. 4; Barbara M. Kelly, *Expanding the American Dream: Building and Rebuilding Levittown* (Albany, N.Y.: SUNY Press, 2004); Kenneth T. Jackson, *Crabgrass Frontier: The Suburbanization of the United States* (New York: Oxford University Press, 1985), chap. 13.

chapter five

GENERAL GEORGE S. PATTON
AND THE WAR-WINNING
SHERMAN TANK MYTH

Nicholas D. Molnar

Thirty years after World War II, General Isaac D. White, the highly respected former commander of the U.S. Army's 2nd Armored Division, was asked to write the introduction to *Sherman: A History of the American Medium Tank*, the seminal work on the most famous American tank of all time. Contrary to what would be expected from a reminiscing former general writing on what was one of the primary instruments of his military success, White pulled no punches and scathingly disparaged the tank. "To those of us who pitted our out-gunned Sherman against German armor," he wrote in 1978, "the book does not entirely indicate the seeming insensitivity on the part of those responsible for the design and procuring of our fighting vehicle." White added bitterly: "Some of us, even at the time, were aware of the bureaucratic and often ignorant wrangling and delays that occurred before our medium tanks were fitted with a tank gun that gave us a reasonable degree of equality against our enemy."[1]

General White's postwar complaints echoed those of many tankers who fought in the Sherman during the war. One tank crew sergeant, after several months in combat, was totally demoralized: "As we go now every man has resigned himself to dying sooner or later because we don't have a chance against German tanks." The disheartened tanker went on to say, "All of this stuff we read about German tanks knocked out by our tanks makes us sick, because we know what prices we have to pay in men and equipment to accomplish this. . . . Our tanks are no match for the Panther and Tiger tanks, and it is just suicide to tackle them."[2] The nickname that American tankers gave the Sherman was equally revealing of their contempt for it. While German panzers were nicknamed after ferocious jungle predators—the Panther and the Tiger—the Sherman's alias was the

Ronson, after a cigarette lighter, because of the tank's propensity to burst into flame as soon as it was hit.[3]

Paradoxically, the Sherman, despite all the derisions and dark-humored nicknames the combat tankers had for it, was celebrated during the war as a symbol of American military might. The government, the media, and the advertising industry had all continually eulogized the Sherman throughout the conflict. Acclaim for the tank filled the pages of countless newspapers and popular magazines across the United States.[4] Reporters and correspondents had no qualms about portraying the Sherman as "the best tank in the world" because many in the profession saw giving such high praise as performing a public service.[5] The *Popular Science* 1942 article on the tank, entitled "America's Tank Family," described the Sherman as "the Army's most versatile tank. . . . It's 360-degree turret, high-velocity cannon, and low silhouette make it a powerful weapon."[6] Another article from the same periodical in 1943, entitled "Why America's Tanks Are the World's Best," praised the Sherman as, "Heavily gunned, fast, and mechanically dependable, . . . more than a match for anything the Germans, Japs, or Italians can send against it."[7] The harshest disparagement of the Sherman came from a *Collier's* article that described the tank as "pathetically ugly, . . . like a fat woman in a hoop skirt."[8]

When the Sherman's powerful image came under fierce attack by combat tankers who were not afraid to make their feelings publicly known after the Battle of the Bulge in December 1944, General George S. Patton, Jr., the celebrated leader of American armored forces and commander of the victorious U.S. Third Army, threw all his weight into maintaining the tank's mythical stature. Although flawed, Patton's defense of the Sherman was effective in stopping public criticism of the tank. Inadvertently, his statements had a much longer-lasting effect. Patton's defense shaped how the Sherman would be remembered by scholars and laymen in the postwar world. Despite evidence from American tankers suggesting that the Sherman tank was an inferior deathtrap, Patton's defense contributed to the tank's being remembered primarily as a war-winning weapon. This essay examines Patton's contribution to the creation of that myth and its reproduction in popular culture.

General Patton was the perfect figure to defend the Sherman. The media portrayed him as a legendary figure throughout the war, first beginning when articles on his exploits appeared in *Life* magazine. Patton's landing in North Africa was described as a mythical knightly charge into the heart of the enemy: "Patton himself had had his landing boat destroyed just as he was about to step into it and, riding in a tank, had personally led his troops through snipers and artillery fire."[9] Patton often played on this medieval warrior image, telling *Life* that if he ever encountered General Erwin Rommel, commander of the German forces in North Africa, "We could make it like the old knightly combats. The two armies could watch. I'd be on one tank, Rommel in another. I'd shoot at him, he'd shoot at me. If I killed him, I'd be the champ. If he killed me—well, he won't."[10] *The New York Times* wrote of Patton: "He hit Tunisia like a whirlwind, amazing men who had never served under him, not to mention the Axis army he attacked. . . . He rages through his command like an indignant lion."[11] Patton was seen as a contemporary knight in shining armor, worthy of commanding the Sherman tank, America's modern-day warhorse, in combat.

Patton's popularity only picked up as the war went on, with major periodicals praising his adventurous exploits. In the process, he earned the reputation as the Army's most successful armored force commander. *Newsweek* described Patton as: "the Army's top tank expert. Fearless and blasphemous, he is loved by his men, who call him 'Old Blood and Guts.'"[12] *The New York Times* gave him its stamp of approval: "When the American tank corps was formed during the last war [World War I], young George Patton was the first officer assigned to it. . . . In other words, General Patton is not a man who suddenly has had to learn about tanks. Now that these great engines of destruction form an important element in a modern army, there is every reason to believe that the right man is in the right place."[13] Because of these flattering portrayals in the media, Patton, in the eyes of the American public, was seen as the most credible authority on tanks and tank warfare.

Patton was sorely needed to fulfill his knightly duties when the Sherman tank came under a series of devastating attacks throughout the media in 1945. By the last year of the war, combat tankers returning home from the battlefront began to openly deride the Sherman as an inferior weapon of war. Hanson Baldwin, Pulitzer Prize recipient and military correspondent for *The New York Times*, led the charge against the war-winning image of the Sherman. In his columns, Baldwin shared some of the harshest condemnations that the combat tankers had for the tank: "We're just outtanked and outgunned, that's all. We don't mind the lack of armor on our tanks as much as the lack of firepower. But it's mighty aggravating to let fly with everything you've got and just have the shells bounce off the front of the Jerry tanks."[14] Another tanker bluntly damned the Sherman and the bureaucratic branches that created it: "German tanks have more firepower and more protective armor than any American tank ever used in combat. . . . It is criminal for a nation to permit its supporting weapons to be inferior to those of the enemy."[15] Baldwin even included an attack on how the Sherman was reported to the American public: "You know, our morale would be a lot better if there weren't so many cock-and-bull stories in the papers about how our tanks are world beaters. You see, when the layman reads that we've knocked out twice as many Jerry tanks as they have of ours, he doesn't realize that it's not our tanks alone that did the job. It's tanks plus artillery, plus planes—plus guts."[16]

Baldwin's acidic criticisms created a ripple effect throughout the American media. Periodicals were no longer afraid to voice anxieties about the Sherman. Major media outlets followed Baldwin's lead, attacking with full force the tank's war-winning image. *Time* wrote of the Sherman: "Toe to toe, the Shermans never could [engage Tiger tanks]. They had to count on getting around on the Tigers' flanks, where the Germans are more vulnerable. In the kind of confined infighting the U.S. Army ran into four months ago [in the Battle of the Bulge], end runs were seldom possible. The smaller Shermans were badly battered."[17] *Life* sarcastically dismissed the Sherman as the worst tank in the world: "[T]he Sherman is simply not in the same company with the Russian and German heavy tanks, nor is it supposed to be. . . . It is a useful tank, the best in the world after the Russian and German."[18] *Newsweek* wrote that German tanks were "the Sherman's masters" and candidly asked its readers, "Must we defeat Germany with inferior weapons?"[19]

Patton immediately rushed to the Sherman's defense, using his stellar reputation to defend the tank's war-winning image. In March 1945, Patton wrote a letter on the virtues of the Sherman to one of his high-ranking Third Army officers, General Thomas T. Handy. Interestingly, much of this personal letter found its way onto the pages of *The New York Times* and the *Army and Navy Journal* only a week after it was written. The letter was quoted in dozens of influential newspapers and periodicals soon thereafter.

Patton accused those who attacked the Sherman as unpatriotic: "It has come to my knowledge that certain misguided or perhaps deliberately mendacious individuals, returning from the theater of war, have criticized the equipment of the American soldier."[20] Patton then began a long tirade in defense of the tank: "It has been stated at home that these tanks are not comparable with the German Panther and Tiger type tanks. This statement is wholly incorrect for several reasons."[21] As evidence of the Sherman's superiority, Patton compared German and American tank casualties: "Since . . . August 1944, when the Third Army became operational, our total tank casualties have amounted to 1136 tanks. During the same period we have accounted for 2287 German tanks, of which 808 were of the Tiger and Panther variety, and 851 on our side were M4 [Sherman]."[22]

Patton continued his defense of the Sherman by praising the tank's reliability: "Had the 4th Armored Division been equipped with Tiger and Panther tanks and been required to make the move from the Saarguemines [France] . . . to Mainz [Germany] it would have been necessary to rearmor it twice; and furthermore, it would have had serious if not insurmountable difficulty in crossing rivers."[23] Patton cited mobility as another asset of the tank: "We must remember that all our tanks have to be transported on steamers and the difference between 40 tons and 70 tons is very marked. The 70-ton tank could never have been brought ashore in landing boats as many of our medium tanks were. Nor could they have marched from the Cotentin Peninsula [France] to the Rhine [River] as practically all of our tanks have been required to do."[24] To cap off the Sherman defense, Patton praised the tank's technological superiority: "In mechanical endurance and ease of maintenance, our tanks are infinitely superior to any tank in the theater of war. The outstanding advantage which our tanks possess over the German tank is the mechanical traverse and stabilizer, through the use of which we get most of our kills."[25]

At first glance, Patton's defense of the Sherman seems foolproof. How could the Sherman be an inferior tank if the Third Army used the tank to achieve its victories? There is no denying that Patton's Third Army was extremely successful. The role of the Sherman in achieving that success is another matter. Patton, with a classic sleight of hand, linked the success of the Third Army with the image of Sherman tank. When one scrutinizes the evidence, it becomes obvious that the success of the Third Army's Shermans can be attributed to a variety of circumstances that had nothing to do with the tank itself.

One of the most obvious anomalies was that the Third Army was activated in France after the heavy hedgerow fighting in Normandy, during which the First Army's Shermans, already in France, sustained massive casualties. It became almost impossible for the armored divisions of the First Army to recover their combat effectiveness because of the poor replacement system. This did not happen to the Third Army's 4th Armored Division, widely considered to be the most successful armored division in military history. In addition to missing the hedgerow combat, the 4th uniquely trained its enlisted men not only in their own duties but also in the responsibilities of soldiers one or two ranks above them.[26] Green replacements new to the unit received the same rigorous training. When the division began to take casualties, its Shermans could maintain their combat effectiveness.

Patton cites the success of the 4th Armored Division of the Third Army as evidence of the Sherman's superiority. He fails to point out that a major factor in the 4th's success was how it was employed. As the spearhead of the Third Army, the 4th Armored Division was launched against weak points in the enemy's defenses. After it penetrated those points, the division wreaked havoc throughout the rear echelons of the German forces. The mind-set of the combat tankers in the 4th reflected this type of mission. Because they operated behind enemy lines, tank commanders were ordered to keep their tank hatches open in combat so that they could better understand the terrain and enemy around them. One of the most famous tank commanders of the 4th Armored Division, Colonel Creighton Abrams, sometimes threatened to weld open the hatches of inexperienced tank commanders when he caught them buttoning up (closing the tank commander's hatch) in action.[27]

Unlike the 4th Armored Division, other tank units in the Army were forced to use their Shermans as sledgehammers against static German defenses. The independent tank battalions, often attached to the infantry divisions, had a very different function: that of mopping up. Cleaning up the pockets of enemy resistance was truly the dirty work of the Army's advance, which satirical author Kurt Vonnegut accurately described as "the divinely listless loveplay that follows the orgasm of victory."[28] The Shermans of the 712th Independent Tank Battalion once had the job of mopping up in the wake of one of the 4th Armored Division's victorious drives. Tankers in the 712th were ordered to not peek their heads out of their tank turrets because snipers from prepared defenses often fired on and killed those who did. In one instance, after a tanker had been warned to button his hatch, a sniper's bullet immediately struck him, killing the man instantly.[29] In a mopping-up action, Shermans played by a totally different set of rules in order to survive.

Compared with other tank units, the 4th Armored Division had a number of other advantages that contributed to its success. The division's employment in the enemy's rear areas ensured that its Shermans had room to outmaneuver German tanks, a necessary requirement for them to have a chance in tank-to-tank combat. In open terrain, the Shermans could employ their principal advantage over German tanks: sheer numbers. A platoon of five Shermans would often engage one German tank, doing everything possible to try to outflank and encircle it. The Shermans would then fire on the German tank's vulnerable side and rear areas, places where even the shells of the 75mm cannon would not ricochet. Outflanking tactics somewhat compensated for the Sherman's inferior armament, but not totally. One sarcastic tanker put it best: "A tank gun should be able to destroy its opponent frontally. While it is desirable to hit a tank on the sides, no tank fights or advances sideway."[30]

Tank crews in other Army units knew all too well that outflanking tactics were not employable in every encounter with the enemy. In such situations, Shermans had to slug it out head-on against prepared defenses, handcuffed by their inadequate armament and poor armor protection. A tanker in the 2nd Armored Division described one such encounter: "We were moving down the road in a Sherman . . . firing all weapons, when we saw a German Mark IV tank twenty yards away back off to permit a German Mark V [Panther], thirty-five yards away, to fire on us."[31] What happened next was truly terrifying: "We fired . . . at the Mark V [Panther] and hit him on the front slope, left side, and it bounced off. He then hit us twice. The first shot hit just below the driver's hatch, went through two layers of sandbags, the armor plate, and exploded inside. The second shot hit slightly below the first with the same effect."[32] The Panther was not done. Targeting another Sherman in the tank column: "The tank behind us, a Sherman, . . . fired upon the Mark V [Panther], hit him on the front part of the turret and the . . . shell bounced off. The Mark V [Panther] then hit the . . . tank on the front plate, just to the right of the driver, went through a single layer of sandbags and pierced the armor plate."[33] Even though the Shermans had got off the first shots at point-blank range, they were still destroyed because they were no match for a German tank in a frontal encounter. Combat tankers forced into fighting confined battles such as these found no solace in being told by their superiors that they should have outflanked the enemy.

Without a doubt, the 4th Armored Division's unique advantage was its overwhelming air support from the XIX Tactical Air Force. These two units had a unique bond and a mutual respect for one another, unlike anything ever seen before in the Army. General Otto Weyland, commanding general of the XIX, had great admiration for the division: "4th Armored became one of our favorite outfits. They took immediate and full advantage of friendly air power and didn't whimper if they got a bloody nose in an engagement. Air-Ground teamwork was terrific."[34] One day, when a XIX pilot was shot down ahead of one of the 4th Armored Division's columns, tanks unhesitatingly fought ahead to rescue the downed pilot. Heroic acts such as these were paid back in kind with devastating aerial assaults from the Thunderbolt (P-47) fighter-bombers that made mincemeat out of German tanks unlucky enough to be caught in their crosshairs.[35] Combat tankers loved the support they received from the Thunderbolts, with one enthusiastically declaring: "Our best weapon, and the boy that has saved us so many times, is the P-47."[36]

The XIX performed more than just tank busting for the 4th Armored Division. Patton used the XIX to protect the flanks of the Third Army's advances. Patton often told his troops: "Forget this goddamn business of worrying about our flanks. . . . Some Goddamned fool once said that flanks must be secured and since then sons of bitches all over the world have been going crazy guarding their flanks. We don't want any of that in the Third Army. Flanks are something for the enemy to worry about, not us."[37] Although conservative commanders became distressed about protecting their flanks with ground forces, Patton used aerial reconnaissance from the XIX to ensure that advance units of the Third Army could operate well behind enemy lines without worrying about organized counterattacks. Patton wholeheartedly trusted the XIX with this vital role, once telling its commander during an operation: "You guard my right flank. . . . You hit it with the air and watch it; we are going straight east."[38]

All these advantages resulted in unparalleled success for the 4th Armored Division, and the Third Army greatly benefited from having such a unique unit as its spearhead throughout the war. When Patton defended the Sherman, he used the best example of armored warfare to make his point. Most other tank units would not be so lucky as to engage the Germans under these conditions. Patton's argument for the Sherman falters if examples outside the Third Army are used to illustrate the tank's battle prowess. During the hedgerow fighting in Normandy, the Allies lost a total of 2,405 tanks, twice as many tank casualties as the Third Army during the entire war.[39] Patton's example of the Sherman's success turns a blind eye to the combat tankers who were slaughtered because of the use of such an inferior tank.

After the successes of Patton's most poignant examples are detached from the Sherman itself, arguments for the tank's technical superiority dissolve into thin air. Patton argues that it would be difficult to ship heavy tanks from the United States to Europe. For the most part, he is right; heavy tanks like the Panther (45 tons), Tiger (55 tons), and King Tiger (70 tons) would have been more difficult to ship than the relatively lightweight Sherman (35 tons). However, there is one glaringly obvious flaw in his argument: American tankers did not ask, nor did they want, monster tanks like the Panther, Tiger, and King Tiger. The combat troops wanted their Shermans to have the capability to destroy their heavyweight German adversaries. Improved versions of the Sherman equipped with the diesel engine and armed with the 90mm supervelocity cannon (two improvements suggested by tankers but never seriously pursued by the Army's bureaucratic branches) would not have come close to the massive tonnage of the German behemoths, making it just as shippable as the undergunned Sherman that the combat tankers were forced to fight with. After arriving in Europe, improved versions of the Sherman would have made the trip across France and into Germany just as easily as its inferior counterpart.

Patton makes a strong case for the Sherman's reliability, citing the great distances that the Third Army traveled as evidence. Having a tank that could travel thousands of miles without breaking down is an undeniable asset. However, serious questions arise as to whether this is an inherent quality of the Sherman itself or the product of a combination of factors unrelated to the tank.

Constant repairs were performed on the Sherman by maintenance troops that followed in the wake of the Army's advance. The maintenance troops did whatever was necessary to keep the tank running, whether it was changing a spark plug in the Continental engine or replacing an entire Ford engine. Maintenance duties on the Sherman were no cakewalk because spare parts for critical components of the tank were often lacking. As a result, maintenance troops found it necessary to throw Army regulations out the window and rummage through the carcasses of destroyed Shermans for usable parts.[40] One pragmatic maintenance officer commented on the necessity of cannibalization: "One tank in combat was a lot better than two on the dead line waiting for spare parts."[41]

In contrast, the ability of German maintenance troops to cannibalize their tanks for spare parts was greatly inhibited.[42] In Europe, disabled German tanks with salvageable parts were left in the field by maintenance troops who were themselves retreating in the face of the Army's advance.[43] Also, Allied air forces enjoyed air superiority and wreaked havoc on the German supply lines, ensuring that the supply of spare parts would be further diminished.[44] The lack of spare parts meant that German tanks with only minor problems could not be repaired and were rendered useless.[45]

Proper maintenance is integral to any vehicle's reliability, especially a tank. If a tank is taken care of, it will have a much longer service life compared with a tank that is run into the ground. The Sherman's reliability stemmed from the outstanding maintenance performed on the tank, having nothing to do with its inherent design.

Another factor that contributed to the Sherman's reliability was the inordinately high rate in which it was destroyed in combat. Because of the massive losses taken by tank units, combat tankers were receiving replacement Shermans at an alarming rate. The maintenance troops of the 3rd Armored Division calculated that fresh vehicles were sent to the front lines every 25 hours.[46] Some combat tankers had five or six Shermans shot out from under them, each replaced with a brand new tank. Colonel Abrams of the 4th Armored Division, credited with the most tank kills in World War II, went through seven Shermans before the end of the conflict.[47] The Sherman was replaced so often that it never had the chance to wear out.

Patton's assertion that the Sherman's inherent reliability enabled it to make the trip across France and into Germany is simply false. The reliability of the Sherman can be attributed to a combination of outside factors, not to the tank itself.

In his defense of the tank, Patton argues that the Sherman possessed numerous technical advantages over the German behemoths. One of them was mechanical traverse technology, which enabled the Sherman to speedily swivel its main armament toward the enemy. German tankers had to slowly hand-crank their turrets to move them.

According to the combat tankers, mechanical traverse technology did not make a difference in battle. One tanker declared, "[A]lthough the Mark V [Panther] has a much slower traverse . . . it had never been their experience that it was not sufficiently fast enough to track any of our tanks, other than an M4 traveling at a very high speed."[48] Other tankers in the same unit "had no experiences where the speed of traverse actually affected the outcome of an encounter with a German tank."[49]

Tankers on the battlefront disagreed with Patton's assessment that mechanical traverse technology was an advantage in combat situations. The reason for this difference of opinion is clearly illustrated during an encounter with a German tank:

> A Panther . . . had its gun turret turned ninety degrees from the forward position. [The Sherman] fired the first round . . . and struck the Panther square in the middle of its forward glacis plate. . . . When it was over, the tank commander realized that the round had ricocheted and not penetrated the tank. He quickly reloaded, fired the second round, and struck the glacis plate again as the German slowly turned its turret in his direction. Before the Panther could get its gun zeroed in on the M4, the tank commander got off a third round, with equal results. The Panther was finally able to fire its high-velocity 75mm, which penetrated the M4 tank like a sieve.[50]

In combat, mechanical traverse technology was nullified by the Sherman's technical disadvantage of inferior armament. Because the Sherman's rounds bounced off the hulls of German tanks, getting off the first few shots did not decide the outcome of battle. One disgruntled tanker put it best: "We have power-driven turrets that the enemy doesn't. But because of our gun it's not much of an advantage."[51]

Another technical advantage Patton advocates in defense of the Sherman is gyrostabilizer technology. Gyrostabilizer technology, in theory, enabled the tank to shoot accurately while moving. Because the main gun in most tanks wobbled violently while the tank was in motion, tanks usually stopped to fire in order to increase the accuracy of the shot. Gyrostabilizer technology was invented as a solution to this problem.

Patton obviously failed to read the numerous reports from the battlefront that contradicted his assertion that gyrostabilizer technology was an advantage in combat. Most combat tankers felt it was useless. One independent tank battalion declared: "After the first fire, it was never possible to re-adjust the stabilizer satisfactorily, making it therefore most undependable. None of the men appeared to have had sufficient training on how to handle this unit. Manuals were issued, but the men still did not master the mechanics of the stabilizer to adjust it for desired fire. Because of this defect, the gyrostabilizer unit was seldom used and the 'stop and shoot' method was generally adopted."[52] Other combat tankers had even more disparaging remarks, including "not suitable for precision firing, . . . can fire better with it turned off, . . . always stop when firing to give better chances of hitting target, . . . [and] do not consider it worthwhile to retain."[53] The most telling example of the combat tankers' feelings for gyrostabilizer technology comes from the 1st Armored Division, in which it was reported that "the gyrostabilizer units were removed in all the tanks . . . and shipped back to Ordnance."[54]

Although riddled with numerous flaws, Patton's letter in defense of the Sherman reassured the American public that the tank was still a war-winning weapon. Those who ridiculed the tank simply could not muster an effective counter to Patton's argument. The chief of the Ordnance Department, who himself was facing severe criticism for the shortcomings of the Sherman, expressed his personal thanks to Patton: "There has been so much talk based upon opinion rather than facts with respect to tanks . . . . Your letter . . . to General Handy has certainly cleared the air with respect to tank characteristics and vicious criticism which is going around in this country about tanks in the way nothing else possibly could. It is a great service to the country to send the letter as you did!"[55] Criticisms of the Sherman sharply subsided after Patton's defense of the tank appeared in the media.

Patton's letter was not the only venue in which he espoused his problematic arguments in defense of the Sherman. He directly manipulated the media correspondents who tagged along with the Third Army during its operations in Europe. During a press conference the same week in which he wrote the letter, he forthrightly asked reporters for positive publicity for the Sherman.[56] Interestingly, Patton gave them almost a carbon copy of the arguments he made in his letter. His advocacy work seems to have paid off because a week later, he declared at another press conference with the same correspondents: "I first want to thank all of you for helping me out with those remarks I asked you to make about weapons. I read several editorials from home and while I was not quoted, it was damn well said."[57] It should come as no surprise that Patton wrote of the media shortly before his death, "I permitted the newspaper correspondents to question me. I did this weekly during active operations and always had them on my side."[58]

All of Patton's efforts to defend the Sherman proved wildly successful in stopping criticism of the tank in the media. Patton waged the propaganda war magnificently, using his personal influence to drastically change the direction of the debate. The fervor with which he defended the tank raises an important question: What were Patton's motivations in defending such an inferior tank?

Patton believed that media attacks on the Sherman had a destructive effect on the morale of the combat tankers. He felt so strongly about this point that he often emphasized it to the reporters who followed him. "We have the best tanks in the world and there is no doubt about it, and it has a bad effect on people back home when we say otherwise," he once told them. "Any talk that our army is inferior to the German Army is not only a malignant lie, but it has a bad effect on the soldier."[59] Troop morale would prove one of Patton's main concerns as a leader throughout his military career.

To Patton, troop morale went hand in hand with combat success. He strongly believed, "In my opinion we will only win this war through blood, sacrifice, and high courage. In order to get fighters we must develop the highest possible Esprit de Corps. . . . To die willingly, as many of us must, we must have tremendous pride not only in our nation and in ourselves but in the unit in which we serve. . . . [It] is of vital moment to our ultimate victory."[60] In Patton's mind, high morale translated into superb results in combat. If Patton admitted that the Sherman was an inferior weapon of war, the morale of the combat tankers would have been devastated.

Patton defended the war-winning image of the Sherman out of pure pragmatism. He had the foresight to realize that the Sherman would remain the workhorse of the Army until the end of the conflict. Covering up the tank's problems seemed a better solution than revealing it as a total failure. Acknowledging that the Sherman was a deathtrap would have shattered the morale of the combat tankers who would be fighting with the tank until the war was over.

Although he never revealed his personal views publicly, Patton had many of the same criticisms of the Sherman as the combat tankers. Patton was well aware of the tank's tendency to burst into flame when hit by enemy shells. On multiple occasions, he directly contacted the bureaucratic branches voicing his concerns. In North Africa, he pleaded with the chief of the Armored Force for diesel engines: "The day before yesterday we knocked out six M-6's [Tigers] at a cost of four of our M-4's [Shermans]. It certainly looks to me as if we must go to Diesel, as in every case, the tank hit burned."[61] In Europe, he wrote to the chief of the Ordnance Department complaining that the measures taken to prevent ammunition fires were a failure: "It seems to me that too many tanks burn. I should be willing to give up 20% of the ammunition space to reduce the number of burned tanks."[62]

Patton also realized that the Sherman's main armament was totally inadequate in combat against German tanks. After being questioned by media correspondents on the subject, he inadvertently blurted out: "About the tanks, if you had a village 1500 yards long and put a Tiger tank at one end and one of our tanks at the other, our tank would get licked but anybody that does that is a damn fool!"[63] Just as he did with the fire problem, Patton directly contacted the bureaucratic branches voicing his concerns. In North Africa, he suggested to the chief of the Armored Force: "If you get some 3-inch guns, place them in M4's and add another set of armor plate to the front silhouette, we will have a very powerful tank and tank-destroyer."[64]

Patton once remarked to an ordnance officer in Europe, "Ordnance takes too God Damn long seeking perfection at the expense of the fighting men, and you can tell that to anyone at Ordnance."[65] His commentary could accurately describe his feelings toward the other bureaucratic branches, because none of his suggestions to improve the Sherman were ever implemented.

Patton's media defense of the tank was therefore far from an accurate reflection of his personal views. Although most of his public arguments were flawed, ironically, they would become the foundation of the war-winning Sherman myth.

The first histories of the Sherman after the war stand out because of their portrayal of the tank in such a positive light, using Patton's media defense as evidence of the tank's superiority. *Tanks Are Mighty Fine Things* (1946) had no qualms about wholeheartedly defending the Sherman: "[The Germans] were not whipped by quantities alone. Our tanks were better and we used them more intelligently."[66] The ace in the hole of this argument was, of course, Patton: "No one was more outraged by the critics of the Sherman tank than was the late George Patton and no one was better qualified to reply. [Patton's letter to General Handy cited in full]."[67] *Weapons of World War II* (1947) used the very same method to make its point: "[The Sherman] tank was gradually developed into one of the most reliable track-laying tanks in the world's history. . . . Praise of the M4 medium tank was universal in all theaters and it would take many pages to record adequately the performance of this important weapon of war. Concerning its use in Europe, General Patton wrote . . . [another of Patton's letters praising the Sherman cited in full]."[68]

Just like Patton, the authors of these histories had their own pragmatic motives for defending the Sherman. Chrysler, a major manufacturer of Shermans during the war, commissioned the writing of *Tanks Are Mighty Fine Things*. Obviously, it would not be in the best interests of the automobile manufacturer to deride one of its major contributions to the war effort. *Weapons of World War II* blindly praises the Sherman for similar reasons. Written by General Gladeon M. Barnes of the Ordnance Department, the Sherman was presented as the "best tank in the world" because it was seen as a reflection of his engineering prowess, as well as that of the entire Ordnance Department. Declarations in Barnes's diaries that the Sherman was "a waste of Government money" were replaced with heaps of praise for the tank as a result.[69] In both cases, the war-winning Sherman myth was perpetuated to further personal agendas.

Unfortunately, the Army's official histories of World War II, popularly known as the *Green Books*, were a powerful reinforcement of the war-winning Sherman myth. Although admitting the defects of the tank more readily than their historical predecessors, Patton's flawed arguments are clearly echoed in the *Green Books* defense of the Sherman. *The Ordnance Department: Procurement and Supply* espouses a classic Patton argument: "The Sherman was more mobile and mechanically reliable than German medium tanks, and had greater flexibility and rapidity of fire."[70] *The Ordnance Department: Planning Munitions for War* points out, just as Patton would, "The Sherman had qualities not even remotely duplicated in any German vehicle. . . . In point of reliability, it similarly outshone both the notoriously undependable Tiger and the Panther."[71]

With the major histories of the tank advocating or failing to refute the war-winning Sherman myth, it was only a matter of time before this premise became accepted as historical fact.[72] Eventually, these flawed arguments permeated what would prove to be most people's contact with the Sherman after the war: popular culture. Once again, the Sherman became a media darling, a symbol of strength and victory.

The Sherman is often utilized as an image of power within the visual media. In the 1983 movie, *Tank*, set in contemporary America, a crazed Army sergeant played by popular actor James Garner blows an automobile sky high with the Sherman's 75mm cannon and then smashes the tank through a building, immediately reducing it to a pile of rubble. One of the main reoccurring storylines in *G.I. Combat*, the long running DC comic book series, is that of a Sherman tank haunted by the ghosts of U.S. Civil War Generals J. E .B. Stuart and William T. Sherman. On almost every occasion, the crew of the Haunted Tank encounters some type of German heavy armored vehicle and destroys it with relative ease.[73] More recently, the entire plot of a 2006 episode of the television cartoon series *Family Guy* revolves around the main character, Peter Griffin, rampaging around his hometown of Quahog, Rhode Island, in an antique tank that looks strikingly similar to the Sherman.[74]

The war-winning Sherman myth is also found in less obvious places. A radio-controlled toy tank, for sale in 2007, comes in a carton with a caption on it that declares: "The hero of the Detroit Arsenal is back! The M4 Sherman tank is ready to take your living room the same way it rolled to victory in Normandy, 1944."[75] Post services from countries around the world, including Luxembourg, Belgium, India, the Marshall Islands, and, of course, the United States, have issued commemorative postal stamps bearing the image of victorious Shermans.[76]

The most intriguing place where the war-winning Sherman myth rears its head is within music lyrics. Successful musicians, such as They Might Be Giants, used the Sherman in this manner in 1986: "Hats off to the new age hairstyle made of bones / Hats off to the use of hats as megaphones / Speak softly, drive a Sherman tank / Laugh hard, it's a long way to the bank."[77] Similarly, The Infected uses the Sherman in almost the same way in 1990: "You lie and yo breath stank / So bad it makes it hard to think / You lie and yo breath stank / Rolls me over like a Sherman tank."[78] The best example of the war-winning Sherman myth being reproduced in music comes from the band Mr. Shiraz, who titled its 2005 debut album, "I'm Invincible! I'm Built Like a Sherman Tank. Somebody . . . Try . . . And . . . Stop Me!"[79]

Popular culture distributes the war-winning Sherman myth to wider audiences than the work of scholars will ever reach. In September 2006, in a nationally televised college football game, Rutgers fans cheered on running back Brian Leonard as he smashed through multiple South Florida defenders to gain a first down. As fans of the home team voiced their disapproval with boos and hisses, all the awe-struck ESPN sportscaster could remark was that Leonard "looked like a Sherman tank on that run!"[80] With that remark, made more than a half century after the end of World War II, television viewers were introduced to the Sherman for the first time as a symbol of strength and power. Seemingly forgotten was the other much-less flattering image that the tank was, as one bitter soldier succinctly put it, a "ridiculous thin-walled undergunned piece of shit."[81]

Although the origin of the war-winning Sherman myth lies with General Patton and with scholars who utilized his flawed arguments, the myth has taken on a life of its own in popular culture, assuming the guise of the true history of the tank, discarding reality to the historical wayside. Patton's defense of the Sherman in 1945 was a success beyond even his wildest imagination, influencing not only how his contemporaries viewed the tank, but how future generations came to remember it.

NOTES

I thank Professor John Whiteclay Chambers II for his guidance in the preparation of this essay.

1. General Isaac D. White, foreword to R. P. Hunnicutt, *Sherman: A History of the American Medium Tank* (Belmont, Calif.: Taurus Enterprises, 1978), 5.

2. Sergeant Moore (no first name given), quoted in Brigadier General Isaac D. White to Dwight D. Eisenhower, *Report on United States vs. German Armor*, March 1945, reprinted in published form as Major General Isaac D. White, *Report on United States vs. German Armor* (Bennington, Va: Merriam Press, 2001), 47.

3. Ronson Company History, www.fundinguniverse.com/company-histories/Ronson-PLC-Company-History.html (accessed February 6, 2007).

4. Examples of newspapers and popular periodicals that carried articles during World War II praising the Sherman and American tanks in general are *American Magazine*, *Atlanta Constitution*, *BusinessWeek*, *Chicago Tribune*, *Collier's*, *Fortune*, *Life*, *Los Angeles Times*, *Newsweek*, *New Yorker*, *The New York Times*, *Popular Mechanics*, *Popular Science*, *Saturday Evening Post*, *Science Newsletter*, *Time*, *Washington Daily News*, *Washington Post*, and *Washington Times Herald*.

5. Richard W. Steele, "The Great Debate: Roosevelt, the Media, and the Coming of the War, 1940–1941," *The Journal of American History* (June 1984): 69–92.

6. "America's Tank Family," *Popular Science*, June 1942.

7. Arthur Grahame, "Why America's Tanks Are the World's Best," *Popular Science*, March 1943.

8. Frederick C. Painton, "Here Comes Gabriel—Fighting with a Yank Tank Crew," *Collier's*, July 17, 1943.

9. John Field, "Patton of the Armored Force," *Life*, November 30, 1942.

10. Ibid.

11. Frank Kluckhohn, "Always Go Forward!" *The New York Times*, April 4, 1943.

12. "American Commanders Under General Eisenhower," *Newsweek*, November 16, 1942.

13. Kluckhohn.

14. Hanson Baldwin, "American Tanks—I," *The New York Times*, March 18, 1945.

15. Baldwin, "American Tanks—II," *The New York Times*, March 19, 1945.

16. Baldwin, "American Tanks—I."

17. "New Tank," *Time*, March 19, 1945.

18. "The Battle of the Tanks," *Life*, March 26, 1945.

19. "Must We Defeat Germany with Inferior Weapons?" *Newsweek*, February 26, 1945.

20. General George S. Patton to General Thomas T. Handy, letter, March 19, 1945, quoted in "Tank Inferiority Denied by Patton," *The New York Times*, March 28, 1945; General George S. Patton to General Thomas T. Handy, letter, quoted in *The Army and Navy Journal*, March 31, 1945.

21. Ibid.

22. Ibid.

23. Ibid.

24. Ibid.

25. Ibid.

26. Steven J. Zaloga, *US Army Tank Crewman 1941–45* (Oxford, United Kingdom: Osprey Publishing, 2004), 14.

27. Zaloga, 28.

28. Kurt Vonnegut, *Slaughterhouse-Five* (New York: Dell Publishing, 1969), 66.

29. O. J. Brock, quoted in Aaron Elson, *Tanks for the Memories: The 712th Tank Battalion in World War II* (Hackensack, N.J.: Chi Chi Press, 2001), 147.

30. Baldwin, "American Tanks—II."

31. Gunner William J. Marcheski, quoted in White, 71.

32. Ibid.

33. Ibid.

34. Hanson Baldwin, *Tiger Jack* (Ft. Carlson, Ky.: Old Army Press, 1979), 65.

35. Ibid.

36. Sergeant Harold E. Fulton, quoted in White, 74.

37. Ladislas Farago, *Patton: Ordeal and Triumph* (New York: Ivan Obolensky, 1963), 447, quoted in Carlo D'Este, *Patton: A Genius For War* (New York: Harper-Collins, 1995), 623.

38. Polk Oral History, United States Army Military History Institute, quoted in D'Este, 638.

39. Steven J. Zaloga, *M4 (76mm) Sherman Medium Tank 1943–65* (Oxford, United Kingdom: Osprey Publishing, 2003), 16.

40. Belton Y. Cooper, *Death Traps: The Survival of an American Armored Division in World War II* (Novato, Calif.: Presidio Press, 1998), 33.

41. Ibid.

42. General Burkhart H. Mueller-Hillebrand, *German Tank Maintenance in World War II* (Washington, D.C.: Center of Military History, United States Army, 1988), 2.

43. Ibid., 37–39.

44. Ibid., 4, 34.

45. Ibid., 44.

46. Cooper, xiii.

47. "Sum and Substance," *Armor*, September–October 1950, quoted in Lida Mayo, *The Ordnance Department: On Beachhead and Battlefront* (Washington, D.C.: Office of the Chief of Military History, 1968), 334; Zaloga, 50.

48. Lieutenant Colonel John A. Bell, quoted in White, 24.

49. Ibid.

50. Cooper, 176.

51. Baldwin, "American Tanks—II."

52. Excerpts of Technical Intelligence Reports on the Sherman Tank, December 9, 1944, Entry 646A, Box Number A746, Records of the Office of the Chief of Ordnance—Record Group 156, National Archives II, College Park, Md. (hereafter, RG 156, National Archives).

53. Colonel George M. Dean to Representatives of the Armored Center, Resume of Report by Colonel George M. Dean on His Two-Month Tour of Battle Fronts in the European Theater of Operations, April 7, 1945, Entry 7.8, Box Number 6, Records of Headquarters Army Ground Forces, Armored Center—Record Group 337, National Archives II, College Park, Md. (hereafter, RG 337, National Archives).

54. Excerpts of Technical Intelligence Reports on the Sherman Tank, December 16, 1944, Entry 646A, Box Number A746, RG 156, National Archives.

55. General Levin H. Campbell to General George S. Patton, letter, March 30, 1945, Box 34, George S. Patton Papers, Manuscript Division, Library of Congress, Washington D.C. (hereafter, Patton Papers, Library of Congress).

56. General George S. Patton, Jr. to Media Correspondents, transcript of meeting, March 17, 1945, Box 53, Patton Papers, Library of Congress.

57. General George S. Patton, Jr. to Media Correspondents, transcript of meeting, March 30, 1945, Box 53, Patton Papers, Library of Congress.

58. Diary of General George S. Patton, Jr., September 22, 1945, Box 3, Patton Papers, Library of Congress.

59. General George S. Patton, Jr. to Media Correspondents, transcript of meeting, March 17, 1945, Box 53, Patton Papers, Library of Congress.

60. General George S. Patton, Jr. to General Lesley J. McNair, letter, May 2, 1942, Box 12, Patton Papers, Library of Congress, quoted in D'Este, 414.

61. General George S. Patton, Jr. to General Jacob Devers, letter, July 16, 1943, Box 34, Patton Papers, Library of Congress.

62. General George S. Patton, Jr. to General Levin H. Campbell, letter, March 21, 1945, Box 34, Patton Papers, Library of Congress.

63. General George S. Patton, Jr. to Media Correspondents, transcript of meeting, March 17, 1945, Box 53, Patton Papers, Library of Congress.

64. General George S. Patton, Jr. to General Jacob Devers, letter, March 26, 1943, Box 34, Patton Papers, Library of Congress.

65. General George S. Patton, Jr., quoted in Lida Mayo, *The Ordnance Department: On Beachhead and Battlefront* (Washington, D.C.: Office of the Chief of Military History, 1968), 337.

66. Wesley W. Stout, *Tanks Are Mighty Fine Things* (Detroit, Mich.: Chrysler Corporation, 1946), 82.

67. Ibid.

68. General Gladeon M. Barnes, *Weapons of World War II* (New York: D. Van Nostrand Company, 1947), 209.

69. General Gladeon M. Barnes, Medium Tank T20 Series Diary, February 28, 1944, Entry 646A, Box Number A744, RG 156, National Archives.

70. Harry C. Thomson and Lida Mayo, *The Ordnance Department: Procurement and Supply* (Washington, D.C.: Office of the Chief of Military History, 1960), 263.

71. Constance M. Green, *The Ordnance Department: Planning Munitions for War* (Washington, D.C.: Office of the Chief of Military History, 1955), 283.

72. Some historical studies that have recognized the Sherman's inadequacies are Charles M. Bailey, *Faint Praise: American Tanks and Tank Destroyers During World War II* (Hamden, Conn.: Archon Books, 1983), 118, 146; John Whiteclay Chambers, editor-in-chief, *The Oxford Companion to American Military History* (New York: Oxford University Press, 1999), 58, 712; R. P. Hunnicutt, *Sherman: A History of the American Medium Tank* (Belmont, Calif.: Taurus Enterprises, 1978), 512–13; William L. O'Neill, *A Democracy at War: America's Fight at Home and Abroad in World War II* (Cambridge, Mass.: Harvard University Press, 1995),

350–53, 370–73; and Steven J. Zaloga, *Sherman Medium Tank 1942–45* (Oxford, United Kingdom: Osprey Publishing, 1978), 14–18. Unfortunately, these studies have not sought answers to the major dilemmas that plague the tank's unfinished history, and when they have, these inquiries have never been fully answered.

73. *G.I. Combat* (New York: DC Comics, 1957–1987). *G.I. Combat* is the second-longest–running war comic book series of all time, with 288 issues published during its long 30-year tenure. Almost all of the final 94 issues (1978–1987) have the haunted Sherman tank on the cover. Prior to these issues, the type of vehicle used by the crew was the M5 Stuart light tank—this one haunted by only General J. E. B. Stuart.

74. This particular reference to the Sherman occurred in an episode titled "Hell Comes to Quahog" of the television cartoon series *Family Guy*, first aired on September 24, 2006, FOX Network.

75. Radio-Controlled Sherman Tank distributed by Hobbytron.com, www .hobbytron.com/130ScaleRemoteControlM4A3ShermanTank.html (accessed February 6, 2007).

76. Sherman commemorative postage stamps in India referenced in Deepkamal Kaur, "Commemorative Stamps on Defense Forces Released," *Chandigarh India Tribune*, March 28, 2006. Sherman commemorative postage stamps in Luxembourg, Belgium, the Marshall Islands, and the United States referenced in Patton Commemorative Stamps and First Day Covers, the Patton Society, www .pattonhq.com/stamps.html (accessed February 6, 2007).

77. This particular reference to the Sherman occurred in the song titled "Rhythm Section Want Ad" by They Might Be Giants in 1986.

78. This particular reference to the Sherman occurred in the song titled "You Lie and Your Breath Stank" by The Infected in 1990.

79. Mr. Shiraz references the Sherman in its 2005 debut album, "I'm Invincible! I'm Built Like a Sherman Tank. Somebody. . . Try. . . And. . . Stop Me!"

80. Rutgers vs. South Florida, nationally televised college football game, first aired on September 29, 2006, ESPN Network. The author heard this particular reference to the Sherman while watching the game on television.

81. Brendan Phibbs, *The Other Side of Time: A Combat Surgeon in World War II* (Boston, Mass.: Little, Brown, 1987), 75.

chapter six

NAVAL GUNFIRE SUPPORT IN OPERATION NEPTUNE: A REEXAMINATION

Barbara Brooks Tomblin

Historians have devoted considerable attention to the planning and execution of Operation Neptune/Overlord, the Allied cross-channel invasion in June 1944. Although numerous books and articles have been written about the experience of Allied navies off Normandy on D-Day, naval gunfire support for the American beaches, code-named Utah and Omaha, deserves further examination, especially with regard to the experience of Allied warships in the Mediterranean theater during the years prior to June 6, 1944. For, as Captain Roger Hill, Royal Navy, has written in his memoirs of the war, "The invasion was the culmination of all the developments, inventions, organization and lessons learned, from the early commando raids, North Africa, Sicily, Salerno, the tragedy of Dieppe, and the failure at Anzio."[1]

This study of naval gunfire support during Operation Neptune will focus on the two American sectors at Normandy endeavoring to reexamine the planning and execution of naval fire support in light of amphibious experience gained in the Mediterranean prior to June 1944. In planning and preparing for Operation Neptune, Allied planners had the advantage of important precedents as well as lessons learned and recommendations made by amphibious commanders in the Mediterranean. In action reports written after each of the four major invasions in the Mediterranean, senior commanders included assessments of naval gunfire support during each operation and made specific recommendations about mine clearance; naval bombardments; close-in gunfire support; anti-aircraft discipline; aerial reconnaissance and spotting of naval gunfire; and defense against air, submarine, and E-boat attacks.

Although U.S. Navy Chief of Naval Operations Ernest J. King had originally assumed that the Royal Navy would provide most, if not all, of the
naval gunfire support for the Normandy operation, by the end of 1943, it
had become apparent that the U.S. Navy would have to provide some heavy
warships and destroyers for Operation Neptune. Consequently, the final
operation plan (op plan) for Neptune assigned a bombardment group composed of battleships, cruisers, monitors, and destroyers to each of the two
American task forces of the Western Naval Task Force. Rear Admiral Don
P. Moon's Task Force 125, tasked to bring General Lawton Collins's VII
Corps to Utah Beach, had a bombardment group under the command of
Rear Admiral Morton Deyo, which included three heavy cruisers (U.S.S.
Quincy, U.S.S. *Tuscaloosa*, and H.M.S. *Hawkins*), the battlewagon *Nevada*,
the monitor H.M.S. *Erebus*, the light cruisers H.M.S. *Enterprise* and H.M.S.
Black Prince, the Dutch gunboat *Soemba*, and 10 destroyers. *Tuscaloosa*,
Enterprise, *Erebus*, and *Soemba* were veterans of the Mediterranean War, as
were most of the destroyers. In addition, Don Moon had a support craft
group commanded by Lieutenant Commander L. E. Hart (USNR), flying
his flag in *LCH 209*.

Rear Admiral John Lesslie Hall, Jr.'s Task Force 124, the O Assault
Force (for Omaha), enjoyed similar support from a bombardment group
under command of Rear Admiral Carleton F. Bryant. Admiral Bryant had
two American battleships (U.S.S. *Arkansas* and U.S.S. *Texas*), four light
cruisers (H.M.S. *Montcalm*, H.M.S. *Glasgow*, H.M.S. *Bellona*, and the
French cruiser *Georges Leygues*), and 11 destroyers. He, too, had a close
support craft group under the command of Captain Lorenzo S. Sabin, who
had commanded the Gaffi Attack Group during the invasion of Sicily in
July 1943. For the assault on Omaha Beach, Captain Sabin had a mixture
of 7 LCRs, 5 LCGs, 9 LCT(R)s , 28 LCPs, 9 LCT(A)s, and 10 LCT(HE)s—all
small support craft that were more-recent versions of the landing craft
(rocket) and other flak and gun ships developed in 1943–1944 as the result
of amphibious experience in the Mediterranean and Pacific theaters.[2]

UTAH

The Americans code-named the sector closest to the Cherbourg peninsula
U, or Utah, sector. The op plan called for Admiral Don P. Moon's Task
Force 125 to land Major General J. Lawton Collins's VII Corps on Utah

Beach at 0630 on D-Day. Although the Germans had assembled less-formidable defenses on Utah than on Omaha, the Utah assault groups faced opposition from 28 German coastal fortifications with 110 guns. The Germans counted on the low-lying, flooded areas behind Utah Beach to act as a natural defense, but inland from the beachhead had also located another 18 batteries and could employ a number of mobile 88mm guns.

To silence these German gun batteries and emplacements in Utah sector, the op plan specified that 40 minutes prior to H-hour, Admiral Deyo's battleships and cruisers would open fire on selected targets from a range of 11,000 yards, the destroyers from 5,000 yards. At H-hour minus 40 minutes, *Nevada* and *Quincy*, with their secondary batteries, and *Enterprise*, *Shubrick*, and *Hobson*, with their main batteries, would commence rapid fire on the beaches. Just 10 minutes prior to H-hour, heavy hitters *Nevada* and *Quincy* would plaster the beaches again with their main batteries, and LCT(R)s would fire 5,000 5" rockets over the heads of the leading assault waves onto the shore. VII Corps commander Major General Collins anticipated that this naval gunfire would knock holes in the concrete seawall along Utah Beach.[3]

Just after midnight on June 6, 1944, Admiral Morton Deyo's Utah bombardment group approached the French coast and anchored between the transports and the shore, prepared to protect from enemy fire the troop transports, as well as the mine craft tasked to sweep the approach channels, fire support areas, and boat lanes to within a mile of the shore. Onboard the 13,600-ton *Baltimore*-class cruiser U.S.S. *Quincy*, her 1,142 officers and crew had been at general quarters since midnight expecting to be fired on by enemy coastal guns. John R. Blackburn, the *Quincy* air control officer, recalled, "We fully expected this to happen when we came within range and had a plan (of questionable value) to provide counter-battery fire in the event that the coastal batteries cut loose with their 6-to 11-inch guns."

At midnight, the *Quincy* set condition Zebra, and at 0130, the cruiser anchored. Keeping an hour-by-hour journal of events on D-Day, *Quincy* crewman Fred King wrote at 0145: "Before going to G.Q. we saw bomb explosions reflected in the sky on the distant horizon. A channel had been swept of mines and was marked by red and green lights dimly lit." Fred King could see heavy anti-aircraft fire from the beach directed at Allied bombers. "We can feel it when the block-busters drop, even when 9 miles out," he wrote. German gun batteries covering Utah Beach, however, remained silent.[4]

The quiet was short-lived. At 0505, a shore battery opened fire on the destroyers *Fitch* and *Corry*. When a large caliber battery at Saint Vaast began shooting at the yard-class minesweepers (YMSs) sweeping for mines 3,500 yards offshore, *Black Prince* quickly took the battery under fire. German batteries targeted U.S.S. *Nevada* as well. Lieutenant Olsen recalled seeing the shells land all around the *Nevada*. "We learned later that we were straddled twenty-seven times by shells and never hit. We had been shelled for what seemed like ages before we saw our main battery of 14-inch guns being trained and ready to open fire." On *Quincy*, John Blackburn heard the "splat" of a shell landing 1,000 yards from the cruiser. "The next salvo of enemy projectile landed even closer—only about five hundred yards short this time."[5]

Below deck at his battle station with a repair party, Fred King could not see the action but was kept informed by the *Quincy* chaplain, who gave the crew a play-by-play over the ship's loudspeaker. In his diary, King explained, "[W]e are being fired on by shore batteries but luckily they are falling short or wide of us. We are standing by to open fire on beach as soon as our spotting plane gets range." Impatient, King wrote at 0534: "Other ships are now firing on the beach, but we have not commenced firing as yet. Why? Let's get them before they get us!"

Soon Fred and his repair party, on their feet and wearing helmets, gas masks, and lifebelts, could hear muffled gunfire. "0537: Commenced firing! Look out, Hitler!" he noted in his diary. According to John Blackburn, who could see the beach from his station in air spot, salvoes from *Tuscaloosa* and *Nevada* silenced the enemy batteries firing at them. "They closed up shop when the big stuff started going off around them."

When shells from enemy batteries started near missing the cruisers, Admiral Deyo decided to move up the scheduled pre-landing bombardment. King recalled: "At 6 am we opened fire at 11 miles on our predetermined targets which were covering Utah Beach, and silenced them with our first salvoes."[6]

Fred King kept track of the bombardment in his diary: "0600: We made a direct hit on shore battery." It was probably a machine gun emplacement on Green Beach, *Quincy*'s intended target according to John Blackburn. "[T]the destroyer *Benson* had already been shelling the beach for some time," Blackburn recalled. "Bomb clouds of dust and rubble obscured the beach, but I could see where the salvos from the tin can were landing. Since she was much closer, and better able to see what she was shooting at, we would just plunk ours in nearby—one four gun salvo every fifteen seconds." Blackburn watched and called the spots into the plotting room.

Ten minutes later, King added, "0610—A smokescreen now being laid by low flying planes screening us from the beach. 0611—Another direct hit for the Mighty Q on #2 target. Our 8″ battery is doing most of the firing which is contrary to plan. We fellows here on damage control are stretched out on the deck. In case of a hit, we won't be too good a target."[7]

Unfortunately, AA (anti-aircraft) fire shot down one of the aircraft assigned to lay a protective smokescreen over the ships off Utah. As Emil ("Moe") Vestuti, a fire controlman on U.S.S. *Corry*, recalled, "there were two planes flying by laying smoke to protect the boats that were coming up and as this one plane was getting ready to cover us, it got shot down and that left us exposed. Then it seemed like everything on the beach just concentrated on *Corry*." In an interview just after D-Day, the destroyer's 33-year-old commanding officer, Lieutenant Commander George Dewey Hoffman, told Edward R. Murrow, "We were about 4,000 yards off-shore when the coastal batteries opened up." The German batteries took aim on the destroyer ahead of *Corry*, the U.S.S. *Fitch*. "Then the guns ranged on us. It was about a half hour before H-hour. The first shell splashes were short." When asked about the effectiveness of German gunners, Quartermaster Third Class Robert E. Powell, a crewman on the U.S.S. *Fitch* sky lookout, replied, "Oh they are doing lousy. They're shooting, but they aren't coming anywhere near us."[8]

Targeted by enemy guns, *Corry* fired back, expending 400 rounds as she zigzagged to avoid enemy shells. The *Corry* skipper also told Murrow that the ship was moving "very slow—we were taking as much evasive action as we could, but we had to stay within our prescribed area, for it was our job to support the troops about to go ashore."

According to Lieutenant Commander Hoffman, after silencing the German battery firing on her, *Corry* began to shell her assigned targets, "which were German pillboxes and machine gun positions. We eliminated a couple of them, and then another battery opened fire on us." Hoping to better observe the enemy gun battery in the improving visibility, Lieutenant Commander Hoffman ordered *Corry* gunners to fire faster. "[We] increased our rate of fire," he told Murrow. "Empty powder tanks came pouring out of turrets. We exchanged fire for about ten minutes, pouring it on the shore batteries, and then we were hit——three larger projectiles entered almost simultaneously." Lieutenant Commander Hoffman rang for full speed and "gave a hard right rudder to clear the area to assess damage, stop leaks, and put out fires before returning. The rudder jammed. The ship speeded up and began going in circles."

Down in the forward engine room, Machinist Mate Grant Gullickson could hear the guns firing. "All of a sudden, the ship literally jumped out of the water! As the floor grate came lose, the lights went out and steam filled the space." According to some sources, *Corry* had detonated a mine. Then, Lieutenant Commander Hoffman told Murrow, he sent officers and men aft to steer by hand, and they managed to get the destroyer headed back seaward, "but we lost all steam, and the engines stopped." He "ordered the ship's boats put over" to tow *Corry* clear, and *Quincy* fired white phosphorus shells to cover *Corry*, but by then, John Blackburn recalled, *Corry* was "mortally wounded . . . and sinking rapidly." At 0641, Hoffman gave the order to abandon ship. "The main deck was awash, due to the rapidity of the flooding of all the engineering spaces except one. We got away in good order, placing wounded in boats." *Fitch* and *Hobson* took the enemy guns under fire while they rescued survivors. *Butler* also picked up some *Corry* crewmen. *Corry* suffered 24 men killed, 59 wounded.[9]

To protect them from long-range German gun batteries, the Utah assault group's transports had anchored 11½ miles from shore, making the landing crafts' run to the beaches a very long, exposed one. As a novel feature of this assault, planners had included eight LCTs, each carrying four British-designed duplex drive (DD) amphibious tanks to provide immediate artillery support for the troops ashore. PC-1176 and PC-1261 were to guide the LCTs to within 5,000 yards of the beach, after which they were to launch their DDs. By the time they began moving toward Omaha Beach on D-Day, however, German shore batteries, recovering from the shock of surprise, had begun returning the slugging salvoes of the naval fire support ships, "raising great gouts of water as they plumbed for the correct range." James Arnold watched in horror as an enemy shell made a direct hit on the PC-1261, the Green Beach control vessel. "The little 173-foot hull seemed to disintegrate in a belch of flame and noise. I doubt if a man aboard survived." Unfortunately, PC-1261's loss, probably to a mine, not a direct hit, deprived the tanks of their primary control vessel. Also hit by a mine, LCT-597 sank quickly, taking all four of her duplex drive tanks with her. On board LCC-60 nearby, Lieutenant Vander Beek recalled, "We were but a few yards away and felt the explosion's potent shock waves course through our craft." Mines claimed other victims. James Arnold, headed toward the line of departure in LCI(L)-530, wrote later, "Just before we jockeyed into position, a terrific explosion to starboard a few hundred yards rocked our LCI. It was the LCT-707. She had hit a mine, turning her completely over. Then all hell seemed to cut loose." Although commanders at the time blamed artillery fire for some of these losses, they almost certainly struck mines. Lieutenant (junior grade) John B. Rich in PC-1176 took over and led in the remainder of the LCTs with DDs, wisely launching them much closer to shore than the recommended three miles. Launched in smoother waters near shore, all 27 landed shortly after the first wave touched down on time at 0630.[10]

Just prior to the LCTs' arrival, 341 Ninth Air Force B-26 Marauders, flying parallel to the coast at very low altitude, had clobbered enemy positions. In sharp comparison to the Sicily landings, when trigger-happy gunners on ships offshore shot at aircraft carrying airborne troops, AA recognition and discipline during the Normandy operation was excellent, aided by better communication and the white and black invasion stripes painted on all the C-47s carrying paratroops and other aircraft taking part in the invasion. In addition to this successful air bombardment, four LCGs (landing craft, gun) had closed the beach flanks to provide close-in support, and LCT(R)s (landing craft, tank, with rocket launchers mounted) had fired off a stream of rockets. This intense bombardment should have done the trick, but a strong tidal stream had swept the landing craft south of the line of departure. The first wave of troops came ashore unopposed but confused about their location. Studying his maps, Brigadier General Theodore Roosevelt Jr. concluded they were about 2,000 yards south of their designated point on Utah Beach. By some stroke of luck or providence, the soldiers had come ashore in an area weakly defended by the Germans. Had they waded onto the proper beach sector, they would have been met by fire from two German beach batteries.

Fortunately, Utah Beach had few beach obstacles, and UDTs (underwater demolition teams) exploded any found on the beaches. By 0800, they had cleared 700 yards of beach, but soon after the second wave landed, enemy guns stepped up their fire on the beaches, causing some casualties. When James Arnold's landing craft hit the beach, he recalled, "German 88's were pounding the beachhead. Two U.S. tanks were drawn up at the high-water line, pumping them back into the Jerries." The destroyer *Shubrick* located one battery firing on the beaches, and at 0820, shelled it into silence. Then, about noon, German batteries on the eastern side of the Carentan estuary began firing on the beaches, prompting *Herndon, Hawkins,* and *Soemba* to return fire. H.M.S. *Hawkins* zeroed in on a battery of four 155mm guns and four 75s, and *Soemba* made contact with Rangers on Pointe du Hoc who needed fire support. Not to be left out, *Herndon* neutralized batteries near Grandchamp, which had been harassing the boat lanes.

According to Arnold, the NOIC for Utah Beach, about noon "an officer wearing the single star of a brigadier general jumped into my 'headquarters' to duck the blast of an 88." Announcing that he was Teddy Roosevelt, the general told Arnold, "If you have any authority here, I wish you would stop bringing my troops down on Red Beach. They're being slaughtered. The navy ought to know better than to send them into that sector where the darn Krauts have them bracketed." Although not supposed to function as NOIC until the assault phase was over, Arnold agreed to shift the landing waves to Green Beach. "It was remarkably successful too, until German spotters finally notified their batteries to shift their fire over to Green Beach. That was some three hours later."[11]

General Roosevelt's troops moved inland to make contact with the paratroopers who had dropped earlier, and succeeding assault waves came ashore quickly despite a rapidly rising tide. By evening of D-Day, the U.S 4th Division had secured the beach and advanced some six miles inland, suffering only 197 men killed or wounded. Throughout D-Day and into the evening, gunfire support ships, aided by aerial spot planes, provided fire support to the troops on Utah Beaches. U.S.S. *Quincy* fired 585 8″ rounds on D-Day, assisting paratroopers of the 101st Airborne, bombarding batteries north of the beaches, and firing on enemy troops along the Carentan road. In his diary, 21-year-old Fred King kept a running account of *Quincy* shoots. "1300—We are the only ship firing now, our gunfire had been the most accurate of all, demolishing all our targets with one or two salvos." Noting that *Quincy* had a large new battle flag flying from the mainmast, King wrote: "Shells litter the deck, as proof of the heavier firing we did this morning. One of the German shells missed our stern by only 20 feet, besides several other near misses."[12]

Benefiting from prior experience in the Mediterranean where SOC and OSU catapult planes were vulnerable to German fighters and friendly AA fire, the Allies had organized five squadrons of Mustangs and RAF Spit-fires to provide air spot for gunfire support ships in Utah sector. (The Curtiss SOC Seagull scout-observation plane was a catapult-launched sea-plane flying from battleships and cruisers to spot gunfire or conduct recon-naissance. The Vought OS2U Kingfisher catapult-launched observation floatplane was the main shipboard observation aircraft used by the U.S. Navy in World War II.) The op plan called for the planes to work in pairs, one pair over the beaches while another returned to refuel and a third pair was en route to relieve the first. These fighter aircraft could remain over the beaches for only 45 minutes, making them a poor substitute for car-rier-based aircraft with pilots trained in aerial spotting. Nonetheless, these fighters did offer some air cover, and being land-based avoided earlier problems such as those experienced by carrier-borne planes from escort carriers during the Salerno invasion. These aircraft had proved vulnerable to accidents in light wind conditions.

Ensign Charles P. Rozier's duty station on U.S.S. *Tuscaloosa* as assistant main battery plotting room officer and his battle station in Fire Control Plot gave him a vital role in *Tuscaloosa* D-Day naval gunfire support opera-tions. The cruiser's air spotter confirmed that *Tuscaloosa* shells were falling on a German supply column. When the spotter reported a large column of trucks coming down the road, Ensign Rozier said, "[I] picked off a point three nautical miles(beyond) the current target, measured the difference in bearing with [my] parallel arm plotter, and gave the plotting room office the spot, 'up six thousand, left three and one-half degrees.'" Plot cranked the spot into the Main Battery Mark Eight range keeper and fired a spot-ting round. Charles Rozier said. "To our surprise and my delight, the spot from our Spitfire pilot was 'twelve o'clock, 50, fire for effect.'" According to the Spitfire pilot spotting the cruiser's fall of shot, "rounds were falling into the road and damaged trucks were stopping the advance." *Tuscaloosa's* shoot on German infantry an hour later achieved similar results. "Mission successful, resistance was heavy; you knocked hell out of them." Rozier recalled, "Words like that kept our spirits at a high level."[13]

By 1800 hours on D-Day, Admiral Moon's task force had put 21,328 troops, 1,742 vehicles, and 1,695 tons of supplies on Utah Beach. Admiral Morton Deyo's Allied bombardment group, composed of American, Brit-ish, and Dutch ships, had made a significant contribution to the success of these landings on Utah Beach. Thanks to the air forces' bombing of the beach, naval gunfire, and coastal defenses manned by one German static regiment, manned largely by reservists and foreigners, the U.S. 4th Division suffered only 197 casualties on D-Day. Mines proved far more deadly than German shell fire to Allied ships and landing craft off Utah Beach. Losses from both mines and shell fire included the U.S.S. *Corry*, PC-1261, three LCTs, and two LCIs sunk.[14]

OMAHA

In simultaneous landings, on D-Day morning, Rear Admiral John Lesslie Hall, Jr.'s Task Force 124 put General C. R. Huebner's 16th RCT (regimental combat team) of the U.S. 1st Infantry Division, the 115th and 116th RCT of the U.S. 29th Infantry Division, as well as the 2nd and 5th Ranger Battalions, ashore on the second American sector at Normandy, O, or Omaha. Rear Admiral Carleton F. Bryant commanded the bombardment group for the O Assault Group. For Operation Neptune, Admiral Bryant had the firepower of not one, but two battleships (*Texas* and *Arkansas*), four light cruisers (H.M.S. *Bellona*, H.M.S. *Glasgow*, H.M.S. *Montcalm*, and H.M.S. *Georges Leygues*), U.S.S. *Emmons*, and DesRon 8's eight destroyers. For the initial assault period, his bombardment group also included three British destroyers (H.M.S. *Tanatside*, H.M.S. *Talybont*, and H.M.S. *Melbreak*). Captain Harry Sanders' escort screen would serve as reserve gunfire support ships.[14]

Captain Lorenzo Sabin's Close Gunfire Support Group, an assortment of shallow draft, armed landing craft including nine LCT(R)s, provided close-in fire support. Three minutes before touchdown on the beaches, these LCT(R)s were to fire a rocket barrage over the heads of the first wave as they approached shore. Theoretically, this rocket barrage would destroy many of the beach obstacles in Omaha sector and stun enemy defenders, lessening opposition to the first assault waves.

Task Force 124's approach to Omaha Beach went much as planned. "On the night before the invasion, minesweepers preceded our heavy bombardment group across the English Channel," Rear Admiral Bryant recalled. Early on D-Day morning, the bombardment group approached the French coast. "We anchored in our proper position about 1 a.m. to await dawn, the hour when the bombardment was to start," the admiral recalled. "It was an eerie night. The full moon was shielded from us by a cloud layer. Those conditions produced a kind of half-twilight."

As Admiral Alan G. Kirk's flagship *Augusta* neared her bombardment position off the coast, the lack of German opposition to the invasion forces took Kirk by surprise: "There was no German gunfire against the ships, against the transports . . . we had devoted quite a lot of attention to areas where we thought the Germans had heavy guns in the naval sense, 6-inch or bigger, and there weren't any. . . . Nor were there any German air attacks. We'd expected that."

Officers and crews on the bombardment ships found the waiting nerve-wracking. On the destroyer *McCook*, Lieutenant Jerry Clancy told reporter Martin Sommers, "What I can't understand is why they don't fire on us." Sommers later wrote that "we all wished they would start firing, so we could start firing back. That would be better than waiting."[15]

At 0530, however, alert German gunners spotted the invasion craft in the early morning gloom and opened fire on the most obvious target, the battlewagon *Arkansas*. Within minutes, other enemy batteries took aim at the destroyers *Emmons* and *Doyle*, which could not return fire until their air spot planes arrived overhead. "German 155mm rifles, far on the left flank, were pumping shells around the pre-invasion task force, raising towers of foam ominously close," a *Yank* reporter wrote. The French cruiser *Montcalm* opened fire first, but when the spot planes made contact, *Arkansas* and the tin cans (destroyers) *Doyle, Harding, Baldwin,* and *Emmons* began shelling the German gun emplacements. Fortunately, by 0551, they had silenced them.

The pre-landing naval bombardment, scheduled to commence at 0550, called for the heavy hitters *Texas, Arkansas, Glasgow, Montcalm,* and *Georges Leygues,* with their longer-range ordnance, to fire on enemy artillery batteries behind Omaha Beach. On D-Day morning, *Arkansas,* an old World War I battleship with a main battery of 12 12″ guns, took station 4,000 yards off Omaha Beach and at 0552 opened fire, shattering a German radar station, a machine gun position, and a fortified house, while the British cruiser *Glasgow* put 219 rounds into the bluff above Les Moulins. To soften up the two beach exits to Saint Laurent and Coleville, Admiral Bryant had the French cruiser *Georges Leygues* and the British destroyer *Tanatside.* They liberally plastered the bluff near the location of today's military cemetery with 6″ and 4″ shells. *Montcalm* blasted away at Port-en-Bessin for 10 minutes and then shifted fire to enemy emplacements behind the western end of Omaha Beach.

Admiral Bryant assigned his other battleship, U.S.S. *Texas*, with her 14″ guns, the mission of shelling an emplacement of large-caliber guns reported to be on Pointe du Hoc. *Texas* arrived off the coast about 0440 on June 6 and took station 12,000 yards offshore near Pointe du Hoc. She opened fire at 0550 with her main battery, cratering the area near the battery reputed to be "the most dangerous battery in France." The German guns did not reply because as the Rangers who climbed the cliffs at Pointe du Hoc discovered, the guns were not even there! Meanwhile, with her secondary battery, *Texas* zeroed in on targets at the western end of Omaha Beach, "a ravine laced with strong points to defend an exit road." From LCT(A)-2227, Ensign Victor Hicken saw the *Texas* open fire. "We went in right in front of the bow of the battleship *Texas* when it fired a full salvo. It was just like a giant door slamming, and it really shook me up. You could actually see the shells flying through the air toward the shoreline." *McCook* joined the battleship, firing on a pillbox and anti-tank guns on one side of a road exit from the beach to Vierville sur Mer. Several small support craft, LCG-424, PC-568, and LCT-464, also fired on German emplacements, but neither their effort nor that of the battleship *Texas*, which fired 190 rounds, knocked out these stubborn German defenses.[16]

Satterlee and *Talybont* also took position off Pointe du Hoc and from a range of 5,000 yards began firing to soften up enemy defenses in preparation for the Ranger assault. Destroyers *Thompson*, *McCook*, and *Carmick*, spread out in Fire Support Area 3 at the western end of Omaha Beach, opened fire on targets from Pointe de la Percee to Dog Beaches and the bluffs behind Easy Green Beach. To their east, *Tanatside*, *Emmons*, *Baldwin*, and *Harding* shelled pre-selected targets on Easy Red and Fox Green while *Doyle* shelled a cliff above Fox Red Beach exit and *Melbreak* roughed up a crossroads in Saint Honorine. *Doyle* continued to fire blindly until H-hour, and *Melbreak* even kept shelling the village of Saint Honorine past H-hour. In the destroyer *Baldwin*'s Combat Information Center, Lieutenant Davis C. Howes could hear the sound of gunfire. "We continued firing, and still no opposition. Where was the mighty German air force, the shore batteries whose positions we had plotted on the chart in front of us? Surely there must be some opposition!"[17]

Describing the bombardment, Admiral Bryant wrote, "Our time came shortly before six o'clock in the morning. The naval vessels opened up on shore defenses; it was a noisy time and *awesome*. After our allotted time, our fire ceased, and we awaited calls from our fire-control officers sent ashore in the landing parties, but none came. Later we learned that nearly all had been killed." Admiral Bryant and others on the *Texas* bridge stood by helplessly. "From our distance offshore we could see men, tanks, guns and landing craft on the beach, but we were unable to tell friend from foe." Bryant said they could see a group of men at the foot of the cliffs but could not tell whether they were "Germans or ours. Nothing was moving. We knew instinctively that something was wrong."[18]

Although not at first apparent to those offshore on the transports, fire support ships, or even on Admiral Hall's flagship *Ancon*, something had gone terribly awry at Omaha Beach. The reasons seemed puzzling to many observers offshore. The scheduled rocket barrage seemed to have gone off as planned. Watching from the British light cruiser *Bellona*, Peter Walker remembered, "Seeing the rocket ships close inshore firing salvo after salvo of rockets in quick succession was an awesome sight."

The nine rocket craft assigned to Omaha Beach had, indeed, sent off their 5" rockets as planned to pulverize the beach and, temporarily at least, to stun any German defenders. Larry Carr, who commanded the 14 former Royal Navy LCT(R)s for Operation Neptune, recently told the author, "I was on the bridge of the command rocket ship and gave the order to fire which was carried out when each vessel was 3500 yards from the beach front. We fired rockets to land 300 yards ahead of the first wave of troops." LCT(R)-423 let go her barrage of 1,000 rockets at Hamel-au-Pretre midway between the two beach exits to Vierville and Saint Laurent and off the eastern beaches of Omaha. LCT(R)-447 put another thousand rockets into the bluff above Easy Red and Fox Green sectors. Between 0623 and 0632, three LCTs with 1,000 rockets each also fired barrages on Fox Green beach and enemy strong points in this sector.

Although it was impressive to witnesses, several D-Day historians have concluded that this rocket barrage failed to knock out any German obstacles or defenders. According to historian Joseph Balkoski, "for all their noisy fireworks, the rockets accomplished little." Stephen Ambrose and Adrian Lewis also cited witnesses affirming Balkoski's argument that "most rockets fell into the sea short of the beach, harming no one and failing to break up any obstacles or wire." Larry Carr, however, insists that most of his rockets were fired accurately. "Each ship had radar to help calculate the exact time of firing. We were to fire the first rockets at the water's edge to a depth of 300 yards on completion. I estimate that less than 5% of the rockets were defective and landed far short of the projected range but our mission was considered successful which was the reason we were later used in southern France." The official action report confirms Carr's observations. It states, "Rocket fire was excellent in general. Rockets from two of the craft appeared to be short. Many rockets exploded shortly after launching. Conversation with a few Army personnel who landed early indicated they considered the rocket fire their best cover."[19]

While naval bombardment attempted to soften up Omaha's beaches, USAAF's B-24 Liberators assigned to drop bombs on 13 selected German targets, including strongpoints on Omaha Beach, made their runs. Despite extremely poor weather conditions, the bombers made their bomb runs without incident. Yet, to everyone's amazement, not one bomb hit Omaha Beach. Orders sent out the night before D-Day by VIII Air Force Headquarters had instructed the Liberator pilots and bombardiers to delay their drop by several seconds to avoid hitting the first waves of landing craft. The concern of air commanders about the difficulty of precision bombing through the heavy overcast seemed reasonable at the time, but their caution resulted in most of the 329 Liberators' bombs falling a mile or more inland, failing to neutralize coastal fortifications but "destroying only crops and cattle."[20]

As the bombardments died down, the first waves of landing craft neared shore. Allied planners had placed great hope for close-in fire support on the ability of LCTs to approach the shore and launch their duplex drive tanks, which would then churn to the beaches and provide first-wave assault troops with far heavier firepower than rifles and machine guns. Tragically, the DD tank plan failed to work as envisioned. Lieutenant Dean L. Rockwell commanded Group 35, the first group of LCTs assigned to the 116th Infantry's Dog Green, White, and Red Beaches. "Before leaving Portland the question had been raised by this command as to the course to pursue in the event of a sea too rough for launching," he wrote. In the end, the Army left the decision to the senior army officer for each battalion, Captain Elder of the 743rd and Captain Thornton of the 741st. Observing the choppy, two-foot seas on D-Day morning, Lieutenant Rockwell decided against launching his DDs. In his report, he wrote, "At 0505 this command contacted Captain Elder via tank radio, and we were in perfect accord that the LCTs carrying tanks of the 743rd Battalion would not launch, but put the tanks directly on the designated beaches." Joining up with some LCTs with standard battle tanks, Lieutenant Rockwell's LCT-535 guided the LCTs toward the beach, and LCT-535 touched down at

0629. "Despite fairly heavy machine gun and larger caliber gunfire, all tanks, save one, were landed successfully on the correct beaches," Rockwell noted in his report. However, Lieutenant (junior grade) Phil Bucklew in the lead LCT, determining that they were aiming for the wrong beach, ordered them to go ashore to the right. All 28 DDs and 14 standard tanks then hit Dog White and Green with their guns blazing.

Dubious all along about the feasibility of the DD tanks, in his op plan, General Leonard T. Gerow had wisely included 16 LCT(A)s carrying regular Sherman tanks. Captain Lorenzo Sabin commanded the 16-LCT group. Tossed about and scattered by the rough seas, however, only 10 of his 16 LCTs managed to arrive off Omaha Beach without incident. "During the approach to the beach," Captain Sabin wrote, "LCT(A)-2229 was sunk, presumably due to flooding, at a position about two miles off Dog Red beach. Two officers, four men, and three Army personnel were lost." As they neared the transports the LCTs split into two groups. PC-658 guided eight of the LCTs to the 116th Infantry's sector on the western section of Omaha Beach, and LCC-20 led the rest toward the 16th RCT's beach in the eastern sector. As Ensign Victor Hicken recalled, his LCT(A)-2227 landed "smack on" Dog Green, but they could not get the anchor winch to retract. "A mortar shell blew off the ramp. And at that moment the heavy fire eased. I think Company A, 16th Regiment was landing and took the fire from us. In a sense we were saved by their sacrifice."[21]

After a three-hour ordeal, tossing in the choppy seas, the first assault wave of 50 landing craft with Company C, 2nd Ranger Battalion, and Company A of the 116th Infantry, 29th Division neared Dog Green and Dog White sectors of Omaha Beach off Vierville. The Royal Navy's 551 Assault Flotilla lifted them to the beach in armed LCAs. Lieutenant Jimmy Green, who joined the 551 Landing Craft Flotilla at Plymouth in early 1944, arrived off Omaha Beach on D-Day morning in the LSI *Empire Javelin*. "I was the leader of the first wave and it was my task to land A Company of 116th Infantry regiment at Vierville sur Mer at 05:30 on 5 June. We were referred to in the flotillas as the 'The Suicide Wave,' something we felt with pride represented the danger we faced rather than the prospect of casualties." Green wrote that they had trained day and night, even in the fog, and that "many of the men had taken part in earlier landings in the Mediterranean." The 551 Flotilla had six LCA and two LCAs from H.M.S. *Prince Charles* carrying two platoons of C Company 2nd U.S. Rangers.

"The officer commanding A Company, 116th Infantry Regiment was Captain Taylor Fellows who I believe served in the National Guard at Bedford, Virginia. He was very serious, thoughtful officer who seemed a lot older than our sailors who were in their late teens and early twenties." Captain Fellows sought Green out on *Empire Javelin* and "spoke to me of his concern that this would be the first time that he and his Company would see action and asked me to give them every support." Jimmy Green assured Captain Fellows that "if we saw any Germans we could certainly open fire with our Lewis guns."

Jimmy Green's LCAs rail-loaded (landing craft were lowered and kept at the level of the ship's rail, loaded, and then lowered and launched into the ocean) Captain Fellows' men on *Empire Javelin* as planned and set off for Omaha Beach. Lieutenant Green's LCA "went flat out and crunched to a halt some 20 or 30 yards from the shore line. The beach was so flat that we couldn't go any further so the troops had to go in single file up to their waists in water and wade to the shore through tide runnels." Captain Fellows and his men left the LCA opposite Vierville sur Mer. "They all made the beach safely," Jimmy Green said, "and formed a firing line at a slight rise. At this time there was lull in the German firing. They had been plopping mortar shells around us and firing an anti-tank gun but suddenly they ceased firing. A German veteran told me recently that they had been ordered to preserve ammunition." Suddenly, Captain Fellows's men began taking heavy German small arms and machine gun fire, which cut Captain Fellows down immediately and killed or injured at least 100 of his company.

Only eight of the Company B 743rd Tank Battalion's 16 M4s beached at 0630 on Dog Green at the mouth of Vierville draw. Tanks of Companies A and C, however, managed to land on Beach Dog White and Dog Red. T/5 Robert Jarvis, who landed on Omaha Beach from an LCT in a tank of Company B, 743rd Tank Battalion, recalled, "I finally had a free slack moment in firing to look around. I figured by our firing that the beach should be pretty well secured. . . . As I was watching, the surf rolled a body of a sailor alongside our tank. I recognized the sailor as being one of the crew of our LCT. . . . It was then that I realized everything was not going according to schedule."[22]

Landing craft nearing Dog Green grounded some 30 yards short of the beach, forcing the weary, seasick soldiers to jump into the sea under a hail of fire. Many sank under their heavy load of equipment or were shot as they came off the LCVPs. German machine guns and mortars also tore into the troops landing near a beach exit between Dog Red and Easy Green sectors opposite Les Moulins, but here smoke from a grass fire obscured some of the G.I.s from enemy fire. Unfortunately, Lieutenant Commander Joseph H. Gibbons's Naval Combat Demolition Units, scheduled to land at H-hour plus three minutes to clear obstacles from sixteen 50-yard gaps in the beaches, also took heavy enemy fire. "The gunfire was intense, but we were successful in clearing initially six gaps 50 yards each and three semi–partially cleared gaps." Enemy fire from an 88mm gun scored a direct hit on the rubber boat carrying 300 pounds of additional explosives for one of Gibbons's crew: "[T]he concussion therefrom set off the explosives on the obstacles which in turn killed all members of the crew with the exception of one man who had gone up the beach to place markers to guide in subsequent craft."

A few tanks actually made it onto the beach, providing cover for some fortunate infantrymen who advanced behind them. However, by 0700 commanders realized that German fire had decimated most of the first wave to land on Omaha Beach. Almost all the men of Company A had been killed or injured. Company E had ended up far east of their assigned sector, Company F was scattered with many killed or injured, and Company G had also come ashore in small clusters. According to the official army history, only two of the three companies of the 2nd Battalion, 116th Infantry had landed within their regimental zone, and one company had lost a fourth of its men within the first 45 minutes. Company E had landed so far to the east of its assigned Easy Green and part of Easy Red sectors that the men got mixed up with troops from the 16th RCT.[23]

East of the 116th RCT's beaches, initial assault waves from *Henrico* and *Empire Anvil* landed on the 16th Infantry's beaches, Easy Red and Fox Green. At 0500, Captain Thornton, the senior army officer of the 741st Tank Battalion, decided to launch into the sea the DD tanks being carried by Lieutenant (junior grade) J. Barry's LCTs. Launched into the sea some 5,000 yards from shore, most DD tanks foundered in the moderately heavy seas when their canvas "bloomers" collapsed. Only five of the 32 tanks tasked with providing firepower on Omaha's eastern beaches actually got ashore. Landing craft approaching Omaha Beach in successive assault waves also encountered heavy fire. Some foundered or were hit. "Many of our LCVPs didn't make it back, particularly those whose crews had been recently assigned to our ship and lacked the landing experience most of us had had at Sicily and Salerno, Italy," wrote Robert E. Adams, a 25-year-old boat coxswain serving on board the U.S.C.G. *Samuel Chase*. Adams felt he was not only a practiced coxswain, but lucky. "My boat grazed one of the German's telephone pole beach obstacles. On top, so close I could almost touch it, was a teller mine. It could have blown us all to bits. So our first landing was successful—but just barely."

Intense enemy machine gun and mortar fire greeted landing craft bearing the second assault wave touching down on Omaha Beach at 0700. Many units arriving on the beach found themselves scattered and leaderless when enemy fire wiped out their commanders and sergeants. The rising tide and enemy fire had rendered many of the radios useless, further complicating the task of reorganizing units. For at least a full hour after touching down, enemy fire pinned down vehicles and troops of the second wave on the western Omaha Beaches, making any progress inland all but impossible. After the eighth wave came LCIs, LCMs, and DUWKS (pronounced "ducks"). LCI-489 arrived off Omaha Beach with five other LCIs around daybreak. James Roland Argo, a pharmacist mate (ship's doc) on board the LCI-489, recalled, "Actually our LCI didn't land up on the beach, which was the goal of LCIs. We hit an obstacle in the water and were not able to get right up on the beach. Lieutenant (H.H.) Montgomery was surveying where he wanted to direct fire. Suddenly all hell broke out. Montgomery yelled, 'Get off the bridge' and we abandoned the bridge immediately." As he explained, "German bunkers that were supposed to have been blasted out in an air raid weren't. Fire started coming from everywhere. To make things worse, the water was very rough." Describing the obstacles, Argo wrote, "Wood timbers/cross ties and barbed wire were attached to mines. One of the first things I remember seeing just before all hell broke out was a couple of dead men draped over these obstacles in the shallow water. Later I learned that these men were sent in to clear and mark channels for other landing craft and us." One by one, DUWKS carrying artillery to help support their advance foundered or were hit by enemy shell fire and by 0830 serious congestion on the beaches had forced the beachmaster to close the western beaches to incoming vehicles.[24]

Offshore, Admiral Bryant's fire support ships, ordered to cease fire at H-hour, sat idle. Until they contacted their shore fire control parties (SFCPs), the destroyers could not lend support to the embattled G.I.s on Omaha, but some of these SFCPs had landed on the wrong beach sectors, and many of them had suffered heavy casualties. Few of the destroyers managed to fire during this critical first hour and a half. Using visual observation of the enemy gun flashes, however, at 0716 *Thompson* fired four salvoes on a German field gun shelling the beachhead. When the enemy gun resumed firing at 0724, she retuned fire and reported it silenced.

Although by now most naval commanders realized that the assault on Omaha Beach had run into serious trouble, smoke, and haze, the failure to get shore fire control parties ashore and set up had deprived Admiral Bryant's fire support ships of opportunities to render effective fire support. As Admiral Bryant recalled, "The beach was a most alarming sight. Tanks were burning, ships were burning, every so often a larger explosion would indicate a hit on an ammunition dump. That was very frustrating, because we had all sorts of gun power but didn't know how to use it."[25]

Finally, at 0810, *Carmick* made contact with her SFCP, which requested fire support. She fired a ranging salvo well inland, but experienced difficulty with her radio transmitter and lost contact. The team had left the SFCP's radio key open and, although those on *Carmick* could clearly hear the team's conversations and "the whine of enemy machine gun bullets over their foxhole," they could not relay messages to the men ashore. Fortunately, about 0830, *Carmick*'s commanding officer, Commander Robert O. Beer, observed some American tanks near the breakwater firing on a bluff. Breaking the cease-fire order, he ordered *Carmick* to put a few salvoes on the same spot. This tactic of cooperation with the tanks proved very successful.[26]

In the meantime, Lieutenant Colonel James E. Rudder's Rangers at Pointe du Hoc struggled to get a hold on their sector. They had landed at 0708, 35 minutes late because of a navigation error and strong currents and in full view of German defenders at the top of the steep cliffs. Motor Launch 304 closed the edge of the cliffs and blazed away at the enemy defenders. At 0728, a Ranger SFCP made contact with the destroyer *Satterlee*, enabling her to use her guns to keep the Germans back far enough for the Rangers to scale the cliffs and seize the 155mm gun battery, which proved a mere decoy. The Americans subsequently found her guns in a field several miles inland from the beaches. Later on D-Day, *Satterlee*, *Harding*, and *Thompson* assisted the Rangers in repelling several counterattacks.

At 0733, the *Hunt*-class destroyer *Talybont* departed as scheduled for the screen, and within the hour, *Doyle* made contact with her SFCP only to learn they had no targets in sight. *McCook*, on the other hand, got into the action at 0839 polishing off a German pillbox "with direct hits," and at 0901, *Emmons* fired air bursts at a German patrol boat. By now, German shore batteries had begun firing back on the destroyers. An enemy shell, from either an 88mm or 105mm gun, struck the *Baldwin* at 0820. "Number one gun was set afire by a small hit," Davis Howes recalled. "Our motor whaleboat was smashed by another shell. Bang, bang, we fired a couple of rapid salvoes. The battery that had fired on us was out of action and we soon had the fire out, and were okay, except for the loss of the boat." These shoots by destroyers off Omaha Beach were the exceptions during that crucial period from 0800 to 0900.[27]

As for the smaller, close-in support landing craft, the reports indicate that LCT-30 did aggressively beach on Fox Green beach about this time with her 20mm gun blazing. However, the LCFs (landing craft, flak) in Captain Sabin's group, designed to repel aircraft attacks, had little to do on D-Day given the lack of response from the *Luftwaffe*. All except one of the LCG(L)s, however, managed to take up their positions off the beachhead by H-hour, and at least one did get into the action. Nearing Omaha Beach to land troops of Company A, 116th Infantry, Sublieutenant Jimmy Green, a wave commander with the 551 Assault Flotilla, spotted a pillbox on the beach through his binoculars. Green recalled that he was "thinking that if it was manned we were going to be in trouble. There was a loud bang in my right ear and I turned to see a LCG [landing craft gun] blazing away with its 4.7s and scoring direct hits on the pillbox. I wished it could have stayed longer, but it disappeared as quickly as it had arrived." The LCGs might have been able to render more effective close-in support had they been assigned a Shore Fire Control Party, but as Adrian Lewis has pointed out, LCG(L)s "were not tied into the naval gunfire support system so could only fire on visually identifiable targets of opportunity." In his action report, Captain Sabin wrote of the LCG(L)s: "Gun ships have a definite value for close inshore work but their fire control system is too crude."[28]

Just before 0900, Captain Harry Sanders's flagship *Frankford* arrived off Easy Red sector from the screening area north of the transport area. When *Frankford* closed the beach, Sanders, a veteran of the Mediterranean war where he had commanded the destroyer screen during the Anzio campaign, realized the gravity of the situation on Omaha. At 0900, he ordered all destroyers to get into action and assist the beleaguered troops. This galvanized the tin cans, and for the next few hours, *Frankford* and the other destroyers were busy locating and firing on any available German targets. "We proceeded in to probably 1000 yards and tried to contact our shore-fire control party," *Frankford* gunnery officer Lieutenant Owen F. Keeler recalled. "For reasons that became obvious later, we never had clear targets on the beach. Unfortunately the German camouflage was excellent, so from a distance we could not see who was where or pinpoint anything to shoot." The destroyer's D-Day action report noted, "Consequently, all fire, with one exception, was made on targets of opportunity." *Frankford* found fire control assistance in an unlikely place. "Then one of our light tanks that was sitting at the water's edge with a broken track fired at something on the hill," Lieutenant Owen Keeler explained. "We immediately followed up with a five-inch salvo. The tank gunner flopped open his hatch, looked around at us, waved, dropped back in the tank and fired at another target. For the next few minutes he was our fire-control party."

Meanwhile, under control of airborne spotters, Admiral Bryant's flagship *Texas* shifted her major-caliber fire inland to interdict enemy reinforcement activities and to destroy batteries and other strongpoints farther inland. At midday, *Texas* closed to within 3,000 yards off Omaha Beach to fire on snipers and machine gun nests in a defile off the beach. As Admiral Bryant recalled, "At about the middle of our sector was a gully up which our men and equipment were to go to get inland. But nothing was going up it. A mass of men were huddled at the seam and nothing moved." Bryant said he finally got permission from Admiral Hall "to fire a few 14-inch shells up the gully. The ship fired perhaps a half dozen rounds, and they had immediate effect. Soon we could see Germans coming down the gully with their hands up. Then our men, guns, trucks, and so forth began to move up the gulch." By noon of D-Day, the army had opened four major breaches in the German defenses.[29]

Aerial spotters gave the battleship *Texas* and other Navy fire support ships invaluable assistance locating targets and adjusting their fire. Anticipating the need for accurate information about enemy targets for gunfire support ships, Allied planners had arranged for air spot from single-seat fighters, an innovation that had been developed successfully in the Mediterranean. These fast, maneuverable fighters, which replaced the slow, vulnerable ship's catapult aircraft, played an important spotting role on D-Day. The Air Spotting Pool, commanded by Commodore E. C. Thornton (RN), included the 34 Tactical Reconnaissance Wing, which as of June 1,

1944, had 101 Spitfires and Seafires in five naval and two air force squadrons. The U.S. Navy had two squadrons, No. 26 and No. 63, at Lee-on-Solent, the only two American squadrons to fly Spitfires. Their pilots were experienced floatplane pilots and aircrews from Navy battleships and cruisers. The first Seafire mission on D-Day flew off at 0441 to spot for heavy warships participating in the invasion, followed by fighters from No. 3 Fighter Wing, flying spotting and recce missions for both U.S. Navy and Royal Navy ships off the beachhead. About noon on June 6, the three Mustang 1A squadrons (No. 268, No. 2 RAF, and No. 424 RCAF), arrived at Lee-on-Solent and completed 96 sorties.[30]

Naval gunfire support off the Normandy beachheads continued well into D-Day and thereafter. With her shore fire party either killed or wounded, *Emmons*, for example, spent the remainder of D-Day looking for targets of opportunity. Observing German naval infantry marching down the street of Port en Bassin, the destroyer opened fire with her 40mm guns and "broke up the formation and the sailors dived into the surrounding houses." When *Emmons* responded to a request from Admiral Bryant to shoot off a church steeple in Coleville without damaging the church, even her best efforts failed. After firing 11 rounds, the next two shook the tower, clipped it off, and set it crashing into the church nave.

Late on D-Day afternoon, *McCook* began firing on a pillbox atop a cliff overlooking Omaha Beach. After receiving several direct hits from the destroyer's 5″ shells, the German defenders came out of their pillbox waving white flags. According to the BBC, "This occasion is one of the very few in history of war when troops on land have surrendered to a warship." On the light cruiser, H.M.S. *Bellona*, Peter Walker remembered, "As the army advanced, *Bellona* fired her guns inshore at targets spotted by aircraft and forward observation officers off shore. There was a Fleet Air Army Officer and an Artillery Officer in the operations room who communicated with them. The stench of burnt cordite permeated the whole ship."[31]

Offshore, General Omar Bradley had anxiously awaited reports on the progress of the landings, but with communication with Omaha Beach "thin to nonexistent," he had received only scattered reports. From these, Bradley had garnered the impression that the Americans had been repulsed at Omaha. Finally, at 1330, he got a heartening message from Lieutenant General Gerow that the troops on Omaha were, in fact, advancing. "Thank God for the United States Navy!" General Gerow told Bradley.[32]

For the first few hours on Omaha Beach, however, American troops had been pinned down under the cliffs, unable to move into the heavily defended draws. Deprived of most of their artillery and tank support, they had taken heavy losses to German machine gun, mortar, and shell fire before Allied commanders realized the desperate nature of the struggle and ordered Allied destroyers to close the beaches and knock out enemy pillboxes and other defenses. In early 1944, following the landings at Anzio-Nettuno in Italy, Admiral John L. Hall had predicted the very situation in which the Americans on Omaha Beach found themselves on D-Day morning. In his action report, Admiral Hall offered a word of caution, "The risk of daylight landing must be accepted against accurate heavy gunfire, minefields, and numerous beach obstacles, which will probably completely disorganize the assault waves."[33] Admiral Hall's observations proved uncannily true for the Americans landing on Omaha Beach on June 6, 1944. Were Admiral Hall's recommendations taken to heart by the Allies in planning Neptune/Overlord? And to what extent did they make use of the lessons learned in four major amphibious operations in the Mediterranean prior to D-Day?

In planning and preparing for Operation Neptune, Allied planners had the advantage of numerous, important precedents as well as lessons learned and recommendations made by amphibious commanders in the Mediterranean, such as Admirals Henry K. Hewitt, John Lesslie Hall, Alan G. Kirk, and Lyal Davidson. Although a detailed, complete study of the planning process for naval gunfire support in Operation Neptune has yet to be written, some evidence suggests that the Commander in Chief Allied Expeditionary Force (ANCXF), Admiral Sir Bertram H. Ramsay, and his staff may not have taken full advantage of this body of amphibious knowledge gained in the Mediterranean war. Historians Alan Millet and Williamson Murray have concluded that neither Generals Bradley and Eisenhower nor Admiral Ramsay was particularly interested in lessons learned to date in the Pacific theater, which they considered "bush league stuff."[34]

In a postwar interview, Admiral Kirk, who commanded Task Force 122, the Western Naval Task Force, for Neptune, offered this insight on the planning process: "All the planning was done in Norfolk House by Admiral Ramsay and his staff in the minutest detail." U.S. Navy officers found the British planning procedure disturbing because, as Admiral Kirk recalled, the U.S. Navy War College trained them to issue "broad directives from the top to principal commander, who worked out their plans and submitted them to the topside fellow for approval and then passed it downward. Each fellow did the details with his staff. The British didn't do that." In the Mediterranean, Admiral Kirk and Admiral Hewitt had followed the American system for planning. For Operation Neptune, Kirk attempted to follow his training, but in working with the British encountered difficulties. "My staff officers would from time to time make comments, 'We could do it better this way or that way.' And these were never accepted by Admiral Ramsay's staff. In fact, we got some rather tough little comments back, directed against me for allowing these younger officers in their turn to speak out against the voice of the commander in chief." Kirk recalled the process was "a little bit touchy, a little bit awkward." His comments raise doubts about the extent to which planners of the Normandy operation took into consideration lessons and recommendations based on Allied experience of naval gunfire support in the Mediterranean.

One must assume, however, that Allied planners for Operation Neptune had access to numerous action reports and other studies based on the experience gained in the four recent amphibious operations in the Mediterranean. Lessons learned and recommendations made by Allied commanders in the Mediterranean about naval gunfire support fall into five categories: naval bombardments; close-in gunfire support; mine clearance; air spot; and defense against air, submarine, and E-boat attacks.[35]

Whether to include in the op plan provisions for a pre–H-hour naval and/or air bombardment of the immediate invasion area proved one of the most contentious issues for senior commanders in the Mediterranean theater. For Operation Torch, the first Mediterranean operation in November 1942, the Americans made no provision for naval bombardment prior to the actual landing of troops on the beaches of French Morocco or inside the Mediterranean at Oran and Algiers. Although Torch planners anticipated that Vichy French forces might oppose the landings, they hoped that diplomacy would forestall any open hostilities. In the event of French resistance, however, Allied intelligence had provided naval commanders with the location of enemy defenses, such as gun batteries, airfields, and warships. Concerned about the presence of the French battleship *Jean Bart* in the harbor at Casablanca and others warships at Dakar, Allied planners had also arranged for a covering force composed of battleships and cruisers to be included in the Western Naval Task Force (TF 34). Each of TF 34's three attack groups assigned to land troops along the Moroccan coast also had its own fire support group. The two amphibious landings inside the Mediterranean were joint U.S.-British operations supported by fire support groups and Force H, a covering force composed of three British battleships, a battle cruiser, two aircraft carriers, and four light cruisers screened by destroyers.[36]

Admiral Hewitt's Western Task Naval Force arrived off the Moroccan coast in the early hours of November 8, 1942, largely unobserved, but the first assault waves in all three locations alerted Vichy French batteries, which promptly opened fire. After these initial exchanges of gunfire, U.S. Navy fire support ships responded to requests for gunfire support from the Army ashore or to counter offensive moves by French warships.

Hoping to catch the French defenders at Oran and Algiers by surprise, the Allies did not attempt a pre-landing bombardment in either location. Both of these joint British-American landings achieved tactical surprise, but when the troops came ashore, Vichy French forces briefly opposed their advances, and shore batteries opened fire on Allied ships. In addition to opposition to the assault waves, French forces repulsed attempts by Rangers and commandoes to force the harbors at Oran and Algiers.[37]

Despite resistance from French forces during Torch, Allied planners decided against a pre–H-hour bombardment for the next Mediterranean operation, the invasion of the island of Sicily, code-named Operation Husky. U.S. Army commanders remained resistant to any bombardment that might alert the enemy and continued to press for a pre-dawn assault. H-hour was therefore again set for the pre-dawn period of darkness, but planners did not preclude pre–H-hour gunfire by cruisers and destroyers against enemy searchlights or gun batteries firing on the landing craft. Nor did the op plan rule out barrages by specially equipped landing craft carrying 5″ rockets designed to neutralize or destroy mines and beach defenses.[38]

In the third major Allied amphibious operation in the Mediterranean theater, code-named Avalanche, on September 9, 1943, Rear Admiral John L. Hall's Southern Attack Force (TF 81) landed two regimental combat teams of the U.S.VI Corps on four beaches along the Gulf of Salerno on the Italian mainland. To support the American landings in the southern sector, Rear Admiral Lyal Davidson had the veteran fire support ships *Philadelphia*, *Savannah*, *Boise*, and *Brooklyn* and the destroyers of Desron 13. Once again, however, planners made no provision in the op plan for pre–H-hour naval or air bombardments although a one scout boat with rockets was tasked to fire on the American beaches. The British sector's Northern Attack Force at Salerno had three *Hunt*-class destroyers positioned just a mile off the beaches to provide close gunfire support and an LCR to fire a rocket barrage just prior to touchdown on Uncle Red Beach.

The Allies' decision not to employ a naval bombardment prior to H-hour proved a fatal one. "The effect of the stubborn German resistance on the beaches was a shock and considerably confusing to our troops," Lieutenant Harrie James told Admiral Hall. Having spoken with many of the troops and to several Army officers, Lieutenant James felt many "rightly or wrongly" connected the lack of pre-landing naval bombardment with the Italian surrender and "felt they had been 'let-down' in the sense that naval pre-landing bombardment was withheld because of the armistice."[39]

Despite the intensity of German opposition to the Salerno landings, Allied planners again decided against a pre–H-hour bombardment for their next amphibious operation in January 1944—a left-hook landing south of Rome at the resort town of Anzio-Nettuno designed to outflank the German held Gustav Line. Planners reasoned that the Anzio area would be lightly defended and that a night assault would achieve surprise, allowing General John P. Lucas's VI Corps and the troops of the British First Division to get ashore and establish a wide beachhead before the enemy could react and reinforce the area. Inasmuch as the Germans failed to oppose the initial landing of Allied troops on the Anzio beaches and the Allies achieved total surprise, a pre–H-hour bombardment would have been ill advised. But by the winter of 1944, amphibious operations in the Pacific, especially the Tarawa landings, and the cumulative experience of the Allies in three Mediterranean invasions had convinced Neptune/Overlord planners to include at least some pre–H-hour naval bombardment in hopes of destroying or temporarily silencing some of the German batteries, machine gun nests, and other coastal defenses in Normandy.

Although acknowledging the importance of pre–H-hour naval bombardment to success in amphibious operations, Admiral Hall had warned after the Salerno operation that a heavy bombardment by warships was not "a panacea for all the troubles in the form of enemy resistance which may beset an assault force. It may, and probably will, knock out some of the beach defenses, but it most certainly will not eliminate them all . . . and it most certainly will destroy the last vestiges of surprise, tactical or otherwise." On D-Day at Normandy, Admiral Hall's comments proved insightful indeed to the Americans and the British as well. On June 6, 1944, pre-landing H-hour air and naval bombardments failed to silence or neutralize many of the enemy's batteries and pillboxes and did not allow the first waves of troops and tanks to come ashore unopposed.[40]

Naval gunfire support in the Mediterranean theater prior to the spring of 1944 had not included any large-scale, pre–H-hour naval bombardments. Thus, Allied planners for Operation Neptune lacked specific information about their effectiveness in the Mediterranean. They had accumulated a body of knowledge, however, about other aspects of naval fire support. In each of the Mediterranean landings, gunfire support ships had quickly responded to enemy fire prior to the arrival of the first assault wave. Fire support ships also shot out enemy searchlights and then stood by for fire requests from their own shore fire control parties (called "forward observation officers" in the Royal Navy) or Army units established on the beachhead. Occasionally, calls for supporting fire came from beachmasters or other naval units. In the first few hours of an assault, many of these calls requested that fire support ships silence or neutralize large enemy shore batteries firing on the beaches, on incoming landing craft, or on transports in the transport area. As D-Day progressed, naval fire support ships focused increasingly on targets such as enemy mortars and machine gun nests, mobile batteries, troop concentrations, vehicles, and armored columns identified by spotter aircraft or Army units.

When French shore batteries opened fire on approaching landing craft in the Northern Attack Group (TG 34.8) during Operation Torch in November 1942, the wisdom of including gunfire support ships in the op plan became obvious. Happily, for the troops in the vulnerable landing craft, the destroyer *Eberle* quickly returned fire with her 5"/38-caliber. When a French battery took aim on the destroyer *Roe*, the light cruiser *Savannah* intimidated it with her 6" battery. Although a few enemy shells landed near the transport *Henry Allen*, the other transports managed to retire to seaward before being hit. Landing craft of the Center Attack Force off Fedhala, Morocco became targets for French batteries as well, prompting fire support group ships to expend hundreds of rounds trying to knock out these shore defenses. The light cruiser *Brooklyn*, for example, shot 757 rounds of 6" ammunition against the Skerki Battery. As some naval commanders had feared, counterbattery fire by U.S. Navy ships off Morocco occasionally fell near American troops, but overall cases of friendly fire were few. At Safi, the commander of the Southern Attack Force, Admiral Lyal Davidson, wrote in his action report that the "exchange of gunfire" took place in "complete darkness and only the intermittent flashes of enemy battery could be used as a point of aim." During the Normandy operation, gunnery personnel on Allied ships used similar visual observation of gun flashes and even the glint of sun off the binoculars worn by German officers.[41]

In his after-action report, Captain Robert Emmet, Commander Center Attack Group (Com TG 34.9), wrote, "The cruisers and destroyers assigned specified Fire Support Missions executed them successfully." As an example, Captain Emmet cited *Brooklyn*'s rapid silencing of a battery of four 138mm guns near Pont Blondin with her 6" guns. Control vessels and destroyers also played a key role in close fire support during the Fedhala landings. In his action report, Captain Emmet particularly noted the effectiveness of American destroyers' main batteries of 5"/38-caliber guns against French 105mm and 75mm batteries firing on the landing beaches "except in a few cases where certain guns were protected by reverse slopes from fire from the westward."[42]

Certain French gun batteries, however, called for the large-caliber guns of heavier warships. Arguing that in Batterie Railleuse and the 155mm battery south of Safi, the enemy had "the means of offering great resistance to the landing operations," Admiral Davidson wrote, "The early neutralization of these two batteries, due to the accuracy of counter battery fire by the battleship *New York* and light cruiser *Philadelphia*, had an important bearing on the success of the whole operation." In his history of the Moroccan landings, historian Samuel Eliot Morison argued that the *New York*'s effective counterbattery fire on Batterie Railleuse "helped disprove the popular notion that battleships had become obsolete and useless." Allied planners duly noted the success of the *New York* and included battleships whenever possible in future amphibious operations, including Operation Neptune.

Although Admiral Davidson commended his Southern Attack Force ships for demonstrating the "effectiveness of naval gunfire neutralization of shore batteries," he failed to mention that his cruisers and destroyers had not scored any direct hits. Captain Paul Hendren, commanding the cruiser *Philadelphia*, candidly noted, "It is next to impossible to make direct hits on individual guns of a shore battery."

To silence such batteries, Captain Hendren concluded that "dive bombing . . . appeared to offer a much better chance of putting the individual guns out of action." He recommended a combination of intensive bombardment by naval gunfire for a few minutes, "using plane spot and followed immediately by check fire and dive bombing." Hendren also suggested a gas shell to "assist in rapid neutralization of such a battery." Allied planners for Operation Neptune/Overlord would have done well to heed Captain Hendren's advice and not rely so heavily on the results of naval bombardment to reduce enemy gun emplacements and batteries in Normandy.[43]

In another important development for future amphibious operations, Northern Attack Force fire support warships off Medheia and Port Lyautey discovered that their gunfire could be effective against more than enemy shore batteries or stationary gun emplacements. For example, when Rear Admiral Monroe Kelly's fire support ships received call fire requests against French truck columns and armored counterattacks, they responded with accurate fire. The cruiser *Savannah* broke up one enemy effort "with a blistering barrage of air-spotted 6-inch." Furthermore, the battleship *Texas* "probably made true believers of some Army men when she broke up a French attempt to truck some infantry to the front."

Admiral Davidson considered gunnery operations during the landings at Safi a success "beyond reasonable expectations." He attributed this success, in part, to the element of surprise, the extreme accuracy of naval gunfire even during darkness, the volume and rapidity of fire, and the enemy's lack of will to resist. The admiral confirmed the effectiveness of plane spot and called the use of large, unrestricted fire support areas a "definite step forward. This gives the ships a chance to make long firing runs, unhampered by numerous turns." These fire support areas would become standard for future Mediterranean amphibious operations. Davidson also recommended that the naval attack force have control of the air and that aircraft be employed for night bombing of batteries "because ships' gunfire during darkness cannot be replied upon." Noting that the Southern Attack Group had suffered from a lack of good maps, the admiral suggested that a standard map or mosaic with the M-square system already superimposed be issued well in advance to all units connected with the problem of naval gunfire.[44]

On July 10, 1943, the Allies invaded the island of Sicily. For this second major amphibious operation in the Mediterranean war (Operation Husky), each of the task forces for the American sectors, Dime, Joss, and Cent, had its own fire support group composed of cruisers, destroyers, and in the Cent sector the British monitor H.M.S. *Abercrombie*. Although the op plan did not call for a pre–H-hour bombardment for the American sectors in Sicily, planners tasked fire support ships to provide close support for the infantry as it came ashore, secured beachheads, and advanced inland against opposition from the Italian defenders of Sicily and their more determined German allies.

The Joss attack group also had the services of one British landing craft flak (LCF-12). As the name implies, the British used this type of craft for anti-aircraft purposes as well as for convoy escort and beach patrols during amphibious landings. LCFs were fitted with four 40mm Bofors and eight 20mm Oerlikon guns, manned by Royal Marines. On D-Day for Operation Husky, LCF-12 escorted troops of the U.S. 7th Infantry to their beaches in the Joss sector.[45]

In addition to LCFs, the Joss Attack Force had close gunfire support from the new LCG(L), an old LCT decked over to carry two 4.7″ naval guns. Gaffi Attack Group had three LCGs, Molla Attack Group one, and Salso Attack Group another three LCGs. The Navy intended them as floating gun batteries to provide close-in support until the Army could get its artillery ashore. Fortunately, by midmorning on D-Day during Operation Husky, LCTs had beached, bringing the U.S. 3rd Division's divisional artillery ashore and one tank company of the 66th Armored Regiment. However, in future amphibious operations, especially those at Salerno, Italy, and at Omaha Beach in Normandy, delays in the arrival of division artillery and tanks would prove costly.[46]

Six of the new rocket launching craft, dubbed LCT(R)s, made their debut in the Sicily landings. Developed after the failed British raid on Dieppe, these new rocket craft were designed to drench landing beaches with 5″ rockets, tearing up mines and beach obstacles and hopefully stunning or silencing enemy machine gun nests and other defenses. The original LCT(R)s—decked over LCTs—carried 800 (later 1,110) 5″ rockets in fixed batteries with a range of 3,000 yards. Because the early LCT(R)s could not aim their rockets and had to fire them over the heads of the approaching assault waves, the rocket barrages often proved inaccurate.[47]

Opportunities for fire support occurred early on D-Day in the Dime sector, with the cruiser *Boise* and the destroyer *Jeffers* opening on an enemy gun position on the beach at 0400 by observing its gun flashes. A half-hour later, Axis aircraft made their first appearance over the Gela Area. The destroyer *Maddox*, on patrol at the outward edge of the invasion area, suffered a direct hit and sank.

When dawn came on D-Day, the light cruisers *Savannah* and *Boise* catapulted their O2U spot planes for reconnaissance duties and to observe the fall of shot. At 0930, a battery began shelling the LSTs (landing ship tank) on Red 2 and Green 2, prompting *Boise* and *Jeffers* to open fire on the battery, silencing it. Admiral Hall ordered *Boise* to close the beach to fire on a battery enfilading troops, and she responded by closing to 3,000 yards, locating the guns behind a dune and silencing them.[48]

In addition to neutralizing enemy shore batteries and machine gun positions near the beaches, U.S. Navy fire support cruisers and destroyers in Dime sector off Gela found themselves instrumental in stopping two Axis armored thrusts at the invasion beaches on D-Day. Lieutenant C. G. Lewis, piloting *Boise*'s spot plane, first sighted the tanks on Niscemi Road at 0830. He called for naval gunfire, and from 1050 to 1108, *Boise* fired on the tanks from ranges of 11,550 to 13,600 yards. Captain Hewlet Thebaud, commanding the fire support group for the Gela landings, also ordered *Savannah* to move into the FS Area 2 to assist in repelling the tank attacks. H.M.S. *Abercrombie*, a British monitor, joined Admiral Davidson's Cent fire support ships on the morning of D-Day and saw plenty of action, firing on a target north of the Impari River at 0730 "with great effectiveness."

Communications difficulties on the monitor and the need to service the cruiser *Philadelphia*'s spot planes silenced the *Abercrombie* until 1248, when she resumed bombardment aided by an American SOC spot plane flown by Lieutenant Commander E. D. Stephenson (USN). He and Aviation Radioman 2/C Dwight Piersen volunteered to provide aerial observation for the British monitor despite the danger of being attacked by enemy aircraft, which had already shot down two of *Savannah*'s spot planes. With Lieutenant Commander Stephenson's assistance, H.M.S. *Abercrombie* silenced one strong point, but on returning to the *Philadelphia*, two Me-109s overtook the SOC and shot her down into the sea off Yellow Beach. Neither Stephenson nor his radioman survived.[49]

In Joss sector, which included landing beaches both north and south of the town of Licata, enemy batteries quickly got the range of approaching landing craft, prompting Admiral Richard Conolly to order two destroyers in to lay a protective smokescreen. Except for a few British LCTs converted to gunboats or LCFs, the Navy had no naval gun fire support immediately available for Red Beach because the destroyers *Roe* and *Swanson* had earlier collided while chasing down some radar contacts off Porto Empedocle.

At about 0542, the Red beachmaster signaled the Gaffi Attack Group commander, Captain Lorenzo S. Sabin in LCI-10, "Enemy field artillery getting close. Hold the wave. Give us support." Sabin then called on one of the destroyers for support, and *Buck* responded. She closed the beach to 6,400 yards and silenced enemy guns firing on Red Beach. Captain Sabin later reported that when *Buck* closed the beach, her wake freed LCI-218, which had grounded on a false beach. *Buck*'s close-in gunfire support set an important precedent for the role of American destroyers at Omaha Beach.[50]

After D-Day, both U.S. Navy and Royal Navy fire support ships continued to provide gunfire support for the troops advancing inland or along the Sicilian coast. On D-Day plus 1, for example, a column of Italian tanks attacked troops of the 180th Infantry, who called for naval support. The cruiser *Savannah* quickly responded. From his battle station on *Savannah*, Pharmacist Mate Richard O. Sharon recorded the action in his diary: "0830—We are now firing our main batteries in an attempt to break up a German tank formation moving up on our troops. 0900—Our firing has been reported as successful. 1000—We are now firing three turret salvos on the beach so must have the range." *Savannah* pumped 126 rounds into the Italians and blew about one-half of their support troops to shreds.[51]

U.S. Navy cruisers and destroyers continued to support the Army for the remainder of the campaign in Sicily, shelling enemy troops and positions along the north coast of the island while Royal Navy destroyers fired on Axis tanks, gun batteries, and troop concentrations on the road leading north from Catania. Naval gunfire support during Operation Husky received accolades from senior naval commanders and Royal Navy midshipmen alike. "Direct and indirect bombardments of towns and large area targets by more than one ship without F.O.O. observation were of considerable assistance to the army and the early capture of Malilli in particular was due to this form of support," Admiral Troubridge wrote. Midshipman Frank Wade felt that the Army-Navy shore bombardment being exhibited in Acid sector proved the "new procedures were working." Prior to Husky, he said, "the army had been very leery of naval shore bombardment and support and there had been several nasty incidents when we fired into our own troops." Indeed, Operation Husky quashed most doubts about the use of naval gunfire support in amphibious assaults. "The naval bombardment in Operation Husky completely won the confidence of the Armies of both British and American in naval supporting fire," the final report noted.[52]

Allied warships had made important contributions to the success of operations in Sicily, but during the next Allied amphibious operation in the Mediterranean, naval gunfire support would prove a decisive factor in securing a beachhead on the Italian mainland at Salerno. In Operation Avalanche, which took place on September 9, 1943, Rear Admiral Hall's Southern Attack Force (TF 81) landed two regimental combat teams of the U.S. VI Corps on four beaches along the Gulf of Salerno. Rear Admiral Davidson's task group (TG 81.5), which included the veteran light cruisers *Philadelphia, Savannah, Boise,* and *Brooklyn,* the British monitor *Abercrombie,* and Commander E. R. Durgin's Desron 13, provided four fire support groups. The U.S. Army had rejected Admiral Hewitt's offer to provide close-in gunfire support from rocket craft or small gunboats, such as LCGs. In their op plan for Avalanche, however, the British had included a pre–H-hour naval bombardment by Royal Navy cruisers, a monitor, and destroyers prior to the landing of Lieutenant General Sir R. McCreery's X Corps on six beaches to the north of the American sectors at Salerno.[53]

As the ships of the Avalanche assault groups steamed toward Salerno, news of an armistice with Italy gave rise to rumors that Allied forces would come ashore virtually unopposed in the Gulf of Salerno. These optimistic predictions did not fool most commanders on board the transports and warships, but convinced many of the embarked troops that the Italians would welcome them with open arms. In reality, the invasion did not take the Germans by surprise. They had sent troops to take over Italian coastal defenses, and when the first waves of American troops touched down on Red, Green, Yellow, and Blue Beaches off Paestum in the Gulf of Salerno between 0335 and 0342 on D-Day, the Germans opened up on them with a barrage of mortar, machine gun, and 88mm shell fire. A barrage of 34 rockets fired on Green Beach constituted the only pre-landing fire in the American sectors. Without close-in gunfire support, the troops had to wait for the arrival of their 105mm artillery to come ashore in DUWKS and their tanks in LCTs. "There is fierce opposition all along the beaches," correspondent Al Newman wrote, "Most of the troops pinned down by enemy fire. 'Hell of an armistice, isn't it' comments one naval officer."[54]

DUWKS put some artillery and tanks ashore, but enemy fire drove off LCTs carrying tanks of the 751st Tank Battalion and hit many vehicles on the beaches. Enemy gunfire also delayed until noon the arrival of tanks being carried aboard LSTs. Admiral Hall's ships had taken station offshore to provide gunfire support for the embattled troops on the beaches, but an overly ambitious minesweeping plan had left some of the boat lanes and fire support areas unswept by H-hour, preventing the approach of fire support cruisers and destroyers and depriving the first assault waves of much needed gunfire support. As a result, by dawn of D-Day, German machine gun, mortar, and shell fire from enemy batteries and tanks had pinned American troops down on Green, Yellow and Blue beaches.

Despite the desperate need for naval gunfire, Rear Admiral Davidson had just one fire support ship, the destroyer U.S.S. *Ludlow*, in position in Fire Support Area One behind the assault waves, but she could not proceed until a minesweeper led her in through the enemy minefield. Beyond the minefields at a long range of 25,000 yards, the 15" monitor *Abercrombie* fired on an enemy battery using air spot around 0825, again on tanks at 1025, and at 1112. *Ludlow* finally safely negotiated the minefield but experienced the further frustration of being unable to contact her SFCP. She did, however, by using top spot, respond to requests from shore for gunfire against several bridges in the path of advancing German tanks.[55]

With the situation touch and go on the beaches, Admiral Davidson contacted the Minesweeper Group (TG 81.8) commander, Alfred Richards, and, ignoring Richards's protests that he had completed only one sweep and the area was "thick with mines," the admiral demanded that Richards guide his flagship *Philadelphia* through the minefield toward shore. He complied, and by midmorning of D-Day, Admiral Davidson had his gunfire support ships in position, but the lack of contact with SFCPs ashore and poor visibility caused by haze and smoke limited their effectiveness. These conditions forced Davidson's ships to rely for target information and spotting on "hazy descriptions" and visual observation from top spot (visual observation high up in the ship, either from lookouts or from a director tower) or spot planes. Fortunately, the campaign for Sicily had taught the Navy the value of air spot, and provision had been made in the Avalanche op plan for aerial observation for fire support ships by specially trained P-51 Mustang pilots flying from airfields in Sicily. Using their own cruiser spot planes and Army P-51s, Davidson's ships fired on a variety of prearranged targets or enemy gun batteries and tanks located by their gun flashes.[56]

To the north of the American sectors off Salerno, Rear Admiral Richard Conolly's Northern Attack Force also encountered stiff enemy opposition. At 0121, a German battery opened fire on Admiral Conolly's flagship, the U.S.S. *Biscayne*, and one shell hit LST-359, inflicting 50 casualties. Connolly ordered a smoke screen laid and told his fire support ships to return fire. The British Army had not objected to a pre–H-hour naval bombardment in their sector, so at 0315, three *Hunt*-class destroyers commenced firing on pre-selected targets. LCGs and special LCAs (hedgerow craft) then fired 5″ rockets, but these rockets cleared only a six-yard–wide path, and LCG fire straddled at least one rocket LCA. Another rocket craft fired on the wrong beach, causing troops following behind her to land on Sugar Amber beach instead of Uncle Green.

This pre-landing bombardment may have destroyed or temporarily silenced some enemy batteries, but at H-hour, troops arriving on British beaches also encountered German artillery and machine gun fire, as well as mines on the beaches. Heavy fire from 105mm and 155mm guns peppered arriving LSTs and other landing craft. LCI-221, for example, reported receiving 81 shrapnel hits. In addition to shore batteries, the Germans had tanks lying in wait to fire on the beaches with their 88mm guns. One large landing craft, LST-315, was struck four times by 88mm shells. Furthermore, this heavy enemy fire only increased with daylight when targets became more visible to German gunners.[57]

This stiff German resistance hampered the debarkation of troops on British Uncle Red beaches and prompted calls to Allied warships for fire support. When German 88mm guns firing on the beaches delayed the arrival of LCTs carrying the Army's field artillery, naval gunfire support became all the more necessary, but initially, British fire support ships were out of range and also experiencing delays in contacting their shore parties (forward observation officers, FOOs). H.M.S. *Lookout* managed to fire on visible enemy targets, however, and H.M.S. *Nubian* opened up on enemy guns and machine gun nests from a range of 7,500 yards. The cruiser *Uganda* targeted some enemy tanks as well.[58]

By midday on D-Day, Admiral Davidson's fire support ships had contacted their SFCPs in the American sectors and could answer requests for fire support to stop a series of tank-supported enemy counterattacks on the beachhead. The destroyer *Edison's* skipper had developed some inventive tactics against enemy tanks. According to crewman Richard Groscup, "The only way we won the fight was to head to shore at full speed and then came a turn so we could give a broadside of our six 5" guns and then go full in reverse. Our Captain Hap Pearce used this tactic throughout all our Mediterranean engagements." Going in to within 5,000 yards of shore, *Edison* was "so close to the beach we had to be careful not to go around," Groscup recalled. Closing the beaches proved risky, too, as the monitor *Abercrombie* discovered when she struck a mine and suffered enough damage to have to retire to Palermo for repairs.

The cruiser *Philadelphia* fired on a group of 35 German tanks observed by a spot plane to be hiding in a copse adjacent to Red Beach; and, according to Lieutenant W. R. Austin, who was ashore during the engagement, the cruiser knocked out at least 20 percent of the enemy tanks. During the afternoon of D-Day, *Bristol* and *Woolsey* also took on German tanks forming north of the Sele River. The ability of warships such as these to locate and break up enemy troop and tank formations proved vital to Allied success at the Salerno beachhead.[59]

The issue remained in doubt for days at Salerno, however, and Allied fire support ships remained on call and in action for over a week supporting the Allies' tenuous hold on the beachhead and assisting troops as they tried to advance inland.[60]

German aircraft repeatedly harassed naval gunfire ships supporting the Salerno operation, but these ships also fell victim to mines and submarines. The tug *Moreno* hit a mine and had to be towed from the Gulf of Salerno; a submarine torpedoed and sank the destroyer *Rowan*; a new German FX1400 radio-controlled (or glide) bomb heavily damaged the cruiser *Savannah*; and a glide bomb hit H.M.S. *Uganda*. Another glide bomb damaged the British battleship *Warspite*, which had to be towed to Malta for repairs.

The hard-fought Salerno campaign yielded some important lessons for the Allies. As Lieutenant Commander Harrie James wrote after the Salerno operation in 1943, "For the first time our assault forces were met by German troops in well prepared defensive positions right down on the beach area." James predicted that unless knocked out by a pre–H-hour bombardment, they "can hold up the advance of our assault troops and pin them down on beach areas which in turn impeded the unloading over these beaches." The American experience at Omaha

Beach in 1944 confirmed James's predictions. The Navy also discovered off Salerno that amphibious operations could be costly in terms of ships sunk or damaged and lives lost because of offshore minefields, fire from enemy shore batteries and 88mm tank guns, determined air attacks including those by the new radio-controlled glide bombs, and well-placed torpedoes fired by enemy submarines. Although DUWKS brought much needed artillery to shore—and some tanks, carried in LCMs, managed to get ashore in the early hours of the Salerno invasion—Operation Avalanche proved that an amphibious operation against a determined, well–dug-in enemy needed more firepower for the initial assault waves than even the new LCT(R)s could provide. The use of smokescreens helped shield landing craft and fire support ships from enemy fire to some extent, and aircraft flown from escort carriers near the beaches were a huge improvement over the lack of air cover in Husky, but problems persisted with SFCPs failing to get ashore and set up, radios not functioning to contact the fire support ships offshore, and ensuring timely air spot and replenishment of ammunition.[61]

Although the Allies had planning for Operation Neptune/Overlord well underway by January 1944, amphibious landings at Anzio-Nettuno, Italy, on January 22 of that year yielded some valuable lessons and confirmed the correctness of Allied amphibious doctrine. Both U.S. Navy and Royal Navy assault forces for the Anzio landings, code-named Shingle, had gunfire support teams. Assault forces of General John Lucas's U.S. VI Corps had a Gunfire Support Group (TG 81.8) under the command of Captain Robert Cary. Anticipating joint American and British fire support groups used in Overlord/Neptune, Task Group 81.8 was a joint task group composed of the veteran American cruiser *Brooklyn* and British cruiser *Penelope*, escorted by Captain Harry Sanders's Desron 13. In the British sector off Peter beaches, the British 1st Infantry Division had support from H.M.S. *Orion* and H.M.S. *Spartan*, the old Dutch gunboats *Flores* and *Soemba*, and eight destroyers.

Once again, planners for Operation Shingle did not opt for a pre–H-hour naval bombardment, but LCT(R)s fired rocket barrages. In his supplementary report, Admiral Frank Lowry, commanding Task Force 81, wrote, "The entire approach and landing was [sic] made without opposition. As far as is known, the element of surprise was preserved up to the time rockets were fired. No supporting fire was laid down." Because Lowry considered rocket fire "extremely effective" during the Anzio landing, he recommended that "LCT(R)s should discharge their rockets between H minus 7 and H minus 5 minutes when landing boat wave is 1000 to 2000 yards from the beach."[62]

Although the Allied landing at Anzio-Nettuno took the Germans by surprise, allowing General John Lucas's troops to come ashore almost unopposed on January 22, 1944, the German commander, Albert Kesselring, quickly reinforced the area. German artillery, including guns mounted on railroad cars, the famous Anzio Annies, repeatedly shelled the beachhead, transport, and fire support areas, and the *Luftwaffe* sent bombers and fighters over Anzio on a regular basis. During the Anzio landings, British ships operated with American SFCPs and vice versa, and the results proved very satisfactory. According to Admiral Lowry, "The ability of Naval Support Units to deliver interdiction fire on road junctions, highways, crossroads and bridges, denied certain strategic points to the enemy and probably determined the eventual enemy defense line out of range of naval guns."

Other than mines, which damaged *Mayo* and sank YMS-30 and LCI-32, the most effective enemy weapon against Allied shipping and fire support vessels off Anzio during the long campaign at the beachhead proved to be the new German radio-controlled glide bomb. German mother aircraft carrying these early versions of guided missiles appeared over the beachhead on D-Day plus 1. Although Allied fighters chased many of the raiders away, glide bombs scored a direct hit on the British destroyer *Jervis*, and an aerial torpedo claimed the *Janus*, which capsized and sank. The presence of fighter-director teams and special radio-jamming equipment (known as "Y-service") on the destroyer escorts *Frederick C. Davis*, *Herbert C. Jones*, and British H.M.S. *Ulster Queen* helped reduce the risk of attack from German glide bombs but could not eliminate it. On January 29, 1944, a glide bomb hit a new heavy British cruiser, H.M.S. *Spartan*, which subsequently sank.[63]

Devising better tactics against German glide bombs as well as conventional aircraft was a priority to naval commanders in the Mediterranean, but in all four Allied invasions in the Mediterranean prior to June 1944, the provision of effective tactical air support to ground forces and aerial observation and spotting to fire support ships also proved critical to operational success. In the absence of Allied airfields within range of the landing beaches, arrangements for air support for Operation Torch relied on ship catapult planes and naval carrier aircraft. U.S. Navy carrier planes from the U.S.S. *Ranger* and three escort carriers (*Santee, Sangamon, Suwanee*) provided anti-submarine warfare (ASW) and combat air patrols, were used as strike aircraft, and answered requests for fire support from air liaison parties ashore. They quickly established air superiority over the Moroccan beaches, and Navy dive bombers proved extremely useful in engagements with Vichy French gun batteries. The OSU and SOC catapult aircraft on American battleships and cruisers did yeoman service in Torch, but proved slow and vulnerable to enemy fire. Inside the Mediterranean, the Royal Navy's Fleet Air Arm carriers *Avenger, Argus, Furious, Dasher,* and *Biter* provided air cover for the joint American-British landings in Oran and Algiers. These landings had the advantage of some air support from the British base at Gibraltar, but in Morocco on D-Day, "aircraft carriers carried the whole weight of air protection."[64]

Planners for the invasion of Sicily, anxious to provide adequate air support, had the use of land-based aircraft flying from bases in North Africa, eliminating the need for aircraft carriers. Despite these resources, a lack of Allied fighter cover cursed the U.S. Navy on D-Day off Sicily. Axis planes bombed and strafed ships and landing craft alike in hit-and-run raids, usually not picked up by Allied radars, and enemy fighters harassed the catapult aircraft spotting for the gunfire support ships. Enemy fighters repeatedly attacked these highly maneuverable old scout planes, catapulted early on D-Day to spot for the cruisers and the British monitor *Abercrombie*. One skilled pilot managed to outmaneuver two Me-109s, but the cruiser *Savannah* lost three spot planes and one pilot, Lieutenant C.A. Anderson, to German fighters on July 10, 1943. The vulnerability of cruiser catapult aircraft to enemy fighters off Sicily prompted Admiral Hewitt to advise they not be used as spot planes in future amphibious operations, but Admiral Davidson rose to their defense.[65]

To provide air support for the Salerno operation, the Allies once again resorted to carrier-borne aircraft from two fleet carriers (*Formidable* and *Illustrious*) and five escort carriers, but also employed Spitfires and P-51s flying from bases in North Africa. The short range of these fighters meant they could remain over the beaches only a short time, so planners counted on capturing the small Montecorvino airfield at Salerno on, or within a short time after, D-Day. When British troops failed to capture and hold the airfield, air support became more difficult. Furthermore, light airs in the Mediterranean and inexperienced pilots resulted in many accidents. Despite these problems, senior officers reported that air coverage prior to the departure of the assault forces off Salerno was "superior to that in Husky" and air defense by friendly fighters "excellent." Three fighter director ships, tasked to vector Force V's Seafires onto targets, took part in Operation Avalanche, but air support suffered from malfunctioning fighter director equipment. Landmasses ashore at Salerno made for poor radar information, and British radar scopes, which lacked a planned position indicator (PPI) scope, prevented the two fighter director ships, *Palomares* and *Ulster Queen*, from providing enough early warning of air raids. Allied experience at Salerno prompted recommendations that PPI scopes be fitted in the radar equipment aboard all fighter director ships and that GCI (ground control intercept) radar be added to all forward destroyers.[66]

The final Mediterranean invasion prior to D-Day in Normandy, Operation Shingle, had minimal air support. Fortunately, General Lucas's VI Corps troops came ashore almost unopposed, seized the small harbor of Anzio immediately, and secured the beachhead promptly. However, when Allied troops failed to press inland and the Germans sent fresh reinforcements to Anzio-Nettuno, the Allies were in for a grueling four-month campaign. They needed fire support from both Royal Navy and U.S. Navy cruisers and destroyers during this period on an ongoing basis as well as an alert defense against enemy air raids. Operation Shingle had excellent cooperation between British and American shore fire control parties, and Admiral Lowry wrote, "Army fighter pilots used Army procedure to adjust fire for both British and U.S. Ships. . . . [It] is amazing that the results could be so satisfactory." Admiral Frank Lowry commended the air warning system at Anzio, which in the first 30 days detected all but one of 30 German air attacks. He credited this success to a combination of centralized control for radar reporting, Y-service reports, and fighter direction cleared through the air plot of a fighter director ship. Clearly, Allied air defense had come a long way since the invasion of Sicily![67]

To provide effective naval gunfire support in amphibious operations, the Navy had to not only protect its warships, transports, and landing craft from air, submarine, and E-boat attack, but also promptly clear enemy-laid minefields off the beaches that limited maneuvering for fire support ships. In the four Mediterranean operations prior to June 1944, neither the U.S. Navy nor the Royal Navy lost a warship to enemy shell fire although enemy fire from mortars, shore batteries, and German 88mm guns damaged or sank numerous large landing craft, such as LSTs, LCTs, and LCI(L)s, off the beaches. Mines, however, sank the sweeper *Portent* and YMS-30 off

Anzio and heavily damaged the British *Abercrombie* at Salerno, the mine-sweeper *Staff* off Sicily, and the destroyer *Mayo* off Anzio. Although not a glamorous mission, mine clearance proved to be a crucial component of any amphibious operation, and yet the U.S. Navy came to operations in the Mediterranean sorely lacking in minesweepers and the trained, experienced personnel to man them.

In addition to mine clearance, for future operations the Allies had to devise better anti-aircraft tactics, such as smoke screens and jamming of radio signals for glide bombers, and they needed to develop landing craft that could come in very close to shore to neutralize or destroy enemy machine gun nests, mortar emplacements, and gun batteries that had not been eliminated by pre–H-hour bombardments. The invasions of North Africa, Sicily, and Salerno had also shown a continuing need for naval gunfire long after D-Day to support ground forces by neutralizing enemy tanks, mobile guns, or batteries camouflaged and hidden from aerial and other forms of reconnaissance.[68]

To what extent did the operation plan for naval gunfire support for Neptune/Overlord reflect the knowledge of amphibious warfare gained in the Mediterranean from 1942 to early 1944? As experience in the Mediterranean had clearly shown, sweeping enemy sea mines in the approaches, boat lanes, and transport and fire support areas had to be a priority in any amphibious operation. D-Day historian Stephen Ambrose has correctly pointed out that bombardment ships off Omaha and Utah "were at anchor because the swept area was too narrow to allow maneuvering, meaning the Navy regarded mines as more dangerous than the German batteries." His comment reflects the wartime experience of the U.S. Navy and Royal Navy prior to Operation Neptune, which confirmed that danger from sea mines far exceeded that of shell fire from fixed enemy gun batteries.[69]

Operation Neptune planners had every reason to be deeply concerned about the problem of sea mines and mine clearance. The Germans had been laying mines in the English Channel for most of the war, prompting Allied minesweepers to expend considerable effort to sweep them. Planners also knew that German mine-laying would be focused on possible beachheads along the French coast. "No weapon that the enemy might have employed before D day against our forces caused me more anxiety than the potentialities of minelaying," Admiral Ramsay wrote. "Mines were employed defensively on a considerable scale in the Bay of the Seine during the months prior to D-Day and caused the naval plan largely to be framed round the requirements for sweeping our forces through the enemy's minefields." Ramsay noted as well that the Germans had increased mine-laying efforts during the six weeks prior to D-Day using "aircraft on a scale which had not been attempted for over two years and introducing two new types of mines."

Realizing that minesweeping for Neptune would require a major effort and that the Americans needed most of their minesweepers for the Pacific War, planners had to rely primarily on British minesweepers and mine craft. In fact, the majority of the 302 fleet sweepers and mine craft for Neptune were British, the U.S Navy providing only 32 sweeps. The resources and planning devoted to minesweeping during Operation Neptune paid off, however. Although on D-Day, mines claimed PC-1261 and 16 landing craft, and may have struck *Corry* off Utah Beach, no warship fell victim to mines off Omaha, nor did enemy minefields compromise naval gunfire support as they had in the campaigns for Sicily and Salerno. Although some landing craft struck mines or mines attached to obstacles at Omaha, most of the vessels lost to mines were sunk or damaged in the period just following June 6, 1944. Hitler's refusal to allow the Germans to lay the new, very-difficult-to-sweep pressure mines contributed as well to the low figure of Allied ships mined during Operation Neptune.[70]

The difficulties facing the Americans at Omaha Beach cannot be traced to mines or to any one tactical failure, but to a combination of factors, including the decision to mount a daylight assault, the failure of the air forces to actually bomb Omaha Beach, the inherent difficulty in destroying encased shore batteries with ships' gunfire, the unexpected discovery of a veteran German division defending Omaha Beach, and the ineffectiveness of the specialized landing craft and loss in the rough seas of duplex drive tanks that planners counted upon for close-in gunfire support.

The decision by Neptune planners to mount a daylight assault preceded by air and naval bombardment represented a departure from every major Mediterranean operation to that point. Although American naval commanders in the Mediterranean had been advocating pre–H-hour naval bombardments since the Torch operation in November 1942, they had not received authorization to use pre-landing bombardment in any of the Mediterranean invasion prior to Normandy. As a result, they had little evidence of its effectiveness. The experience of gunfire support ships during Operation Torch had, however, shown that fixed shore batteries were difficult to destroy by naval gunfire alone, and Admiral Hall had warned that some enemy defenses would survive any pre-landing bombardment. Neptune planners failed to take seriously these warnings about the ineffectiveness of naval gunfire on fixed gun emplacements.

As this chapter has shown, on June 6, 1944, the pre–H-hour naval bombardment did not, in fact, knock out all of the German gun batteries and defenses capable of firing on Omaha Beach. Historians disagree as to the accuracy of the pre–H-hour naval bombardment at Omaha Beach. In his study of intelligence during World War II, F. H. Hinsley argued that the "[Neptune] bombardment was not marked by great accuracy; the naval gunfire scored few direct hits and the bombing of the beach, carried out in overcast conditions, was only partly successful." In his assessment of the 35-minute naval bombardment prior to H-hour at Omaha, however, naval historian Samuel Eliot Morison wrote that, "under the hazy and smoky conditions, the shooting was excellent." D-Day historian Stephen Ambrose also disputed any lack of accuracy from naval guns. He quoted a British seaman, Ian Michie, who was on the cruiser *Orion* on D-Day, June 6, 1944. "Our shooting was very good and direct hits were soon being recorded. We scored thirteen direct hits on the battery before shifting target." Others have also indicated that their ship scored direct hits. Ambrose, who visited the Normandy invasion sites, does not disagree. "They took many direct hits, dozens in some cases, but even the 14-inch shells failed to penetrate."

As F. H. Hinsley noted, "deficiencies in intelligence," in particular the failure of Allied intelligence to detect that the principal enemy gun positions on the beaches had been constructed to give enfilading fire, contributed to the problems on Omaha Beach. These gun batteries could not fire directly out to sea on warships or transports, but were placed to fire down the beaches from the flanks. "Had this been known the naval fire plan would have been differently framed," he wrote.[71]

Samuel Eliot Morison's arguments cast doubts on Adrian Lewis's suggestion that more heavy warships should have been included in the bombardment for Omaha. Morison argues that the anchorage and fire support areas off Omaha Beach were already "too crowded," limiting maneuvering room and restricting gunfire. "No more ships would have been used—there was too much crowding as it was," he wrote. Collisions between warships had, in fact, occurred during Mediterranean fire support missions. The destroyers *Roe* and *Swanson* collided off Licata in Operation Husky, and *Philadelphia* and *Laub* collided during naval gunfire support missions along the Italian coast in May 1944. In determining the number of fire support ships to assign to assault task forces, planners therefore had to consider the risk of collision as an important factor. Furthermore, little evidence suggests that more heavy warships off Omaha Beach would have been able to silence or destroy the majority of the casemated, fixed German batteries. Had H-hour been postponed to 0730, it might, as Samuel Eliot Morison suggested after the fact, have given "naval gunfire more time to play on beach defenses." Admiral John L. Hall had argued in vain for a two-hour naval bombardment, but this would not have eliminated the problem of warships using valuable time and ammunition to pound German guns on Pointe du Hoc and at the southern end of Utah Beach at St. Martin de Varreville, which were not, after all, even in place.[72]

The short duration of the pre-landing naval and air bombardment was a compromise between the need for neutralizing shore defenses and maintaining the element of surprise. The wisdom of landing the first Normandy assault waves in daylight, rather than under cover of darkness as the Army had long insisted, reduced the element of surprise and made the arriving troops and tanks more vulnerable to enemy gunfire. In his final report, Admiral Ramsay defended the decision to make a daylight landing in Normandy, which, he wrote, was "in accord with experience in the Pacific against strong defences, when the assaulting force possessed decisive naval and air superiority, and I am convinced that this is the correct answer under these conditions." He did admit, however, that planners made this decision prior to the discovery of beach obstacles on the Normandy landing sites and that there "was no general agreement as to a daylight attack." Two "vain efforts" made later to change it failed.

According to Admiral Ramsay, the Normandy bombardment ships were to begin their bombardment missions on D-Day when it was "light enough to spot his fall of shot visually" but "if possible, fire should be withheld until it was light enough for air observation." Allied experience in the Mediterranean had shown that daylight enhanced visual observation for naval gunfire support ships, an important element given that shore fire–control parties needed time to get ashore and set up. The Allies had also learned that the most reliable spotting came from trained pilots flying ship-borne catapult planes or single-seat fighters (Spitfires and P-51 Mustangs) flying from either carriers or land bases, preferably the latter because they had proven to be far less vulnerable to attack by enemy aircraft.[73]

Action reports by senior naval commanders in the Mediterranean had also warned that smoke and haze could be a negative factor in identifying targets, spotting the fall of shot, and avoiding firing on friendly troops. Fortunately, by June 1944, many Allied naval crews had gained experience in visual observation during Mediterranean operations. During the Normandy operation, in the smoke, without observation from aircraft or SFCPs, Allied gunnery personnel were also able to use similar visual observation of gun flashes.

Operations Torch, Husky, Avalanche, and Shingle had demonstrated that enemy shore batteries would, and could, fire on approaching transports, landing craft, and gunfire support ships. Furthermore, experience in the Mediterranean indicated that machine gun, mortar, and shell fire often increased after daylight when targets became more visible. On the positive side, these four major amphibious operations had also provided Allied warships with invaluable practice in returning fire from shore batteries and bombarding pre-selected fixed enemy positions, as well as demonstrating the effectiveness of American 6″ cruisers and of modern destroyers with 5″/38-caliber guns against shore batteries, pillboxes, tanks, and other enemy defenses. The Torch operation had encouraged the Navy to include ships like *Brooklyn, Philadelphia, Boise,* and *Savannah* in the next three amphibious operations, along the north coast of Sicily, and in support of the breakout from Anzio along the Italian coast. These amphibious operations gave ample evidence that destroyers could close the beaches and knock out specific targets using aerial observation, information from SFCP or army units, or visual observation.

The effectiveness of naval gunfire support in the Mediterranean may well have encouraged some Neptune planners to assume they had sufficient fire support off Omaha Beach. Admiral Hall, who felt strongly that he did not have enough firepower for the operation, also had enough confidence in the ability of American destroyers to argue forcibly for the inclusion of more destroyers in the op plan for Neptune. His faith in them was born out during the struggle for Omaha Beach.[74]

Fire support lessons learned in the Mediterranean taught the Allies that the critical time in an amphibious operation is the first few hours after H-hour, when assault forces might have to secure the beachhead without adequate support from their own artillery and tanks and before SFCPs could get ashore and set up to request gunfire support. The Sicily landings demonstrated the value of close-in gunfire support, and they strongly indicated the need for further development and production of small, shallow-draft, armed craft like the LCT(R)s, LCFs, and LCGs. Prototype LCT(R)s had proven useful in Operation Husky, which also revealed that rocket fire could be inaccurate and depended on the crews of the individual LCT(R) firing on the correct beach at the assigned time.

Furthermore, by design, the LCT(R)s's 5" rockets could not neutralize or destroy machine gun nests, mortar emplacements, and other fixed defenses. "Rockets cannot destroy a pill box, for example," notes Larry Carr, who commanded the rocket flotilla at Normandy. "It took 26 seconds for rockets to travel 3500 yards and the only power it had was the explosion itself. Therefore we could only hope to destroy light beach defenses such as barbed wire, mines, etc." The Navy did expect rocket barrages to stun enemy troops. "Each ship fired 1044 5" projectiles in a matter of three minutes which was expected to have a deadly effect on the enemy troops," Larry Carr explained. As promising as rocket barrages seemed to naval commanders in 1944, experience in the Mediterranean had clearly indicated that they were not always 100 percent accurate or effectively employed. Yet Allied planners expected rockets to clear broad expanses of beach, such as those at Omaha and Utah Beach in Normandy. On the other hand, eyewitnesses and some military historians have underestimated the effectiveness of rocket barrages on D-Day in Normandy, which, according to Larry Carr and the official report, fell for the most part on the beaches and provided good cover for the infantry. It should also be noted that the most damaging enemy resistance on Omaha Beach came not from barbed wire, beach obstacles, land mines, or even small arms, but, as Captain Lorenzo Sabin himself has written, from "machine-gun fire from pillboxes . . . accompanied by intermittent artillery fire coming from emplacements in openings in the hill." Captain Sabin also recalled that "mortar fire was deadly accurate causing by far the greater part of our casualties." Rockets were not designed to be effective against any of these targets.[75]

Allied plans to bring standard tanks and DD tanks to shore in LCTs on June 6, 1944, with the first wave to provide close-in fire support before the arrival of division artillery met with mixed results. Many of the DDs foundered and sank in the rough seas, and quite a few of those who crawled onto the beaches did not survive withering enemy shell and mortar fire. Without artillery or tank support, soldiers wading ashore and trying to cross the wide, open expanse of Omaha Beach made easy targets for

German gun batteries, machine guns, mortars, and small arms. Allied aircraft did lay smokescreens to cover ships and landing craft, but coverage was uneven. In some cases, smoke from smokescreens or naval shells setting fire to grasses obscured the navigational marks on the beaches to arriving landing craft crews. Although small armed landing craft such as LCGs lay offshore to provide close-in support, their gun crews failed to locate targets in the smoke and haze, were afraid to fire and hit friendly troops, or found that their LCGs beyond the range of enemy batteries on the cliffs and behind the beachhead. Reports from the Mediterranean landings may have led Neptune planners to expect more from these small craft than they could deliver. Off Omaha Beach, some LCGs did fire before the arrival of the first waves of the troops. For example, LCG-687 fired 220 rounds on the eastern flank of Omaha Beach; LCG-811 and PC-553 fired on enemy pillboxes at Omaha; and PC-567 fired on pillboxes behind a seawall. In the Mediterranean, LSTs armed with 40mm Bofors guns had actually fired on German beach defenses and even tanks, but with no LSTs scheduled to land during the first few hours of the Normandy assault, their guns were not available to suppress any German fire.[76]

In addition to the development of small, close-in support craft, naval gunfire support in the Mediterranean had seen significant improvements in the training and combat experience of SFCPs, including the development of special grid maps for spotting of fire, improved radios (which in the earlier landings had often malfunctioned), the addition of walkie-talkies for fire parties, the inclusion of army artillery officers on naval fire support ships, and the assignment of SFCP personnel to airborne units. Furthermore, British forward observation officers had worked in the Mediterranean with U.S. Navy fire support ships and vice versa. They had also learned to cooperate with Army artillery observers and Piper Cub aircraft pilots—all useful experience for the Normandy campaign. Senior naval officers in the Mediterranean had repeatedly recommended more training and rehearsals as keys to successful amphibious operations. Allied planners for Operation Neptune had obviously taken these recommendations seriously for naval forces assigned to the cross-channel attack benefited from longer training periods and more realistic rehearsals than those in prior operations in the Mediterranean theater. Tragically, however, in April 1944, during one of the full-scale rehearsals off Slapton Sands (Exercise Tiger), German E-boats managed to attack and torpedo three LSTs, killing more than 700 men.

In the 18 months prior to Neptune, Allied navies had also developed better tactics and acquired additional ships to protect their amphibious forces against enemy air, submarine, and E-boat attacks. Experience in the Mediterranean had made Allied officials keenly aware of the risk to ships and landing craft from air attack, including the new FX-1400 glide bombs, and resulted in new radio-jamming techniques, increased reliance on smokescreens, and other defensive tactics. To conceal their warships from naval gunfire, fire from shore batteries, or air attack, the British had developed the tactic of laying smokescreens. The U.S. Navy had adopted the British use of smokescreens during Operations Husky and then used it extensively during Operation Avalanche and throughout the Anzio campaign. By 1944, most Allied ships and even smaller craft had Bessler smoke generators; and off Anzio, the Navy had instituted a smoke patrol to lay smoke during pre-dawn and dusk periods. Yet off Normandy, the use of smokescreens was only partly effective in protecting Allied ships from attack, as the fate of the *Corry* illustrates. Fortunately, unlike in the Mediterranean theater, the Allies possessed air superiority over weakened German air forces during the Normandy operation.

The risk of submarine and E-boat attack to Neptune shipping remained, however, a real concern, especially after the losses inflicted on Allied landing craft during the rehearsal off Slapton Sands. Axis submarines had accounted for numerous losses of Allied warships, transports, landing craft, and cargo vessels in the Mediterranean, and Italian MAS boats and German E-boats had also harassed Allied shipping in that theater. German E-boats did make a halfhearted attack against the eastern flank early on D-Day, sinking a destroyer, the Norwegian *Svenner*. In air attacks on June 7–8, 1944, a radio-controlled glide bomb hit and sank the U.S.S. *Meredith*, but the real danger from German E-boats came in the days after the invasion when they torpedoed the LST-538 and sank LST-376, LST-314, and the tug *Partridge*. Mines claimed the destroyer *Rich* and the netlayer *Minster*, and they damaged the sweeper *Tide* and LST-499. A mine struck *Glennon*, later polished off by a German shore battery.[77]

And, finally, during Operation Neptune, commanders offshore lacked accurate information about the situation on the beaches, especially Omaha Beach, because of communication difficulties caused by casualties to shore fire control parties and radios. Hoping, even assuming, that the pre–H-hour naval bombardment, rocket barrages, and air bombardment would have silenced most of the Germans defenses, Allied planners had ordered fire support destroyers to cease firing at H-hour and not to resume until they had contacted their SFCPs. A few destroyers did not heed the cease-fire order but, seeing troops pinned down on the beaches, visually located targets and opened fire. However, uncertain about how much opposition the troops were encountering on Omaha, senior commanders delayed bringing in more fire support until Captain Harry Sanders realized the gravity of the situation and ordered his destroyers to close the beach and support the embattled troops on Omaha. In the meantime, some Army commanders on the beaches had found soft spots in the enemy's defenses and had decided to scale the cliffs rather than move inland as planned through the heavily defended draws.

In conclusion, as this reexamination of naval gunfire support for Utah and Omaha Beaches in Operation Neptune/Overlord has shown, the Allies benefited considerably from the experience of amphibious warfare in the Mediterranean. Some of the recommendations and lessons learned in the Mediterranean, especially in regard to the need for pre-landing naval bombardment, better training and rehearsals, the increased use of smokescreen and jamming of radio-controlled enemy bombs, and the use of trained aerial spotter fighter aircraft, were heeded; others were not. Allied planners for Operation Neptune failed to take into account the difficulties encountered by gunfire support ships in destroying, or even scoring direct hits, on gun emplacements in the Mediterranean and the inherent weaknesses in close-in support craft such as LCT(R)s, LCGs, and LCFs. These, coupled with the failure of the air forces to drop bombs on Omaha Beach, the difficulties faced by DD tanks and other landing craft in the rough seas, and the unexpected arrival of a veteran German division to defend the beach, made the struggle for Omaha Beach a bloody one indeed.

NOTES

1. Roger Hill, *Destroyer Captain: Memoirs of the War at Sea 1942–45* (London: Grafton, 1986), 249. Major sources for Operation Neptune include *The Invasion of Normandy: Operation Neptune, United States Naval Administration in World War II, Commander U.S. Naval Forces Europe*, Vol. V, Part IV, Neptune Operations Plans (Washington, D.C.: U.S. Navy, 1945); Samuel Eliot Morison, *Invasion of France and Germany*, vol. IX (Urbana: University of Illinois, 2002), *History of United States Naval Operations in World War II*; Gordon A. Harrison, *Cross-Channel Attack: The European Theater of Operations, U.S. Army in World War II* (Center

For Military History, U.S. Army, Washington D.C.: 1993); Stephen Ambrose, *D-Day* (New York: Simon & Schuster, 1995); Joseph Balkoski, *Omaha Beach* (Mechanicsburg, Penn.: Stackpole Books, 2006) and *Utah Beach* (Mechanicsburg, Penn.: Stackpole Books, 2006); Adrian Lewis, *Omaha Beach: Flawed Victory* (Chapel Hill, N.C.: The University of North Carolina Press, 2003); Paul Stillwell, ed., *Assault on Normandy* (Annapolis, Md.: Naval Institute Press, 1994); and John T. Mason, ed., *The Atlantic War Remembered* (Annapolis, Md.: Naval Institute Press, 1991). In his study of the Allied landings on Omaha Beach, Adrian Lewis argues that, "For the Normandy invasion, the Allied commanders ignored tested doctrine and thus ignored the cumulative body of knowledge in amphibious operations gained through hard fought battles in North Africa, Sicily, and Tarawa." In Chapter 3 of his book, Adrian Lewis elaborates on the cumulative knowledge of amphibious operations and doctrine gained in the Mediterranean and at Tarawa in the Pacific theater, but he does not focus on naval gunfire support.

2. Morison, *The Invasion of France and Germany*, XI, Appendix I. Of the 6,939 ships, merchant vessels, and landing ships and craft participating in Operation Neptune, 79 percent were British or Canadian, 16.5 percent American, and 4.5 percent other Allies. His 4 LCGs, 13 LCTs, 12 LCS, and 20 LCPs would provide close-in gunfire support. Other specialized landing craft accompanied the Minesweeper Group, Beach Red, and Beach Green Assault Groups. In addition, both task forces for Utah and Omaha Beaches had a screen of destroyers, destroyer escorts, frigates, and trawlers to provide defense against enemy submarines, to furnish anti-aircraft protection, and possibly to serve as reserve gunfire support vessels.

3. Morison, XI, 95; Balkoski, *Utah Beach*, 54; *The Invasion of Normandy: Operation Neptune*, 317; Harrison, *Cross-Channel Attack, Chapter VII: German Defense Measures, 1944*. These deadly "88's" had plagued previous Allied ships and landing craft in previous amphibious operations in the Mediterranean. According to the Neptune plan, the object of the bombardment was to neutralize coastal defense and inland batteries, especially those capable of bringing fire to bear on the approach channels and transport areas; to destroy beach defenses during the final approach and assault; and to support the army after the assault by engaging hostile batteries, enemy formations, or defended areas.

4. John R. Blackburn, "The Best Seat for a Really Big Show," in Paul Stillwell, ed., 99–100; Fred D. King, "The Quest of the U.S.S. *Quincy*," http://www.uss quincy.com; Admiral Alan G. Kirk, "Command from the Flagship *Augusta*," in Mason, ed., *The Atlantic War Remembered*, 366. *Quincy* was armed with nine 8" guns and had a secondary battery of 12 5" guns and an array of AA weapons.

5. Ambrose, *D-Day*, 267; John R. Blackburn, "The Best Seat for a Really Big Show," in Paul Stillwell, ed., 99–100; D-Day: Europe's Liberators, http://www .portsmouth.co.uk/. Alan Pile, a crewman onboard H.M.S. *Hawkins*, recalled. "We had guns from 1919 with superb 1944 crews." *Hawkins* had opened fire at 0538 on a battery of four 155mm guns across the Carentan estuary, securing several hits. At 0600, she shifted her guns to Pointe du Hoc. The *Hawkins* was, indeed, a World War I vintage cruiser built at Chatham dockyard and completed in 1919. In 1944, she had a crew of 749 men commanded by Captain J. W. Jocelyn, DSC. In March of 1944, *Hawkins* was recalled from the Indian Ocean to England to be refitted with enhanced radar and close-range AA armament. According to a history of the cruiser, "The new crew worked up quickly in May and June on the coast of Northern Ireland and South Devon to provide the additional fire support needed when the operation [Neptune] was increased to a five division landing." H.M.S. *Hawkins* in http://wartimehistory.com/. *Quincy* was also firing on the beaches. "The belch of nitrous brown smoke and yellow flames from the *Quincy*'s two forward turrets gave us the reassuring feeling that at least we were in the fray and doing something about those pesky gun emplacements that were firing at us," John Blackburn wrote.

6. Morison, XI, 96; Blackburn, in Stillwell ed., 102–03; Fred King, "The Quest of the U.S.S. *Quincy*," diary entry for June 6, 1944; Balkoski, *Utah Beach*, 80. *Quincy*'s action report states that, "at 0530 the ship was taken under fire by shore battery 13A. Four enemy salvoes landed 2,000 to 2,500 yards short." "Her main battery commenced fire at 0550 on Target 20, an artillery headquarters."

7. King diary entry, June 6, 1944; Blackburn, Stillwell ed., 102–03. "About 50 friendly planes from England now overhead," Fred King wrote. "Chaplain says they are P-38s, an air umbrella. Says also that all the ships are pouring shells into the beach and that is an all-American team in a single wing-back formation; the NEVADA, QUINCY, & TUSCALOOSA in tailback position."

8. Moe Vestuti, interview, Edward R. Murrow, "Captain Hoffman CBS Radio Interview, June 9, 1944," in http://www.uss-corry-dd463.com/d-day_u-boat_ photos/d-day_accounts.htm; Thomas B. Allen, "The Gallant Destroyers of D-day," *Naval History Magazine*, June 2004: 2. From the cruiser *Quincy*, John Blackburn was watching *Corry*'s ordeal. The *Quincy* was then ordered to fire smoke projectiles. "It took us a while to start blasting out the 5″ white phosphorous shells that might provide something of a curtain for the stricken destroyer," he recalled. "We had to empty the antiaircraft shells from our ammo hoists and bring up the white phosphorous from the magazine and lower handling room."

Hoffman also wrote, "When all were clear I stepped into the water, but the current kept pleating the swimmers around the ship, during which time they were subjected to endless shelling, which further increased our losses."

9. Edward R. Murrow, "Captain Hoffman CBS Radio Interview, June 9, 1944," in http://www.uss-corry-dd463.com/d-day_u-boat_photos/d-day_accounts .htm; Ambrose, 266; Allen, "Gallant Destroyers of D-day," *Naval History,* June 2004; Hoffman interview, usscorry-dd463.com/d-day; Blackburn, in Stillwell ed., 104; Morison, XI, 96, 106, 108. Lieutenant Commander Hoffman was the godson of Admiral George Dewey. Robert Powell spoke too soon, for just then, a large-caliber enemy shell landed near the destroyer. As Thomas B. Allen wrote in his article about destroyers at Normandy, "The ship began evasive maneuvering at high speed." Looking down, Powell "could see the shells hitting the water where we would have been if we had not made a turn." Thomas B. Allen: "They claimed *Corry* hit a mine." Morison wrote that *Corry* "struck a mine amidships." "The explosion almost cut her in two." Ambrose also wrote that *Corry* hit a mine. However, Hoffman in his interview, the action report, and the *Corry* Web site all claim she was hit directly by large-caliber shells. Her action report stated she was "hit by two 6–8-inch projectiles from a land battery at approximately 0630." Witnesses testified that the explosion threw the men on the bridge backward and that a mine exploding under the ship would have driven the middle of the ship upward. However, the official report went with the mine explanation, some believe because Allied officials wished to discredit German marksmanship. *Corry* survivors stated that at least ten men in the water were killed by enemy gunfire.

10. Ambrose, 267; Commodore James E. Arnold, "NOIC Utah," in Stillwell, ed., 89–91; Harrison, *Cross-Channel Attack,* 304; Morison, XI, 98; Balkoski, *Utah Beach,* 201–06. Balkoski says the LCT was LCT-593; Morison says it was LCT-597. Balkoski also claims 27 DDs came ashore. Harrison states that 28 DD tanks came ashore about 15 minutes late, "But, as it turned out, the assault troops had no immediate need for them."

11. Morison, XI, 98, 104–05; Arnold, in Stillwell, ed., 89–90; 104–06; Balkoski, *Utah Beach,* 83, 88–89, 180–84, 192. Balkoski argues that despite warnings, coxswain of landing craft did not take into account the strong current off Utah. Smoke and haze from the bombardments made identification of landmarks on the flat shore line at Utah Beach very difficult, and the main control vessel, PC-1261, hit a mine, taking her out of action. By the time *Glennon* arrived to relieve her at 1046, German gunners had been silenced, and she received only one call for fire. H.M.S. *Hawkins* claimed to have put two batteries at Grandcamp Maisy out of action on D-Day, but according to the "Atlantic Wall in Normandy" Web

site (http://www.atlantikwall.org.uk/omaha.htm), "the three casemates show no sign of damage from the front, only superficial damage from the east."

12. Morison, XI, 104; Fred King, "U.S.S. Quincy": At 0615, King wrote, "The 5″ battery now starts in earnest, rocking the ship from side to side as they all fire at once. Mounts 1, 3 5 & 6, total of 8 guns." "0835: Just made direct hit on our number three target on first salvo. 1135: A lull in the fighting since early this morning. Just announced that a shore battery that had been firing on us has been 'taken care of.' We only fire intermittently now, and have done so for the past three hours or more."

13. Charles Rozier USNA site; Morison, XI, 104, 106; *The Invasion of Normandy: Operation Neptune*, 31; Captain John A. Moreno, "The Death of Admiral Moon," in Stillwell, ed., 228. The Allies had 104 single-seat fighters available on D-Day. Morison claims *Nevada*, *Black Prince*, and *Erebus* continued to fire for 50 minutes after H-hour. However, according to Captain John Moreno, at H-hour, *Erebus* "trained one turret, fired one salvo, and then disaster struck. One gun failed to return to battery. She was loaded up with prisoners of war and returned to home waters, her crew completely disconsolate." *Tuscaloosa*, for example, expended 487 rounds of 8″ on D-Day in 16 shoots. Although enemy batteries tried to hit the cruiser *Tuscaloosa*, they never came closer than 300 yards from her. The battleship *Nevada* got off 337 rounds of 14″ and another 2.693 rounds of 5″ shells.

14. Vice Admiral C. F. Bryant, "Battleship Commander," in Stillwell, ed., 183; Morison, XI, 102, 106; Balkoski, *Utah Beach*, 185, 312. Balkoski attributed the Allied success at Utah in large measure to "overwhelming numbers and terrain unfavorable to the defender." He also noted that the 4th Division was "one of the most highly trained outfits in the U. S. Army in the spring of 1944." The German 709th Division was "a mediocre outfit with questionable morale and limited mobility, spread so thinly over a coastal sector more than thirty miles in length that only a portion of a single battalion received the brunt of the Americans' ferocious assault on the morning of June 6."

15. Bryant, "Battleship Commander," in Stillwell, ed., 183; Peter Walker, H.M.S. *Bellona*: Action on D-day, WW2 BBC People's War, February 28, 2004; Ambrose, 262; Peter Elliot, *Allied Minesweeping in World War 2* (Annapolis, Md.: Naval Institute Press, 1979), 115–16. Admiral Bryant later recalled, "Omaha Beach shelved sharply upward toward a road, and then cliffs rose two hundred feet to the countryside. On the far right side of Omaha was a high cliff on which the enemy batteries were believed to be located. These were the primary target of the larger naval vessels; the destroyers close to shore had as their assignment the machine gun emplacements in the cliffs." The modified *Dido*-class cruiser

H.M.S. *Bellona* was part of Bryant's bombardment group. Peter Walker was an Asdic (sonar) operator on the *Bellona*. "Eventually we were briefed about D-Day and the ships proceeded to Normandy. As soon as we cleared harbour, paravanes [mine countermeasure devices] were streamed, and then as we got into the Channel we went to actions stations. I was the Action Lt. Operator on the Asdic (sonar) and as far I can remember operated in the mine detecting mode as we approached the beaches. *Bellona*'s duty was to support OMAHA beach, the American sector."

16. Morison, XI, 121–22; William Kirkland, *Destroyers at Normandy* (Norfolk, Va.: Naval Historical Foundation, 1994), 22; Balkoski, *Omaha Beach*, 83; John A. Lorelli, *To Foreign Shores* (Annapolis, Md.: Naval Institute Press, 1995), 227. According to Morison, Vol. XI, 122: ". . . the volume here [at Omaha] and elsewhere was not enough to attain the desired results, because not enough time was allowed of the bombardment—the Army did not want it to start before daylight." Once again, as they had in the Mediterranean theater, Army commanders had refused to agree to a daylight naval bombardment. Kirkland noted that not a single protected battery suffered serious damage form this pre-landing bombardment.

17. Kirkland, 22–23; Davis Howes, "Dread of the Unknown," in Stillwell, ed., 114–15; Edward B. Billingsley, "The *Emmons* Saga," U.S.S. *Emmons* Web site; Adrian Lewis, 17. Lewis's diagram of the boat lanes and fire support ships is helpful but not complete. *Emmons, Frankford, Baldwin, Harding, Thompson*, and *Bellona* are missing. *Endicott* did not take part; *Emmons* replaced her. Thirteen minutes prior to the scheduled pre-landing bombardment, a German shore battery east of Port en Bessin shelled the U.S.S. *Emmons*, straddling her with approximately 10 3″ or 4″ shells. The destroyer returned fire, silencing the battery, at least for awhile.

18. Vice Admiral Carleton Bryant, "Battleship Commander," in Stillwell, ed., e-mail letter to author from Larry Carr, July 26, 2005. Admiral Kirk's flagship, *Augusta*, also fired on D-Day morning commencing at 0618, 21 rounds on one target, another 30 rounds on another target at 0643. See *USS Augusta* War Diary, June 6, 1944, on the U.S.S. *Augusta* Web site (www.internet-esq.com/ussaugusta/index.htm).

19. Peter Walker, H.M.S. *Bellona*; BBC Wars and Conflict, World War Two, http://www.bbc.co.uk/history/worldwars/wwtwo/; email letter to author from Larry Carr, July 26, 2005; Balkoski, *Omaha Beach*, 84; Lewis, *Omaha Beach: Flawed Victory*, 218–19; Morison, XI, 122–23; Lorenzo Sabin, "Close-in Support at Omaha Beach," in Stillwell, ed., 59. PC-567 also fired on a pillbox behind a

seawall, and two tanks on board the LCT-2050 fired 300 rounds as well. Sabin also wrote that "due to excessive dispersion, however, the rockets inflicted very little damage on the enemy." He did say they were a morale booster to the assault troops. Sabin also blamed late arrivals of LCT(R)s for a lack of training. In his book, Adrian Lewis also concludes that the rockets failed to destroy any beach obstacles, mines, or German defenses.

20. Balkoski, *Omaha Beach*, 85–96; Morison, XI, 124; Harrison, 300–01. According to Harrison, the medium bombers bombing Utah Beach had, "slightly better results, although a third of all bombs fell seaward of the high-water mark, and many of the selected targets were not located by pilots."

21. Balkoski, *Omaha Beach*, 103, 106; Lewis, 250–53; Commander LCT-6 Flotilla 12 and 26 action report of LCT 20, June 29, 1944; Commander Group 35 LCT-6 Flotilla 12 action report, July 1, 1944; Harrison, 309; Morison, XI, 134. Prior to D-Day, Lieutenant Rockwell made a study of DD tanks, found that they were "basically sound," but recommended an escort vessel with the most recent navigational equipment escort them to within 1,000 yards of the beaches, that the LCTs should not carry additional cargo, and that all LCT(DD) crews should be trained thoroughly. According to the op plan, the first wave was to leave the line of departure, marked by subchasers (SCs) and patrol craft (PCs) about 4,000 yards off Omaha Beach, and guided by other small craft make their run into the beach. After touchdown at 0631, the first waves of troops would be followed immediately by 14 UDT teams tasked to blast lanes through the beach obstacles, allowing succeeding waves of landing craft to come in with the tide and beach. At 0700, one half-hour after the arrival of the first wave, the second wave would come ashore followed every 10 minutes by the remainder of the assault units.

22. Jimmy Green, BBC Wars and Conflict, World War Two, http://www.bbc .co.uk/history/worldwars/wwtwo/; Morison, XI, 132, 134; Kirkland, 29; Balkoski, *Omaha Beach*, 109. Green recalled, "in two columns of three like Nelson at Trafalgar with LCA 910 in the head of the starboard column and my second in command Sub Lieutenant Tony Drew at the head of the port column." Morison says that German gunners took aim at the tanks that reached the beach and on the vulnerable landing craft, hit two, and also destroyed several tanks. According to Balkoski, LCT(A)-2124 was hit by a mortar shell, which blew her ramp off and LCT-2229 flooded and sank two miles off Dog Red. When a German shore battery also took pot shots at the U.S.S. *Carmick* at 0647, she quickly silenced it.

23. Harrison, 313–15; Morison, XI, 136; Joseph H. Gibbons interview, Box 11, World War Interviews, Operational Archives Naval Historical Center. Gibbons's

demolition units suffered 41 percent casualties on D-Day. Half of the 16 Army-Navy special engineer task force assault teams got to the shore 10 or more minutes late because of delays in loading from LCTs to LCMs. Only six teams made the beach in "working condition," only five teams hit their appointed sectors, and artillery or mortar fire caused heavy casualties. *Omaha Beachhead* (June 6–13, 1944); The Landings: Center for Military History, 1994, 43.

24. Robert Adams, James Argo, in Wartime Memories Project—The Second World War—Day by Day," http://www.wartimememoriesproject.com/ww2/day-by-day/1944-06-06.php; Lieutenant Dean Rockwell, Commander Group 35, LCT-6 Flotilla 12 action report, July 14, 1944; Harrison, 315; Morison, XI, 137–38. "Our commanding officer was H.H. Montgomery, Lieutenant USNR," Argo wrote. "As I recall, our LCI's ship's complement included four officers and between 25–28 enlisted men." Joseph McCann was a 15-year-old coxswain of a landing craft bringing first wave troops to Easy Red Beach on D-Day morning. He beached his craft, offloaded the troops, and quickly withdrew. "If I hadn't been prepared through North Africa, Sicily, Salerno, I probably couldn't have faced up to that," McCann recalled (*LST Scuttlebutt*, November/December 1998, 37).

25. Balkoski, *Omaha Beach*, 228; Bryant, "Battleship Commander, in Stillwell, ed., 182. For example, on Dog Red Beach, the 2nd Battalion commander had no working radio to assist in rounding up his men.

26. Kirkland, 40–41, 46; Morison, XI, 144–47; Steve Zaloga, *Omaha Beach* (Westminster, Md.: Osprey Publishing, 2003), 64, 66; Edward F. Prados, ed., *Neptunus Rex* (New York: Presidio Press, 1998), 182–83; Ambrose, 386. *Carmick* also opened fire on two German strongpoints overlooking the base of the draw at Les Moulins where a small army detachment was trapped in a house. Seaman 1st Class Robert Giguerre came ashore with the 6th Naval Beach Battalion from LCI(L)-85 in the first wave on Omaha only to be pinned down by enemy fire from a large gun emplacements and two machine gun emplacements. Asked to assist in blowing a gap in an anti-tank ditch, he recalled, "In all I must have thrown six to eight grenades and then got the hell out of there in a hurry because a destroyer was coming in to start shelling the gun emplacement. The shelling from the destroyer just about buried the two machine gun emplacements with sand and mud."

27. Kirkland, 48. Howes, in Stillwell, ed., 114, Morison, XI, 146–48. Morison notes that only 20 percent of the naval fire support ships were used because of lack of information.

28. Balkoski, *Omaha Beach*, 118; Lewis, 242, 244; Jimmy Green, BBC People's War. One LCI(L) went to the wrong beach at Utah and had to return to Omaha.

29. Kirkland, 44, Lewis, 129; Bryant, "Battleship Commander, in Stillwell, 184; http://www.usstexasbb35.com/; Balkoski, 184; Morison, XI, 147–48; Ambrose, 384–85; *Frankford*'s war diary noted cryptically, "Throughout the morning and afternoon rendered direct fire support at targets of opportunity on beach DOG Red and DOG White." *Texas* turned her 14" guns on Pointe du Hoc while *Satterlee*'s guns pummeled the western flank and H.M.S. *Talybont* fired on machine gun nests and pillboxes between Pointe du Hoc and Pointe de la Percee. In position just 2,200 yards offshore, *Thompson* also participated in the pre-landing bombardment of enemy batteries on Pointe de la Perce.

30. Eric Brown, *The Seafire* (London: Allan, 1973), 63–64; Morison XI, 104. Lee on Solent's total for the day was 435 sorties. In the spring of 1944, No. 885 and 886 Squadrons were refitted with the first Seafire LIIIs and No. 808 and 897 Squadrons with Spitfire LVS's.

31. Peter Walker, H.M.S. *Bellona*; BBC Wars and Conflict, World War Two, www.bc.co.uk/history/war/dday/clockwatch_lowshtml; Edward Baxter Billilngsley, *The Emmons Saga: A History of the USS EMMONS (DD457-DMS22)* (iUniverse, 2005). There was at least one incident, perhaps more, of friendly fire from destroyers trying to assist the troops by firing on targets but hitting some of Major Thomas Dallas's 1st Battalion 116th RCT, 29th Infantry Division troops just west of Vierville draw, see Balkoski, *Omaha Beach*, 324–25. Peter Walker also recalled, "On several occasions *Bellona* returned to Plymouth to get more ammunition and change the gun barrels because of wear." Walker also noted, "At night *Bellona* went close inshore and did the night firings. The Gunners' Mate said that the ammunition was of recent design and was flashless. Gun flashes from the older ships would have given their position away."

32. Morison, IX, 150, 152, 320; Balkoski, *Omaha Beach*, 237; Lewis, 29. First Division artillery finally began landing at 1600, and the 26th RCT came ashore at 1930 on D-Day. H.M.S. *Glasgow* expended 505 rounds, aided by plane spot; *Montcalm* fired at various targets on D-Day, and *Arkansas* fired a total of 350 rounds.

33. Commander Eleventh Amphibious Force, J. L. Hall, Amphibious Assault Operations, February 25, 1944, Box 1, RG 313, N.A.; Morison, Vol. XI, 143, 150; Balkoski, *Omaha Beach*, 57–58; Ambrose, 269; F. H. Hinsley, vol. III, Pt. 2, 130; McGeorge Bundy, "Ultra Warnings," and Sabin, "Close-in Support at Omaha Beach," in Stillwell, ed., 30, 61. Observers offshore found the bombardment and rockets impressive, but the resulting smoke and haze obscured the enemy fire on the approaching landing craft and on the beaches. Communication with

SFCPs and others on Omaha Beach was spotty, and at first, Admiral Bryant did not realize the perilous situation on Omaha. On D-Day, Admiral Kirk sent a boatload of officers including McGeorge Bundy in toward the beaches "for a look." Bundy did not observe very much and told Kirk that the others were giving him more information than they actually had. Moving to within a 500 yards of shore, about H plus 5 hours, Captain Lorenzo Sabin observed the deadly accurate mortar and machine gun fire on the beaches and asked permission from Admiral Hall to lay down another rocket barrage, but Hall refused.

34. Williamson Murray and Allan R. Millett, *A War to Be Won: Fighting the Second World War* (Cambridge, Mass.: Harvard University Press, 2001), p. 419; Harrison, 161–65. According to World War II historians Murray and Millett, Admiral Ramsay and Generals Eisenhower and Bradley do not appear to have been particularly interested in lessons learned in the Pacific. In the spring of 1944, General George C. Marshall, U.S. Army Chief of Staff, sent Major General Charles Cortlett from the Pacific to advise Bradley and other senior commanders about the experience gained in the assaults on Attu and Kwajalein. Corlett received a less than enthusiastic reception. As Murray and Millett concluded, "None of the senior U.S. commanders, including Eisenhower and Bradley, displayed the slightest interest in learning anything about his experiences in the Pacific. In fact, prevailing attitude was that anything that had happened in the Pacific was 'strictly bush league stuff' of no use to those planning operations in the European Theater." It is interesting to note that General Corlett expressed concern about the lack of fire support in the plans for Neptune. He also told senior commanders that they had underestimated the ammunition required to support the invasion.

35. Admiral Alan G. Kirk, "Command from the Flagship *Augusta*," in Mason, ed., 354; Harrison, 164. Harrison acknowledges that in January 1944, Generals Eisenhower and Montgomery had to go back and pick up the planning process where COSSAC had left it in July, but they had "an accumulated mass of special studies which greatly facilitated the problems of revising the master plan and preparing its detailed unit field orders." In his final report, Admiral Ramsay acknowledged the difficulty of joint planning and the view of the Americans that he had exercised too much control over the process. "I am aware that the U.S. Naval authorities had to exercise considerable restraint in submitting to a degree of control by superior authority on a level higher than that to which they were accustomed," Ramsay wrote, but he was unrepentant. "No argument, however, that has been produced since the operation has led me to change my opinion

that full coordination in detail was necessary on the highest naval level," Supplement to the *London Gazette*, October 30, 1947, 5110.

36. Com Task Force 34 serial 00241 Nov. 28, 1942, Operation Torch, Box 135, RG 38, National Archives; CincMed serial 00200 30 March 1943, Center and Eastern Naval Task Forces, Box 1704, RG 38, National Archives; Morison, *History of United States Naval Operations in World War Two*, Vol.. II, *Operations in North African Waters*, 36–40.

37. Tomblin, *With Utmost Spirit: Allied Naval Operations in the Mediterranean, 1942–1945* (Lexington: University Press of Kentucky, 2004), chap. 3; George F. Howe, *Northwest Africa: Seizing the Initiative in the West, U.S Army in World War II, Part Two* (Washington, D.C.: Center of Military History, U.S. Army, 1991).

38. CTF 81 (DIME) Rear Admiral John L. Hall report of Operation Husky, app. D, Lessons, Box 295, RG 38, N.A.; Harrison, 189; Lewis, 74; Tomblin, chap. 7, Conclusion, 474–75. Although fire support ships in Admiral John L. Hall's American sector at Sicily "were able to move about in their areas at will unhindered by Coastal batteries," Operation Husky convinced Hall that silencing enemy batteries "by air or other action is a prerequisite." In his study, Harrison admits that there was doubt among Neptune planners that the plan had adequate naval fire support or "whether naval fire could neutralize enemy defenses to an extent that would 'reasonably assure the success of an assault without the cover of darkness.'"

39. Lieutenant Harrie James, Observations on Avalanche, Box 69, RG 38, N.A; Lewis, 79, 82–85. According to Gordon Harrison, 188–89, based on the experience of night landings in the Mediterranean, the Army initially favored a night landing for Overlord. New considerations such as the slight probability of achieving tactical surprise, enemy radar along the French coast, and the desire of the Navy to have daylight for visual observation for fire support ships, prompted planners to settle on an assault soon after first light.

40. CTG 81, John L. Hall, Box 295, 302, RG 38; Tomblin, chap. 10. In his action report after Avalanche, Hall wrote that the night landing proved its worth and recommended that "night landings continue whenever possible to minimize the effect of well directed enemy coast defense fire." He did, however, also recommend "That prior to such landing the entire beach be covered by adequate naval gunfire."

41. TG 34.8 a.r., Torch, Box 135, RG 38, N.A.; CTG 34.0, Box 138, RG 45, N.A.; U.S.S. *Mayrant* a.r., Box 135, RG 38, N.A. American warships did experience some difficulties with radars, fire control equipment, and communications during Torch. U.S.S. *Mayrant's* skipper recommended that her fire direction radar,

control, and indicator unit be relocated to keep it clear of gun blasts. The first salvo of *Massachusetts*'s 16" guns knocked power out to the Mk4 director radar and then at 0930 power to all radars. Also fumes from lack of ventilation in gun turrets caused some crewmen to fall asleep. In his report, CTG 34.1 noted that "radar sets were all too touchy."

42. CTG 34.9 Capt. Robert Emmet, Commander Center Attack Group, 30 Nov. 1942, Box 137, RG 38, N.A; Lewis, 73–74; Major General Donald M. Weller, "The Development of Naval Gunfire Support in World War II," in Lieutenant Colonel Merrill L. Bartlett, ed., *Assault from the Sea* (Annapolis, Md.: Naval Institute Press, 1993), 269. In his study, Weller argues, "In the North African operations counter-battery fire was the major contribution of supporting ships." Lewis correctly notes that the army ignored Admiral Hewitt's report about the value of naval gunfire support.

43. Morison, II, 149; CTG 34.10, Box 138, RG 45, N.A.; *Philadelphia* a.r., Box 1318, RG 38, N.A. Later inspection of the area showed many shell craters. Hendren wrote, "As an example the battery of three 155 mm guns south of Safi, together with its trench system and underground ammunition storage, embraced an area of approx. 25,000 square feet. The gunpits themselves each embrace an area of approx. 200 square feet or a total of 600 sq. ft. Since the pattern of a 6"/47 salvo at 12,000 yds is approx. 450 feet, it can be readily seen that with perfect fire control and perfect spotting the chance of getting a direct hit is largely a matter of chance. Likewise, since all of the gun and operating mechanism except the muzzle of the gun are below ground level, fragmentation from near misses is not likely to do serious damage to the gun or to personnel in the gun pit. Firing at closer ranges . . . will flatten the trajectory and render a direct hit still more difficult."

44. Morison, II, 76; CTG 34.10, Box 138, RG 38, N.A. Admiral Hewitt had concerns about the amount of armor-piercing (AP) ammunition left in case the French sortied from Dakar to attack invasion shipping. At midday on November 8, *Wichita* had only 20 percent of her AP ammunition remaining, *Massachusetts* just 53 percent. Expenditure of ammunition during naval battles was an issue and argued for a large supply train in future operations. This led to the organization of ammunition depots in North Africa and to the forward deployment of the ammunition ship *Mt. Baker*. See the report of Captain Shepherd on Temporary Duty with Amphibious Forces U.S. Atlantic Fleet (TF 34) 24 Oct.–30 Nov. 1942 Cinclant, Box 3, RG 38, N.A.

45. Hubert Newton Johns to author November 28, 1996; Morison, IX, 27–28; Tomblin, 191–92; Lewis, 81. Johns was a signalman on HM LCF 12. He joined

her in April 1943. In his study, Lewis argues that the Allies did not achieve tactical surprise on D-Day for the Sicily landings, yet Samuel E. Morison (IX, 69–70) points out that although senior Axis commanders expected landings on the island and Axis aircraft did spot the Husky convoys, the poor weather and slow communications kept local Axis commanders in the dark. Furthermore, German search radar operators in Sicily saw the large blips of the approaching Allied convoys but did not report them until daybreak. Morison concludes, ". . . the defenders of Sicily were well enough surprised for Allied purposes."

46. Morison, IX, 104, Tomblin, 186; L. E. H. Maund, *Assault from the Sea* (London: Methuen, 1949), 89–90. *Abercrombie* was ordered to fire on an Axis observation post and strongpoint 8 miles inland, and her skipper, Captain Faulkner, was so eager that he shifted ballast to obtain a higher elevation for his 15" guns. The next day when Niscemi was taken, they found the monitor had hit the enemy HQ.

47. LCT(R)s: Alan Payne, "British Landing Craft of World War II," Naval Historical Society of Australia, www.navyhistory.org.au/british-landing-craft-of-world-war-ii/; LCT(Rocket) in Wikipedia; Tomblin, 418–19; Morison, IX, 129. Morison points out the early rocket craft were 36.8" Higgins craft carrying just two rocket projectiles. Alan Payne who worked on these craft says that Colonel Langley of Combined Operations came up with the design for the LCT rocket craft using 65-pound rockets. Later LCT(R)s were modified LCTs with a set of launchers for British RP-3 60-pound, 3" rockets mounted on the covered-over deck and LCT(R)s with 5" rockets. See Ken Ford, *D-Day 1944* (Westminster, Md.: Osprey Publishing, 2002), 10 for a photo of a LCT(R).

48. U.S.S. *Maddox*, a.r., Box 1219; *Boise*, a.r., Box 857, RG 38, N.A.; Morison, IX, 104–05; *Boise*, a.r, 0616 August 1943, Bombardment of Gela, Sicily, 10–12 July 1943, Box 857, RG 38. *Maddox*'s tragic loss underscored the fact that ships in the outer edge of the invasion area were actually at greater risk than those near shore protected by the umbrella of flak from other ships. According to Brigadier General Andrus some 500 yards away, the fire was terrific.

49. *Boise*, Box 857; Morison, IX, 103–04; *Shubrick*, a.r., Box 1433, RG 38, N.A.; H.M.S. *Abercrombie*, a.r. Box 1706, RG 38, N.A. Meanwhile, the destroyer *Shubrick* had been firing for one-half hour on 25 light Italian tanks rumbling down the Ponte Olivo road. Her SFCP efficiently directed the shoot and credited the destroyer with knocking out three tanks and slowing down the rest. American Rangers then engaged the Italian tanks in town.

50. CTG Joss sector, Box 304, RG 38, N.A.; CTG.86.2 Gaffi attack group a.r., Box 304, RG 38, N.A.; U.S.S. *Buck* a.r.; Morison, IX, 78–79, 80–82, note 12. At

Red Beach, Italian pillboxes opened fire on the approaching LCIs, managing to shoot out the communications and controls on LCI-1 as she approached shore. The LCI returned fire engaging the enemy machine gun nests and holding her own. When the second wave of LCIs closed Red Beach in the pre-dawn darkness to unload troops in the heavy surf, they too caught enemy fire. LCI-5, carrying the 7th Infantry's colonel, found herself the target of heavy machine gun fire. Then an Italian mobile battery put a 90mm shell into the LCI's troop compartment, killing several men. They were about to open fire on the suspected enemy E-boats when *Roe* swerved to miss a minefield and hit *Swanson* at right angles abreast her forward stack. Both ships then retired to Malta and Bizerte for repairs.

51. Morison, IX, 111–12; Richard O. Sharon Pharmacist Mate Second Class, "My Mediterranean Cruise." The destroyer *Glennon* fired on the enemy as well until her shore party was forced to close down.

52. Operation Husky, Naval Commander Force A, report of proceedings, Part IV, Lessons learnt, in Vol. 3 Cunningham's overall report, Box 1706, RG 38, N.A.; Frank Wade, *A Midshipman's War* (Evergreen, Colo.: Cordillera Books, 1994), 210. "Henceforth allowance must be made for even greater use being made of naval support in amphibious operations and subsequent advances along a coast," the report read. Admiral Cunningham wrote that he had ships available to support the British army along the coast, but they were not called upon, a great mistake in his estimation.

53. Tomblin, 478–79; Morison, IX, 249, 261. Admiral Conolly had *Roberts*, *Uganda*, *Mauritius*, *Orion*, and *Aurora* and seven destroyers.

54. Tomblin, 243; Al Newman, "D-day, H-hour," *Newsweek*, September 27, 1943: 21–22.

55. CTF 81, Report on Avalanche, Box 295, RG 38, N.A.; Morison, IX, 261, 266–67; Tomblin, 244–45.

56. CTF 81, Report on Avalanche, Box 295, RG 38, N.A.; Alfred Richards letter to author, February 10, 1970; Tomblin, 250; Lieutenant Harrie James, Box 69, RG 38, N.A.; Susan H. Godson, *Viking of Assault, Admiral John Lesslie Hall, Jr. and Amphibious Warfare* (Washington, D.C.: University Press of America, 1982), 94. According to Admiral Hall's biographer, Susan Godson, Hall ordered small landing craft (LCSs) to turn their machine guns and rockets on enemy shore defenses. She wrote, "The unplanned use of LCSs for close fire support was another innovation in amphibious fighting and perhaps the most notable new feature of gunfire support at Salerno."

57. CTF 81, Report on Avalanche, Box 295, RG 38, N.A.; Tomblin, 257–60.

58. CTG 85.1, Salerno, Box 302, RG 38, N.A.

59. Tomblin, 251, 254; Donahue, *Tin Cans and Other Ships* (North Quincy, Mass.: Christopher Publishing House, 1979), 131; Richard Groscup letter to author, November 20, 1996: "It was this time that we started to fire on the beach with our 5″ guns guided by fire control party. The firing was so rapid that we had to use fire hoses to cool down the barrels." On September 17, eight days into the campaign, the destroyer *Niblack* went so close to shore that crewman James A. Donahue wrote, "We were in very shallow water with the screws churning up sand a few times."

60. Donahue, 129–30; Tomblin, chap. 11, Morison, XI, chap. XIII. In the afternoon of September14, the Germans renewed their attempts to breakthrough by attacking north of the creek, but the newly arrived 1st Battalion, 141st Infantry held their ground aided by artillery and naval gunfire. *Philadelphia* was once more in on the action, firing on designated targets from 1503 to 1610. She was joined by *Niblack*. James Donahue, a member of the destroyer's 5″ gun crew, recorded the action in his diary: "At sundown we got orders from the U.S.S. *Philadelphia* to contact the beach and shell enemy positions. The Germans had advanced and the situation looked grave. A few minutes later all ten fire control parties on the beach secured because they were under heavy German shell fire—the cruisers *Philly* and *Boise* ceased firing. Meanwhile our bombers were laying down a terrific bombardment continually."

61. CTG 81.5, ser 0263, 17 Sept. 1944, Box 297, RG 38, N.A; Lt. Harrie James, Box 69, RG 38, N.A.; Tomblin, 272–73, 279–80, 288–89, 478.

62. Com 11th Amphibious Forces, "Lessons learned from Previous Operations, Box 1, RG 313 US Naval Forces Europe. Admiral Lowry reported that the LCT(R)s fired on Green Beach 5 minutes ahead of schedule, but the rocket craft at Yellow Beach was behind position and did not fire. "The first salvoes of rockets could be seen bursting along the entire length of red and green beaches and if any land mines had been present, would have destroyed many of them. There were few land mine casualties among army personnel." Rocket LCSs were not used in Shingle for "no davit space was available," but the assault boat flotilla leaders' LCSs did have rocket projectors and rockets to use in against individual gun emplacement "when and if they opened fire."

63. Vice Admiral Frank J. Lowry, "The Naval Side of the Anzio Invasion," USNI *Proceedings*, 1954, 23–26; Tomblin, 329–30, 332–33, 339–40.

64. Tomblin, chap. 3, 471; Com Task Forced 34, Nov. 28, 1942, Operation Torch, Box 135, RG 38, N.A.; Kenneth Poolman, *Allied Escort Carriers of World War Two* (Annapolis, Md.: Naval Institute Press, 1988), 37–42; In addition to these missions, in Operation Torch, Allied aircraft played a vital role in defending

the task forces against enemy submarines. Both carrier planes and catapult planes flew anti-submarine patrols or were valuable in spotting the telltale periscopes or torpedo wakes from Italian and German subs.

65. Tomblin, 179–80; Morison, IX, 101–02, 105 note 20; *Boise*, a.r. ser. 061 6 August 1943, Shore Bombardment of Gela Area, Sicily 10–12 July 1943, Box 857, RG 38, N.A. Lieutenant Lewis in his report wrote, "In summary it is my opinion that cruiser seaplanes as now in use are not suitable for such duties even if given fighter protection, especially as it is necessary to stay down within range of even the light AA fire in order to see bursts of the target area." Yet her gunnery officer noted, "If fighter protection had been provided for our spotting plane during the early stages of the invasion, *Boise* fire could have been effective in timely destruction and dispersal of enemy tanks, equipment, and troops approaching Niscemi."

66. Tomblin, 479–80.

67. CTF 81, Adm. Hall action report, Avalanche, Box 295, RG 38, N.A.; CTG 81.6, Adm. Lowry Final comments on Shingle, Box 296, RG 38, N.A; Tomblin, 481–82. Anti-aircraft discipline had as well. When trigger-happy AA gunners on Allied ships off Sicily shot down friendly planes carrying airborne troops, Navy commanders began drilling and better disciplining their AA crews.

68. Tomblin, 241–42. The lack of minesweepers in the Mediterranean was attributable, in part, to the critical need in 1942 for escort vessels. As Commander Alfred H. Richards recalled, his mine squadron had spent most of the war prior to Operation Husky on convoy and escort duties, not on minesweeping. When Richards reported to duty in the Mediterranean in 1943, he found the Allies had nothing in the op plan for clearing mines and Admiral Hall had no mine warfare expert on his staff. "[A]as a matter of fact," he wrote later, "mines having not been any particular problem until this time—they were looked upon as rather insignificant barriers to the more important phases of a landing operation." The forthcoming invasion of Sicily and subsequent landings at Salerno and Anzio alerted Allied naval commanders to the importance of minesweeping.

Fortunately, the Royal Navy had a great deal of experience in the Mediterranean coping with Italian-laid minefields, especially those around the island of Malta. Having suffered numerous warship and submarine losses to mines in the Mediterranean by 1943, the British were very aware of the danger that mines presented. Recent losses to mines included the *Hunt*-class destroyer *Southwold* and the submarine *Olympus*, both sunk, the sweeper *Hebe*, three destroyers, and a merchant ship damaged by mines during Operation Harpoon, *Fantome* mined en route from Alexandria to Gibraltar, and the sweeper *Speedy* mined outside Malta.

69. Alan G. Kirk, "Command from the Flagship *Augusta*", in Mason, 354; Susan Godson, "Preparations for the Amphibious Invasion of Normandy, 1944," in Merrill Bartlett, ed., 317; Ambrose, 268.

70. Elliot, 106–07; Admiral Sir Bertram Ramsay to Supreme Commander Allied Expeditionary Force, 16 Oct. 1944, in Supplement to the *London Gazette*, October 30, 1947, 5113; Balkoski, *Utah Beach*, 74. In January, German E-boats had laid mines in the approach channel to Portsmouth; another minefield was discovered outside Lowestoft in February, and a small field off Newhaven in May "close to the busiest route for invasion shipping." Hitler feared the Allies might find an intact pressure mine and discover how it worked. The Allies also laid their own mines using minelayers and bomber command aircraft. "Considerable success is known to have been achieved by mines laid during this period under 'Maple,' which was really an integral part of Neptune," Admiral Ramsay wrote in his report.

71. F. H. Hinsley, *British Intelligence in World War II*, vol. III, Part One: June 1943–June 1944, (New York: Cambridge University Press, 1984), 130; Harrison, 313; Morison, XI, 124–25; Ambrose, 269. Arguing that the bombardment "was no failure; on the contrary, naval gunfire probably reduced enemy resistance by half to three quarters," Morison also concluded that "it could not reach the targets protected from the sea, or hit targets not spotted beforehand." As it was, naval commanders were concerned that long-range German guns might open fire on their ships off Normandy, especially the large, vulnerable transports, so they had requested the transports be anchored over 11 miles out to sea. This made the run-in to Omaha Beach in the choppy seas that much more exhausting and difficult for troops and boat crews alike and probably contributed to the loss of landing craft and DD tanks.

72. Morison, XI, 124–25; Harrison, 322; Lewis, 26, and "The Navy Falls Short at Normandy," *Naval History Magazine*, 12, no. 6 (December 1998): 34–39. Morison also suggested that H-hour could have been set for 0400. "As Admiral Hall wanted, in order to give the underwater demolition teams time to clear the obstacles." It is interesting to note that when Captain Sabin requested a second rocket barrage be launched onto Omaha Beach, Admiral Hall denied his request for fear the rockets might hit Allied troops. The exact time is unclear. Lewis says Sabin's observations were at H-hour plus 6.

73. Ramsay, *London Gazette*, October 30, 1947. On D-Day at Normandy, this was done by all but one or two ships of the Western Naval Task Force "who found it necessary to open blind fire against certain batteries whose fire was more accurate than was the general case."

74. Lewis, 212–13; R. Admiral Lyal Davidson, CTG 85.1, Box 297, RG 38, N.A. In fact, in his action report following the Salerno invasion, Admiral Lyal Davidson reported that the exchange of gunfire took place in "complete darkness and only the intermittent flashes of enemy battery could be used as a point of aim." The Moroccan landings in Torch affirmed the effectiveness of American destroyers' main batteries of 5"/38-caliber guns against French 105mm and 75mm batteries firing on the landing beaches, "except in a few cases where certain guns were protected by reverse slopes from fire from the westward."

75. E-mail letter to author from Larry Carr; Lorenzo Sabin, "Close-in Support at Omaha Beach," in Stillwell, ed., 61. When General Huebner asked Captain Sabin why the small gunships could not get at the enemy mortars firing on our landing craft and troops at Omaha, Sabin recalled replying that they could not get at the mortars because "their locations were not accurately known, and, further, that their apparent locations were out of the gunships' range."

76. Morison, XI, 121–23. Utah Beach fire support had four LCGs assigned.

77. Morison, XI, 170–73; Vice Admiral John D. Bulkley, "Ike Remembered Me," in Stillwell, ed., 52. Bulkeley's PT went alongside the *Rich* to rescue survivors. Her skipper, a long time friend of Bulkeley, refused to abandon ship, so Bulkeley went up, grabbed him and took his pistol away.

chapter seven

VETERANS TELL THEIR STORIES AND WHY HISTORIANS AND OTHERS LISTENED

G. Kurt Piehler

As the twentieth century came to a close, Americans displayed an increasing interest in the history of the Second World War. Anniversary ceremonies commemorating D-Day in 1994 and V-E Day in 1995 garnered extensive national coverage on all major television networks. Hollywood produced scores of new movies with World War II themes that were box office successes and often achieved significant critical acclaim. The works of Stephen E. Ambrose and other historians of the Second World War found their way onto the bestseller list. There was also a pronounced interest in listening to the voices of the World War II generation. Steven Spielberg has created a foundation to fund a massive oral history program to document the Holocaust. Tom Brokaw's oral histories with selected members of the "Greatest Generation" made it to the bestseller list and spurred renewed public discussion of the role that World War II veterans played in shaping American society after 1945. In 2000, the U.S. Congress established a small but ambitious program in the Library of Congress to preserve the oral histories of World War II–era veterans.

This chapter will show how interest in the veteran's voice is not a phenomenon confined to the closing decade of the twentieth century, but one that originated during the Second World War itself. In fact, historians serving with the U.S. Army developed an extensive and sophisticated program in the later stages of the war to systematically conduct oral histories with combat veterans. Introductory texts in the field of oral history generally recognize the importance of the work of S. L. A. Marshall, Forrest Pogue, and other combat historians to the development of oral history methodology.[1] But most scholars, even practitioners of oral history, do not fully understand how influential the work of oral historians was to shaping the writing of official military history within the United States after the Second World War. Among practitioners of military history, oral history methodology gained an acceptance far sooner than it did in other historical disciplines. The writings of S. L. A. Marshall, the most famous practitioner of the combat interview, not only influenced scholarly debates, but in the aftermath of the Second World War, shaped Army doctrines.

However, controversies surround the work of S. L. A. Marshall. In a seminal 1988 article appearing in *RUSI Journal*, Roger J. Spiller cast doubt on the methodology and conclusions of S. L. A. Marshall's most influential work, *Men Against Fire*.[2] This chapter will not seek to reach definitive conclusions regarding the continuing debate over the veracity of Marshall's work, but instead will seek to trace the far-reaching impact of his work and those of other combat historians in solidifying the place of military history within the U.S. Army. Marshall provided the Army a usable past by offering important lessons learned regarding the nature of combat. His work solidified institutional support within the U.S. Army for military history, especially oral history. After V-J Day, the Army remained committed to producing a highly regarded and thoroughly researched series of monographs documenting the history of the war. Army historians, both military and civilian, continued as a permanent fixture of future conflicts of the Cold War and post–Cold War era.

Army-sponsored military history came of age in the Second World War, and it remained part of a wider movement to mobilize intellectuals in the service of the war effort. The role of scientists in developing the atomic bomb, radar, and other technological advances is best known by the general public and documented by historians. But social scientists and humanists also did their part. Social scientists serving with the Office of Strategic Services used their talents to select bomb targets, developing propaganda aimed at demoralizing the Axis, and analyzing the economic capabilities of the Axis powers. Scholars from the humanities developed a reeducation program aimed at German POWs held in the continental United States.[3]

The Army's sustained interest in military history during the Second World War stands in sharp contrast to earlier institutional attitudes toward history. Until the aftermath of the Civil War, there remained little formal support for military history. In *Soldiers and Scholars*, Carol Reardon presents a growing though uneven use of history by the Old Army after Appomattox as a tool to inculcate a sense of professionalism within the officer corps. It was not until the First World War that the Army employed historians to systematically document the history of a conflict as it progressed. Short of personnel and lacking adequate authority over crucial military records, the Army's historical branch made little progress in fulfilling its mandate. After the signing of the Armistice, the Army's historical branch struggled to produce histories in the face of waning official interest.[4] Moreover, what was permissible for an official historian to write about was sharply circumscribed, and Secretary of War Newton D. Baker mandated in 1919 that monographs could not examine political, diplomatic, or economic issues. A year after the attack on Pearl Harbor, the small staff of the Army Historical Section was still working on the official history of the First World War.[5]

In contrast, there remained several significant patrons among the senior American civilian and military leaders during the Second World War who ensured that official historians would document events as they unfolded. In 1942, President Franklin D. Roosevelt issued directives through the Bureau of the Budget requiring civilian and military departments to preserve the historical record of their wartime contribution. Within the civilian leadership of the War Department, Assistant Secretary of War John McCloy played a decisive role in creating a new historical branch within the Military's Intelligence Division (G-2) to focus solely on documenting the history of the Second World War. Two Army chiefs of staff, George C. Marshall and Dwight D. Eisenhower, offered crucial support to Army historians. Professional historians also lent their support to these efforts, and the American Historical Association was consulted by the Army. Many prominent historians enlisted and found themselves detailed to serve as official historians.[6]

Why this interest in official history? Many of the key decision makers valued history. While still in office, Roosevelt established a presidential library for his papers and oversaw their publication. George Marshall was an avid reader of military history and even corresponded with several prominent historians. As a junior officer, Marshall had assisted General John J. Pershing in writing his memoirs.[7] As a junior officer, Eisenhower had spent time in the late 1920s detailed to the American Battlement Monuments Commission and wrote the official guide to the U.S. World War I battlefields.[8]

In part, the emphasis on recording the war stemmed from a realization in late 1941 and early 1942 that crucial aspects of America's involvement in the First World War had not been properly documented. Many government officials in 1941 looked back to the First World War for precedents on how to carry out mobilization and found that properly documented administrative history did not exist to offer them guidance. Instead, they had to rely on the recollections of former governmental officials from the Wilson administration for an understanding of actions taken over 20 years earlier.[9]

George Marshall regarded official histories, completed shortly after battles and campaigns were over, as way of preserving and conveying the lessons learned to the wider Army. But Marshall also wanted Army historians to write short and accessible battle histories in order to boost morale, especially among the wounded and the families of those who lost loved ones killed in service.[10]

By 1944, documenting campaigns and battles became a major task of Army historians. Not only did they seek to ensure that the documentary record was preserved, but they increasingly used oral history as a research tool to discover what really happened in battle. In an age when historians privileged the written record over oral sources, it is not surprising that a journalist, S. L. A. Marshall, pioneered the after-action interview as a way to reconstruct the history of battle. Marshall, a First World War veteran and a successful writer for the *Detroit News*, served in the Second World War in the Army's Historical Branch. As combat historian for the 27th and 7th Infantry Divisions in the Pacific, Marshall decided that the only way he could learn what really happened during the invasions of Makin and Kwajalein was through group interviews with survivors. Not only would Marshall's findings be disseminated through official channels, but his innovative history would reach a wider public through the bestselling book *Island Victory* and the more controversial study *Men Against Fire*.[11]

The Second World War was not the first time that the federal government sought the testimony of combatants. Throughout American history, soldiers and sailors have written scores of memoirs and personal narratives recounting their experiences. To qualify for pensions, Revolutionary War veterans had to provide the federal government with affidavits recounting their service in considerable detail. These pension applications provide modern historians an invaluable source for understanding the perspectives of the common soldier and sailor in the War for Independence.[12]

But it is striking how skeptical the post-Revolutionary generation remained of the testimony of average soldiers. For instance, the Bunker Hill Monument Committee gathered the testimony of soldiers who survived the battle, but they did not disseminate it to the general public because these accounts were so contradictory.[13] This attitude of the Bunker Hill Monument Committee reflects an earlier sentiment regarding the common soldier that was present in American society: Military and civilian leaders did not view it important to systematically understand what the common soldier thought. During the Revolutionary and Early Republic Eras, there remained sharp class distinctions within the standing army between an officer corps drawn from the elite and the enlisted ranks composed disproportionately from the landless, the poor, former indentured servants, and African American slaves.[14] When Washington's officers formed the Society of Cincinnati to preserve their wartime comradeship, they excluded the enlisted ranks.[15]

Disdain for the rank and file remained even stronger in Europe. The Duke of Wellington viewed his men as the "scum of the earth," and the British Army he served in regularly whipped individual soldiers to death (or near death) for disciplinary infractions. When Wellington's soldiers returned home, few cared to preserve their remembrances for posterity, and many did not possess the literacy necessary to record them in memoirs. One of the few memoirs that were published of the common soldier came into existence because someone took the trouble to record the reminiscence of an illiterate soldier. This lack of respect for the common soldier is revealed in the fact that after the Napoleonic wars ended, British merchants gathered the bones of the soldiers who fell on the battlefields of Europe and ground them into bone meal.[16]

The mass armies raised in the American Civil War and in the world wars were different. In the case of the United States and Great Britain, they were filled with volunteers from the literate middle class who expected to be treated with some measure of dignity. No longer were the bones of the common soldier allowed to rot on the battlefield, but massive efforts were made to create cemeteries for all the fallen, not simply a select few officers. Literate soldiers wrote letters home, kept diaries, and, in the aftermath of war, wrote memoirs. They also told their stories to others.

Journalists were among the first professionals to make interviews with combatants a standard practice of their trade. During the American Civil War, reporters joined armies on their campaigns and relied heavily on interviews with participants for their stories. Newspapers, especially during the Civil War, are filled with published letters from soldiers serving on the front. During the Second World War, some of the most popular and enduring war journalism featured individual servicemen. Within the military, *Stars and Stripes* cartoonist Bill Mauldin captured the mood of many GIs with his cartoons depicting the trials and tribulations of two "typical" infantrymen, Willie and Joe.[17] Ernie Pyle, one of the most widely read civilian war correspondents of the conflict, centered his reporting on trying to understand and recount the experience of the average GIs. Throughout his columns, snippets of conversation by GIs are recorded, and much of his reporting stresses the mundane details of Army life, even when Pyle is reporting on epic events.[18]

When military history emerged as a professional discipline in the late nineteenth century, it embraced a methodology that privileged written documents. This is not unique to military historians but remained a pattern throughout the historical profession. The Historical Section of the Army and of the Navy devoted much of their efforts to preserving and publishing historical records. During the First World War, the War Department appointed a historian who considered collecting the recollections of men after battle, but he never gained the necessary cooperation to undertake this assignment.[19]

As a combat historian, S. L. A. Marshall embraced oral history after he learned firsthand the limitations of documents in outlining what happened in battle. In witnessing the battle for Makin, Marshall recalled in his memoirs how difficult it was as a sole observer to learn what actually happened during the course of a battle. To reconstruct the battle, Marshall decided that the best recourse was to conduct group interviews with all the survivors.[20] In an appendix to *Island Victory*, Marshall laid out a methodology for how an Army historical officer could conduct a group interview with combat veterans. In his view, the interview should come as soon after the battle as possible and include both officers and enlisted personnel. In outlining the methodology, Marshall believed that a consensus would emerge from the varied stories on what actually happened. What is striking about Marshall's account of the methodology is his failure to consider how enlisted personnel might censor themselves about the conduct of their officers during the battle out of fear or respect. Although Marshall believed that one can learn about the crucial role of those killed in battle from survivors, he does not discuss the possibility that the living may not want to speak critically about the dead.[21]

Influenced by the methods and success of Marshall, the Army established a team of combat historians in 1944 to document the impending invasion of Europe. Trained in Washington, D.C., by a University of Chicago historian and Army Major Hugh M. Cole, this team, which included Forrest Pogue, reviewed documents from a recent Pacific campaign and was required to reconstruct a history of the battle from them. From these and other exercises, Pogue recalled that they learned what types of information official records did not provide to historians and what questions should be asked of combatants in order to write an accurate battle account. The first team arrived in England several weeks before the invasion and received access to classified documents outlining landings and subsequent plans. Although combat historians had the opportunity to land on Utah Beach on the first day, Pogue and his colleagues assigned to Omaha Beach were unable to go ashore until D-Day plus 2 and instead conducted interviews with wounded veterans aboard their LST.[22]

S. L. A. Marshall and other combat historians found it difficult to conduct group interviews as the Battle for France unfolded. He conducted many of his interviews with the airborne divisions because these were the only two units that were regularly retired from battle for regrouping. For other interviewers, the fast-moving front, especially after the breakout of Normandy, meant that they had to conduct interviews with combatants still on the line. Pogue recalled his efforts to interview the participants in the battle for St. Lo and how he managed to question a key junior officer just before he was killed in subsequent action.[23]

Soon after the Second World War, S. L. A. Marshall would cause a sensation with his publication of *Men Against Fire* in 1947. This small monograph had a profound impact on both military historians and policy makers. Critically acclaimed when it appeared, Marshall sought to understand what happened to men and units in combat. He made the case for arguing that most men were not aggressive in combat in part because of their reluctance to kill and also because of the isolating nature of modern battle. According to his observations and interviews, Marshall argued that only one out of four infantrymen was using his weapons in combat. Marshall's work influenced the senior military leadership to rethink the nature of combat training and encourage greater emphasis on weapons training during basic and advanced training. Marshall rose to the rank of Brigadier

General and went on to write about the combatant's experience of battle in both Korea and Vietnam.[24]

After his death, several scholars questioned Marshall's research methodology and the validity of his conclusions about the nature of battle. In a widely cited article in *RUSI Journal*, Roger Spiller maintained that the ratio of one-in-four active combatants lacked solid empirical documentation. In reviewing Marshall's notebooks and correspondence, Spiller argues that one cannot find the necessary evidence to support the thesis advanced in *Men Against Fire*. There remained staunch defenders of Marshall, most notably Martin Blumenson and General William DePuy.[25] But in many ways, this criticism of Marshall should not obscure the impact his work had on the practice of military history, especially within the U.S. Army.[26] In the case of the military establishment, all four armed services eventually established oral history programs. During the Korean and Vietnam Wars, the Army deployed historians to conduct after-action interviews. During the Vietnam War, the Marine Corps also developed an extensive oral history program. All branches of the armed services conducted an extensive range of interviews in the Gulf War; Somalia Intervention; the military's response to the attacks of September 11, 2001; and the wars in Afghanistan and Iraq.[27]

Army historians writing authorized histories of the Second World War and subsequent conflicts also embraced oral history to better understand the so-called "general's war." They also had substantial encouragement from their superiors. In a 1946 memorandum commissioning Forrest Pogue to write the official history of the Supreme Headquarters of the Allied Expeditionary Force (SHAEF), Army Chief of Staff Dwight D. Eisenhower observed that "much of the story of SHAEF Headquarters rests in the memories of the officers involved" and authorized him to interview as "widely as possible."[28]

One year later, Eisenhower reviewed a summary of Pogue's interviews with key British military leaders and offered his own reactions to their interviews. When Forrest Pogue's *The Supreme Command* appeared in 1954, it received critical acclaim from reviewers for its high level of research.[29]

But it was not just official histories that embraced oral history sources. Outside the armed services, military historians of the twentieth century drew extensively on oral history sources. Forrest Pogue, after leaving the

Army, conducted an extensive range of oral histories to write his multivolume history of George Marshall.[30] Edward M. Coffman, in his classic account of American involvement in the First World War, conducted a number of interviews with officers and enlisted men.[31] To document the D-Day landing, Stephen E. Ambrose and his colleagues at the Eisenhower Center compiled a massive collection of oral history interviews. Ambrose's work, especially *D-Day, Band of Brothers*, and *Citizen Soldiers*, rests heavily on interviews for evidence.[32]

In a 1953 Army guide on how to train Army historians in the discipline, special attention is given to the value of interviewing participants to reconstruct the past.[33] This official endorsement and use of oral history stands in contrast to prevailing sentiments in other fields. Although Allan Nevins created an extensive oral history program at Columbia University to document the lives of political leaders, intellectuals, and other great men (and a few women), the acceptance of oral history as a source remained limited. For example, Louis Gottschalk's *Understanding History*, a widely used general primer in graduate courses in the 1950s and 1960s on historical documentation and writing, offers no discussion of oral evidence or sources.[34] Not until the late 1960s and 1970s, under the influence of the New Left, did historians and scholars turn to oral history as a way to document the experiences of African Americans, women, and other groups who had been marginalized in the historical record.[35]

Some historians questioned the validity of oral history sources. At the Second National Colloquium on Oral History held in 1967, Cornelius Ryan and Forrest Pogue debated the reliability of interviewing combatants about their wartime experience. What is striking about this debate is that Ryan emerged as a critic of oral history after interviewing hundreds of D-Day veterans for his bestselling account of D-Day, *The Longest Day*. In Ryan's view, oral histories simply remained inaccurate and must be confirmed with printed documentation. To emphasize the limitations of oral history, he observed, "I never found one man who landed on Omaha Beach who could tell me whether the water was hot or cold. I never found one man who landed on Omaha Beach who could tell me the exact time when some incident occurred."[36]

In his defense of oral history, Pogue did not question that oral history had limitations. As he put it, "a man under fire is trying first to survive, second to kill the enemy in front of him, and then only later on to analyze what's happening." But Pogue, in defending the special validity of oral history sources, emphasized the importance of an interviewer's conducting the necessary background research before interviewing a combatant and realizing the limited view of the average soldier. As he put it, why would you ask a soldier who landed on D-Day what time the assault began? As Pogue recalled one soldier's telling him, "Hell, you don't think I had time to look at my watch." In Pogue's view, oral history for all its limitations remained an invaluable tool for gaining the perspective of average soldiers and getting history down "while it's hot."[37]

There were points of agreement between these two historians. Pogue emphasized that an important function of oral history, especially combat interviews, is in reconstructing what happened when records were sketchy or nonexistent. For instance, Pogue recalled how interview teams reconstructed the history in the Battle of the Bulge of several units whose records had been captured or destroyed to prevent them from falling into enemy hands, and oral histories were one of the few ways used to reconstruct their histories. Moreover, Pogue did not discount the value of written sources, maintaining only that they were often fragmentary and incomplete. Many of those interviewed would not survive the war, and if their accounts had not been recorded, the historical record would be poorer. While emphasizing the limitation of oral history sources and the need to read them critically, Ryan also dwelt on the limitations of written ones and recognized the biases inherent in them. As Ryan recounted, an oral history interview with Erwin Rommel's widow proved essential for correcting the historical record of her husband's whereabouts on D-Day. As Ryan noted, German Army records state that Rommel left his headquarters on the day before D-Day to consult with Hitler, but after interviewing Rommel's widow, he learned that the German general had instead returned home for her birthday. To protect Rommel's reputation, his subordinates deliberately fabricated the written record, and only an interview with his widow (and the display of custom-made shoes from Paris he bought as a birthday present) corrected the historical record.

The work of combat historians in collecting oral histories represented a broader interest within the military in understanding the voice of average servicemen and -women. Even before the United States formally entered the Second World War, General Marshall believed that it was essential to better understand the background, attitudes, and opinions of Army personnel. On the eve of Pearl Harbor, many draftees and National Guardsmen remained defiant of military authority and expressed an open desire to go over the hill unless they were released from the military. Over the objections of a number of his subordinates, Marshall turned to social scientists to staff a special office to regularly poll Army personnel on a range of subjects.[38] Created in October 1941, the Research Branch employed social psychologists, sociologists, and statisticians to devise and administer a range of specialized surveys designed to understand the attitudes and performance of American soldiers and airmen. In the introduction to the massive four-volume summary of the work of the Research Branch entitled *Studies in Social Psychology in World War II*, Samuel Stouffer emphasized the practical nature of the work performed by his team. As he noted, many of the over 300 "social engineering projects" addressed specific questions:

> To analyze the factors which led men in the South Pacific not to use atabrine as regularly as the Army thought they should; to investigate attitudes and practices associated with trench foot; to find which of two kinds of huts men preferred in Alaska; to compare preferences for different kinds of winter clothing among front-line troops in Belgium, Luxemburg, and Germany; to learn what radio programs men preferred or what they liked most to read in *Yank* magazine; to assess the needs for different kinds of athletic equipment; to analyze the laundry situation in Panama or attitudes toward the Chinese among troops in India-Burma . . .[39]

The work of the Research Branch was massive, with over one-half million men participating in at least one survey. Before drafting surveys, members of the Research Branch often conducted interviews with servicemen to draw up the right questions. Not only were soldiers and airmen asked to complete surveys that could be statistically tabulated, but they were also given the opportunity to express themselves in free-form narrative answers. One only has to glance through the excerpts of these remarks reprinted by Stouffer to hear some of the authentic, if mediated, voices of the GIs. For example, when soldiers were surveyed on combat motivation, they offered the following responses in interviews or in the narrative sections of the survey:

> Ask any dogface on the line. You're fighting for your skin on the line. When I enlisted I was patriotic as all hell. There's no patriotism on the line. A boy up there 60 days in the line is in danger every minute. He ain't fighting for patriotism.[40]

To highlight the section regarding the weariness of battle-tested veterans and their bitterness over the prospect of continued combat, this response was included:

> We feel that the only opportunity we will have to go home is to get wounded. There is isn't an old man in the company who has any hope or confidence of being able to enjoy life again. I will go AWOL before I will make another invasion. I am willing to do my part, but I don't want to be the sucker while thousands of soldiers will never see action.[41]

On the vital role of comradeship in sustaining combatants, Stouffer included excerpts from this interview conducted by the research staff with a wounded soldier:

> You know the men in your outfit. You have to be loyal to them. The men get close-knit together. They like each other—quit their petty bickering and having enemies. They depend on each other—wouldn't do anything to let the rest of them down. They'd rather be killed than do that. They begin to think the world of each other. It's the main thing that keeps a guy from going haywire.[42]

The breadth of this enterprise is remarkable given the few precedents that existed for the involvement of the social sciences in the military. Although psychologists had played a role in the First World War in devising aptitude tests to screen and place volunteers, the massive public opinion polling undertaken by the Research Branch remained quite suspect until late 1941. For example, in a press release in May 1941, the War Department flatly stated its opposition: "Anonymous opinion or criticism, good or bad, is destructive in its effect on a military organization where accepted responsibility on the part of every individual is instructive."[43]

Samuel Stouffer pointed with pride to the influence his research branch had on shaping the decision-making process in the Army. The creation of the Combat Infantryman's Badge stemmed from the findings of the Research Branch, which showed that a substantial morale problem existed in the ranks of the infantry. The point system of demobilization was devised in large measure from the suggestions and views of the rank and file. According to Stouffer, the Branch collected important data on servicemen's plans after the war that helped policy makers craft the GI Bill.

Space will not allow a full assessment of the Research Branch's influence on Army policy during the war. What is important to recognize is the continuing influence of the Branch's work on the social sciences and history. The expertise of social scientists, especially social psychologists and military sociologists, continued after V-J Day.[44] During the Cold War, social scientists, building on the innovative research on race and the military conducted by the Research Division during the Second World War, played a crucial role in building the case for racial integration and an end to a Jim Crow military.[45]

Studies in Social Psychology in World War II (better known as *The American Soldier*) is a seminal work not only for social scientists, but also for historians. Since 1949, it has remained essential reading for scholars seeking to understand combat motivation and the experiences of men in battle. Stouffer and his colleagues concluded that ideological commitments did not motivate most soldiers to fight in the Second World War. Moreover, the Branch concluded that Army training films had only a limited impact on changing soldiers' attitudes with regard to ideology. Instead, soldiers fought in large measure out of loyalty to their buddies.[46]

Since World War II, memoirs, literary works, histories, and Hollywood films have echoed the sentiments of Stouffer regarding unit cohesion in World War II. Memoirs by William Manchester, E. B. Sledge, and a host of other Second World War veterans emphasize the importance of small group loyalty as sustaining them and their comrades in battle. In scores of novels and films, the ethnically and regionally diverse unit is forged by battle into a brotherhood of arms. Among historians, this theme has been popularized most recently by Stephen E. Ambrose in his bestselling monograph and HBO television series *Band of Brothers*. Another example is Steven Spielberg's film *Saving Private Ryan*, which told the story of the D-Day invasion not as a grand epic, but instead as a story of a small unit striving to accomplish its mission.[47]

When the Research Branch studied combat effectiveness, it concluded that all men eventually had a breaking point. Even soldiers with distinguished records of combat service were not immune to breaking down mentally. Moreover, as the Research Branch and others noted, the problem of battle fatigue was not a minor problem, but a significant drain on manpower. Lunacy, shell shock, battle fatigue, combat exhaustion, and post-traumatic stress syndrome have been various cultural constructs for the inability of combatants to continue to fight. Until the twentieth century, armies often viewed mental illness as a sign of cowardice, and we will probably never know how many deranged men were shot by firing squads.[48]

Armies, at least those of democratic societies, had a more difficult time executing soldiers for cowardice. During the First World War, Britain and France executed soldiers for desertion, but this practice led to enormous public opposition. The United States Army in late 1944 carried out only one death sentence for battlefield desertion, and the execution of Private Edward Slovik continues to engender controversy over the justness of this punishment.[49] Moreover, John Keegan and other scholars make a credible case that battle fatigue—or however one defines the condition where combatants are mentally unable to continue to fight—has been exacerbated by the advent of modern warfare. Modern technology has made battle longer, more deadly, and capable of encompassing vast amounts of territory.[50]

During the First World War, many physicians, confronted with men suffering from shell shock, were convinced that the brain had quite literally been shocked. Although medical opinion remained divided during the war, an increasing number of physicians rejected an organic basis for mental casualties. With shell shock, many surgeons needed to establish whether an individual had even received a shock to the brain. When physicians stressed a psychological basis for shell shock, they sought to abolish the term and developed a new strategy for treatment. For hysterical paralysis, many physicians in Germany and France literally shocked limbs with electric current to get patients to move them. Other physicians, especially those influenced by Freudian psychiatry, adopted a therapy that included a talking cure.[51]

By the Second World War, American military psychiatrists' attack on the problem of battle fatigue initially centered on efforts to prescreen and eliminate from induction into the military those they believed were mentally unstable. Despite this approach, large numbers of men were afflicted with battle fatigue. To treat the milder cases, military psychiatrists increasingly emphasized forward treatment and the importance of reintegrating soldiers as quickly as possible back into the unit. For many soldiers, sleep, warm meals, and the chance to discuss their situation led many to their rehabilitation and their return to combat ranks. For the most traumatized, who required evacuation and hospitalization, many psychiatrists believed it essential for them to recall their battlefield experiences as part of the treatment process. To aid the process, it became a common practice, although by no means universal, to administer drugs or to use hypnosis to encourage traumatized servicemen to recall and expunge past memories. John Huston's powerful documentary *Let There Be Light*, on the treatment of mental casualties from the Second World War, dramatically demonstrated the use of hypnosis to encourage veterans to recall traumatic incidents.

The medicalization of the problem of combat motivation is another sign of a shift in the military's attitudes toward the average combatant. Not only did historians or social scientists emphasize the importance of listening to the average combatant, but so did a significant portion of the Army medical establishment. Of course, the emphasis by all three professions given to the stories, opinions, and traumas of average combatants was intended by the military establishment only to be a way to further the war effort. This interest in the individual underscored a dilemma faced by the Army in the Second World War: the need to ensure that individuals continued to serve and fight. In short, despite all the technological advances, winning the war still took individual combatants to fight it and for them to endure a dreadful battlefield experience. Of course, there were other alternatives. For instance, both the Soviet and German armies devoted few resources to treating battle fatigue and relied on harsh discipline.[52]

Scholars of the world wars have noted how these global wars devalued human life through what one historian has termed "industrial killing."[53] In the Second World War, millions died on the battlefield through the application of flamethrowers, tanks, aerial bombers and fighters, and artillery. Both the Axis and the Allies made civilians legitimate targets of air campaigns. The Nazis established a vast bureaucratic apparatus to methodically kill Jews; the Roma; Slavs; homosexuals; the disabled; and other religious, ethnic, and racial groups. Ideologically, Nazism, Italian fascism, and Japanese militarism devalued the role of the individual as a free agent and viewed individuals as servants of the state.

During the Second World War, American leaders sought to draw a sharp contrast between the totalitarian regimes of the Axis powers and American society. President Roosevelt maintained in public pronouncements that Americans must fight the Nazis and Imperial Japan to prevent world domination and their trampling of individual liberties. Although American propaganda would be far more subdued in the Second World War when compared with First World War efforts, such officially sanctioned works as Frank Capra's *Why We Fight* series made clear the evil character of the enemy. Capra portrayed Germans, Italians, and Japanese as servants of the state and all three regimes as subverting religion to the needs of the state. In contrast, Americans were not servants to the state but enjoyed the basic individual freedoms of speech, religion, press, and the right to a trial by jury. Democracies can raise armies and meet the challenge of tyranny without crushing the democratic ethos of the individual.[54]

The emphasis placed on the individual soldier's story by the American military remained more than simply a crude effort to ensure that soldiers remained in their foxholes. Instead, it reflected a remarkably sincere effort to preserve a democratic ethos in the face of total war. It is also striking how enduring the contributions made by historians, social scientists, and the medical profession were to scholarship. Although historians remain critical of S. L. A. Marshall, nonetheless, the work of the combat historians is an essential source for writing the history of the conflict. Forrest Pogue would play a major role in the establishment of the Oral History Association in the 1960s and in the acceptance of oral history methodology in the wider historical profession. *Studies in Social Psychology in World War II* remains essential reading for military sociologists, but also for historians seeking to understand the experience of combatants. Moreover, the work of military psychiatrists to understand and treat battle trauma in the Second World War and its aftermath played a crucial role in changing American attitudes toward mental illness.

NOTES

1. For example, see Donald Ritchie, *Doing Oral History* (New York: Twayne, 1995), 3.

2. S.L.A. Marshall, *Men Against Fire: The Problem of Battle Command in Future War* (New York: William Morrow, 1947; reprint, 1964). Roger J. Spiller, "S.L.A. Marshall and the Ratio of Fire," *RUSI Journal* (Winter 1988): 63–71. See, also Fredric Smoler, "The Secret of the Soldiers Who Didn't Shoot," *American Heritage* 40 (March 1989): 37–45.

3. Stuart W. Leslie, *The Cold War and American Science: The Military-Industrial-Academic Complex at MIT and Stanford* (New York: Columbia University Press, 1993); Barry M. Katz, *Foreign Intelligence: Research and Analysis in the Office of Strategic Services, 1942–1945* (Cambridge: Harvard University Press, 1989); Ron Robin, *The Barbed Wire College: Reeducating German POWs in the United States During World War II* (Princeton: Princeton University Press, 1995).

4. Carol Reardon, *Soldiers and Scholars: The U.S. Army and the Uses of Military History, 1865–1920* (Lawrence, Kan.: University Press of Kansas, 1990).

5. Bell I. Wiley, "Historical Program of the U.S. Army, 1939–Present [1945]," chap. 1, 1–2, File number 2–3.7, AB. A, Historical Manuscript Collection (HMC), U.S. Army Center for Military History, Fort McNair, Washington, D.C., Xx PT6U

6. Stetson Conn, *Historical Work in the United States Army, 1862–1954* (Washington, D.C.: Center for Military History, U.S. Army, 1980), chaps. 3–6.

7. The assistance rendered by George Marshall to General John J. Pershing is documented in George C. Marshall, *The Papers of George Catlett Marshall*, vol. 1, *"The Soldierly Spirit": December 1880–June 1939*, ed. Larry I. Bland and Sharon R. Ritenour, (Baltimore, Md.: The Johns Hopkins University Press, 1981): 359–77.

8. Dwight D. Eisenhower, *Eisenhower: The Prewar Diaries and Selected Papers, 1905–1941*, ed. Daniel D. Holt and James W. Leyerzapf (Baltimore, Md.: The Johns Hopkins University Press, 1998), chap. 2.

9. Bell I. Wiley, "Historical Program of the U.S. Army, 1939–Present [1945], 6 [I–6]–[I–7].

10. Forrest C. Pogue, "U.S. Army Historical Section Activities in the European Theater, 1944–1946," in *Armed Forces Oral Histories: World War II Combat Interviews* (Bethesda, Md.: University Publications of America, 1989), ix.

11. S. L. A. Marshall, *Island Victory: The Battle of Kwajalein Atoll* (Washington, D.C.: The Infantry Journal, 1945); Marshall, *Men Against Fire* (New York: William Morrow, 1947; reprinted, 1964).

12. John C. Dann, ed., *The Revolution Remembered: Eyewitness Accounts of the War for Independence* (Chicago: University of Chicago Press, 1980). For an example of how historians have used pension applications as evidence, see Lawrence E. Babits, *A Devil of a Whipping: The Battle of Cowpens* (Chapel Hill, N.C.: University of North Carolina Press, 1998).

13. G. Kurt Piehler, *Remembering War the American Way* (Washington, D.C.: Smithsonian Institution Press, 1995), 57; Carol Adele Kelly, ed., *Voices of My Comrades: America's Reserve Officers Remember World War II* (New York: Fordham University Press, 2007).

14. Mark E. Lender, "The Mind of the Rank and File: Patriotism and Motivation in the Continental Line," in *New Jersey in the American Revolution*, vol. 3, ed. William C. Wright (Trenton: N.J.: Historical Commission, 1976).

15. Minor Myers, Jr., *Liberty Without Anarchy: A History of the Society of the Cincinnati* (Charlottesville, Va.: University of Virginia Press, 1983).

16. Samuel Hynes, *The Soldiers' Tale: Bearing Witness to Modern War* (New York: Allen Lane/Penguin Press, 1997), 1–33.

17. Frederick S. Voss, *Reporting the War: The Journalistic Coverage of World War II* (Washington, D.C.: Smithsonian Institution Press, 1994).

18. Ernie Pyle, *Brave Men*, with introduction by G. Kurt Piehler (New York: Henry Holt, 1944; reprint, Lincoln: University of Nebraska Press, 2001).

19. Pogue, "U.S. Army Historical Section," ix.

20. S. L. A. Marshall, *Bringing Up the Rear: A Memoir*, ed. Cate Marshall (San Rafael, Calif.: Presidio Press, 1979), 67–81.

21. Marshall, *Island Victory*, 108–15.

22. Pogue, "U.S. Army Historical Section," x. Pogue also kept a diary of his wartime service, which documents his work as a combat historian. See Forrest C. Pogue, *Pogue's War: Diaries of a WW II Combat Historian* (Lexington: University Press of Kentucky, 2001).

23. Pogue, "U.S. Army Historical Section," xi.

24. F. D. G. Williams, *SLAM: The Influence of S.L.A. Marshall on the United States Army*, TRADOC Historical Monograph Series (Fort Monroe, Va: Office of the Command Historian, U.S. Army Training and Doctrine Command, 1990), 77 88.

25. Martin Blumenson, "Did 'Slam' Guess at Fire Ratios? Probably: A Legend Remembered," *Army* (June 1989): 16–21; William E. DuPuy, "Insights" *Military Review* 69 (July 1989): 96–98.

26. Kent Roberts Greenfield, *The Historian and the Army* (New Brunswick, N.J.: Rutgers University Press, 1954).

27. Robert K. Wright, Jr., "Clio in Combat: The Evolution of the Military History Detachment," *Army Historian* 6 (Winter 1985): 3–6; Stephen J. Lofgren, "The Status of Oral History in the Army: Expanding a Tradition," *The Oral History Review* 30 (Summer/Fall 2003): 81–97.

28. Louis Galambos, Joseph P. Hobbs, Elizabeth F. Smith, et al., *The Papers of Dwight D. Eisenhower: The Chief of Staff*, vol. VII (Baltimore, Md.: The Johns Hopkins University Press, 1978), 1209–10.

29. Louis Galambos, Joseph P. Hobbs, Elizabeth F. Smith, et al., *The Papers of Dwight D. Eisenhower: The Chief of Staff*, vol. VIII (Baltimore, Md.: The Johns Hopkins University Press, 1978), 1570–75. Preston Slosson, review of *The Supreme Command*, by Forrest C. Pogue. *American Historical Review* 60 (January 1955): 393–94.

30. Forrest C. Pogue, "The George C. Marshall Project," in *The Second National Colloquium on Oral History*, ed. Louis M. Starr (New York: Oral History Association, 1968), 82–94.

31. Edward M. Coffman, "Talking About War: Reflections on Doing Oral History and Military History" *Journal of American History* 87 (September 2000): 582–92.

32. William Manchester, *Goodbye, Darkness: A Memoir of the Pacific War* (Boston: Little, Brown, 1980); E. B. Sledge, *With the Old Breed, at Peleliu and Okinawa* (Novato, Calif.: Presidio Press, 1981); Stephen E. Ambrose, *Band of Brothers: E Company, 506th Regiment, 101st Airborne: From Normandy to Hitler's Eagle's Nest* (New York: Simon & Schuster, 1992); *D-Day, June 6, 1944: The Climatic Battle of World War II* (New York: Simon & Schuster, 1994); and *Citizen Soldiers: The U.S. Army from the Normandy Beaches to the Bulge to the Surrender of Germany, June 7, 1944–May 7, 1945* (New York: Simon & Schuster, 1997). Ambrose dedicated *D-Day* to Forrest Pogue and acknowledged his great intellectual debt to this first historian of D-Day.

33. U.S. Department of the Army, *The Writing of American Military History: A Guide*, Pamphlet No. 20–200 (Washington, D.C.: Government Printing Office, 1956), 27.

34. Louis Gottschalk, *Understanding History: A Primer of Historical Method*, 2nd ed. (New York: Alfred A. Knopf, 1969).

35. Roger Horowitz, "Oral History and the Story of America and World War II," *Journal of American History* 82 (September 1995): 617–24.

36. Cornelius Ryan, "A Panel of Historians Discuss Oral History," in *The Second National Colloquium on Oral History*, ed. Louis M. Starr (New York: Oral History Association, 1968), 13–20.

37. Pogue, "The George C. Marshall Project," 82–94.

38. Lee Kennett, *G.I.: The American Soldier in World War II* (New York: Charles Scribner's Sons, 1987), chap. 4.

39. Samuel A. Stouffer et. al., *Studies in Social Psychology in World War II, vol. 1, The American Soldier: Adjustment During Army Life* (Princeton, N.J.: Princeton University Press, 1949), 6.

40. Stouffer, *The American Soldier*, vol. 2, 169.

41. Stouffer, *The American Soldier*, vol. 2, 90.

42. Stouffer, *The American Soldier*, vol. 2, 136.

43. Stouffer, *The American Soldier*, vol. 1, 12.

44. Robin M. Williams, Jr. "The American Soldier: An Assessment, Several Wars Later," *Public Opinion Quarterly* 53 (Summer 1989): 155–74.

45. For an overview of the impact of Stouffer and his teams on developments in the field of psychology and other social sciences, see Ellen Herman, *The Romance of American Psychology: Political Culture in the Age of Experts* (Berkeley:

University of California Press, 1995) and Eva S. Moskowitz, *In Therapy We Trust: America's Obsession with Self-Fulfillment* (Baltimore, Md.: The Johns Hopkins University Press, 2001).

46. For examples of recent historical scholarship drawing on Stouffer's *American Soldier [Studies in Social Psychology in World War II* (Princeton, N.J.: Princeton University Press, 1949)], see Michael D. Doubler, *Closing with the Enemy: How GIs Fought the War in Europe, 1944–1945* (Lawrence, Kan.: University Press of Kansas, 1994); Brenda L. Moore, *To Serve My Country, To Serve My Race: The Story of the Only African American WACs Stationed Overseas During World War II* (New York: New York University Press, 1996); and Gerald F. Linderman, *The World Within War: America's Combat Experience in World War II* (New York: Free Press, 1997).

47. John Bodnar, "Saving Private Ryan and Postwar Memory in America," *American Historical Review* 106 (June 2001): 805–17.

48. Ben Shephard, *A War of Nerves: Soldiers and Psychiatrists in the Twentieth Century* (Cambridge: Harvard University Press, 2001), passim.

49. Shephard, passim.

50. John Keegan, *The Face of Battle* (New York: Viking, 1976).

51. Shephard, passim.

52. Richard A. Gabriel, "Soviet Military Psychiatry" and Robert Schneider, "Military Psychiatry in the German Army," in *Military Psychiatry: A Comparative Perspective*, ed. Richard A. Gabriel (Westport, Conn.: Greenwood Press, 1986).

53. Omer Bartov, *Murder in our Midst: The Holocaust, Industrial Killing, and Representation* (New York: Oxford University Press, 1996).

54. For a sophisticated analysis of the efforts by the Roosevelt administration and the U.S. Army to inculcate a democratic ethos among soldiers, see Benjamin L. Alpers, "This Is the Army: Imagining a Democratic Military in World War II," *Journal of American History* 85 (June 1998): 129–63.

SEMPER PARATUS: THE U.S. COAST GUARD'S FLOTILLA 10 AT OMAHA BEACH

Mark A. Snell

The United States Coast Guard, which can trace its founding to 1790, is the nation's oldest continuous maritime service. The Coast Guard and its predecessors have participated in every war since 1790, including the wars against Saddam Hussein. Yet in 2003, the Coast Guard came under attack by the secretary of defense. A *Washington Post* article appearing on August 31, 2003, claimed, "Defense Secretary Donald H. Rumsfeld has all but decided to remove the U.S. Coast Guard from participation in future wars, a prospect that is devastating morale in the maritime service because of its pride at having taken part in most of the nation's armed conflicts over the past 200 years, defense sources said." Continuing, the article alleged that

> In recent months Rumsfeld, who is considering a number of radical changes in the organization and structure of the U.S. armed forces, has written several increasingly harsh memos raising questions about the Coast Guard's role in wars, officials said. Rumsfeld has expressed dissatisfaction with the fact that last year, when the Pentagon asked whether the Coast Guard could send cutters to the Persian Gulf to protect Navy ships, Coast Guard officials declined, citing budget pressures. . . . Rumsfeld has also noted that the Coast Guard has its hands full attending to its homeland security mission along U.S. coastlines, waterways and harbors.[1]

During the Second World War, the U.S. Coast Guard also had "its hands full" with homeland security, yet its contributions to overseas military operations were extremely valuable, especially the role that it played in amphibious operations. In fact, one of the bloodiest days in U.S. Coast

Guard combat history was June 6, 1944, during the largest amphibious assault of the war. While the men and women of the Coast Guard performed their traditional homeland security missions along the U.S. coastline, their mates in Flotilla 10 of Assault Group O transported and landed troops in landing craft, infantry (LCIs) under intense enemy fire on Omaha Beach. The Latin motto of the Coast Guard is *Semper Paratus*— Always Ready. On that day, they would have to live up to their motto.

The Coast Guard, which had been a branch of the U.S. Treasury Department in peacetime, became a combatant force when Executive Order 8929 transferred the service to the Navy Department on November 1, 1941. In addition to its traditional responsibilities, the USCG then took on roles in anti-submarine warfare and convoy escort, as well as port control and security. Coast Guard sailors also served alongside naval personnel on Navy ships, and entire Coast Guard crews manned other naval vessels, typically transport ships and attack transports, the latter having the ability to carry and launch smaller landing craft, such as landing craft, assault (LCAs) and landing craft, vehicle and personnel (LCVPs: more commonly called "Higgins boats," after their designer and manufacturer, Andrew J. Higgins of New Orleans). The manning of troop transports by Coast Guard crews even predated the transfer of the service to the Navy Department when President Franklin D. Roosevelt gave the authorization on June 3, 1941.[2]

The original Coast Guard crews who served on the transports were transferred from the service's oceangoing cutters, but the men who originally operated the smaller landing vessels were called "surfmen," Coast Guardsmen who previously had served at coastal lifesaving stations and who possessed the boat-handling skills needed to bring a craft through rolling surf onto the beach. These men would then train recruits in the necessary skills as the service expanded during the war.[3] One young recruit attending Coast Guard basic training in St. Augustine, Florida, recalled that assignment to "landing barge" duty, as it sometimes was called, was seen as punishment. According to Marvin Perret, a Coast Guard coxswain who landed troops on Utah Beach on June 6, 1944,

> . . . we were there [basic training] for six weeks and there were rumors around the reservation that "Man, whatever you do, don't mess up" and we were like, "What do you mean?" "Well if you do something out of order or you don't pay attention they may send you to Landing Barge

School." Of course a lot of the kids didn't really know what that was but having been born and bred in New Orleans I had seen Mr. Higgins's crew building these landing craft . . . and I knew darn well what these things were all about, so I was really a step ahead of the guys. . . . They took about 150 of us—we didn't know it at the time—but they had plans for us destined to be boat crew personnel. . . .[4]

In addition to manning transports and Higgins boats, Coast Guardsmen also served as crew members on larger landing vessels, such as LCI and landing ship, tank (LST), as well as a variety of similar types of vessels. (Vessels longer than 200 feet were called ships; shorter vessels were known as craft or boats.) LSTs were flat-bottomed ships with an overall length of 327 feet and were capable of landing tanks and trucks through two bow doors directly onto the beach. An LCI(L)—the "L" stood for large—had an overall length of 158.5 feet, was flat-bottomed, and discharged troops down ramps on both sides of the bow. The LCI(L) was the primary landing vessel of Flotilla 10.[5]

Flotilla 10's LCIs were built in Orange, Texas, by the Consolidated Steel Corporation's Shipbuilding Division. They were powered by eight General Motors diesel engines that provided 1,600 horsepower for two propeller shafts with twin variable-pitch propellers. They required a crew of three officers and 21 enlisted men and could carry up to 188 troops. The LCIs were armed with four 20mm cannons and two .50-caliber machine guns, all intended primarily as anti-aircraft weapons although they could be used in a ground-support role when the vessels were beached.[6] Unlike larger ships, the LCIs were not named, but numbered, such as LCI(L)-94. The LCIs that would make up the flotilla included vessels numbered from 83 through 96, 319 through 326, and 349 and 350 for a total of 24 craft. After the vessels were commissioned, they assembled in Galveston, Texas, where they were formed into an organization originally designated Flotilla 4 (it would be redesignated Flotilla 10 prior to the Normandy invasion). Command of the flotilla went to Commander Miles H. Imlay (USCG).[7]

Miles Hopkins Imlay was 41 years old when he took command of the flotilla. A native of Washington, D.C., Imlay attended Brown University before his appointment to the United States Coast Guard Academy, from which he graduated in 1923. He served in a variety of assignments on cutters and destroyers before the war, and he also taught and coached at the Coast Guard Academy. He was head of the Seamanship Department at his alma mater when the United States entered the war in 1941.[8] Imlay's extensive experience both afloat and at the Academy would serve him well on June, 6, 1944.

"On February 20, 1943, the flotilla departed Galveston, Texas, and sailed for Key West, Florida," recalled a Coast Guardsman assigned to one of the LCIs. Continuing, he remembered:

> The first day out of Galveston, the unseasoned sailors got a taste of bad weather. They suffered that illness where you would have to get to feeling better before you could die. You might say they didn't have any guts. They had lost them over the side or in the bucket on the deck near their bunk. They were seasick! By the time the flotilla arrived in Key West, they had a lot of guts. They had grown up to be men. They became accustomed to the constant rolling, pitching, and turning of these seagoing flat-bottomed Broncos known as Landing Craft Infantry (Large). One sailor later said that LCI stands for "Lousy Civilian Idea."[9]

Lieutenant (junior grade) Arthur Farrar, USCG Reserve (USCGR), even wrote that an LCI "appeared to be a combination of a bad dream and a Buck Rogers creation."[10] On their maiden voyage, the crews of the LCIs quickly realized that the flat-bottomed vessels, which made them ideal for discharging troops onto a beach, were terribly unstable in a rough sea, something they would experience more than once during the war, including the early morning hours of June 6, 1944. Lieutenant (junior grade) Coit Hendley (USCGR), who commanded LCI(L)-85 during the Normandy invasion, recalled that LCIs "are light and large enough to catch every breeze. They have no keel to hold them steady, and the large flat bottom reacts to every little twist of the currents." His nickname for these unwieldy vessels was "the Ugly Ducklings."[11]

After departing Key West, the flotilla sailed to Norfolk, Virginia, in March, where training in amphibious operations began. A half day out of Key West the weather turned nasty. Coit Hendley remembered, "To most of us Ensigns and a large part of the crew, this was to be the first sea duty. It was a rugged initiation. Some say an LCI will roll on heavy dew. In this gale they did everything. They rolled and pitched and shuddered. Sometimes they hit a wave with a jolt like running into a brick wall. The storm lasted four days. . . . The five days of bad seas had made a sorry mess of some brand new Ensigns."[12] At Little Creek and Virginia Beach (the former being the current Little Creek Naval Amphibious Base, and the latter the U.S. Army's Fort Story), "we got our first experience of approaching a beach, dropping a stern anchor, and learning to retract after unloading the troops," wrote a veteran many years later. After the vessels were degaussed to protect them from magnetic mines, on March 31, the flotilla departed, via Bermuda, for French Morocco, where it arrived at Port Lyautey on April 29, 1943. There, it prepared for the invasion of Sicily.[13]

On July 10, 1943, the men of Flotilla 4 discharged their troops near Licata and Gela on the southern coast of Sicily during Operation Husky. German air raids threatened the LCIs nightly, but the only damage that the vessels received was from shore-based machine guns during the landings at Licata. On the night of July 11, the men of the flotilla were involved in one of the tragic episodes of warfare: fratricide. During a German air raid, American C-47 transport planes carrying paratroopers of the 82nd Airborne Division flew over the fleet. At the same time, the Germans had dropped parachute flares to illuminate the ships below. According to one sailor in the flotilla, "The gun crews, blinded by the flares, filled the air with an umbrella of tracers. They could not see what they were shooting at. . . . Every ship in the area opened up with every gun. You could see the planes crashing into the water. It was too late when the planes were recognized as C-47 transports."[14] The cost was high: Twenty-three of 144 planes were lost, more than half that survived were badly damaged, 60 pilots and crewmen perished, and more than 200 paratroopers were killed.[15]

The flotilla also landed troops at Salerno on September 9, 1943, during the Allied advance up the boot of Italy. Some of the vessels were used later to evacuate retreating British soldiers when the Germans staged a large counterattack. Other vessels of the flotilla also made landings on the nearby Isle of Capri. As the war in Italy continued to move farther inland, the flotilla departed and anchored at Gibraltar, where crewmembers were given liberty. According to one old salt,

> The harbor was filled with British and American war ships. Fifty percent of the crew from each LCI was granted Liberty in Gibraltar. The British sailors didn't care too much for the American sailors and it didn't take much to start the disagreements between the two allies. Due to these disagreements and the resulting brawls the flotilla had as many casualties in Gibraltar as we had in all the previous Mediterranean operations. Needless to say we left Gibraltar without another liberty.[16]

The crewmembers of Flotilla 4 did not know it, but they were about to see many more British sailors at their next destination, the ports situated along the south coast of England. The buildup for the long awaited cross-channel attack was about to begin.

The flotilla was headquartered at Greenway House, on the Dart River near Dittisham. Greenway House was novelist Agatha Christie's home; the Coast Guard's temporary occupation of her abode forced her to move into her gardener's house for the rest of the flotilla's stay.[17] For the next seven months, the buildup for the invasion continued unabated, as did training in amphibious operations. Coast Guard Combat Photographer Seth Shepard, assigned to the flotilla, wrote that, "All the invasion veterans of North Africa, Sicily, and Italy, and that included most of the crews of the Coast Guard LCIs in our flotilla, knew that no large scale operation could hope to be even partially successful without the long grind of preparation." Long hours, tedious drills, and realistic training would occupy the members of the flotilla through the winter and spring. According to Shepard, "This meant actual maneuvers along the coast of England—called 'dry runs'—and those million and one little items, plans, stores, orders that must in the end dovetail into the complete pattern."[18] It was during one of these "dry runs" that German torpedo boats attacked and sank two LSTs at the Slapton Sands training area in Devonshire, resulting in 789 dead and 300 wounded. (Imlay's flotilla was not involved in this debacle.) One of the lessons learned from this exercise was that rescue craft would be needed for the actual invasion, and the U.S. Coast Guard got the call, supplying sixty 83' wooden-hulled cutters and nearly 1,000 men for the job.[19]

Training continued. "Beaching and target practices were frequent. Possible and probable casualties were outlined and practices set up to remedy them," wrote Coast Guard Lieutenant (junior grade) Arthur Farrar at the end of 1944. "Many full scale practice operations were made so that landing was natural for both sailors and soldiers. Operations were planned to be as near as possible like the real operation."[20] Meanwhile, extensive alterations were made on all Allied beaching craft (including LCIs), such as the installation of new radios; LSTs even underwent modifications on their bow doors.[21] Routine maintenance was stepped up to ensure that everything was in tip-top shape. On LCI(L)-92, Combat Photographer Shepard wrote, "The daily routine included chipping decks, painting topsides and in the bilges, getting the whole ship in first class condition."

After removing nonessential equipment to lighten the vessels, new invasion gear began to arrive, making it apparent to all that the big day was near at hand. Shepard recalled that "the crew constantly talked of invasion and we all wished that it would hurry up and come. Waiting is tough."[22] Even though the Germans had not resorted to chemical warfare, no chances were taken. "Gas warfare defense received a lot of attention," wrote LCI(L)-85's Lieutenant Farrar. "Each man was given the proper equipment to protect against gas and knew how to use it. He also was taught how to treat himself if he did get gassed. By D-Day there was a definite feeling among the crew that they could take care of themselves."[23]

By mid-May, everyone assigned to the flotilla—and probably everyone else in the Allied assault force—knew that the invasion would soon come. According to the official history of the U.S. Coast Guard during World War II:

> From the Thames Estuary in the east, to Falmouth, near Land's End, in the west, the ports on Britain's English Channel shore were packed with ships and boats of virtually every kind, including types never known before. There were even floating breakwaters and piers to be sunk in place. Invasion craft were everywhere. As the time for the assault drew close, men, machines, equipment, supplies, and ammunition moved south to the various ports. All hands turned to in moving materials and loading the ships. There was little sleep in the last 24 hours before the sailing.[24]

The Germans sensed something important was about to occur, too. Lieutenant Farrar later wrote, "There were several nuisance air raids but three days before D-Day they came over in earnest. There was a lot of shooting and nineteen men in the flotilla received injury from flak. No damage to ships was done by enemy action although there were some near misses by bombs and eleven mines were found in the harbor next morning."[25] During one of the earlier "nuisance" raids, Motor Machinist's Mate, 3rd Class August B. Buncik stuck his head out of LCI(L)-94's steering room hatch when a piece of shrapnel or a spent antiaircraft slug penetrated his helmet and creased his head. The vessel's pharmacist's mate sent him to the hospital, but Buncik would return in time to make the Channel crossing.[26]

The naval component of the invasion of Fortress Europe was code-named Neptune and was under the overall command of Admiral Sir Bertram H. Ramsay of the Royal Navy. Rear Admiral Alan G. Kirk (USN) commanded the Western Naval Task Force with responsibility for the landings on Omaha and Utah beaches, and Rear Admiral Sir Philip Vian (RN) commanded the Eastern Naval Task Force, with responsibility for the landings in the British sector (Gold, Sword, and Juno beaches). Under Admiral Kirk was Rear Admiral John Lesslie Hall Jr. (USN), commanding Task Force O for Omaha, and Rear Admiral Don P. Moon (USN), leading Task Force U for Utah.[27] To support Neptune, a vast armada was waiting like a coiled spring in the waters of the United Kingdom. The Allied fleet included 238 capital ships, 221 smaller vessels, 200 minesweepers, 805 merchant ships, and 4,308 landing vessels. Nearly 80 percent of the fleet comprised British or Commonwealth vessels, and 16.5 percent were U.S. vessels. The rest were French, Dutch, Norwegian, and Polish.[28]

More U.S. Coast Guard vessels and Coast Guard–manned naval vessels took part in Neptune than in any previous operation. Coast Guard–manned vessels included three attack transports (U.S.S. *Joseph T. Dickman*, U.S.S. *Samuel Chase*, and U.S.S. *Bayfield*), 10 LSTs (four of which were assigned to the Eastern Naval Task Force under British command), 24 LCIs, and the 60 vessels assigned to the Coast Guard Rescue Flotilla. The attack transports and some of the LSTs carried LCVPs and other small landing craft that were lowered to the water by onboard davits. Of course, the landing craft themselves were piloted and manned by Coast Guard coxswains and motor machinist's mates. Coast Guard sailors also served on board vessels with Navy crews, such as the attack transport U.S.S. *Charles Carroll*. Not counting the smaller landing craft carried by the transports and LSTs, there were 97 Coast Guard and Coast Guard–manned vessels in the invasion.[29]

"Actual loading of assault troops began on June 1," wrote Admiral Kirk, the Western Task Force commander. "The men were briefed and the ships 'sealed,' and the great armada hung poised on the southern coast of Britain. . . ."[30] The LCI(L)-92 did not receive its cargo of GIs until the early morning hours of June 3. With the troops on board, the vessel was packed like a tin of sardines. "Some of us [Coast Guardsmen] went around trying to find guys from our home towns," recalled Seth Shepard. "J. W. Spring, motor machinist's mate, third class (USCGR), of Fort Worth, Texas, found a fellow Texan from his hometown, and they spent the whole evening talking over old times and, of course, Texas."[31] Everything depended on the weather, which was not cooperating. Admiral Kirk later reported, "D-Day had originally been set as June 5, but due to adverse weather conditions there was a last postponement of 24 hours. Then on the night of

June 5, our last minute air attacks rose to a crescendo, paratroopers made their jumps far inland, and the great armada moved across the Channel."[32]

Flotilla 4 was redesignated Flotilla 10 before the Channel crossing—"No doubt this was to confuse the enemy," recalled one Coast Guard veteran assigned to the flotilla. Motor Machinist's Mate 1st Class (MoMM 1/C) Clifford W. Lewis, onboard the LCI(L)-94, described in his diary the unfolding events on his vessel during the evening of June 5:

> Still waiting patiently although we know much already as to where we are to land, etc. Skipper [Lieutenant Gene R. Gislason] called us all into the crew's quarters and had a long diagram or photograph of the beach on the mess table. All pill boxes, machine guns, mines, and other obstacles [were shown]. Our beach is to be Red Dog, close to Easy Green. He said we could expect plenty of mines & that subs & E-Boats would be active. New weapons were expected and 1950 enemy planes were available for use against us. He wished us the best of luck and then Mr. Mead checked over our names for correct serial numbers & [life insurance] beneficiaries.[33]

The skipper's intelligence briefing was inaccurate concerning the threat level for enemy aircraft, submarines, and E-boats (attack boats larger than U.S. PT-boats, one of which did sink a Norwegian destroyer), but the danger of mines was very real. In fact, the first naval casualty of the invasion occurred when one of the minesweepers, out in front of the fleet, itself struck a mine and sank.[34]

The fleet departed the coast of England while it was still daylight on June 5. After rendezvousing at pre-selected locations, the armada headed for the Normandy coast, with the minesweepers in the lead, followed by destroyers, the LCT flotilla (carrying tanks), a bombardment group of battleships, cruisers, and more destroyers, and then the transports and larger landing vessels, including LSTs and the LCI(L)s. Other types of vessels came along behind the landing craft, including the Coast Guard rescue cutters.[35] Seth Shepard described what he saw as his own LCI(L) was heading out to sea: "Everywhere the ships were beginning to take their positions. LCIs, LSTs, transports, destroyers, escort vessels, even cruisers and battleships. All the LSTs had a large barrage balloon flying above them and the LCIs looked top-heavy with the mass of troops on deck. We all watched the memorable sights of the vast flotillas of ships stretching in every direction." The ships stayed close to the coast until darkness fell. By

8:30 P.M., they were on their way to Normandy. Overhead, transport aircraft, bombers, and fighters were heading to France. "Those planes made us feel more secure and were always a grand sight," wrote Shepard.[36]

Flotilla 10 had been augmented with 12 Navy-manned LCIs for Operation Neptune, bringing the total number of vessels under Imlay's command to 36, with 18 each set to land at Utah and Omaha.[37] Imlay wore two hats for this invasion: In addition to commanding Flottilla 10, he also was deputy commander for Assault Group O-1 (the O stood for Omaha), which was under the overall command of another Coast Guard officer, Captain Edward H. Fritzsche. The other assault groups for Omaha were designated O-2, O-3, and O-4. Assault Group O-2 was under the command of Captain W. A. Bailey (USN). Assault Group O-3 also was commanded by a U.S. Navy officer, Captain L. B. Schulten, but Assault Group O-4 was led by Commander S. H. Dennis of the Royal Navy. Bailey's and Dennis's assault groups carried the soldiers of the 29th Division's 116th Regimental Combat Team (RCT); Dennis also had the responsibility of landing Army Rangers at Pointe du Hoc. Fritzsche's and Schulten's groups would land troops of the 1st Division's 16th RCT. Omaha Beach, itself merely a code name, would be divided into sectors, with Assault Groups O-2 and O-4 landing on Dog Green, Dog White, Dog Red, and Easy Green sectors (as well as Pointe du Hoc), while Assault Groups O-1 and O-3 landed on Easy Red and Fox Green sectors.[38]

Because his main responsibility was as deputy commander of Assault Group O-1, Imlay, now a captain, would be able to concentrate only on the Omaha landings on June 6; after his LCIs destined for Utah Beach arrived at the rendezvous area (10 miles from the beach), he no longer controlled them. Many years later Imlay explained that "a flotilla organization is an administrative, logistics, and training command. It rarely acts as a unified assault unit." On the approach to the rendezvous area, Imlay commanded Convoy Group One, comprising LCIs from two flotillas and 14 Coast Guard rescue cutters.[39] Upon arriving at the rendezvous area, he became Deputy Assault Group Commander responsible for the landings of six LSTs, five LCIs, 53 LCTs, and six rhino ferries (barges of pontoon units propelled by outboard motors, usually carrying heavy automotive and construction equipment).[40] Not only would he not know what happened to the LCIs of Flotilla 10 at Utah, he would not even be able to control his LCIs from Assault Group O-2 after they began landing troops in the other sectors of Omaha Beach.

H-hour on D-Day was set for 0630 hours, but the Coast Guard and naval crews would be preparing to launch much earlier, from between 0100 and 0400, depending on the assault wave to which they were assigned. The LSTs would launch their tanks first, specialized armored vehicles known as "DD tanks" (the "DD" stood for duplex drive, which allowed the tanks to swim with propellers until they got ashore). Next came the Higgins boats and LCIs carrying the assault troops; young Coast Guardsmen also piloted many of the Higgins boats.[41] In his operations order to his convoy, Captain Imlay emphatically reminded his subordinate commanders, "REMEMBER THE MISSION OF THE NAVY IN THIS OPERATION IS TO PUT THE ARMY ON THE BEACH."[42] Doing so would prove extremely difficult. After a rough channel crossing and hours of driving in circles, the LCVPs headed for shore, followed by the LCIs and various other landing vessels. Allied air forces already had bombed the German defenses (although the bombardment was ineffective), and the Navy's battleships, cruisers, and destroyers were pounding away at enemy positions.[43] Seth Shepard wrote that the "LCIs were following each other in a long circular movement. The beach on which we were to land was 16 miles away. . . . At 5:50 A.M. the LCIs of our flotilla formed into two columns and swung in toward land, now hazy as an early morning mist blew in off the channel. . . . By 7 A.M. we knew that the first waves of small landing boats already hit the beaches and we wondered how they were making out."[44] On LCI(L)-94, MoMM 1/ C Clifford Lewis was manning one of the 20mm cannons. Weighted down with helmet, impregnated uniform (in case of a chemical attack), gas mask, cartridge belt, knife, canteens, and life jacket, he could see LCVPs and LSTs returning to the "transport area," where the attack transports were anchored. Coming toward shore in a subsequent wave, he saw that "[s]moke hovered over the beach and a number of ships could be seen burning furiously. Tracer shells began skipping out over the water towards us," he later wrote in his diary. "They exploded very close and shrapnel clattered against the ship."[45] All hell had broken loose on Omaha, and the LCI sailors were about to enter its gates.

After passing the attack transports, the LCIs fanned out and steered toward their designated beaching stations. Smoke, haze, and strong currents made it difficult for the coxswains to keep their vessels on course. The first LCI to hit the beach was LCI(L)-91.[46] Just getting to a point on Dog White sector where the ramps could be dropped had proven to be arduous and hair-raising. The Germans had done a magnificent job of preparing beach defenses, with all sorts of obstructions and mines that could rip huge holes in the sides of landing vessels. Army engineers and Navy demolition teams had tried valiantly to make paths for the incoming craft, but they were largely unsuccessful.[47] Lieutenant (junior grade) Arend Vyn, Jr. (USCGR) snaked the 91 through stakes topped with teller mines (German anti-tank mines) and lowered his ramps at 7:40 A.M. to allow the troops to get ashore, but according to Vyn, "Troops disembarked reluctantly over both ramps in the face of heavy enemy machine gun and rifle fire." The slowness in getting the troops off and the rapidly rising tide forced Lieutenant Vyn to move his vessel forward to keep it grounded. The 91 was "swinging with the tide toward the [mined] stakes on the port bow so the ship was retracted [pulled with an onboard winch back toward its anchoring point]. While doing so, a teller mine was exploded at the port bow injuring a few soldiers but not causing fatal damage to the ship," Vyn wrote in his official after-action report.[48]

Vyn called for assistance from some of the smaller craft in the area, but no help was forthcoming. Because he still had some 60 troops aboard, Vyn raised anchor and moved the 91 about 100 yards west of his original beaching "in an effort to get in beyond the obstructions." Again the ramps were dropped, and the troops began disembarking. At that point, a German shell slammed into the 91 and exploded in the fuel tanks, killing 22 men of the 147th Combat Engineers and five of the Coast Guard crew. Artillery shells splashed around the stricken vessel, and small arms fire rattled off the hull. Vyn saw his ship was dying, so he threw all of his Secret and Confidential correspondence into the raging fire and ordered the survivors to abandon ship.[49] The 91 suffered 11 Coast Guardsmen wounded and seven killed in action, the highest number of casualties of any Coast Guard–manned vessel during the Normandy invasion.[50]

"My heart beat multiplied when I looked over the starboard bow, near the beach," wrote the LCI(L)-92's Seth Shepard, "and saw the Coast Guard manned LCI 91 enveloped in flames and smoke. She was the first LCI to hit that sector of the beach and we were scheduled as the second."[51] The skipper of the 92 was Lieutenant Robert M. Salmon (USCGR). Salmon decided to land in the 91's lee (the side of the ship that is sheltered from the wind) and use the smoke coming from the burning hulk as a screen for his own vessel. Salmon's LCI, like Vyn's vessel, was carrying combat engineers. About 100 yards from the shore, as the 92 was taking intense small arms and artillery fire, a huge explosion rocked the ship's port side:

It, too, had struck a mine. Nineteen of the combat engineers were killed, but none of the Coast Guardsmen. "I saw Army officers pleading with their men to get off as quickly as possible," recalled Combat Photographer Shepard, "The cries of some of the helpless soldiers in the deep water were pitiful. All the while the terrific explosions, fire and heavy smoke filled the air and the littered decks heaved under the impact of still other shells as they ripped through steel plates."[52] Lieutenant Salmon tried to retract his vessel after the surviving soldiers had disembarked, but the fire caused by the explosion had grown too intense, and loss of water pressure prevented the crew from battling the flames. Salmon ordered the 92 abandoned.[53]

Lieutenant (junior grade) Coit Hendley commanded the LCI(L)-85. Some five miles out from the beach, one of the junior officers saw "wreckage . . . floating around [and] numerous life belts and packs were observed. . . . There wasn't any activity to be noted on the beach, but the wreckage told of terrific fighting."[54] The strong tide had pushed the control vessel directing the landing craft away from its designated area, and so Hendley's LCI was directed to the wrong beach. "We actually landed in the left flank of Easy Red or the right flank of Fox Green rather than the right flank of Easy Red as scheduled," Hendley wrote in his after-action report. After grounding the 85 and lowering the ramps, it became apparent that the water was too deep for the soldiers to wade to shore. Lieutenant Hendley backed out his LCI and took it about 100 yards to the right and beached again. At that point, the 85 struck a teller mine that exploded under the bow. Then, according to Hendley, "The port ramp went down and the troops began going ashore. Shells and machine gun fire began to hit us. About fifty troops got down the port ramp before a shell hit it and blew it off the sponsons and over the side. As the starboard ramp had not gone down and the wounded men were jamming the deck, we backed off the beach again."[55]

Although the mine had not caused any casualties, German artillery and small arms fire had wreaked havoc. "A check revealed that we had approximately 15 dead and 30 wounded men all in the forward part of the ship," Hendley reported. "We had been hit approximately 25 times by shells. Fire was starting in troop compartments 1, 2, and 3. Water was coming in slowly from shell holes below the water line and the hole made by the mine." Because the engine room escaped without damage, Lieutenant Hendley ordered his coxswain to back off the beach about 200 yards so that the damage-control party could fight fires and make temporary repairs. The 85's Coast Guard pharmacists' mates and several Army and Navy physicians who had been onboard began tending to the wounded immediately. Because there were still troops waiting to go ashore, a Higgins boat came alongside and ferried a boatload to the beach, but there were assault troops still aboard when Hendley ordered the 85 to head back to the transport area, where it pulled alongside U.S.S. *Samuel Chase* to offload casualties.[56] The famous combat photographer Robert Capa, who had gone ashore with the first wave of the assault and had used all of his rolls of film, decided to hitch a ride back with the 85 to the transport area. Capa later recalled this episode:

> I saw an LCI behind me with a lot of medics getting out and some getting killed as they got out. One place being as bad as another, I waded out and waited in the water for all the medics to get out. Then I climbed aboard and started to change my film. I felt a slight shock and I was all covered with feathers. I thought: "What is this? Is somebody killing chickens?" Then I saw the superstructure had been shot away and the feathers were the stuffing from the Kapok jackets [life vests] of the men who were blown up.[57]

Aboard the *Samuel Chase*, Capa snapped a photograph of the badly damaged 85 below him, the deck still littered with dead and wounded soldiers. When the living and the dead had been transferred to the larger vessel, a tugboat took the 85 in tow, but the latter vessel began to list so badly that the "crew scrambled on board the tug before she went over. She turned slowly on her side and then bottom up immediately," wrote Hendley. "A demolition charge was put in her stern and she went down completely." Luckily for the crew, only four Coast Guardsmen had been wounded during the battle.[58]

Lieutenant Gene R. Gislason (USCGR), the commander of LCI(L)-94, decided to take matters into his own hands. Rather than suffer the fate of his fellow skippers, he decided to discharge his troops elsewhere. Gislason had been a merchant mariner before the war, and at 32 years of age, was older than the other LCI commanders. His crew even gave him an appropriate nickname: Popeye. He had a personal cache of J&B scotch, which he ordered the cook to divvy out to the crew during the assault until it was gone or until they did not want any more. One of the crew members, Motor Machinist's Mate Charles Jarreau recalled, "Popeye looked at our sign [placed by a beach-marking team] and said, 'Hell, I'm not going in there, we'll never get off the beach.' So he aborted the run. The rest of the LCIs in our flotilla went in where they were supposed to go. . . . They were all shot up. Which made our skipper go up in our esteem by one hell of a lot." Carrying men of the 116th Infantry Regiment of the 29th Division, Gislason had his coxswain pilot his vessel about 100 yards down the beach. The 94 then headed in and grounded. The ramps went down and the Germans opened up.[59] MoMM 1/C Clifford Lewis wrote in his diary, "We disembarked our troops and started out when the Skipper noticed we had fouled an LCVP with a line and started back in to assist them. At that moment 3 shells burst into the pilothouse and exploded killing 3 of my shipmates and wounding two including an officer. Couldn't do anymore for the LCVP so we cut the line and started off the beach again after the pilot house was cleared and hand steering put into operation."[60]

One of the dead crewmen was MoMM 3/C August B. Buncik, the unlucky sailor who had been slightly wounded in the head during the German air raid of his port back in England just prior to the invasion. This time, Buncik was decapitated. Cliff Lewis described the gruesome scene in the pilothouse:

Went topside on the boat deck just aft of the pilothouse. The Pharm. Mates were working over a couple of shapeless hulks lying in wire baskets and covered with blankets. It was a horrible sight with blood and flesh spattered over everything. [Seaman 1st Class Jack] De Nunzio had both legs blown off & part of his stomach, but was still living. I helped doc give him plasma, but it was hopeless. He died 15 min. later. Buncik was decapitated and occupied only half a stretcher. [Seaman 1st Class Fletcher P.] Burton [Jr.] was still intact but killed by the concussion. . . . The bodies were later put aboard an LST and were later buried on the beach.

Burton, DiNunzio, and Buncik were the only fatalities on the 94, but two other crewmen were wounded.[61] The three dead men were interred in the Normandy American Cemetery above Omaha Beach, where they still lie.[62] Although Popeye was able to retract and save his vessel, the German gunners had taken a serious toll.

Lieutenant (junior grade) Budd Bornhoft (USCGR) was in command of LCI(L)-93. The 93 had survived its first landing during the morning of June 6 but met its fate during a second trip that afternoon. The tide was quickly falling as the 93 struggled to get over a sandbar on Easy Red. The coxswain was able to pass over it, and the ramps were dropped. Most of the soldiers had disembarked when German artillery began pounding the vessel. Of the 25 troops remaining on board, four were wounded, and one was killed. As soon as the remaining troops had gotten off the 93, Lieutenant Bornhoft ordered his vessel to retract, but the tide had receded so fast that the 93 could not clear the sandbar that it previously had slid over during the trip in. By now, the 93 had taken at least 10 direct hits from German artillery and had struck a submerged mine as well. Small boats evacuated the wounded soldiers, and two of the crew who also had been hit. Finally, Bornhoft ordered the rest of the crew to abandon ship.[63]

The LCI(L)-88 was the first vessel of its type to land on Easy Red, where it beached at 7:35 A.M.. Standard operating procedure for LCIs called for one of the crew to wade ashore with a hand line that was attached to the beach so that the disembarking troops had something to hold onto as they struggled through the surf. This time, the unfortunate Coast Guardsman did not return. According to Lieutenant William B. Cole (USCGR), the 88's skipper, his crewman "was missing in action, believed killed by gunfire while ashore with the life-line for troops, in performance of his assigned duty."[64] In reality, he had been blown to bits. More than five decades later, a Coast Guard veteran of the invasion recalled, "The first casualty was a young seaman who had volunteered to take the man rope ashore. He was hit at the bottom of the ramp and his body splattered over the ship. Since there were no identifiable remains, he was carried as M.I.A. [missing in action] for a year which perpetrated a cruel false hope for his next of kin."[65] Nonetheless, Lieutenant Cole was able to discharge all the troops and begin retracting within four minutes after the 88 had beached, but at 7:39 A.M., "a direct shell hit was received on the starboard side forward, damaging the starboard ramp beyond repair," Cole wrote in his after-action report, "and killing one man, wounding mortally one man of the ship's crew." Despite the damage caused by artillery, LCI(L)-88 was able to withdraw under its own power and was used to ferry casualties and assist other vessels for the rest of the day.[66]

Lieutenant George Hutchinson (USCGR), commander of the LCI(L)-83, thought it prudent not to take his vessel the whole way to the beach because of the underwater obstacles, so he hailed smaller landing craft and began unloading his 1st Division soldiers. After 36 infantrymen had been transported to the beach, Radioman Third Class Leroy Bowen, Jr., recalled

Before another boat could take off a load a shell killed three more men and wounded thirteen. He [Hutchinson] decided to try to ram the obstacles again, when a mine blew a hole in the bottom and forward part of the number one crew compartment, injuring and killing a few more men. We grounded on the beach, dropped our ramps, and the rest got ashore. We abandoned ship and went ashore with the troops.[67]

That evening, the officers determined that the vessel could be repaired. With the ragged puncture from the mine blast patched and with the all pumps operating, the 83 was re-floated. Navy demolition crews cleared the remaining mines and obstacles, giving the 83 a path to back away from the beach. With the assistance of two tugs, the LCI(L)-83 headed back to England on June 7.[68] In addition to the 1st Division casualties on the 83, two Coast Guard crewmen were wounded on June 6.[69]

With the exception of LCI(L)-91, which had one officer wounded, none of the other LCIs in Flotilla 10 suffered casualties.[70] Over on Utah Beach, the Germans resisted only lightly, making the run-in to the beach seem more like an intense training exercise. Back on Omaha, the survivors of the wrecked LCIs became spectators—and in some cases, infantrymen—until they could catch a ride on a returning vessel. Many were forced to remain on the beach until nightfall. Seth Shepard recorded, "The full moon rising back of us gave a hideous light to the dead bodies lying along the beach road. Then we saw bodies stacked up like a lumber pile farther down." Unwounded crewmen would be taken back to England to a survivor's base to await reassignment. The wounded also were taken to England to base hospitals.[71]

The LCIs that had not been hit or had suffered only minor damage remained off the coast of Normandy for several weeks to ferry wounded to other ships that would take them back to England or to bring supplies and replacement personnel ashore. During the night of June 10, LCI(L)-319, sitting off Utah Beach, threaded its way through a minefield with two ammunition barges in tow during a storm. For this feat the skipper of the 319, Lieutenant (junior grade) Francis Xavier Riley (USCG), was awarded the Bronze Star.[72] Several days after the assault, young Cliff Lewis went ashore with some of his shipmates. They tried to go beyond the beach but they were stopped by Army military police who forbade them from going farther inland because "our blue helmets & clothing were a perfect target for snipers who were still active in the area." So instead, they decided to head back. "Once again on the beach we made our way to where our sister ships the 91, 92, & 93 lay broken, twisted & charred by fire," Lewis recorded in his diary. "Seeing them made us realize even more how lucky we were."[73]

During the invasion of Normandy, four of Flotilla 10's LCIs had been sunk, with 35 of the flotilla's crewmembers wounded and 13 killed in action. On all the other Coast Guard–manned vessels, including the smaller landing craft, only three crewmen were wounded and three killed in action.[74] Because of the actions of Flotilla 10's crewmembers and officers on June 6 and during the subsequent weeks, all the LCIs of the flotilla retroactively were awarded the Coast Guard Unit Commendation.

For their bravery, skippers Gene Gislason, Coit Hendley, George Hutchinson, Robert Salmon, and Arend Vyn received Silver Stars. Another LCI skipper, Lieutenant Samuel Allison (USCGR), of the LCI(L)-326, received the Silver Star for volunteering to use his vessel as a control boat after he had discharged his troops. According to his award citation, "he volunteered for this assignment and, in the face of concentrated shell fire and constant threat of exploding mines, effectively directed boat traffic throughout the remainder of the initial assault." Two enlisted men of the flotilla, Seaman First Class Gene Oxley and MoMM 1/C William Trump also received Silver Stars. Both men had braved enemy fire while dragging the anchor lines to the beach so that the troops would have a line to hold onto as they struggled through the surf. Finally, Captain Imlay also received the Silver Star, not only for his cool actions under fire as Deputy Assault Group Commander, but also for his subsequent actions as assistant to the naval officer in charge of one of the beaches in the aftermath of the assault.[75]

"After the beach-head had been secured and the fighting had moved far inland," recalled a crewman on one of the LCIs, "many of the long-term crewmembers were relieved and transferred back to the states. During the latter part of 1944, the remainder of the flotilla departed for Charleston, South Carolina." New crews were assigned, and many of the vessels were repaired, overhauled, or refitted. After training in the Chesapeake Bay, the flotilla—now named Flotilla 35—departed Norfolk in December 1944, sailed through the Panama Canal, and made its way westward to the Pacific Theater, where it remained for the duration of the war, eventually playing a role in the campaign for Okinawa.[76] It was there that a kamikaze plane struck LCI(L) 90, but the vessel was not sunk. None of the vessels that had survived Normandy ever again landed troops under fire. In the Pacific, many were used to lay smoke screens, and others were employed as supply and mail transports. When the war ended, most of the vessels returned to Galveston, Texas, where they were decommissioned in 1946.[77] Sadly, the skipper of LCI(L)-88, Lieutenant William B. Cole, who had survived the carnage of Omaha Beach, was lost at sea on February 3, 1945, during a training exercise off San Clemente Island, California, while trying to rescue another man. His name is listed on Walls of the Missing at the World War II West Coast Memorial in the Presidio of San Francisco.[78]

Captain Miles Imlay did not command Flotilla 35 in the Pacific. After Normandy, he was reassigned to the United States to the staff of the commander, Eastern Sea Frontier, headquartered in New York, as the air-sea rescue officer. He stayed in the Coast Guard after the war and received several plum assignments, including a stint as skipper of the Coast Guard training ship *Eagle* at the United States Coast Guard Academy and as commanding officer of the Coast Guard Receiving Center at Cape May, New Jersey, where Coast Guard recruits receive basic training. He was promoted to admiral before his retirement. On March 12, 1972, Miles Imlay committed suicide at his home in Waterford, Connecticut.[79]

The United States Coast Guard performed many valuable missions during World War II and subsequent wars, and now it has an even more robust role in homeland security in the wake of the terrorist attacks of September 11, 2001. With proper funding, training, and equipment, the men and women of today's Coast Guard could accept and accomplish any mission that the U.S. Navy gives them—if authorized—just as their predecessors had done more than 60 years earlier. Young Cliff Lewis had experienced war on June 6, 1944, and had lost three of his buddies on the LCI(L)-94. His final diary entry describes his last trip to Omaha Beach on July 26, 1944, when he visited the temporary American cemetery where the remains of his shipmates were buried:

Went ashore in evening. . . . Rode LCVP and transferred to a duck [DUKW, an amphibious truck]. Hit Dog Red Beach. Walked up road toward St. Laurent. Visit grave yard. Saw Buncik, DiNunzio and Burton's graves. No.'s A-4–71, A-9–174, 6-1-12. It's fixed up nice and the little white crosses are lined up neatly in 2 directions. A flag pole, a mast from some ship is in the center and flowers are planted around it. (Some colonel paid the French $5 to bring the flowers.) Many more graves being dug. The graveyard is about a mile from the beach and overlooks a pleasant valley.[80]

Semper Paratus—Always Ready, especially in war.

NOTES

1. "Coast Guard Fights to Maintain War Role," *Washington Post*, August 31, 2003.

2. Robert E. Johnson, *Guardians of the Sea: History of the United States Coast Guard, 1915 to the Present* (Annapolis, Md.: Naval Institute Press, 1987), 190, 195–96, 240–41; Stephen E. Ambrose, *D-Day, June 6, 1944: The Climactic Battle of World War II* (New York: Touchstone, 1995), 45–46. Coast Guardsmen also manned U.S. Army transport and cargo vessels.

3. Johnson, 191.

4. U.S. Coast Guard Oral History Program. Interviewee: Marvin J. Perrett, World War II Coast Guard Veteran. Interviewer: Scott Price, Assistant Historian, June 18, 2003 at Coast Guard Headquarters, Washington, D.C.

5. Ambrose, 43–44.

6. USS LCI(L)-83, www.uscg.mil/hq/g-cp/history/WEBCUTTERS/LCI-83 .html (accessed May 15, 2005).

7. "Coast Guard-Manned Landing Craft (Infantry), Large: Flotilla 4/10/35" (written by an anonymous member of the Flotilla), http://www.uscg.mil/hq/ g-cp/history/WEBCUTTERS/LCI_Flotilla4_History.html (accessed May 15, 2005).

8. Official Biographical Sketch of Captain Miles H. Imlay, USCG, Public Information Division, U.S. Coast Guard (Imlay Papers, USCG History Office, USCG Headquarters, Washington, D.C.).

9. Ibid.

10. Arthur Farrar, "LCIs Are Veterans Now," [U.S. Coast Guard Academy] *Alumni Association Bulletin* 6, 9 (December 1944): 181–91.

11. Lieutenant Coit G. Hendley, "D-Day: A Special Report," *The Washington Times*, June 6, 1984.

12. Ibid.

13. "Coast Guard–Manned Landing Craft (Infantry), Large: Flotilla 4/10/35" (written by an anonymous member of the Flotilla), http://www.uscg.mil/hq/ g-cp/history/WEBCUTTERS/LCI_Flotilla4_History.html (accessed May 15, 2005).

14. Ibid.

15. Ibid.; Samuel Eliot Morison, History of United States Naval Operations in World War II, Volume IX: *Sicily—Salerno—Anzio, January 1943–June 1944* (Boston: Little, Brown and Company, 1954), 121.

16. "Coast Guard-Manned Landing Craft (Infantry), Large: Flotilla 4/10/35" (written by an anonymous member of the Flotilla), http://www.uscg.mil/hq/ g-cp/history/WEBCUTTERS/LCI_Flotilla4_History.html (accessed May 15, 2005).

17. Hendley, "D-Day: A Special Report."

18. Seth Shepard, "Invasion: The Story of the LCI (L) 92 in the Invasion on Normandy June 6, 1944," www.uscg.mil/hq/g-cp/history/LCI92.htm (accessed May 13, 2005).

19. Ambrose, 139; Malcolm F. Willoughby, *The U.S. Coast Guard in World War II* (Annapolis, Md.: Naval Institute Press, 1957 [revised printing 1989]), 249.

20. Farrar.

21. Morison, 63.

22. Shepard.

23. Farrar.

24. Willoughby, 239.

25. Farrar.

26. Excerpts from WWII Diary of Clifford W. Lewis, MoMM 1/C, United States Coast Guard, www.uscg.mil/hq/g-cp/history/Normandy_Diary.html (accessed May 15, 2005).

27. Morison, 52.

28. Georges Bernage, *The D-Day Landing Beaches* (Bayeux, France: Heimdal, 2001), 18.

29. Willoughby, 241–42. Willoughby mistakenly wrote that there were 25 USCG LCI (L)s, when in actuality there were only 24.

30. Vice Admiral Alan G. Kirk, "The Invasion of Normandy," in *Pictorial History of the Second World War*, vol. 6 (*Battle Stations: Your Navy in Action*) (New York: Wm. H. Wise & Co., 1947), 245.

31. Shepard.

32. Kirk, 245.

33. Diary of Clifford W. Lewis.

34. Ambrose, 256, 265–66.

35. Ibid., 256–58.

36. Shepard.

37. Scott Price, "U.S. Coast Guard Manned LCI (L)s" www.uscg.mil/hq/g-cp/ history/WEBCUTTERS/USCG_LCI-Index.html (accessed Dec. 14, 2005).

38. Morison, XI, 130, 133, 141.

39. Neptune Operation Order No. 6–44, Western Naval Task Force, Assault Force "O" (Task Force One Two Four), Convoy Group One, LCI (L) & Rescue Craft Section. KCI(L) 87, Flagship, Weymouth, Dorset, 31 May 1944. USCG Historian's Office (hereafter cited as Neptune Operation Order No. 6–44).

40. Miles Imlay, "Historic Greenway House: 1944 and 1973," 6–7. Unpublished memoir. Imlay Papers, USCG Historian's Office.

41. Ambrose, 256–60.

42. Neptune Operation Order No. 6–44.

43. Morison, XI, 123–25.

44. Shepard.

45. Diary of Clifford W. Lewis.

46. Shepard.

47. Ambrose, 369.

48. Arend Vyn, Jr., "Participation in Operation Neptune by USS LCI (L) 91." Written June 10, 1944, www.uscg.mil/hq/g-cp/history/WEBCUTTERS/LCI_91 (accessed May 13, 2005).

49. Ibid.; Frank Vyn, "The Invasion of Omaha Beach: The LCI-91 & Crew," www.uscg.mil/hq/g-cp/history/Vyn_Article.html (accessed Dec. 21, 2005).

50. Casualty worksheet for Normandy, USCG Historian's Office.

51. Shepard.

52. Ibid.

53. Willoughby, 246; Recollections of John Mateyack, crew member on LCI(L)-92, www.geocities.com/lcil_92/Pg16.htm (accessed May 16, 2005).

54. Farrar.

55. Hendley, "After-action report of the USS LCI (L) 85 During Operation Neptune," www.uscg.mil/hq/g-cp/history/WEBCUTTERS/LCI_85 (accessed May 13, 2005).

56. Ibid.

57. Robert Capa, as related to Charles Wertenbaker, cited in Richard Whelan, *Robert Capa: A Biography* (New York: Alfred A. Knopf, 1985), 213.

58. Hendley, "After-action report."

59. Cited in Ambrose, 326–27.

60. Diary of Clifford W. Lewis.

61. Ibid.

62. The Web site of the American Battle Monuments Commission lists the names of service members (and civilians) buried in U.S. overseas cemeteries.

63. "USS LCI (L)-93," www.uscg.mil/hq/g-cp/history/WEBCUTTERS/LCI_93 (accessed May 13, 2005); Willoughby, 246.

64. W. B. Cole, "Action report, Operation NEPTUNE" cited in "USS LCI (L)-88," http://www.uscg.mil/hq/g-cp/history/WEBCUTTERS/LCI_88 (accessed May 13, 2005).

65. A. B. Vernon to Robert W. Kirsch, ed., "The Elsie's Newsletter # 13," USS LCI National Association, June 1995. Vernon was the commanding officer of one of the USCG rescue cutters assigned to Flotilla 10. This letter can be found on the Web site of the 6th Naval Beach Battalion, which has a page dedicated to the LCI(L)-88, www.6thbeachbattalion.org/uscg-lci.html (accessed February 28, 2008).

66. W. B. Cole.

67. Reminiscences of Leroy C. Bowen, Jr., RM 3/C, LCI (L)-83, www. uscg.mil/hq/g-cp/history/LCI83_Rpt.html (accessed May 13, 2005).

68. USS LCI (L) 83, www.uscg.mil/hq/g-cp/history/WEBCUTTERS/LCI_83 (accessed May 13, 2005).

69. Casualty worksheet for Normandy, USCG Historian's Office.

70. Ibid.

71. Shepard.

72. Willoughby, 247.

73. Diary of Clifford W. Lewis.

74. Casualty worksheet for Normandy, USCG Historian's Office.

75. "Coast Guard Heroes at Normandy: selected combat award citations of Coast Guardsmen decorated for valor under fire during the Normandy Invasion," www.uscg.mil/hq/g-p/history/Normandy_Heroes.html (accessed May 13, 2005).

76. "Coast Guard–Manned Landing Craft (Infantry), Large: Flotilla 4/10/35."

77. "USS LCI (L)-90," www.uscg.mil/hq/g-cp/history/WEBCUTTERS/LCI_90 (accessed May 13, 2005). The information concerning decommissioning was found in the individual vessels' histories on the Coast Guard Historian's Office website, such as the one cited here for the LCI(L)-90.

78. A. B. Vernon. The American Battle Monuments Commission is responsible for the World War II West Coast Memorial. This executive agency maintains a database (www.abmc.gov/search/wwii.php) that contains the names of all American dead buried in overseas cemeteries or listed on the walls of the missing. Two World War II memorials, one on the Atlantic Coast and one on the Pacific Coast, list the names of those who lost their lives in American coastal waters during the war.

79. Imlay obituary, USCG Historian's Office.

80. Diary of Clifford W. Lewis.

chapter nine

AMERICAN PACIFISM, THE "GREATEST GENERATION," AND WORLD WAR II

Scott H. Bennett

During NBC's coverage of the fiftieth anniversary of D-Day, I was asked by Tim Russert on *Meet the Press* my thoughts on what we were witnessing. As I looked out over the assembled crowd of veterans, which included everyone from Cabinet officers and captains of industry to retired schoolteachers and machinists, I said, "I think this is the greatest generation any society had ever produced."

TOM BROKAW[1]

Why do we use the term "greatest generation" for the participants in war? Why not for those who have opposed war, who have tried to make us understand that war has never solved fundamental problems? Should we not honor, instead of parachutists and bomber pilots, those conscientious objectors who refused to fight or the radicals and pacifists who opposed the idea that young people of one nation should kill young people of another nation to serve the purposes of politicians and financiers?

HOWARD ZINN[2]

Journalist Tom Brokaw has dubbed the citizen soldiers who endured the Great Depression, won the "good war," and reformed postwar America, the "greatest generation." Both in wartime and in peace, the greatest generation championed liberty, democracy, and progress—at home and abroad. Even though Brokaw stresses the courage, heroism, and sacrifice of the uniformed citizen soldier, he also celebrates civilian contributions to the greatest generation's project of economic recovery, war, and social reform. The greatest generation thesis, though deeply flawed, provides a useful approach to the discussion of World War II pacifism and pacifists.[3]

Less known and uncelebrated, tens of thousands of American pacifists opposed World War II. The pacifist camp included pacifist organizations— notably the Fellowship of Reconciliation (FOR), the American Friends Service Committee (AFSC), the War Resisters League (WRL), and the Women's International League for Peace and Freedom (WILPF)—the historic peace churches (Quakers, Mennonites, and Brethren), and conscientious objectors (COs). Even more than during the First World War, COs were a major element in the antiwar dissent during World War II. To honor their mainly pacifist convictions, at least 43,000 COs refused to take up arms, including 6,000 COs who went to prison, 12,000 who served in Civilian Public Service (CPS), and 25,000 or more who performed noncombatant jobs in the military. Thousands of other nondraft-eligible pacifist men and women opposed the "good war." Pacifists—no less than the citizen soldiers celebrated by Tom Brokaw—condemned Italian fascism, German nazism, and Japanese militarism; they also struggled for freedom, democracy, civil rights, and social justice on the home front and overseas during and after the Second World War. Pacifists, too, are part of the "greatest generation."

PACIFISM AND PEARL HARBOR

"Do not let Japan led us into disastrous war," WRL founder Jessie Wallace Hughan telegraphed President Franklin D. Roosevelt immediately after the Japanese attack on Hawaii. "We urge peace in spite of the Pearl Harbor events."[4] Two weeks later, the WRL declared: "Under no circumstances, regardless of cost to ourselves, can we abandon our principles or our faith in methods that are the opposite of those demanded by war." At the same time, the WRL announced that it had no "intention of obstructing or interfering" with the war. "We respect the will of the government. . . . [and] our fellow citizens to whom war presents itself as a patriotic duty." The WRL recognized that Pearl Harbor, along with the subsequent declarations of war by Germany and Italy, "left no choice for those who believe in military defense."[5] Other pacifist organizations, including the FOR and WILPF, issued similar statements.

Even though pacifists condemned the Japanese strike on Pearl Harbor, they argued that the United States and the Allies were complicit in the developments that had prompted the attack—and, more generally, that had led to the collapse of the interwar international system, to Hitler's rise to power, to Japanese expansionism, and to the Second World War. Contributing to World War II were the unjust Versailles Treaty, Western imperialism in Asia, the Allies' attempts to preserve their own empires while opposing Axis imperial ventures, and support for Nazi Germany as an anticommunist bulwark by Allied governments and corporations during much of the 1930s. One CO summarized this view by quoting pacifist writer Kirby Page: "Hitler caused the war, but the Allies caused Hitler."[6] The United States further contributed to the outbreak of war by stoking Japanese resentment with anti-Asian measures such as the Oriental Exclusion Act, by failing to honor its own neutrality laws, and by selling war materials to Japan. In addition, radical pacifists charged that capitalism, which sanctioned economic competition and imperialism in its quest for markets and raw materials, contributed to the war. Thus, even after the attack on Pearl Harbor, pacifists did not view World War II as a Manichean struggle that compelled their support. Expressing this pacifist view, the FOR declared that "sole guilt" for the war did not rest with Japan.[7]

What about Hitler? Pacifists offered various answers to the so-called "Hitler question" and to the dilemma of resisting tyranny and aggression without armed force. Besides their revisionist argument about the origins of Pearl Harbor and World War II, pacifists opposed war against the Axis powers on ethical and political grounds. Ethically, pacifists wished to honor their usually religious-based pacifist convictions; politically, they also argued that war would sow the seeds of future conflict. Radical pacifists, usually housed in the WRL and FOR, contended that nonviolent methods—including mass strikes, boycotts, demonstrations, noncooperation, and civil disobedience—were more effective than military methods to challenge military aggression and political tyranny. They argued that such techniques could be used to resist Hitler and Japan; here pacifists pointed to the nonviolent methods that had helped to prevent war between Norway and Sweden (1905); to defend Berlin against the Kapp Putsch (1920); to shorten the French occupation of the Ruhr Valley (1923); and, under the leadership of Mohandas Gandhi, to resist the British empire in India.

Of course, to be effective, nonviolent resistance required prior training in pacifist principles and tactics and could not suddenly be adopted or imposed during a crisis. Instead of armed military service, pacifists focused on alternative civilian service, on a quick and just peace, and on reform of the political, social, and economic conditions that were responsible for war and violence. Most pacifists probably would have agreed with Stephen Cary, a Quaker CO and postwar AFSC leader, who later explained: "I became a CO with no illusions that it offered a short-range response to Hitler's evil, but a feeling, too, that the military response was no answer either—unless one thinks that 40 million dead and a continent in ruins qualifies as an answer."[8]

While the American peace and anti-interventionist movements collapsed after Pearl Harbor, the established national pacifist organizations and historic peace churches continued to oppose World War II. Both absolute pacifist organizations (which opposed all wars) and liberal pacifist organizations (which opposed most wars, while retaining the option to support particular conflicts) opposed the Second World War. Absolute pacifist groups included the religious pacifist Fellowship of Reconciliation (1915) and the secular pacifist War Resisters League (1923). Liberal pacifist organizations included the Women's International League for Peace and Freedom (1919, founded in 1915 as the Woman's Peace Party); the American Friends Service Committee (1917); and the Catholic Worker Movement (1933). Similarly, the historic peace churches and their action organizations—the AFSC, the Mennonite Central Committee, and the Brethren Service Committee—opposed the war. Despite the positions adopted by their churches, however, more Friends and Brethren actually served in the Army and Navy during World War II than became COs.

During World War II, pacifists opposed conscription, assisted COs, aided refuges, and lobbied Congress to liberalize the immigration laws to help them enter the country; championed civil liberties for Japanese Americans; repudiated civil defense; opposed war bonds; and condemned the bombing of German and Japanese cities. Pacifists opposed the Allies' policy of unconditional surrender and advocated a just, prompt, and negotiated peace. Pointing out the disastrous consequences of the vengeful Versailles Treaty imposed on Germany after World War I, pacifists argued that only a negotiated peace could stop the mass slaughter—including the extermination of the Jews—and address the conditions that would cause future wars. Conversely, unconditional surrender would prolong the killing and perpetuate the causes of war.

The FOR and WRL organized peace teams to encourage peace action, education, and fellowship among pacifists. In regular meetings, peace teams discussed pacifist texts, current affairs, and the use of nonviolent techniques to advance social justice; they sang peace songs; and they wrote members of Congress and planned peace projects. Peace teams sponsored public meetings; organized study groups; circulated petitions; provided financial support to COs; staged simulated draft board tribunals to give COs the opportunity to rehearse their responses; and distributed pacifist literature, newspapers, and periodicals. Importantly, in the midst of total war, peace teams, along with pacifist organizations, offered fellowship to the tiny pacifist community.

Pacifists also spearheaded wartime human rights campaigns to protect and expand the civil rights and civil liberties of racial minorities, most notably Japanese Americans and African Americans. Pacifist activists and organizations, particularly the FOR and the AFSC, took a leading role in protesting the compulsory relocation and internment of 120,000 Japanese Americans, a policy initiated in February 1942 with FDR's Executive Order 9066. Among these pacifists were Mary Farquharson, FOR's northwest secretary and a WILPF and American Civil Liberties Union (ACLU) socialist pacifist activist in Seattle; Floyd Schmoe, a professor at the University of Washington who quit his job to lead AFSC's efforts to aid Japanese Americans; and Caleb Foote, the FOR's West Coast Youth Secretary. While condemning the internment as an assault on civil liberties and human rights, pacifists worked to assist evacuees and to improve conditions in the assembly centers and relocation camps in which they were detained. Pacifists provided financial and material aid for internees, including games, toys, children books, and sporting equipment. They visited relocation camps; urged colleges to admit evacuees; helped Japanese Americans to resettle in nonrestricted areas east of the Rocky Mountains; campaigned for the right of evacuees to return home; and, with the end of the internment, helped them to resettle and find jobs. During the internment, pacifists supervised the rental of evacuees' homes and businesses, and they protected and tended to their property.

Gordon K. Hirabayashi—a Japanese American pacifist, a Quaker CO, a FOR and AFSC member, and a senior at the University of Washington—in an act of nonviolent civil disobedience and noncooperation, challenged the government's curfew and expulsion. "I consider it my duty to maintain the democratic standards for which this nations lives," he declared in a statement to the FBI. "Therefore, I must refuse this order for evacuation. . . . I am objecting to the *principle* of this order which denies the rights of human beings."[9] Farquharson organized his defense committee, which was financed by donations from Quakers and members of the FOR and ACLU. Convicted by the Federal District Court of Seattle, he appealed his case to the U.S. Supreme Court. Even though the court, in *Hirabayashi v. United States* (1943), ruled against him by 9–0 vote, Hirabayashi's convictions were overturned in 1986 and 1987.

Pacifists also helped to lead a nonviolent wartime African American civil rights movement a decade before *Brown v. Board of Education* (1954), the Montgomery bus boycott (1955–1956), and Martin Luther King, Jr.'s rise to prominence. Pacifists worked with the nonviolent March on Washington Movement (MOWM), led by A. Philip Randolph. Randolph, the nation's most powerful black labor leader, threatened a mass black march on Washington to pressure FDR to end racial discrimination in defense employment, which he did with Executive Order 8802 in June 1941, thereby establishing the Fair Employment Practices Commission. Under the FOR's sponsorship, in 1942, pacifists at the University of Chicago established the Congress of Racial Equality (CORE), which pioneered Gandhian nonviolent direct action and civil disobedience to promote civil rights. CORE's founders included George Houser, one of eight Union Theological Seminary students sentenced to one year in prison for refusing to register for the 1940 draft, and James Farmer, whose divinity deferment made his application for CO status moot. During and after the war, CORE organized biracial sit-ins, boycotts, civil disobedience, and other nonviolent direct action to challenge Jim Crow in housing, restaurants, skating rinks, barbershops, movie theaters, and interstate bus transportation. In CPS and prison, COs also used Gandhian methods to battle racism (as discussed later in this chapter).

The pacifist press remained active during the war. Unlike during World War I, pacifists published a number of periodicals and newspapers during the war without government interference. The FOR published *Fellowship* (1935), its well-established journal and successor to the *World Tomorrow* (1918–1934). *The Conscientious Objector* (1939–1945), which reflected the views of militant COs, covered pacifist developments in the United States and abroad, chronicled radical COs' disillusionment with CPS, and publicized CO social activism in CPS camps and prison. *Pacifica Views* (1943–1947), a four-page weekly "gadfly of C.P.S." published by COs at the Glendora, California, CPS camp, gave COs a forum to discuss pacifist ideas and the application of nonviolent action to social reform. The National Service Board for Religious Objectors (NSBRO) published *The Reporter*, the WILPF published *Four Lights*, and the Catholic Worker Movement, the peace churches, and the Jehovah's Witnesses all published newsletters and/or newspapers. To chronicle the plight of prison COs, Julius and Esther Eichel published the absolutist *Weekly Prison News Letter* (1943), and its successor, the *Absolutist* (1943–1947).

CONSCRIPTION AND CONSCIENTIOUS OBJECTION: THE
SELECTIVE TRAINING AND SERVICE ACT OF 1940

Even before Pearl Harbor, pacifists mobilized to defeat, or at least shape, the first peacetime draft in American history. In September 1940, President Roosevelt signed into law the Selective Training and Service Act of 1940. After lobbying by pacifist organizations, churches, and civil liberties groups, Congress amended the original Burke-Wadsworth bill to include more liberal provisions for COs. Pacifists won two major concessions. The 1940 law granted CO status to any "person who by reason of religious training and belief, is conscientiously opposed to participation in war in any form." This language broadened the Selective Service Act of 1917, which had effectively restricted CO status to members of the historic peace churches. The 1940 law also permitted COs to choose "non-combatant service" under military control or "work of national importance under civilian direction."

The Selective Service, in collaboration with the historic peace churches, created Civilian Public Service to provide alternative service under civilian control for COs who rejected noncombatant military service. In October 1940, to coordinate administration of the CPS camps, the historic peace churches established the NSBRO. Under the terms of the agreement between the federal government and the peace churches, the government contributed equipment and facilities, and the peace churches maintained the camps and covered the $35 monthly expenses for COs unable to pay for their own room and board. The peace churches raised more than $7 million to support CPS; the Mennonites contributed $3.1 million, the Friends $2.3 million, and the Brethren $1.6 million.[10]

The pact between the government and the peace churches recognized the right of conscientious objection; at the same time, it was a politically pragmatic agreement. Mindful that public opinion was hostile toward COs, the government did not want to be viewed as being too lenient toward objectors. Besides, the government had learned from its experience during World War I, when 450 absolutist COs had refused military service, had been court-martialed, and had waged protests, including work and hunger strikes, at Fort Leavenworth and other military prisons. In 1940, the government offered conscientious objectors better treatment in order to respect individual conscience and to avoid the burden of handling principled and often difficult objectors. For COs, the World War II conscription law was a marked advance over the Selective Service Act of 1917. Most religious pacifists, particularly traditional religious pacifists and members of the historic peace churches, embraced CPS as a huge improvement over their plight during the First World War.

Although the peace churches assumed financial and administrative responsibility for CPS, policy control remained in the hands of military officers assigned to the Camp Operations Division of Selective Service rather than church-appointed civilian camp directors, who were pacifists or sympathetic to pacifists. Military control of CPS, which angered radical COs, was symbolized by the July 1941 appointment of Colonel (later General) Lewis B. Hershey, who replaced Clarence Dykstra, the former president of the University of Wisconsin, to head Selective Service.

Pacifists created advisory agencies to provide legal advice and other assistance to young men seeking CO status. The NSBRO, supported by the peace churches and other religious groups, offered the most extensive advisory service. Other agencies included the Metropolitan Board for Conscientious Objectors, which advised COs in the New York City area, and Legal Service for Conscientious Objectors, which was absorbed by the nonpacifist ACLU. The ACLU, which considered conscientious objection a civil liberty, also operated the National Committee for Conscientious Objectors. In addition, pacifist organizations and peace churches had their own committees on CO issues. Such agencies helped draftees complete Form 47, the Selective Service document used by applicants seeking CO status to submit evidence to support their claim; they assisted COs who wished to appeal Selective Service decisions; and they worked with the Justice

Department to win probation and parole for imprisoned COs. For instance, Albert Dietrich's local draft board denied his request for CO status on grounds that he was a secular and not a religious objector. With NSBRO's assistance, Dietrich mounted a 20-month campaign of appeals, hearings, and letters that eventually led General Hershey to recognize his religious motivations and grant him CO status. In 1946, Dietrich, a Methodist who served in three CPS camps, thanked NSBRO for its advice and support. "In those dark days when I was having so much difficulty with my draft case," he wrote, "it was a source of real comfort to me to know that you were backing me and doing all you could do for me in Washington."[11]

THE CO COMMUNITY, NONCOMBATANT MILITARY SERVICE, AND CO SOCIAL ACTIVISM IN CPS AND PRISON

World War II COs were a diverse lot. The vast majority were religious objectors who represented various denominations, including the historic peace churches, nonpeace church Protestants motivated by social gospel theology, Catholics, Jews, Black Muslims, Hopi Indians, and Jehovah's Witnesses. Constituting more than 60 percent of all prison COs, the Jehovah's Witnesses were not absolute pacifists because they were willing to battle for the Lord at Armageddon; all Jehovah's Witnesses draftees claimed ministerial deferments and most accepted prison when their request was denied. In addition, a small number of secular COs—political, philosophical, and humanitarian—did not meet the religious test established by the 1940 conscription law; this group, which included pacifists and nonpacifist objectors, totaled less than 6 percent of COs. Nonpacifist COs included African Americans who refused to serve in a Jim Crow military, Puerto Rican nationalists who refused induction to protest Puerto Rico's colonial status, Japanese Americans who refused induction to protest their incarceration, and socialists who refused to participate in what they called a "capitalist" war. For instance, Carlos Cortéz, an atheist antiwar socialist who did not win CO status because he opposed the war on socialist rather than on religious grounds, served 18 months in Sandstone Federal Penitentiary. Notwithstanding the war's democratic rhetoric and Nazi challenge, Cortéz rejected "the idea of shooting another worker" on political and ethical grounds.[12]

In addition to divisions between religious and secular COs and divisions within the religious CO camp, so-called "service," "resistant," and "absolutist" COs took different approaches toward CPS. Most service COs were members of the historic peace churches who accepted CPS as a genuine attempt by the government to respect pacifist convictions. They welcomed the opportunity to apply religious ideals and serve people through hospital work, firefighting, relief activities, public health and conservation projects, and other humanitarian assignments. Service COs embraced wartime civilian service; they rejected calls to resist CPS policies and attempts to transform the larger society. Resistant COs, usually radical political and religious objectors, championed social reform, civil rights, and civil liberties; and they led nonviolent protests in CPS and prison to advance these goals. Within the resistant camp, social action COs sought to promote social justice and transform society along socialistic lines. Finally, a small number of absolutist COs refused all cooperation with conscription and the war effort. Absolutists, who refused to register for the draft, complete a military physical examination, or report to CPS, ended up in jail. Resistant, social action, and absolutist COs were often members of the WRL and, to a lesser extent, of the FOR.

In CPS and prison, radical pacifist COs used nonviolent Gandhian methods—work strikes, hunger strikes, and noncooperation—to challenge Jim Crow, conscription, censorship, and the myriad policies that dehumanized prison and gutted the original vision of CPS. Significantly, CPS and prisons served as laboratories of social activism that enabled COs to develop the techniques of nonviolent direct action and civil disobedience that transformed pacifism and infused postwar social movements.

Between 1941 and 1947, 12,000 COs served in 151 CPS camps nationwide. CPS camps were often former Civilian Conservation Corps camps; these rural camps deliberately isolated COs from population centers—a decision motivated, in part, by FDR's political concerns about anti-pacifist sentiment, a mood captured by a sign posted in a barber shop near a CPS camp in West Compton, New Hampshire: "NO SKUNKS ALLOWED So You CONSCIENTIOUS OBJECTORS Keep to Hell out of this Shop!"[13]

In CPS, COs performed various jobs, including reforestation, dam construction, agricultural labor, and soil conservation, an enterprise that involved planting seedlings, digging ditches, and grading highways. COs also worked on public health projects to improve sanitation and eradicate diseases like hookworm and typhus. For instance, in Florida, the Mulberry CPS camp built 2,500 portable outdoor toilets to combat hookworm. Elsewhere, some 240 COs served in dangerous firefighting units. Smoke jumpers parachuted from airplanes to fight forest fires, a job that enabled COs to provide an important service while demonstrating their own courage. "I felt I wasn't a coward, but I wanted a chance to demonstrate it in a very dramatic way," one CO smoke jumper recalled.[14] Other units battled forest fires with water pumpers and hand tools.

The desire to perform work of national importance, as well as the urge to demonstrate their willingness to assume dangerous risks and sacrifices, led more than 2,000 COs in CPS to volunteer for work in mental hospitals and 500 more (in CPS and prison) to serve as human guinea pigs in medical experiments. Perhaps COs' greatest contribution to the national welfare was their work in 41 mental hospitals and 17 schools for the mentally deficient in 12 states. COs and in some cases, their wives, girlfriends, and paid female staffers known as CO Girls, or COGs, ameliorated the wartime labor shortage that led to understaffing and worsening conditions for the nearly 600,000 people confined to these institutions. After visiting several mental hospitals, Frank Olmstead, the WRL field secretary, published an account of one. Left alone in the building where incontinent patients were housed, he was surrounded by 300 inmates. Half were naked, most had huge sores but no shoes, others had swollen feet from urine poisoning, and some acted out their perversions. Other COs recounted how some inmates were left in their own feces for extended periods; after their feces dried, they could not stand or roll over without stripping the skin from their bodies.

Without doubt, COs and COGs improved conditions. Working as many as 100 hours per week in mental hospitals, COs—and in some cases, COGs—changed beds, dressed sores, prepared meals, fed patients, monitored inmates, and maintained the buildings and grounds. In schools for mentally deficient boys, CO housemasters tried to create a loving and nurturing home-like atmosphere. The COs also taught the boys vocational skills, which enabled some to win paroles and lead independent lives. By applying nonviolent principles and treating inmates with care and respect, COs humanized mental hospitals.

In addition to their work in mental hospitals, 500 COs volunteered to serve as human guinea pigs for medical and scientific experiments sponsored by the Office of Scientific Research and Development and the Office of the Surgeon General of the Army. Using COs as live subjects, scientists conducted uncomfortable and often dangerous experiments designed to cure, control, or treat malaria, typhus, pneumonia, and hepatitis. Other tests studied the results of extreme heat, cold, and altitude, or experimented with malnutrition and starvation. Jim Peck, a prison CO who participated in a hepatitis experiment that permanently damaged his liver, later explained: "I viewed it as an opportunity to do a small part in helping to discover a cure for a disease which . . . plagued people in many parts of the world, particularly the near east."[15] By volunteering as human guinea pigs, COs demonstrated that pacifists, no less than GIs, risked their lives to advance noble ideals and serve humankind. Indeed, during World War II, 30 CPSers died—though not from medical experiments—and 1,500 were discharged for physical disabilities without compensation.

Pacifists also initiated a program for humanitarian work overseas. The peace churches sponsored schools in CPS to train COs for overseas relief and reconstruction assignments during and after the war. The program prepared COs to work in refugee settlements, in displaced persons programs, and in reconstruction projects. In April 1943, Selective Service approved a plan, drafted by historic peace church–affiliated colleges already offering such programs, to establish a CPS overseas relief and rehabilitation training program. To administer the program, in May 1943, Selective Service established CPS camp 101 (actually a college training program) in Philadelphia, with side camps at Quaker, Brethren, and Mennonite colleges. Meanwhile, led by Mennonite Robert Kreider, an advance team for a CPS relief unit sailed for China.

Congress torpedoed these initiatives, however. In June 1943, Congress adopted the Starnes Amendment to the 1944 War Department appropriation bill, which prohibited COs from participating in overseas relief programs and from training for these programs on college campuses. Representative Joseph Starnes (D–Ala.), a member of the House Subcommittee on Military Appropriations and a military veteran whose son was fighting in the Pacific, opposed the CO project for several reasons. He did not want to divert military resources, including military transport, to nonmilitary projects; he did not want to allow COs to attend "soft" college training programs while drafted GIs, including his son, were risking their lives overseas; and he did not want COs "glamorized" by foreign service.[16] In a letter to a CO registered in the training program, Starnes declared "that only fighting men and fighting equipment should be sent overseas as representative of this government"; in the same letter, he observed that his son, whose college education had been interrupted, was risking his life on the battlefield "to preserve freedom and liberty."[17] In addition, Starnes resented Eleanor Roosevelt's political influence and the role that she reportedly played in developing the program—all without consulting Congress. With passage of the Starnes Amendment, the Selective Service closed CPS 101, and the CPS team en route to China (and service with the Friends Ambulance Unit) returned.[18]

Looking ahead to postwar needs and opportunities, the peace churches continued to operate informal training schools in CPS. After the war, pacifists engaged in overseas humanitarian work; this included a cattle boat program in which CPSers participated in a United Nations Relief and Rehabilitation Administration initiative to transport livestock to Europe to rehabilitate war-ravaged herds. These humanitarian programs demonstrate that pacifists, though rejecting military service, made positive social contributions.

Most pacifists initially viewed CPS as an opportunity to transform ideals into action and to build humane, democratic, self-governing Christian communities based on pacifist values and relationships. In accord with the so-called "second mile" principle that taught Christians to embrace sacrifice during a time of national crisis, the historic peace churches and other traditional pacifists welcomed CPS as an occasion for religious witness and service. Some COs devoted their free time to reading, lectures, and discussions on peace, nonviolence, and social justice. At Big Flats, New York and Powellsville, Maryland, COs established Schools of Nonviolence. Often, the titles of camp newspapers reflected CO ideals and concerns: *School of Cooperative Living*, the *School of Pacifist Living*, and the *School of [Cooperative] Industrial Relations*. At Waldport, Oregon, poet William Everson founded the Fine Arts Camp, a community of CO poets, writers, painters, and other artists who produced impressive cultural magazines such as *The Compass* and *The Illiterati* and contributed to the postwar San Francisco Renaissance, which preceded and influenced the '50s Beat Movement.

Although most COs supported CPS, some radical COs challenged the program. Resistant and social action COs—usually political objectors or religious pacifists outside the peace churches—were often members of the WRL and/or the FOR. They attacked CPS's shortcomings, including the arbitrary camp management, the role of the peace churches in administering CPS camps against the will of secular pacifists, and the military control of CPS. Significantly, CPS did not provide compensation for COs, support for dependents, medical insurance, or workmen's compensation, which led radical COs to condemn CPS as "slave labor" and "involuntary servitude." Radicals also charged that CPS too often failed to provide sufficient work of national importance, as required by the 1940 draft law. Indeed, much CPS work entailed trivial jobs such as clearing brush and planting saplings, which led one WRL leader to observe that "70% of the projects could be done by able-bodied morons."[19] COs demanded the same compensation awarded to GIs, allotments for their dependents, a choice between religious and government camps and between paid and unpaid work, and increased "detached service" to allow COs to perform work of national importance outside the camps—in hospitals, firefighting, community service, and overseas relief and reconstruction projects.

To protest CPS, resistant COs resorted to work strikes,[20] work slowdowns,[21] hunger strikes,[22] individual appeals, mass petitions,[23] unionization,[24] legal challenges, and walkouts. In April 1943, discontented COs in CPS and other pacifists organized the Chicago Conference on Social Action to discuss CPS problems and issues. Even though General Hershey prohibited them from participating, 40 COs, most from AFSC-administered CPS camps, risked imprisonment and attended the meeting. The peace churches, which administered the camps, imposed furlough punishments against the AWOL COs, in part to forestall more drastic action by the Selective Service. The Chicago conference achieved little, but it demonstrated the increasing radicalization of non-peace church COs and marked a growing rift between resistant COs and the peace churches that administered CPS.

Several COs went to court to challenge CPS's constitutionality. Invoking the First, Fifth, and Thirteen Amendments, COs argued that CPS curtailed religious freedom; denied COs liberty and freedom without due process because GIs were paid but not civilian COs; imposed "slave labor" and "involuntary servitude"; and exceeded congressional authority because the camps were placed under military rather than civilian control. However, in several cases, notably *Roodenko et al. v. U.S.* (1944) and *Kramer et al. v. U.S.* (1945), appeals courts rejected—and the U.S. Supreme Court refused to review—these arguments.

In 1942, COs began to walk out of camps. In numerous walkout statements, they expressed their disillusionment with CPS, detailed their grievances, and announced their decision to cease compromising with CPS, NSBRO, Selective Service, conscription, and the war government. Walkout statements, which anticipated the Nuremberg principle of individual responsibility, emphasized the importance of acting on one's ideals and refusing to support—even implicitly—the war machine, totalitarianism, and slave labor. Philip Isely remarked: "By remaining in CPS, I not only acquiesce (and thereby give tacit support) to conscription and continued war, but I also fail to make the positive choice of devoting my full-time efforts towards ending the war and building a peaceful and cooperative society." Julian Jaynes anticipated the moral imperative behind the Nuremberg principle: "In so far as I accept public decisions, I am responsible for them unless I remove my guilt by opposition . . . [and by] civil disobedience against all war encounters." John H. Abbot denounced the insignificant leaf raking, the "involuntary servitude," and the "unhealthy state-church-individual relationship" that marked CPS: "I ask for the freedom which our men are fighting for on many shores, not to sit idly by for the duration, as I would be in jail, but [to] serve fellowmen [sic] to the limits of my ability. I can not do that while confined in C.P.S." Jessie Wallace Hughan, whose nephew walked out of CPS and served a one-year prison sentence, later saluted COs who walked out: "Those boys . . . are the shock troops of war resistance." Similarly, WRL chair Evan Thomas declared that COs who walked out of CPS—and into jail—"are rendering a great service to the struggle for freedom in America and the entire world."[25]

Racism was another issue that concerned COs. Even though the peace churches endorsed racial equality, and even though CPS in general was racially integrated, public opinion in some Southern communities made racial integration in CPS camps difficult. On occasion, the peace churches compromised with Jim Crow sentiment on grounds that even segregated CPS projects would help blacks and whites alike. For instance, the Mennonite Central Committee established a public health unit in Mississippi that excluded black COs. In Maryland, the AFSC bowed to local objections by transferring a black CO assigned to the Powellsville camp. In CPS, COs protested racism; for instance, in Maryland, COs assigned to the Cheltenham School for Delinquent Boys defied the school's Jim Crow policies, which were eventually abolished. Elsewhere, COs disregarded local Jim Crow customs and socialized with blacks. For instance, at Mulberry, in central Florida, COs invited blacks to their camp, leading locals to call them "nigger lovers" and one Mulberry camper to denounce racism as "America's number one problem."[26]

In response to pressure from secular pacifists who opposed the peace churches' religious monopoly over CPS, the government established three government-run camps at Mancos, Colorado, at Lapine, Oregon, and at Germfask, Michigan, which later moved to Minersville, California. Resistant and social action COs—disgusted with what they considered the peace churches' collaboration with the government and conscription—often transferred to these camps. Radicalized by CPS, Minersville COs emblazoned their protest on the camp's welcome sign: "Here Men Are Conscripted At Forced Labor Without Pay, Without Allotment, And Without Accident Compensation"; to punctuate their charge, next to this, they inscribed the Thirteenth Amendment: "Neither Slavery Nor Involuntary Servitude Except As A Punishment For A Crime Shall Exist Within The United States."[27]

Even some camp directors and authorities became disillusioned with CPS. Paul Voelker, the Germfask camp director, resigned to protest insulting charges about Germfask COs in *Time* magazine. "I have found the Selective Service treatment of men in this CPS camp to be the re-establishment of slavery in our nation and the punishment of men whose conscience does not permit their participation in war," Voelker declared. "As a liberty-loving American citizen and ex-serviceman, I cannot take part in the administering of a system of unpaid, forced labor." Similarly, the superintendent of an incarceration facility told a CO jailed after walking out of CPS: "You COs may be glad when [the] war's over, but not half so much as I who yearn for good old days of simple murderers and bankrobbers for prisoners."[28]

Besides the 12,000 COs in CPS, 6,000 objectors served prison terms; one of every six men in federal prison during World War II was a CO. Prison COs included objectors who had refused to register for the draft, had been denied CO status by their draft boards (often because their objection to war was based on secular rather than religious grounds), or had started in CPS before disillusionment and radicalization led them to refuse to cooperate with CPS officials or to walk out of camp—which made them "AWOL" and often led to their trial and imprisonment. It is important to note that the 6,500 local draft boards often differed in determining who qualified as a "genuine" conscientious objector. Like CPSers, prison COs waged dramatic nonviolent direct action protests—work strikes, boycotts, and hunger strikes—to honor conscience, defend civil liberties, and advance social justice. More specifically, they protested racism, censorship, dehumanization, what they considered totalitarianism, lousy food, and other prison ills. Several hunger strikes generated considerable publicity, including an 82-day liberty-or-death fast by Stanley Murphy and Lou Taylor, a 248-day fast by Igal Roodenko, a 9-month fast by Bent Andresen, and several fasts totaling 426 days by Corbett Bishop.

During the war, radical pacifist COs were often thrown into segregated jails. Confronted with Jim Crow racism, they led a wartime civil rights movement. Prison COs repeatedly challenged Jim Crow. For instance, at the Federal Correctional Institution in Milan, Michigan, Milton Kramer was threatened with a 10-year sentence for smuggling out a letter that denounced Jim Crow blood banks. At Sandstone Federal Penitentiary, COs organized a petition drive that persuaded officials to integrate their segregated dining table and dormitory. Elsewhere, COs often ignored prison rules and sat with black inmates during meals, movies, and other social events before guards intervened and removed them to solitary confinement—or, in prison parlance, the "hole." The most significant prison rebellions against Jim Crow were organized by COs at Danbury Federal Correctional Institution in Connecticut, the Lewisburg Federal Penitentiary in Pennsylvania, and the Ashland Federal Correctional Institution in Kentucky.

In 1943, 23 COs at Danbury waged a 135-day work strike to end Jim Crow in the prison dining room. To isolate them from other inmates, officials confined the strikers to the entire second floor of one wing of the prison and assigned them to individual cells. Throughout their prolonged isolation, the strikers developed study groups, leisure activities, and a covert communications system; they engaged in spirited debates; and they published a handmade newspaper titled *The Clink*. The pages of *Life* magazine, when hand-washed, yielded enough ink to print *The Clink*'s cartoons, poetry, drawings, and articles. To buttress morale and solidarity, Jim Peck composed a protest song entitled "Jimcrow Must Go!" that compared German Nazism with American Jim Crow. Accompanied by a guitar that Lowell Naeve built from a mixture of oatmeal and ground newspaper cooked on a radiator, at night, COs sang "Jimcrow Must Go!" and other songs.

During their work strike against Jim Crow, the Danbury COs mounted parallel strikes. Through hunger strikes, they obtained newspapers, magazines, books, longer yard periods, open cell doors, and hot food. They also waged a successful strike against the segregated prison barbershop, whose white and black barbers limited their work to the heads of their own race. The strikers refused Jim Crow haircuts until, in Peck's phrase, "our hair outgrew the patience of the prison officials."[29]

Shortly before Christmas 1943, after an 18-week work strike, the warden agreed to integrate the prison dining room. "It's over, it's over," Peck declared. "We've smashed them."[30] Indeed, even under inhospitable prison conditions, the strike showed the potential of nonviolent protest. Writing later, Peck observed: "It seems to me that the campaign against racial discrimination may be counted as one of the most important contributions of COs in World War 2."[31]

Both at Lewisburg and Ashland, Bayard Rustin, a black CO, led protests against Jim Crow and other ills. Upon his arrival at Ashland in 1944, Rustin was assigned to a segregated cell block, separated from white COs on the floor above. After numerous protests, Rustin was permitted to visit the white COs on the upper floor on Sunday afternoons. A white inmate who opposed integration warned Rustin not to return. When Rustin returned the following week, the white inmate attacked him with a stick, repeatedly clubbing him over the head. COs moved to disarm the inmate, but Rustin told them to stop. Eventually, the attack ceased. According to a CO witness, the white inmate "was completely defeated and unnerved by the display of nonviolence, and began shaking all over, and sat down."[32] The violence actually advanced integration because the warden, in response to the attack, reversed prison policy and permitted unlimited interracial visits. Later, Rustin cited this incident as an example of effective nonviolent resistance.

In June 1945, Rustin renewed his attack on Jim Crow by leading 12 COs on a hunger strike to protest the segregated mess hall. In August, prison authorities tried to break the strike by transferring four COs, including Rustin, who was sent to Lewisburg, where he continued his Ashland hunger strike for several days. At Lewisburg, Rustin continued to wage protests against Jim Crow and other prison problems. (Rustin was not the first CO to protest Jim Crow at Lewisburg; in 1943, for instance, COs had organized a boycott and work strike against racial segregation.)

Recollecting his prison experience, Rustin expressed the COs' optimistic sense of purpose, which transformed imprisonment into a liberating struggle for justice:

> We used to say that the difference between us and other prisoners was the difference between fasting and starving. We were there by virtue of a commitment we had made to a moral position; and that gave us a psychological attitude the average prisoner did not have. He felt either that he had done something wrong, and that he should be punished for it, or that he had done nothing wrong, and society was brutalizing him. We had neither the guilt nor the feeling of being brutalized. We had the feeling of being morally important; and that made us respond to prison conditions without fear, with considerable sensitivity to human rights. We thought we were making a contribution to society, in the same way that Gandhi, who was our hero, had said to a British judge: "It is your moral duty to put me in jail." That was our feeling. It was by going to jail that we called the people's attention to the horrors of war.[33]

Besides opposing Jim Crow, COs also protested censorship, foul food, dehumanizing routines, and infringements on their pacifist convictions. For instance, at Sandstone, CO protests persuaded authorities to abolish the *lockstep*, a procedure that required inmates to walk together in tight formation. At Danbury, Jim Peck led several food boycotts that prompted officials to remove disgusting food from the menu. On another occasion, he refused to paint red, white, and blue signs for the prison victory garden on grounds that it was war propaganda; for this, officials sentenced him to 10 days in the hole. David Dellinger was punished with the hole for refusing to respond when summoned by his prison number and for not remaking his bed after a guard tore off the sheets and ordered him to make it as soldiers did. More successfully, Dellinger participated in a sport strike. Dellinger and several other COs, including star pitcher Don Benedict, played on Danbury's softball team. Before the season's final game, which the warden badly wanted to win, Dellinger and other COs were placed in the hole for demanding a one-hour work break to demonstrate support for a nationwide student strike (originating in the mid-1930s) against conscription and military preparedness. Benedict refused to pitch unless the COs were released from solitary; the warden capitulated shortly before game time. Led by Benedict's no-hitter, Danbury won.

COs also challenged prison censorship, most notably at Lewisburg. At Lewisburg, six COs—including Dave Dellinger and Paton Price—staged a 65-day hunger strike against prison censorship. They demanded the abolition of mail censorship and the right of all inmates to obtain writing materials and uncensored books and magazines while accepting the right of officials to screen mail to detect escape plots, blackmail, drugs, and pornography. Dellinger announced: "We are not eating because under the prison system it is the only method we have of calling for an end to censorship" that perpetuated "prison abuses" and "a totalitarian [prison] system." In a letter to his family, Paton Price acknowledged the GIs "valiant" willingness to die in the "fight for freedom"—and explained that he could do no less. Just as he would "not submit" to fascism in Germany, he must fight the evil of prison censorship "with the most powerful weapon I have: my life." However, unlike the "bloody military way" and the "holocaust of war," Price advocated nonviolent resistance. "Pacifism is not 'a way out,' it is another, a better way of fighting evil," he declared. The 64-day hunger strike—during which the COs were force-fed—ended in a compromise settlement favorable to the strikers.[34]

Besides the 12,000 COs in CPS and the 6,000 COs who served prison terms, another 25,000 to 50,000 COs entered the military where they performed noncombatant work, usually as medics.[35] Actor Lew Ayres, who became a pacifist while making the antiwar film *All Quiet on the Western Front*, was the best-known noncombatant CO.

Noncombatant COs chose military service for various reasons. Some COs believed that noncombatant military service offered more opportunities than CPS to save lives and perform meaningful social service, including preparation for postwar foreign relief work. For instance, one noncombatant CO, in a reference to a soil conservation project on the Blue Ridge Parkway, considered it "absurd" to compare the "ward work in hospitals and assistance at operating tables near the front lines to manicuring Crabtree Meadows"; during World War II, COs performed soil conservation work at Crabtree Meadows, a section of the Blue Ridge Parkway.[36] Other COs were influenced by family and friends, who regarded noncombatant military service as more "respectable" than CPS—and less harmful to future careers. Financial considerations led some COs to enter military service instead of CPS. GIs—including CO noncombatants—received salaries, insurance, and allowances for dependents; however, in CPS, COs not only worked without compensation, but they had to pay monthly upkeep stipends. Finally, some COs became Army noncombatants to prove that they were not cowards.

After January 1943, most noncombatants were limited to service in the Medical Corps although this assignment included clerical and other support work. Before 1943, COs were assigned to different branches; they worked in communications, transported food, and served as clerks. In part, the Army and Selective Service hoped that assigning all COs to the Medical Corps, which in effect guaranteed them meaningful humanitarian work, would appeal to their desire to aid the victims of war and persuade them to choose noncombatant military service rather than CPS.

COs serving in front-line positions with the Medical Corps often showed great courage under combat. Orville Cox, a Seventh-day Adventist serving on Guadalcanal, was cited for crawling toward Japanese machine gun and rifle fire to assist two wounded infantrymen. Desmond Doss, another Seventh-day Adventist assigned to medical work, was the first CO to receive the Congressional Medal of Honor. He repeatedly risked his life to tend to wounded GIs. During the Battle of Okinawa, Doss was wounded twice while ministering to injured comrades. His citation, which referenced the 1st Battalion's assault on Maeda Escarpment, a 400' sheer cliff held by the Japanese, read: "As our troops gained the summit, a heavy concentration of artillery, mortar and machine gun fire crashed into them, inflicting approximately 75 casualties and driving the others back. Pfc. Doss refused to seek cover and remained in the fire-swept area with the many stricken, carrying them 1 by 1 to the edge of the escarpment and there lowering them on a rope-supported litter down the face of a cliff to friendly hands." Not surprisingly, the citation concluded that Doss became a "symbol" throughout his division "for outstanding gallantry far and above the call of duty."[37]

War II pacifism was a gendered experience. Only men were conscripted; thus, only draft-eligible men could become COs, a stance that conferred moral status among pacifists. The wartime (and postwar) pacifist movement lionized male COs—particularly resistant and absolutist COs—and their sacrifice and social activism in CPS and prison. However, pacifist women, too, were conscientious objectors who made important contributions to the pacifist movement and the nation. Although exempt from the draft, women offered emotional, intellectual, and financial support to sons, husbands, lovers, and brothers in CPS and prison. About 2,000 pacifist women took jobs in or near the CPS camps of their spouses and boyfriends; other women visited. Other CO wives met to provide mutual support and assistance. In addition, women held leadership positions and roles in the WILPF and in mixed-gender pacifist groups. Similarly, women played important roles in non-pacifist groups that supported COs, such as the ACLU's National Committee of Conscientious Objectors (NCCO), which provided COs legal assistance. For instance, at the NCCO's Washington branch, Vivien Roodenko, a radical pacifist active with the WRL and SP, managed the office, did secretarial work, and liaisoned with the Bureau of Prisons, Selective Service, and the War Department on CO cases and issues.[38]

Still, the contribution of draft-exempt male and female pacifist activists, who were also conscientious objectors, often lost some of its luster next to front-line COs. For instance, after World War II, militant COs took over the leadership of the WRL. Frieda Lazarus, the chair of the WRL's CO Problem Committee who disagreed with civil disobedience and other positions advocated by these former COs, denounced the emergence of a moral hierarchy that assumed that "only former prison men [COs] know what sacrifice for a cause means."[39] Like other egalitarian social movements, the peace movement was not immune to sexism.

AMNESTY CAMPAIGN

Even after World War II ended, COs remained in CPS and prison. From 1945 to 1948, the Committee for Amnesty led a three-year campaign to obtain amnesty for the 6,000 World War II prison COs and to win the release of those who remained in jail. The amnesty campaign served as the epilogue of the radical CO wartime struggle and the prologue of militant postwar pacifist activism. COs played key roles in the Committee for Amnesty and the amnesty campaign. As convicted felons, prison COs lost important civil liberties. Although penalties varied by state, prison COs were commonly forbidden to vote; hold political office; qualify for civil service; and practice medicine, law, or dentistry. The Amnesty Committee organized imaginative protests, including picketing in prison garb to pressure President Harry S. Truman to grant a presidential amnesty to all prison COs. For its advocates, amnesty was a human rights and civil liberties issue, one that involved freedom, justice, and conscience. Significantly, COs in prison took an active role in the campaign. For instance, at Sandstone, Igal Roodenko waged a 248-day hunger strike for amnesty. Explaining his action, Roodenko observed that to him and other hunger strikers: "Freedom and democracy are not merely Fourth-of-July phrases for us . . . This has led us . . . to fasting for freedom."[40] Though unsuccessful, the Committee forged a grassroots social movement that spurred Truman to liberalize his pardon policy, which considered on an individual basis the cases of prison COs.

CONCLUSION, SIGNIFICANCE, AND LEGACY

World War II pacifism is significant for several reasons. First, even though pacifists did not prevent nor influence the course of the Second World War, COs did gain experience and expertise in Gandhian nonviolent direct action, including noncooperation and civil disobedience. Indeed, CPS camps and prison cells served as laboratories of wartime social activism, a development that transformed the pacifist movement and influenced postwar social activism.

Second, COs did valuable social and humanitarian work, sometimes at significant personal risk. In CPS—despite the trivial nature of some work assignments—COs made important contributions in reforestation, dam construction, agricultural labor, soil conservation, firefighting, public heath, and mental hospitals. As human guinea pigs, CO volunteers risked their lives and health in medical experiments designed to develop vaccines and treatments. COs also volunteered for dangerous smoke jumping and firefighting assignments. In overseas combat zones, noncombatant COs in the medical corps placed themselves in harm's way to save wounded GIs.

Third, pacifists defended civil liberties, including the rights of conscientious objection and political dissent. They persuaded Congress to liberalize provisions for conscientious objection in the 1940 conscription law; provided legal aid to COs; defended the constitutional rights of Japanese Americans; defied prison censorship and dehumanizing prison policies; challenged those elements of CPS that seemed to violate civil liberties and equal treatment; campaigned for postwar amnesty for prison COs; and, throughout the war, articulated an ethical-political-humanitarian dissent against armed violence. In so doing, pacifists strengthened civil liberties and the American libertarian tradition.

Fourth, pacifists championed the African American civil rights movement. They founded CORE; supported the MOWM; and, in CPS and prison, CO protests prompted officials to integrate Jim Crow facilities, most notably prison dining rooms.

Fifth, pacifists led a wartime and postwar "revolution in mental health care": this, according to Alex Sareyan, a CO at Connecticut State [Mental] Hospital and a postwar health professional.[41] In 1950, former COs helped establish the National Association for Mental Health (1950), which improved the training of mental health care professionals, enhanced the standards of care for the mentally ill, and promoted the awareness and effective treatment of mental illness.

Sixth, the postwar pacifist movement moved beyond traditional political and educational methods, adopting the nonviolent direct action techniques that marked CO protests in CPS and prison and infused postwar social activism—both pacifist and nonpacifist. Pacifists, particularly former COs, provided leadership to a number of postwar social movements, including the peace movement, the civil rights movement, the anti-nuclear movement, the African liberation movement, the environmental movement, and the civil liberties movement. They founded Pacifica Radio (1949), which pioneered noncommercial radio and broadcast dissident voices, and *Liberation* (1956), an influential journal that in the late 1950s provided a voice of radical dissent and served as a seedbed for the New Left. Indeed, as historian James Tracy has argued, during and after World War II, COs were instrumental in "forging a new radicalism" that transformed America.[42]

No less than GIs, World War II pacifists served their nation and the world. Both during and after World War II, both at home and abroad, pacifists have helped to advance freedom, democracy, and social justice. They, too, are part of the "greatest generation."

BIBLIOGRAPHICAL ESSAY

This is not a comprehensive bibliographical essay; rather, it lists the works that I found most helpful for this survey on pacifism and World War II.

With several exceptions, I have not listed journal articles in this biblio-graphical essay, nor have I listed manuscript collections, primary documents, or the pacifist press, although I have occasionally cited these sources in the Notes. To keep the endnotes to a minimum, I have sourced only direct quotations, usually with published secondary or primary sources. In places, this essay borrows from my earlier work on pacifism and COs:

Army GI, Pacifist CO: The World War II Letters of Frank and Albert Dietrich (New York: Fordham University Press, 2005)

Radical Pacifism: The War Resisters League and Gandhian Nonviolence in America, 1915–1963 (Syracuse, N.Y.: Syracuse University Press, 2003)

"Free American Political Prisoners: Pacifist Activism and Civil Liberties, 1945–1948," *Journal of Peace Research* 40 (July 2003): 413–33

"Workers/Draftees of the World Unite! Carlos A. Cortéz Redcloud Koyokuikatl: Soapbox Rebel, WWII CO, & IWW Artist/Bard," in Victor Sorell, ed., *Carlos A. Cortéz Koyokuikatl: Soapbox Rebel & Artist* (Chicago: Mexican Fine Arts Center Museum, 2002), 12–56

MAJOR STUDIES THAT DISCUSS WORLD WAR II PACIFISM, INCLUDING CO SOCIAL ACTIVISM IN CPS AND PRISON

Mulford Q. Sibley and Philip E. Jacob, *Conscription of Conscience: The American State and the Conscientious Objector, 1940–1947* (Ithaca, N.Y.: Cornell University Press, 1952)

Albert N. Keim, *The CPS Story: An Illustrated History of Civilian Public Service* (Intercourse, Penn.: Good Books, 1990)

Lawrence S. Wittner, *Rebels Against War: The American Peace Movement, 1933–1983*, rev. ed. (Philadelphia: Temple University Press, 1984)

James Tracy, *Direct Action: Radical Pacifism from the Union Eight to the Chicago Seven* (Chicago: University of Chicago Press, 1996)

Stephen M. Kohn, *Jailed for Peace: The History of American Draft Law Violators, 1658–1985* (Westport, Conn.: Greenwood Press, 1986)

Cynthia Eller, *Conscientious Objectors and the Second World War: Moral and Religious Arguments in Support of Pacifism* (New York: Praeger, 1991)

Bennett, *Radical Pacifism*

Bennett, "Free American Political Prisoners: Pacifist Activism and Civil Liberties, 1945–1948"

Peter Brock and Nigel Young, *Pacifism in the Twentieth Century* (Syracuse, N.Y.: Syracuse University Press, 1999)

Charles Chatfield, *For Peace and Justice: Pacifism in America, 1914–1941* (Knoxville: University of Tennessee Press, 1971)

Glen Zeitzer and Charles F. Howlett, "Political Versus Religious Pacifism: The Peace Now Movement of 1943," *The Historian* 48 (May 1986): 375–93

Gretchen Lemke-Santangelo, "The Radical Conscientious Objectors of World War II: Wartime Experience and Postwar Activism," *Radical History Review* 45 (Fall 1989): 5–29.

IMPORTANT RADICAL PACIFIST CO MEMOIRS AND ORAL HISTORIES

Larry Gara and Lenna Mae Gara, eds., *A Few Small Candles: War Resisters of World War II Tell Their Stories* (Kent, Ohio: Kent State University Press, 1999)

Heather T. Frazer and John O'Sullivan, eds., *"We Have Just Begun to Not Fight": An Oral History of Conscientious Objectors in Civilian Public Service During World War II* (New York: Twayne, 1996)

David Dellinger, *From Yale to Jail: The Life Story of A Moral Dissenter* (New York: Pantheon, 1993)

James Peck, *We Who Would Not Kill* (New York: Lyle Stuart, 1958)

Peck, *Underdogs Vs. Upperdogs* (New York: AMP&R Publisher, 1980)

Lowell Naeve and David Wieck, *A Field of Broken Stones* (Glen Gardner, N.J.: Libertarian Press, 1950)

Peter Brock, ed., *"These Strange Criminals": An Anthology of Prison Memoirs by Conscientious Objectors from the Great War to the Cold War* (Toronto: University of Toronto Press, 2004)

Deena Hurwitz and Craig Simpson, eds., *Against the Tide: Pacifist Resistance in the Second World War: An Oral History* [1984 WRL Peace Calendar] (New York: War Resisters League, 1984).

MEMOIRS AND ACCOUNTS BY HISTORIC PEACE CHURCH MEMBERS

Melvin Gingerich, *Service for Peace: A History of Mennonite Civilian Service* (Akron, Penn.: The Mennonite Central Committee, 1949)

Harry R. Van Dyck, *Exercise of Conscience: A WWII Objector Remembers* (Buffalo, N.Y.: Prometheus Books, 1990)

Gordon C. Zahn, *Another Part of the War: The Camp Simon Story* (Amherst, Mass.: University of Massachusetts Press, 1979)

Alex Sareyan, *The Turning Point: How Men of Conscience Brought About Major Change in the Care of America's Mentally Ill* (Washington, D.C.: American Psychiatric Press, 1994)

Robert S. Kreider, *My Early Years: An Autobiography* (Kitchener, Ontario, Canada: Pandora Press, and Scottdale, Penn.: Herald Press, 2002).

BIOGRAPHIES OF RADICAL PACIFIST WORLD WAR II COS AND OTHER RADICAL PACIFISTS

John D'Emilio, *Lost Prophet: The Life and Times of Bayard Rustin* (New York: Free Press, 2003)

Jervis Anderson, *Bayard Rustin: Troubles I've Seen* (New York: HarperCollins, 1997)

Daniel Levine, *Bayard Rustin and the Civil Rights Movement* (New Brunswick, N.J.: Rutgers University Press, 1999)

Andrew Hunt, *Nonviolent Revolutionary: The Life and Times of David Dellinger* (New York: New York University Press, 2006)

Jo Ann Ooiman Robinson, *Abraham Went Out: A Biography of A .J. Muste* (Philadelphia: Temple University Press, 1981).

DESMOND T. DOSS AND OTHER COS WHO PERFORMED NONCOMBATANT MILITARY SERVICE

Sibley and Jacob, *Conscription of Conscience*, 86–98

Booton Herdon, *The Unlikeliest Hero: The Story of Desmond T. Doss, Conscientious Objector, Who Won His Nation's Highest Military Honor* (Mountain View, Calif.: Pacific Press, 1967)

Larry Smith, *Beyond Glory: Medal of Honor Heroes in Their Own Words: Extraordinary Stories of Courage from World War II to Vietnam* (New York: W. W. Norton, 2003), 90–107

Desmond T. Doss, "The Miracle Day," in Patricia W. Sewell, ed., *Healers in World War II: Oral Histories of Medical Corps Personnel* (Jefferson, N.C. & London: McFarland & Co., 2001), 63–66

Jennifer Frost, "Conscientious Objection and Popular Culture: The Case of Lew Ayres," in Peter Brock and Thomas P. Socknat, eds., *Challenge to Mars: Essays on Pacifism from 1918 to 1945* (Toronto: University of Toronto Press, 1999), 360–69.

CONSCRIPTION AND LOCAL DRAFT BOARDS

Lee Kennett, *G.I.: The American Soldier in World War II* (New York: Charles Scribner's Sons, 1987)

George Flynn, *The Draft, 1940–1973* (Lawrence, Kan.: University Press of Kansas, 1993)

Flynn, *Lewis B. Hershey, Mr. Selective Service* (Chapel Hill, N.C.: University of North Carolina Press, 1985)

John W. Chambers, "Conscientious Objectors and the American State from Colonial Times to the Present," in *The New Conscientious Objection: From Sacred to Secular Resistance*, ed. Charles C. Moskos and John W. Chambers, (New York: Oxford University Press, 1993), 23–46

LITERATURE ON WORLD WAR II (AND OTHER) COS

Brock, *Pacifism Since 1914: An Annotated Reading List* (Toronto: Peter Brock, 2000)

PEACE CHURCHES

Guy F. Hershberger, *War, Peace, and Nonresistance* (Scottdale, Penn.: Herald Press, 1944)

Hershberger, *The Mennonite Church in the Second World War* (Scottdale, Penn.: Mennonite Publishing House, 1951)

Albert N. Keim and Grant M. Stoltzfus, *The Politics of Conscience: The Historic Peace Churches and America at War, 1917–1955* (Scottdale, Penn.: Herald Press, 1988)

Perry Bush, *Two Kingdoms, Two Loyalties: Mennonite Pacifism in Modern America* (Baltimore, Md.: The Johns Hopkins University Press, 1998)

Paul Toews, *Mennonites in American Society, 1930–1970: Modernity and the Persistence of Religious Community* (Scottdale, Penn.: Herald Press, 1996)

Proceedings of Pendle Hill Conference on Quakers and CPS, November 4–7, 1996, *Friends in Civilian Public Service: Quaker Conscientious Objectors in World War II Look Back and Look Ahead* (Wallingford, Penn.: Pendle Hill, 1996)

Robert F. Horton, ed., *Profiles of Conscience: Stories and Statements of War Objectors*, prepublication ed. (Washington, D.C.: National Interreligious Service Board for Conscientious Objectors, 1990)

CATHOLIC WORKER MOVEMENT

Patricia McNeal, *Harder Than War: Catholic Peacekeeping in Twentieth-Century America* (New Brunswick, N.J.: Rutgers University Press, 1992)

Mel Piehl, *Breaking Bread: The Catholic Worker and the Origin of Catholic Radicalism in America* (Philadelphia: Temple University Press, 1982)

WOMEN, GENDER, AND THE WILPF

Marian Mollin, *Radical Pacifism in Modern America: Egalitarianism and Protest* (Philadelphia: University of Pennsylvania Press, 2006)

Rachel W. Goossen, *Women Against the Good War: Conscientious Objection and Gender on the America Home Front, 1941–1947* (Chapel Hill, N.C.: University of North Carolina Press, 1997)

Carrie A. Foster, *The Women and the Warriors: The U.S. Section of the Women's International League for Peace and Freedom, 1915–1946* (Syracuse, N.Y.: Syracuse University Press, 1995)

Harriet H. Alonso, *Peace as a Women's Issue: A History of the U.S. Movement for World Peace and Women's Rights* (Syracuse, N.Y.: Syracuse University Press, 1993)

Heather T. Frazer and John O'Sullivan, "Forgotten Women of World War II: Wives of Conscientious Objectors in Civilian Public Service," *Peace & Change* 5 (Fall 1978): 46–51

Timothy Stewart-Winter, "Not a Soldier, Not a Slacker: Conscientious Objectors and Male Citizenship in the United States during the Second World War," *Gender & History* 19 (November 2007): 519–42

WORLD WAR I BACKGROUND (ON CONSCRIPTION AND PACIFISM)

John W. Chambers, *To Raise an Army: The Draft Comes to Modern America* (New York: The Free Press, 1987), which focuses on the First World War but surveys the draft from colonial America to the 1980s

Frances H. Early, *A World Without War: How U.S. Feminists and Pacifists Resisted World War I* (Syracuse, N.Y.: Syracuse University Press, 1997)

TREATMENTS OF CO GUINEA PIGS, MENTAL HOSPITAL WORKERS, AND FIREFIGHTERS

Todd Tucker, *The Great Starvation Experiment: The Heroic Men Who Starved So That Millions Could Live* (New York: Free Press, 2006)

Sareyan, *The Turning Point*

Robert C. Cottrell, *Smokejumpers of the Civilian Public Service in World War II: Conscientious Objectors as Firefighters for the National Forest Service* (Jefferson, N.C.: McFarland & Co., 2006)

Mark Matthews, *Smoke Jumping on the Western Fire Line: Conscientious Objectors during World War II* (Norman, Okla: University of Oklahoma Press, 2006)

Roy Wenger, ed., *CPS Smokejumpers, 1943–1946—Life Stories*, 3 vols. (Missoula, Mont.: privately printed, 1990–1993)

THE PACIFIST ROLE IN DEFENDING AND ASSISTING JAPANESE AMERICANS

Robert Shaffer, "Opposition to Internment: Defending Japanese American Rights During World War II," *The Historian* 61 (1998): 597–619

Shaffer, "Cracks in the Consensus: Defending the Rights of Japanese Americans During World War II," *Radical History Review* 72 (1998): 84–120

DOCUMENTARY FILM ON WORLD WAR II COS
"The 'Good War' and Those Who Refused To Fight It" (Paradigm Productions, distributed by Independent Television Service, 2002)

THE "GREATEST GENERATION" THESIS
Tom Brokaw, *The Greatest Generation* (New York: Random House, 1998)

NOTES

1. Tom Brokaw, *The Greatest Generation* (New York: Random House, 1998), xxx.

2. Howard Zinn, "The Greatest Generation?" *Progressive* (October 2001): 12.

3. The greatest generation thesis presents a romanticized and idealized view of World War II—one that reinforces the notion that the conflict was the "good war" (and often without the quotation marks inserted by Studs Terkel). Here, my argument focuses neither on the historical accuracy of the greatest generation thesis nor on whether we should use this phrase. Rather, I argue that if we use the phrase—and most Americans do—then pacifists and COs should be included. For criticism of the greatest generation thesis by a World War II veteran, see Howard Zinn, "The Greatest Generation?" *Progressive* (October 2001): 12–13. Historian Thomas Childers also takes issue with the phrase in the last volume of his trilogy, *The Best Years of Their Lives: Coming Home from World War II and Beyond* (Boston: Houghton-Mifflin, 2009). Childer discusses his views in Tim Hyland, "Q&A: Thomas Childers," *Penn Current*, February 7, 2008, 1; and Art Carey, "For Many Vets, Peace Never Came," *Philadelphia Inquirer*, May 28, 2007.

4. Hughan, quoted in Scott H. Bennett, *Radical Pacifism: The War Resisters League and Gandhian Nonviolence in America, 1915–1963* (Syracuse, N.Y.: Syracuse University Press, 2003), 74.

5. A Communication from the Executive Committee to the Members of the WRL, December 19, 1941, Abraham Kaufman Papers, Swarthmore College Peace Collection, Swarthmore, Pa. (hereafter SCPC).

6. Joe Dell quoted in Cynthia Eller, *Conscientious Objectors and the Second World War: Moral and Religious Arguments in Support of Pacifism* (Westport, Conn.: Praeger, 1991), 158.

7. For "sole guilt," see the FOR statement on Pearl Harbor, "Our Way in the Midst of War" [December 1941], excerpted in Jessie Wallace Hughan, "Our

U.S.A. Movement Since Pearl Harbor: December 7, 1941 to May, 1942," May 27, 1942, Minutes of WRL Executive Committee, War Resisters League Papers, SCPC.

8. Cary, quoted in Robert F. Horton, ed., *Profiles of Conscience: Stories and Statements of War Objectors*, prepublication edition (Washington, D.C.: National Interreligious Service Board for Conscientious Objectors, 1990), 27, copy at SCPC.

9. Hirabayashi, quoted in *Fellowship*, July 1942, 112.

10. For peace church contributions to CPS, see *The Reporter*, August–September, 1947, 1.

11. Dietrich, quoted in Scott H. Bennett, ed., *Army GI, Pacifist CO: The World War II Letters of Frank and Albert Dietrich* (New York: Fordham University Press, 2005), 44.

12. Cortéz, quoted in Scott H. Bennett, "Workers/Draftees of the World Unite! Carlos A. Cortéz Redcloud Koyokuikatl: Soapbox Rebel, WWII CO, & IWW Artist/Bard," 7, in Victor Sorell, ed., *Carlos A. Cortéz Koyokuikatl: Soapbox Rebel & Artist* (Chicago: Mexican Fine Arts Center Museum, 2002).

13. For a photograph of this sign, see "The 'Good War' and Those Who Refused to Fight It" (Paradigm Productions, distributed by Independent Television Service, 2002), www.pbs.org/itvs/thegoodwar/ww2pacifists.html (accessed December 12, 2008); the original photo is at SCPC.

14. Norman Kriebel, quoted in Heather T. Frazer and John O'Sullivan, eds., *"We Have Just Begun to Not Fight": An Oral History of Conscientious Objectors in Civilian Public Service During World War II* (New York: Twayne, 1996), xxv.

15. James Peck, *We Who Would Not Kill* (New York: Lyle Stuart, 1958), 154.

16. For "soft," see *The Conscientious Objector*, August 1943, p. 8; for "glamorized," see Mulford Q. Sibley and Philip E. Jacob, *Conscription of Conscience: The American State and the Conscientious Objector, 1940–1947* (Ithaca, N.Y.: Cornell University Press, 1952), 228.

17. Starnes quoted in *The Reporter*, August 1, 1943, 2.

18. For the CPS overseas relief program, including the China Unit and the College Training Program, see *The Conscientious Objector*, April 1943, June 1943, August 1943; *The Reporter*, July 1, 1943, August 1, 1943, December 15, 1943, January 1, 1944, July 1, 1945, July 15, 1945; E. Raymond Wilson, *Uphill for Peace: Quaker Impact on Congress* (Richmond, Ind.: Friends United Press, 1975), 35–55, 342; Sibley and Jacob, *Conscription of Conscience*, 187–89, 228; and Nicholas A. Krehbiel, "Relief Efforts Denied: The Civilian Public Service Training Corps and the Starnes Amendment, 1942–1943" (unpublished manuscript). I am indebted

to Krehbiel, who emphasizes the Eleanor Roosevelt factor, for sharing his research with me. Interestingly, a number of influential leaders approved the CPS foreign relief program and opposed the Starnes Amendment, including President Franklin D. Roosevelt, Secretary of War Henry L. Stimson, Assistant Secretary of War John J. McCloy, General Joseph W. Stilwell (commander of U.S. forces in China), General Lewis B. Hershey (Selective Service director), Representative Everett M. Dirksen, and Senator Harry S. Truman.

19. Frank Olmstead, quoted in Bennett, *Radical Pacifism*, 84.

20. For instance, a dozen COs at the CPS camp in Big Flats, New York, initiated a work strike to protest the lack of car insurance for COs who drove government trucks during work assignments; without insurance, they were personally liable if someone were injured in an accident. Exacerbated by another incident between COs and a project manager, the men went on a work strike. Louis Taylor and Stanley Murphy, Big Flat COs involved in these events, later walked out of camp, and in prison, escalated their protest against conscription and the treatment of COs with a celebrated 82-day "liberty or death" hunger strike.

21. Because work strikes and walkouts could result in prison, some COs turned to work slowdowns, which they compared to a general strike and the nonviolent slowdown tactics championed by the Industrial Workers of the World. For instance, John Lewis advised COs to reduce the work tempo by requesting detailed instructions before starting assigned tasks. "We got to be experts at not working," recalled Germfask CO Roy Kepler. "We became experts at digging a hole that never got dug, or a trench." For the Kepler quote, see Deena Hurwitz and Craig Simpson, eds., *Against the Tide: Pacifist Resistance in the Second World War: An Oral History* [1984 WRL Calendar] (New York: War Resisters League, 1984), at May 14–17, 1984, copy in WRL Papers, Series B, Box 7, SCPC.

22. For instance, in October 1943, Igal Roodenko began a work-and hunger strike at Mancos—one of many that he waged—to support six Lewisburg COs who were conducting a political fast to protest prison censorship. After 13 days, Roodenko was arrested for refusing to work and jailed. After his conviction and unsuccessful appeal, in April 1945, he started a three-year sentence in Sandstone Federal Penitentiary, where he continued his nonviolent protests until his release in February 1947.

23. Besides writing individual letters, rebellious COs circulated mass petitions to press their demands for maintenance provisions, the same compensation awarded to GIs, a choice between religious and government camps, and the reform of CPS. One petition garnered 1,800 signatures; another, 900.

24. Max Kampelman led a campaign to establish a CPS trade union; the effort enrolled 500 workers in 25 locals.

25. For the quotations in this paragraph, except for Evan Thomas, see Bennett, *Radical Pacifism*, p. 101. For the Thomas quote, see Lawrence S. Wittner, *Rebels Against War: The American Peace Movement, 1933–1983*, rev. ed. (Philadelphia: Temple University Press, 1984), 78.

26. For both quotes, see Bennett, *Army GI, Pacifist CO*, 43.

27. For a photograph of this sign, see Robert Cooney, and Helen Michalowski, eds., *The Power of the People: Active Nonviolence in the United States* (Culver City, Calif.: Peace Press, 1977), 101.

28. For both quotes in this paragraph, see Bennett, *Radical Pacifism*, 107.

29. Peck, 122.

30. Peck quoted in Lowell Naeve and David Wieck, *A Field of Broken Stones* (Glen Gardner, N.J.: Libertarian Press, 1950), 144.

31. Peck, 129–30.

32. Rustin quoted in Anderson, 107.

33. Rustin quoted in Anderson, 109.

34. Dellinger and Price quoted in Bennett, *Radical Pacifism*, 129.

35. Because Selective Service did not keep centralized records, the exact num ber of noncombatant COs remains unknown, but Sibley and Jacob, who maintain that the total is "almost certainly" more than the 25,000 reported by the Selective Service, estimate the number at between 25,000 to 50,000. See Sibley and Jacob, 86.

36. CO quoted in Sibley and Jacob, 92. Crabtree Meadows is located in North Carolina's Blue Ridge Mountains on a stretch of the Blue Ridge Parkway, which originated as a New Deal project. Even though some COs dismissed as trivial soil conservation work at Crabtree Meadows, such wartime projects, although less urgent than frontline battlefield assignments, made a valuable contribution to America.

37. For Doss's Medal of Honor citation, see U.S. Army Center for Military History, at www.history.army.mil/html/moh/wwII-a-f.html (accessed December 12, 2008).

38. Currently, I am editing the World War II letters of radical pacifist siblings Vivien Roodenko and Igal Roodenko. An extended, archival-based, introduction will provide biographies of the Roodenkos and their peace and justice activism.

39. Lazarus quoted in Bennett, *Radical Pacifism*, 168.

40. Roodenko quoted in Scott H. Bennett, "'Free American Political Prisoners': Pacifist Activism and Civil Liberties, 1945–1948," *Journal of Peace Research* 40 (July 2003): 428.

41. Alex Sareyan, *The Turning Point: How Men of Conscience Brought About Major Change in the Care of America's Mentally Ill* (Washington, D.C.: American Psychiatric Press, 1994), 266.

42. James Tracy, *Direct Action: Radical Pacifism from the Union Eight to the Chicago Seven* (Chicago: University of Chicago Press, 1996); the quote is taken from the title of Chapter 2. For another statement of this argument, see Bennett, *Radical Pacifism*, chaps. 4–8.

chapter ten

FOREIGN POLICY EXPERTS AS SERVICE INTELLECTUALS: THE AMERICAN INSTITUTE OF PACIFIC RELATIONS, THE COUNCIL ON FOREIGN RELATIONS, AND PLANNING THE OCCUPATION OF JAPAN DURING WORLD WAR II

Yutaka Sasaki

INTRODUCTION

An article published in a leading Japanese newspaper reported that John Dower's prize-winning book *Embracing Defeat* became "must reading" among high-ranking officials in the White House just before the outbreak of the Iraq War in early 2003. Dower's book is a grand narrative of the American occupation of Japan (1945–1951), historically rated as a highly successful model of "democratization from above." That is to say, the American occupation of Japan succeeded in transforming a semi-feudal, authoritarian society into a modern democracy in a relatively short period. It is understandable that officials in charge of policy toward Iraq would eagerly attempt to understand why the case of Japan was so successful as they began their planning for the postwar occupation of Iraq by American forces.[1]

As this stepped-up concern reveals, there has recently been renewed interest among official circles and in the U.S. and Japanese media in the successful occupation of Japan, caused by the thus far less than successful

American military occupation of Iraq. On the surface, similarities between the two occupations do exist. The American government regarded both Japan and Iraq as warlike nations whose political and religious institutions were founded on values and belief systems alien to those of Western societies. It posited the main goals of each of these occupations as the twin agendas of demilitarization and democratization, aiming to transform the countries into pro-American democracies.[2]

As far as scholarly interest in the American occupation is concerned, however, Japanese as well as American historians of various political and ideological persuasions had already produced a vast amount of work on the planning, execution, and results—intended as well as unintended—of the American occupation of Japan.[3] Such intense scholarly interest in the American occupation of Japan comes as no surprise because it was truly a pivotal event in the entire history of U.S.–Japan relations, laying the foundation of the current highly integrated state of bilateral relations.

In this connection, historians and social scientists of left-liberal persuasions have tended to point out the limitations of the domestic reforms instituted during the American occupation, arguing that the potential for transforming Japanese political and economic systems in fundamental ways was rather abruptly thwarted by ongoing Cold War concerns that sought to make Japan a staunch American ally in the Western camp. Thus, for these scholars, the American occupation of Japan was something of a "missed opportunity" to genuinely transform Japan into a progressive democracy.[4] On the other hand, conservative or right-wing scholars have continued to argue that many of the occupation reforms, including the new constitution, were thrust upon the Japanese by the Supreme Command for the Allied Powers, led by General Douglas MacArthur, and were responsible for the weakening, or worse, the destruction of a time-honored Japanese national polity with a "uniquely Japanese" identity and national pride.

While being mindful of the differing historical assessments of the occupation of Japan, this chapter focuses on its unofficial planning by two influential American foreign affairs think tanks: the Institute of Pacific Relations (IPR) and the Council on Foreign Relations (CFR). Based in Manhattan, both private organizations served as focal points during the war for the activities of foreign policy experts and intellectuals. Significantly, both organizations began discussing the treatment of a defeated

Japan in the latter half of the Asia–Pacific War in their international conferences, study meetings, and research projects. By engaging in these activities, foreign policy experts and intellectuals who gathered around the IPR and the CFR exchanged information, knowledge, and ideas with strong policy orientations. Furthermore, some of them had connections with the official world and the memoranda and proceedings of their discussions were sent to concerned agencies in Washington. Undoubtedly, the IPR and CFR became two key deliberative locations of information for the official world, including the State Department.

In dealing with the activities of the IPR and the CFR during World War II, this chapter places the following questions at the center of analysis. What concrete measures did foreign policy experts propose for demilitarizing and democratizing Japan, including measures to institute political reforms and industrial control? What prospect did they envision for the future place of Japan in the international order in the Far East? How did they tackle the dilemma of reconciling the international community's cooperation with the pursuit of American national interests and security in dealing with a defeated Japan? To what extent did their activities influence official occupation policies adopted by the U.S. government? How did they try to utilize their expertise to fill the public need for informed discussion on important foreign policy issues? This chapter addresses these questions by examining the activities of the IPR and the CFR in the war years, thereby aiming to shed light on the thoughts of foreign policy experts on presurrender planning and policy toward Japan.

I. DISCUSSION OF THE FUTURE OF JAPAN AT IPR'S WARTIME CONFERENCE

As the first multinational nongovernmental organization dedicated to unofficial studies of Asia-Pacific affairs,[5] the IPR scrupulously yet steadily geared its activities toward an analysis of hot and controversial current political issues following the outbreak of the Sino–Japanese War in the late 1930s.[6] The outbreak of all-out war in the Pacific accelerated this trend, drawing the IPR deep into political debates over the issue of peaceful international settlements and contemporary foreign policy questions. One of the clear manifestations of this was that the IPR decided to officially proclaim that the organization would no longer uphold nonpartisanship as its guiding principle. Immediately after the Pearl Harbor attack by the Japanese Imperial forces, Ray Lyman Wilbur, then chairman of the American Council of the International IPR, made the following statement concerning its policy:

> The immediate job of the American people is the prosecution of war against the military imperialism of Japan and the other Axis powers, whose defeat is the condition of any peaceful adjustment in the Far East and elsewhere. The tradition of the I.P.R. does not permit "neutrality" in this issue; on the contrary, military aggression in complete disregard of the rights of other peoples contradicts anything the I.P.R. has stood for.[7]

In accordance with this wartime policy, which made no pretense of scholarly neutrality or moral relativism, the American Council pledged its full resources in support of the "democratic war effort" of the U.S. government. Above all, because the American Council of the IPR was the only major private organization specializing in Asia-Pacific problems, its intellectual and human resources were soon in great demand. Indeed, after Pearl Harbor various government agencies turned to the IPR for factual data, up-to-date information, publications, and consultation concerning the Far East and the Pacific. As a socially engaged private, unofficial organization and also perhaps with its drive for influence, the international IPR set out to engage in a variety of wartime activities, including a few major international conferences in the hope of creating a lasting peace in that part of the world. One of the most fiercely debated issues was the treatment of Japan after its defeat.

As far as the IPR's deliberations of the treatment and the future of Japan are concerned, the Ninth Conference of the IPR, held in Hot Springs, Virginia, in January, 1945 (hereafter cited as the Hot Springs Conference) was of special significance. Although the previous IPR conference (the Eighth Conference of the IPR held in Mont Tremblant, Canada, in 1942) touched on the issues surrounding the execution of warfare—military, economic, and psychological—against Japan,[8] the Hot Springs Conference placed the subject of the future of Japan on one of its main agendas.[9] Because the IPR was an international organization composed of several national councils, representatives of various IPR-affiliated national councils participated in this conference, including the Americans and British.

The Hot Springs Conference, attended by some 150 representatives from 12 countries, followed the pattern established at the Mont Tremblant Conference and included a large number of government officials, albeit in private capacities, from the membership countries. In fact, some of the delegations from the other countries were theoretically "private," but actually quite clearly "official."

The American delegation was headed by Philip C. Jessup, professor of international law at Columbia University and the former Chairman of the Pacific Council, the central governing authority of the international IPR. The delegation was composed of 28 members, of whom seven were officials. They included John Carter Vincent and Ralph Bunche of the State Department, Frank Coe and Ruppert Emerson of the Foreign Economic Administration, Admiral T. C. Hart of the Navy General Board, Navy Department, Major General Frank R. McCoy, and Congresswoman Frances P. Bolton. As in the previous conferences, academics, including William C. Johnstone of George Washington University, Owen Lattimore of Johns Hopkins University, and Grayson Kirk of Columbia University, became the members of the American delegation. Frederick V. Field, former Secretary of the American Council, Lawrence Salisbury, editor of *Far Eastern Survey*, and Raymond Dennett, Secretary of the American Council, also joined the American delegation. Chatham House, whose Far Eastern Committee served as the British national council of the IPR, sent a higher percentage of participants from the official world than any of the other national councils. These people included Air Marshall Sir John Baldwin, Commodore A. W. Clarke, a commander of the Royal Navy, Sir Paul Butler, a member of the Far Eastern diplomatic service, Sir George Sansom (a noted Japan specialist) from the British embassy, and Arthur Creech-Jones, Labor MP. The British group also included a number of heavyweight businesspeople, including Sir Andrew McFadyean (Chairperson and Director of the British North Borneo Company), Wilfred Andrews (company director, farmer, and fruit grower), and Victor Farmer (Director of Imperial Chemical Industries Ltd).[10]

Other national councils also sent current and former government officials and dignitaries. The Chinese delegation consisted of both Chungking and Washington officials as well as scholars. The chairman was Dr. Chiang Mon-Lin, former Minister of Education. Yunchu Yang, Director of the Department of Eastern Asian Affairs, and Chung-Fu Chang, Director of the Department of American Affairs, both in the Ministry of Foreign Affairs, were among the Chinese delegates. Shih Hu, a notable philosopher and former ambassador to the United States, was also a member. The Indian Council of International Affairs, the Indian branch of the IPR, sent only five delegates, but they included Mrs. V. L. Pandit, Nehru's sister, and also ex-minister of public health, local self-government, United Provinces, and Pandit H. N. Kunzru, President of Servants of India Society and a member of the Council of State. The Canadian and European Councils sent high-ranking government officials to the Hot Springs Conference, too. Canada sent 15 delegates, among whom were H. F. Angus, professor of political science and economics at the University of British Columbia and also a special assistant to Under Secretary of State for External Affairs H. L. Keenleyside, a former Assistant Under Secretary of State for External Affairs, and E. H. Norman, a Japan specialist in the Far Eastern Division of the Department of External Affairs. The French group was headed by Paul Emile Naggiar, former ambassador to Moscow and China, and the Dutch delegation by Dr. Frans H. Visman. a former high-ranking official in the Netherlands Indies Civil Service.[11]

As far as the organization of the Conference was concerned, four round tables were set up at the Hot Springs Conference, with each round table averaging 35 members. The five main topics considered at the round tables were

Treatment of Japan
Economic recovery and progress in Pacific countries
Cultural and race relations
The future of dependent areas
Collective security

Although there were no verbatim records of the round table discussions, as was the case with the other IPR international conferences, there are a couple of firsthand accounts and reports written by participants of the conference in which they concretely recorded the contents of the round table discussions on Japan. Of particular value is a document filed to the State Department by Robert Fearey and Knight Biggerstaff, two Far Eastern scholars affiliated with it. In addition, two American participants, Raymond Dennett and William C. Johnstone, wrote a brief confidential memorandum and an article, respectively, that described the contents as well as the atmosphere of the entire conference. Thus, the following is an analysis of round table discussions on the future of Japan at the Hot Springs Conference, based on these sources, as well as on the postconference official report, *Security in the Pacific: A Preliminary Report of the Ninth Conference of the Institute of Pacific Relations, Hot Springs, Virginia, January 6–17, 1945.* In doing so, this section of the chapter will examine the American delegations' views on major issues surrounding peace settlements with Japan, especially in comparison with those of the British delegation. In addition, important views on major issues regarding the treatment of Japan expressed by delegates of other national councils, including those of the Chinese, Indians, and Canadians, will be included in the analysis.

According to Raymond Dennett, Secretary of the American Council, the most salient feature of the round table discussions on Japan was the sharp disagreement between the American delegates and their British counterparts over key questions concerning the treatment of a defeated Japan. Whereas the British group advocated minimum interference in Japanese political and economic life so that Japan could become a stable country that would contribute to the economic life of the Far East, Dennett observed that the American group "laid more emphasis upon the necessity for a series of fundamental changes in Japanese life which would eradicate as thoroughly as possible the origins of Japanese military and political expansion." Indeed, the Americans "inclined to think that there was no real objection to a period of chaos and instability in Japan provided our goals were achieved in the end."[12] In the same vein, commenting on the atmosphere of the round table discussions on Japan, Fearey and Biggerstaff reported that the American delegation was extremely surprised by the British approach and then went on to criticize them.[13] As a result, the contour of the arguments over how to deal with a defeated Japan was tinged with the tone of what was called a hard peace versus a soft peace.

THE NATURE OF SOCIAL, ECONOMIC, AND POLITICAL CHANGES
IN A DEFEATED JAPAN

The participants centered their discussion on a diversity of major postwar issues concerning a defeated Japan, including the period of immediate measures, disarmament, economic problems, implications of Japan's economic readjustments for trade policies of other nations, and the effect of these measures on Pacific security.

Yutaka Sasaki : 299

As far as the basic aims of the United Nations on the war against Japan were concerned, consensus emerged in the round tables: Japan must be defeated totally, and defeat would be followed by total disarmament, including all arms, munitions, and the elimination of the Army and Navy. Japan would be deprived of all its territorial possessions and mandated islands. The armistice, or terms of surrender, would have to be signed for Japan by the highest authorities, including the Emperor himself. There was also agreement that the occupying forces should be representative of all the United Nations engaged in the war against Japan, including contingents from the Philippines and other Asian nations. Furthermore, it was recognized that there should also be a so-called "spiritual disarmament," meaning that the Japanese people should be persuaded to shed their militaristic propensities through education and economic advancement. It was also generally recognized that war plants should be destroyed or turned over to Asian countries as reparations or converted to the production of peacetime goods. At the same time, it was stressed that reparations should not be used as a means of repressing Japan forever.[14] Within the purview of these general agreements, however, there took place considerable discussion, with resultant disagreements over certain key policies to be applied to a defeated Japan, in terms of specific objectives as well as concrete methods.

First, varying opinions were expressed as to the character of a postwar Japanese regime and as to the direct and indirect means that might be employed by the United Nations to deal with, guide, influence, and assist the Japanese in promoting the growth of a democratic and peaceful nation. One school of thought promoted by the members of Chatham House (the British group) held that a postwar Japanese regime might include some moderate military leaders and some of the great industrialists, for the sake of maintaining internal stability in Japan in the immediate postwar years. In their view, the most logical group with whom the United Nations should deal would be the large industrialists associated with the *Zaibatsu* (the great financial houses), arguing that they might well emerge at the initial stage of the occupation as a focal point of collaboration with an Allied military authority. Thus, according to this view, the old ruling class, except for chauvinistic militarists, should be preserved for the creation of a stable Japan.[15]

A corollary to this argument was that the occupation forces should interfere minimally in Japanese political and economic life so that the country could as quickly as possible become stable and start making its contributions to the economic prosperity of the Asia-Pacific region. Indeed, they expressed the view that because Japan's transformation into democracy must be a slow growth that would be dependent on the achievement of strategic and economic security, it might take a long time for Japan to reorganize its life along democratic lines. As George Sansom, the Japan expert of the British group, argued, "the Japanese will seize any opportunity to move towards liberalism and democracy if it is presented. We must wait and see as regards precise steps to be taken. But any changes must be organic and cannot simply be imposed." Therefore, the supporters of this school argued that it would be undesirable for the United Nations to try to do too much in the way of instituting democratic reforms within Japan.[16]

A diametrically opposed view was expressed by the American delegation. It held that if only minimum or isolated changes were accepted as desirable in moving Japan toward democratic development, there would be a strong likelihood that the old ruling group would come back to regain power and would succeed in blocking further political and economic reforms along democratic, liberal, and peaceful lines. They stressed the point that the present ruling class would never acquiesce to agrarian reforms or tolerate the development of a strong labor movement, resulting in the perpetuation of the present deplorable conditions facing farmers and laborers.[17]

To prevent the old autocratic group from becoming entrenched in power again, the American members maintained that there must be radical political and economic changes, including agrarian reforms and the dissolution or at least the weakening of the power of the *Zaibatsu*. Furthermore, in contrast to the view presented by the members of Chatham House, the Americans argued that the achievement of immediate stability should not be regarded as more important than the necessity of fundamental changes in the political and social structure of Japan that could be brought about to ensure the emergence of a peaceful and democratic Japan (under a United Nations policy of support for liberal and democratic forces). According to this view, the best safeguard for the United Nations against future Japanese aggression was to promote "the earliest possible growth of democratic forces within Japan, even though this growth might be accompanied by some internal disorder and instability." This was essential for Japan to complete "her unfinished revolution." By counting on the upsurge of progressive forces—societal elements composed of leaders of farmer-labor movements, intellectuals, lower ranks of the bureaucracy, small businessmen, and left-wing groups—within Japanese society, the American delegation insisted, the democratic potential could be made possible in a defeated Japan. In their view, the role of the occupation authority was not to suppress mass demonstrations and protests directed at the ruling class but to support them vigorously.[18]

These views advanced by the American delegation found strong support among Chinese, Canadian, and Australian members. In particular, the Chinese views were very close to those of the Americans. They argued that there was a need for Japan to reform itself completely—from its political setup to its industrial structure—so that it would never pose a threat to its neighboring countries. Like the Americans, they expressed distrust of the ruling class in Japan and argued for the necessity of the growth of popular progressive elements that must be sought in every social group, including farmers and laborers. Furthermore, in the view of the Chinese delegation, the political, social, and economic turmoil that were likely to befall Japan was something that should be tolerated as a necessary cost for Japan to transform itself into a peace-loving nation. In the words of Chiang Mon-Lin, "there will be a period of turmoil, of revolution and counter-revolution in post-war Japan. A truly stable government will come later, perhaps much later—maybe the second or third government after the armistice."[19]

On the other hand, the Indian delegation repeatedly supported a policy of relative leniency for Japan. Cognizant of their status as a representative of the so-called "Asiatic" nations, the Indians defended their position based on the following two points. First, harsh treatment of Japan would likely be viewed in Asia as something meted out by Western powers to an Asiatic nation, thus taking on racial overtones. Second, lenient treatment, not harsh treatment, would enable the United Nations to win the confidence of the Japanese people, who must be counted on in Japan's pursuing peaceful and cooperative policies in the future.[20]

ISSUES SURROUNDING THE FUTURE ECONOMIC RECOVERY
OF A DEFEATED JAPAN

These issues bore a direct relevance to the pace of Japan's economic recovery, of the transformation of the Japanese economy, and of the concomitant modifications of Japan's social and political regime conducive to peace, all related to considerations of security. Two distinct views developed on this issue, too, at the round tables. Indeed, there was a strong division of opinion between the Americans and the British about the question of Japan's economic future.

One school of thought supported by the members of the British delegation argued that Japanese economic life must be allowed to recover fairly soon after the initial occupation. The adherents of this position maintained that a severe repression of the Japanese economy would most likely lead to a prolonged period of instability marked by political and social unrest, which in turn would pose a threat to the security and stability of the Far East. Therefore, they argued that positive measures should be instituted at an early date to allow the Japanese to start peaceful trade and economic relations with other nations, including China. The British also argued that it would be necessary to preserve and use the *Zaibatsu* for Japan's economic reconstruction, at least in the short run, although they expressed the hope that the Japanese people would eventually be successful in bringing the *Zaibatsu* under some measure of control. In any event, a British member noted that Japan, stripped of territorial possessions and heavy industries, would not be able to maintain its already low standard of living unless the United Nations would be prepared promptly to offer it opportunities to engage in foreign trade, thereby establishing its place in the world economy.[21] This view was basically supported by the Indian delegation: In their view, a reformed Japan should be permitted to reenter the family of nations as soon as possible. As one Indian member argued, Japan should not be barred from enjoying the conditions necessary to participate in the prosperous and peaceful world order to be established after the cessation of hostilities.[22]

Such a view stood out in a stark contrast to the second view promoted by the American delegation. The Americans regarded the prospective Japanese economic plight with much less alarm, expressing their grave concern that a speedy recovery of Japanese industry in the postwar period carried dangers because of the chance of its being quickly converted to war production for rearmament. They also put emphasis on the necessity of transforming the whole Japanese setup of economic institutions and habits that contributed greatly to the present war. In particular, they argued for limiting the monopolies or *Zaibatsu*, and reorganizing the agrarian system, which would eventually result in raising the living standard of the bulk of ordinary Japanese. Their view was strongly colored by the memory of the last decade, which had witnessed Japan's ominous rise to an aggressive power. As one member who subscribed to this view put it, "The whole trade of the 1930's was part of Japan's mobilization for war" and "the whole meaning of our experience is that we cannot trust her to come back freely."[23]

Not surprisingly, the Chinese delegation strongly supported these rather stringent economic measures. Commenting on the treatment of *Zaibatsu*, one Chinese member stated that "definite steps should be taken to break up the large family trusts." Referring to the plight of ordinary farmers in pre-war Japan, another Chinese member suggested that "the Allies should give maximum aid to the farmers by reductions of rent and interest charges." At the same time, several Chinese members emphasized that the economic recovery of Japan should not allow the living standard of Japan to exceed those of China and other nations in the Far East; the recovery and improvement of the standards of living in the latter countries should take precedence over those of Japan in the postwar world. The Canadian delegates also concurred with these views.[24]

DEBATE OVER THE FUTURE OF THE IMPERIAL THRONE

Perhaps no issue regarding the treatment of Japan generated more heated discussion than the future of the Imperial institution and the postwar position of the Emperor. On this issue, too, the available evidence indicates that the American delegation and the British delegation presented markedly contrasting views.

There was general agreement that the institution of the Imperial Throne in its present form posed a grave danger to the prospects for democratic growth and was hardly compatible with the development of a peaceful Japan. It was therefore agreed that the Imperial institution should be stripped of its myth and traditions of Imperial divinity and also be divorced from the idea of the "divine" racial mission of domination over Asia (*Hakko-ichiu*), which militarists and reactionary societies used to justify their aggressive maneuvers. When it came to the question of whether the Imperial institution could be safely left to evolve into something innocuous, however, there was considerable disagreement.

On the one hand, the viewpoint promoted by the members of the British delegation at round table discussions maintained that the Imperial institution might evolve into a constitutional monarchy if the necessary constitutional changes, including the elimination of various practices such as the right of direct access to the throne by service ministers, were enforced. In addition, these members tended to subscribe to the view that although the Emperor had been used as a tool by the militarists, the Imperial system was in itself passive, and the Emperor should not be held responsible for the actual execution of policy. They also argued that the Emperor was the one element of continuing stability in Japanese life and that any attempt to eliminate the institution by an outside authority would risk throwing the country into revolution and would surely boomerang.[25] It is to be noted that this view was totally congruent with the main arguments of the Chatham House study on the future of Japan, entitled "Japan in Defeat," which was submitted as one of the data papers of the British delegation. In it, the Chatham House group contended that "a constitutional monarchy with a liberal administration might be the most favorable solution in the interests of Japan and the world" and that "[n]o alternative to a monarchical system, under the present Emperor or some other member of his family, is likely to provide that focus of stability which will be essential if the State is not to dissolve into chaos in the impending crisis."[26]

On the other hand, the view held by most members of the American delegation was that the Imperial institution was and would be "an instrument used by Japan's most reactionary elements," serving as the foundation of Japan's excessive nationalism and Japanese militarism. As a result, they advocated the desirability of the abolition of the institution, eliminating it from the Japanese body politic.[27] It is worth noting that William Johnstone, one of the principal members of the American delegation, developed essentially the same view in his data paper entitled "The Future of Japan." After examining both arguments for and against retaining the Imperial Throne in postwar Japan, Johnstone stated that the Imperial Throne was one of the elements that had contributed to Japanese militarism and aggression, and therefore would pose a threat to a peaceful Japan. Thus, he argued that the United States should "devise policies directed toward the abolition of the Imperial Throne and to reject any policy of 'using' the Throne for the establishment of a peaceful Japan."[28]

Perhaps the most vocal American member who argued for the desirability of the abolishment of the Throne was Owen Lattimore. In his view, ordinary Japanese were not so firmly attached to the Emperor, and a considerable number of them would be ready to jettison the Imperial institution. Foreign observers of hereditary monarchy in Asia had a propensity, he argued, to overrate the degree of its spiritual hold on the general population, but history showed that there were numerous instances of hereditary monarchy having been overthrown. Lattimore further argued that under no circumstances should the United Nations attempt to make use of the Emperor for any purpose. Such a move on the part of the United Nations would be dangerous because it might indicate to the Japanese that the United Nations had a respect for the Emperor, thereby acknowledging his authority.[29]

Lattimore was not alone in advocating the abolishment of the Imperial institution. A substantial proportion of the Chinese delegates were in favor of the elimination of the Imperial institution, arguing that that would be indispensable for the development of a peaceful and democratic Japan. For instance, Hu Shih said, "I believe personally that removal of the Emperor would be the first step in greater political maturity in Japan. It would be the first step in the re-education of the Japanese people." In the same vein, Shao Yu-ling, Secretary of the National Military Council, remarked, "I believe personally that it is desirable that the Emperor should go, and that the Japanese people will not be as reluctant to see him go as some imagine."[30]

While Lattimore and a few others proposed "some intriguing theoretical procedures for the United Nations action to abolish the Imperial Institution," including one of sending the Emperor to the countryside, or to China or London in exile, thereby removing the core of excessive nationalist inspiration from Japan,[31] it was generally agreed in the end that the wise procedure would be for the United Nations to let the Japanese people decide the future of the Imperial Throne for themselves. Consequently, the participants "dodged rather than settled" this sensitive issue.[32]

The preceding analysis has revealed that at the Hot Springs Conference stark differences of opinion about the key issues of the postwar settlement were brought out into the open among delegates of different national councils, especially between the Americans and the British. While the Americans maintained that the essential goal of the United Nations was to bring about a drastic change in the internal social setup of Japan, the British expressed strong doubt as to whether the United Nations should attempt to make any drastic changes in Japan.

The important question remains as to the extent, if any, to which the Hot Springs Conference influenced actual policies adopted toward Japan in the immediate years after World War II. It is worth noting that several government officials attended the Conference as members of the American delegation. In addition, as noted, two other officials of the State Department (Fearey and Biggerstaff) participated in it in the capacity of members of the conference secretariat, indicating that the State Department closely watched the deliberations of the Conference. It should be added that *Security in the Pacific*, the official report of the Conference, was sent to a diversity of government agencies. A confidential report written by Philip Jessup even reached none other than the U.S. president.[33]

As Dower has aptly pointed out,[34] because there was a complex struggle over the basic policy orientation toward Japan within the State Department and other governmental agencies in charge of making actual policies in the immediate years before and after World War II, it is difficult to assess the precise practical effects of the Hot Springs Conference on policy making. It can be said, however, that the radical line between the diagnosis of Japan's past and the prognosis for Japan advocated by the American delegation was at odds with the views held by the Committee on Post-War Programs, the State Department's agency that had the power to formulate long-range postwar policies. In fact, by the end of 1944, two important policy orientations regarding the treatment of Japan had already been gradually taking shape in the deliberations of the committee: One was that a defeated Japan would be allowed to restore its industrial capacity, consistent with the requirement to sustain the population, and to be eventually admitted to the family of nations. The other is that the Imperial institution would be preserved and utilized as a focal point of stability of the polity of Japan.[35] Given this, it is no wonder that the two State Department officials (Fearey and Biggerstaff) made the observation that "many members of the American delegation believed that the State Department's approach to Japanese problems, as evidenced by what they had read about its attitude on the Emperor, the Zaibatsu, etc., was similar to that of the British. . . . The Department view was less conservative than the British only in that it was thought not to place so much emphasis on a short period of occupation and disapproved of Japan retaining an army."[36]

Thus, available evidence indicates that the significance of the Hot Springs Conference for officialdom lay in that it served as a sounding board for a variety ideas with regard to the treatment of Japan, while at the same time setting the boundaries of the debate about the important issues on its treatment.

The Council on Foreign Relations dealt with a variety of issues involved in the postwar occupation of Japan as part of its large-scale research project entitled "Studies of American Interests in the War and the Peace" (commonly designated as the "War and Peace Studies," or WPS), started in the summer of 1939. This project was especially noteworthy in that it was conceived and carried out in direct collaboration between the CFR and the State Department. Indeed, the WPS originated in a visit by Hamilton Fish Armstrong,[37] editor of *Foreign Affairs*, and Walter H. Mallory, Executive Director of the CFR, to the State Department on September 12, 1939, to offer "aid on the part of the Council as might be useful and appropriate" and "a cross-section of expert opinion to supplement its [the State Department's] official information and opinion."[38]

In contemplating the WPS, the steering committee chaired by Norman Davis (the President of the CFR),[39] classified a variety of issues concerning war and peace into four general categories: security and armaments, economic and financial problems, political problems, and territorial problems. Four groups of experts were formed: namely, the Security and Armaments Group, the Economic and Financial Group, the Political Group, and the Territorial Group. Each group was headed by a *rapporteur*, who would oversee the activities of the group. In addition, a research secretary was assigned to each group, who would direct research and prepare documentation for the group. The steering committee of the WPS selected individual members based on their experience and competence to deal with particular subjects. In each group, specialized subjects were assigned for expert investigation to qualified members of the group or occasionally to outside experts.[40]

Although the WPS initially directed its resources toward the analysis of postwar issues concerning European peace settlements, it also became concerned with Far Eastern settlements, especially those vis-à-vis Japan, as the war progressed.[41] In its deliberations on peace settlements and security in relation to Japan, the WPS tackled a variety of issues within the framework of security principles and measures against Japan. These issues included the methods of demilitarization and democratization of Japan, industrial control and Japan's economic recovery, the disposition of the Japanese overseas territories (including the mandated islands), and the treatment of the Japanese Emperor. It is to be noted that of the four groups, the Security and Armaments Group (hereafter designated as the Armaments Group)[42] played a central role in producing memoranda on these issues. What follows is therefore an analysis of discussions, as well as memoranda, by WPS participants, especially by the members of the Armaments Group, of major issues concerning peace settlements vis-à-vis Japan. In addition, relevant memoranda produced by other groups will be analyzed for the purpose of comparison whenever necessary. Particular attention will also be paid to major voices and representative opinions, as well as fresh ideas in regard to each topic.[43]

SECURITY PRINCIPLES, ARRANGEMENT, AND INDUSTRIAL CONTROL VIS-À-VIS JAPAN

In regard to this subject, the Armaments Group produced two memoranda, one in late 1943 and the other in the middle of 1944. The first memorandum, authored by Hanson W. Baldwin, the military editor for the *New York Times*, focused exclusively on security policy toward Japan.

During a discussion of the draft memorandum, Baldwin posed such fundamental questions to the members of his group as "Should Japan be forced to remain excluded as a potential member of a Pacific security organization for the indefinite future?" and "What kind of military and industrial controls should be maintained over Japan?" While laying out these questions, Baldwin also made the point that in dealing with the security problem in the Far East, there was a need to take into account two major factors regarding the war: Russia and China. The ensuing discussion by the members of the Armaments Group noted the "inherent difficulty of keeping Japan in a militarily weak but economically prosperous condition." The members recognized that unless Japan was offered an opportunity to create a stable and prosperous national economy, the chance of the growth of political liberalism would become slim. They were, however, aware that an economic revival could be achieved only through the restoration of industrial strength, the backbone of modern military power. In the end, the members adopted the formula that "Japan should be allowed as great a degree of economic prosperity as would be compatible with continued disarmament."[44]

One of the difficult questions regarding the method of control over Japan was, of course, how to carry out the military occupation of Japan.

On this question, Baldwin explained to the members that such an occupation should be as effective as possible, proposing a two- to five-year period of occupation. His proposal drew a variety of responses from the members. Edward P. Warner, the expert on aeronautics, for instance, suggested all controls except a prohibition on an aircraft industry might be abandoned if a liberal Japanese government would be in power. On the question of the duration of occupation, Joseph C. Green, then special assistant to the Secretary of State, argued that although a brief occupation would be necessary to impress on the Japanese the completeness of their defeat, the actual occupation should be terminated after a few months at most, and thereafter the troops of the Allies should retreat into a few strategic points. Green stressed further that there should be representation among the occupying forces of the troops of all the countries engaged in fighting Japan, including China.[45]

The Baldwin memorandum that was transmitted to Washington after revision distinguished the immediate postwar policy from the long-range policy. As for the former, the memorandum argued that to achieve the twin objectives of demilitarization and demobilization of all Japanese armed forces, the military occupation of the main islands of Japan would be necessary "to bring home to the Japanese people the completeness of their defeat" and that "occupation of the main islands of Japan might be undertaken by mixed national contingents drawn from the forces of all nations which had contributed to the defeat of Japan." At the same time, such a military occupation should not be carried out as a punishment of Japan—as retaliatory in nature or long, protracted, and exacerbating—and it should be as brief as is constant with the effective accomplishment of the two purposes.[46]

Furthermore, touching on the spiritual aspect of the demilitarization of Japan, Baldwin supported the idea that the occupying forces would make an effort "to seek out and eliminate some of the traditional forms and institutions which in the past have tended to perpetuate the Japanese feudal-militaristic caste." His memorandum also argued that the occupying forces should encourage the growth of "liberal elements" in Japan, which would lead to the growth of "new political thought." With respect to long-range policy toward a defeated Japan, the memorandum stated that Japan should not be saddled with too severe reparations or with economic punishments that would likely create "the leaven of discontent." On the issue of the industrial control of Japan, the memorandum placed a fairly strict prohibition on the development of a variety of industries, recommending that Japanese aviation and shipbuilding industries, and manufacturing equipment for heavy steel and synthetic oil should be prohibited.[47]

On the other hand, the Baldwin memorandum is noteworthy in that it made clear reference to the gradual induction of Japan into a general international security organization. Such a prospect was dependent, it asserted, on sincere collaborative actions on the part of Japan, mentioning that "the sooner she can be prepared for collaboration . . . the better hope for the peace of the world." By way of summary, Baldwin stated that although Japan should be reduced to "the status of a second-class power" by these control measures, the treatment of Japan and that of Germany should be identical, so that "there should be no feeling that one is more harshly treated than the other because one is Oriental and the other is not."[48]

The second memorandum was authored by Major George F. Eliot, the military correspondent for the *New York Herald Tribune*, who explained during the discussion that the basic thesis of his memorandum was that there should be a "drastic de-industrialization of Japan." Significantly, some of the principal members of the group raised strong objections to the "drastic" aspects in Eliot's memorandum.

Commenting on the general thesis of the memorandum, Baldwin argued that depriving Japan of aircraft industries and enforcing reasonable limitations on merchant shipping would be enough to prevent the resurgence of Japan as a dangerous military power. Most vocal was Armstrong, who argued that the American people would not support the policy of a ruthless deindustrialization that would result in the starvation of many Japanese. Furthermore, the stringent control of Japanese imports of raw materials proposed by Eliot's memorandum might not be supported by the Chinese, who, in his view, would want to export raw materials to Japan.[49]

A few other assumptions in Eliot's memorandum came under heavy criticism. One was his insistence that Japan be allowed to maintain virtually no armaments. Armstrong stressed that Japan would need a greater policing force to maintain internal order than "a few ornamental swords," as proposed in the memorandum. According to Green, the police should be allowed to have at least a limited number of small arms, including submachine guns, for the purpose of maintaining local order. This view was shared by Army General Frank R. McCoy, who argued that it would be unwise to make an "overly categorical and precise statement" in this matter. Another assumption in the memorandum that prompted criticism was the statement about the proposed total ban on aviation industry and manufacture or use of aircraft within Japan. On this, both Theodore P. Wright, the aviation expert and Warner suggested that in place of the "absolute air prohibition" it would be better to sell the Japanese a limited number of commercial aircraft for domestic use.[50]

Even after making suggested changes as a result of this discussion, Major Eliot's memorandum in its final form recommended "drastic" security and control measures for Japan. As to the armaments that Japan should be allowed to retain, Major Eliot flatly stated that "my answer would be in one word: none, of any shape more formidable than the minimum required for local police services." On the other hand, perhaps reflecting the suggestion made during the discussion, he inserted a sentence: "These should be limited to such small arms as may be necessary to enable the police to maintain order." On the issue of industrial control of Japan, Eliot stuck with his original position, recommending the following:

> The Japanese aircraft industry should be completely wiped out.
> Factories directly concerned with the manufacture of heavy weaponry should be dismantled.
> Shipyards should likewise be dismantled except for a fixed annual capacity to maintain foreign trade within carefully restricted limits.
> The construction or acquisition of vessels of war should be forbidden to Japan.
> By general agreement among the powers concerned, the importation by Japan of raw materials, including iron, steel, oil, should be rationed so as to make it impossible for Japan to accumulate a war reserve of these materials.[51]

The harsh nature of Eliot's recommendations is also evident in his insistence that Japan should not be allowed to grow as an industrial economy through trade with other countries in the region. Indeed, he stated that the growth of "a militaristic and aggressive Japan" by forming economic ties with China, India, and South Asia would result in consequences to the world that "may be even more disastrous than those of the present war." In addition, the Elliot memorandum emphasized the need to be vigilant over the economic activities of Japan in the foreseeable future, proposing to create a "joint control commission" after the end of military occupation for the purpose of overseeing imports to Japan.[52]

It is to be noted that a memorandum commissioned by the Economic and Financial Group as a whole advocated a much more liberal treatment of a defeated, demilitarized Japan in the postwar period. The author of the memorandum was Elizabeth Schumpeter, a historian of the Japanese economy and wife of the famous economist Joseph Schumpeter. In her memorandum, Schumpeter argued that Japan must be allowed to retain her industries to maintain her large and growing population. For this purpose, she stressed the need for Japan to have access to export markets providing her with sufficient funds for the purchase of raw materials, to have an adequate merchant marine, and to share international economic enterprises. Furthermore, she endorsed the idea that Japan should become an "industrial center in East Asia."

Indeed, she argued that Japan should be permitted to retain her heavy industries and her merchant marine not only so that she would be able to pay for essential foodstuffs and raw materials but also so that she "may contribute substantially to the industrialization of the rest of the Orient and will reduce to a minimum economic dislocations in those areas which had close trade relations with Japan." Interestingly, Schumpeter justified her recommendations by arguing that Japan should become a stable industrial democracy as a counterweight against the possible aggrandizement of Russian influence in the Far East.[53] It should be pointed out that the members of the Economic and Finance Group headed by Alvin Hansen, the noted Keynesian economist at Harvard, endorsed the content of this memorandum without making any serious objections.[54] Thus it can be observed that the Economic and Finance Group endorsed the concept of economic internationalism, which envisioned an economic order in which nation states would be economically interdependent on one another through free trade and without economic barriers, thereby achieving prosperity and peace.

THE DISPOSITION OF JAPAN'S TERRITORIES, INCLUDING
THE MANDATED ISLANDS

In the meantime, the Armaments Group placed on its agenda the issue of the disposition of the Japanese mandated islands[55] as part of its discussion of security policy on Japan. The Armaments Group identified the crux of the issue to be the antinomy between exclusive American control and international control over the Japanese mandated islands.

Following the initial meeting on this issue, the Armaments Group asked Grayson Kirk, a political scientist at Columbia University, to prepare a short memorandum on this subject, and his conclusion emphasized the desirability of exclusive control over the Japanese mandated islands by the United States. It was the issue of the desirability of exclusive control over the islands that caused a heated debate among the members of the Armaments Group. Stacy May, the deputy director of the Social Sciences Division of the Rockefeller Foundation, argued that the danger in an insistence on exclusive privilege of the islands lay in that other powers might make the same claims with respect to specific areas, endangering the development of a genuine international policing arrangement. According to Wright, the establishments of military bases under exclusive American control might be incompatible with the no-aggrandizement provisions of the Atlantic Charter, arguing that the wording of the draft memorandum "exclusive or predominant control by the United States" should be modified by deleting the world "exclusive." The only dissenting opinion was expressed by Baldwin, who remarked that given the essential strategic importance of the Japanese mandated islands, the future security of the United States should insist on paramount control over the islands after the present war.[56]

The Kirk memorandum transmitted to Washington first pointed out that Japan had violated the mandate obligations not to establish naval bases, also emphasizing that the islands should not fall under the control of any power likely to use them for aggressive military purposes. It went on to explain why the United States should take responsibility or control over the islands, while taking into account several hypothetical situations. The first possibility was that the security of the Pacific would be entrusted primarily to the United States, while other powers would play a collaborating role. A second possibility was that a regional or a broadly international organization was established and that all governmental functions and responsibilities except those relating to security might be placed under direct international authority. A third possibility was that powers other than the United States may not feel any necessity for American military protection. A fourth possibility was that a regional international organization for the Southwest Pacific would be created to internationalize security responsibility, with the United States playing a dominant role in military operations. The final situation was one in which no international security arrangements for the future would be worked out. Following the examination of these hypothetical situations, Kirk concluded that each of them pointed to the desirability of the United States' assuming full responsibility for the security of the Pacific by acquiring control over the Mandated Islands. However, the wording of the conclusion faithfully reflects the Armaments group's view, by replacing the word "exclusive" with "predominant." Indeed, the conclusion stated that "the United States must retain predominant control over the mandated islands, consistent with any agreements which the United States may make with respect to international policing or security arrangements."[57]

The Political Group headed by Whitney H. Shepardson, the Director of the CFR, also took up the subject of the disposition of the Japanese mandated islands. The members of the group were deeply split into two camps over this issue, with one group supporting the idea of unilateral and exclusive control over these islands by the United States and the other preferring the jurisdiction of an international authority. The result was the production of two memoranda whose general tenors and theses were completely different.

The original memorandum was prepared by Arthur Sweetser, former League of Nations official and Deputy Director of the Office of War Information, who essentially argued that the mandated islands constituted a kind of international domain, to be subjected to the control of an international authority. Some members of the group, however, expressed their opposition to this thesis. The most vocal critic was Henry M. Wriston, President of Brown University. He argued for the outright cession of the islands to the United States, suggesting that what the United States needed was the agreement from Great Britain and France because two countries had agreed to transfer these islands to Japan under the Treaty of Versailles. According to Carter Goodrich, professor of economics at Columbia University, the American people would demand exclusive control of the islands after "having shed [American] blood to clinch control of the Islands from Japan."[58]

In spite of these dissenting opinions, Sweetser stood his ground firmly, insisting that it would be "preposterous" to argue that the outright retention of these vitally important islands by the United States would not constitute "territorial aggrandizement" and that the United States had a moral and legal obligation not to take unilateral action irrespective of the treaty rights of other nations or of the international community.[59] Because of the disagreement over this issue among the members, the Political Group transmitted two antithetical memoranda.

The first memorandum, collectively authored by the Political Group, stressed the need to consider this issue from three points of views: the trend of American public opinion, relations with other governments, and the development of the general international organization. As to the first point, the memorandum recognized that public opinion was divided on this issue, with one group demanding outright annexation and the other favoring the placement of the islands under international supervision. As for the second point, if the U.S. policy were construed as one of territorial annexation, observed the memorandum, other governments would "be encouraged, and indeed, in some cases, obligated, to do likewise." Finally, touching on the third point of view, the memorandum argued that the development of the general international organization would "be appreciably affected by the decision as to whether these islands remain at least partially an international domain, . . . , or are removed from such domain and made an outright possession of a single country." In conclusion, it recommended that "if the United States, even though maintaining naval and strategic control of the islands and assuming responsibilities for native government, is prepared after the war to agree to some sort of United Nations' relationship to the territories, there would seem every advantage in so declaring to the world at the earliest possible moment."[60]

The second memorandum, authored by Henry Wriston, strongly advocated the outright annexation of the islands by the United States. According to Wriston, for the United States to annex these islands would not constitute "'aggrandizement' in the sense in which that word is employed in the Atlantic Charter." In justifying his argument further, Wriston stressed the vital strategic importance of the islands. In the author's view, the problem is "not civil, but military," with only the United States and Japan having a deep interest in the islands. Noting that the United States "had to sacrifice Wake, Guam, and the Philippines to Japan at the outset of this war" because of the lack of adequate bases in the Western Pacific, Wriston pointed out that the United States should possess the islands because possession would entail the "major responsibility for applying force" in the Far East. In short, "[a]nnexation by the United States is the simplest solution and the one most likely to contribute to stable peace," he concluded.[61] It can thus be seen that Wriston's memorandum presented a new view of the strategic frontier of the United States as one that should be extended beyond Hawaii to include the Western Pacific so that the United States could assume responsibility for the protection of trans-Pacific air route bases, including the one in the Philippines.

THE TREATMENT AND THE FUTURE OF THE EMPEROR
AND THE IMPERIAL INSTITUTION

This politically sensitive subject was seriously explored by the Armaments Group in the years 1944 and 1945. Julius Pratt, a diplomatic historian at Union College, prepared a memorandum on this subject, which served as a springboard for discussion. It should first be noted that in this draft memorandum, the author concluded that the forceful abolishment of the Imperial system would do more harm than good in reshaping Japan into a stable democracy. Not surprisingly, the discussion centered around the question of whether the Emperor and the Imperial system should be subjected to harsh treatment. The discussion record reveals that the majority of the group agreed with the main conclusion of the Pratt memorandum.

For example, Green urged the participants to consider the reverse procedure in a hypothetical situation, namely, the procedure in which a victorious Japan would force the American people to change the whole complex of their religious and political beliefs by substituting Christianity with the Shinto faith and by banning the American Constitution. According to Green, this was nothing but a "palpable absurdity," analogous to seeing the victorious Americans interfering deeply with the fundamental aspects of Japanese religious and political ideology. Baldwin expressed the view that the Allied nations should avoid doing any harm to the Emperor and the Imperial system, suggesting also that any possible military advantage of using the Throne should be considered carefully and that it would be unwise for the Allies to treat the Emperor as a war criminal and to punish him as an act of retribution at the end of the war. Although Armstrong expressed the only dissenting voice against the soft treatment of the Emperor, the general view of the group was that there should be a distinction between war policies and a policy of punishment after the end of the war and that the latter policy should be avoided.[62]

At the beginning of the memorandum sent to Washington, Pratt pointed out that there were conflicting opinions about the treatment of the Emperor and the Imperial system, noting especially that the Chinese media were the most vocal in arguing for the harsh treatment of the Japanese Emperor. True enough, he observed, the Emperor, whose family line supposedly remained unbroken for ages eternal, was viewed in the eyes of his subjects as a divinity, and Emperor worship was closely connected with Shinto, the center of Japanese religious life. Pratt also recognized that these characteristics of the Imperial system prompted the supporters of harsh treatment of the Emperor to argue that the only way to rid Japan of militarism was to abolish the Imperial system, together with the cult of the Emperor worship with which militarism was allegedly inextricably bound.[63] In the wake of these observations, however, the memorandum argued against any forms of harsh treatment of the Emperor and his immediate family.

First of all, the humiliation or execution of an individual Emperor by conquering powers would more likely result in investing the Emperor with "the sanctity of martyrdom" than "to subject him to loss of face in the eyes of the Japanese." Furthermore, Pratt argued that the development of democracy in Japan would be possible within the framework of the Imperial system by citing the historical precedent in Japan, when democratic forces of the country had in the past tried to create a genuine parliamentary system "within the Imperial system, not by its overthrow." In Pratt's view, "if democracy comes to Japan, it will have to come slowly, by evolution from within." For these reasons, he stated that "In neither politics nor religion is there any reason to believe that a harsh treatment of the Japanese Emperor would contribute to the reforms in Japanese thought or institutions desired by the United Nations."[64]

In addition, Pratt examined the legal status as well as the actual practice of power afforded to the Emperor, to examine the possible responsibility of the Emperor for the present war. According to him, a distinction should be made between the status of the Emperor in the Meiji Constitution and the actual practice of that power. To be sure, the memorandum pointed out, the Constitution of 1869 prescribed that the Emperor alone was accorded the right to make war and peace and to conclude treaties. These were, however, powers only on paper. In actual practice, "the powers exercised personally by the Emperor have borne no resemblance whatever to those of a Hitler or a Stalin. They have fallen far short of those of a President of the United States and have probably not exceeded those of a King of England." According to Pratt, from the seventh century A.D. to 1868, governmental power was in the hands of civil bureaucrats and generals, while the emperors were "at best heads of ceremonial courts without power and at worst were poverty-stricken victims of neglect." After the Meiji Restoration, which abolished the shogunate and restored the Emperor to "his rightful place at the head of the government," Pratt observed, "real power passed very largely into the hands of civil and military bureaucrats—descendants of the samurai class who had engineered the Restoration and the modernization program." Thus, the locus of real power lay in the hands of bureaucrats and the men around the Emperor "who could use his symbolic value for their own ends, who have controlled the government of Japan," and who were "the real shapers of Japanese policy since 1931, and hence the real 'war criminals.'"[65]

Pratt's memorandum thus emphasized the following two points. First, there should be no thought of punishing him as a war criminal, nor should he be singled out for deliberate attack. Second, any attempt to depose the Emperor as a symbol of Japanese nationalism would surely boomerang.[66]

As these discussions on the treatment of the Emperor and the Imperial system reveal, the Armaments Group ended up advocating the preservation of the Imperial system, not because it was an essential ingredient to promote liberal democracy in Japan, but because there was simply no substitute for it in bringing about political stability in Japan. In any event, the Armaments Group manifested a very cautious attitude toward a drastic transformation of the body politic of Japan by outside forces while taking into account the specificity of Japanese historical development surrounding the Imperial system.

There remains the question of WPS's influence on the official policy making by concerned government agencies, including the State Department. There is evidence, although of a circumstantial nature, to suggest that the WPS project—its memoranda and personnel—influenced a series of postwar planning committees and research agencies established within the State Department. As stated before, all the WPS memoranda were sent to the State Department and also circulated among appropriate governmental agencies.[67] It is worth noting that the Division of Special Research and the subcommittees established within the Advisory Committee on Postwar Foreign Policies, both of which were established within the State Department in 1941, utilized WPS memoranda in their meetings.[68] Further, key CFR members participating in the WPS, including Norman Davis, Isaiah Bowman, and Hamilton Fish Armstrong, became members of two State Department committees in charge of presurrender planning: the Advisory Committee on Postwar Foreign Policy and the Committee on Post-War Programs (established in January 1944). The research secretaries of the four groups of the WPS were at first loaned to and subsequently became full-time staff of the Division of Special Research through a special arrangement between the CFR and the State Department. They also functioned as the research staff of the subcommittees of the Advisory Committee on Postwar Foreign Policies.[69] Their influence in the Division of Special Research was so great that some career officials, including Harry Notter, the assistant head of the Division of Social Research, resented their influence, which caused serious friction in the division.[70]

It is also interesting to note that high-ranking officials of the State Department commended the WPS in appreciation of its contribution to the State Department's planning. For instance, Secretary of State Cordell Hull wrote to Norman Davis, saying, "The excellent memoranda which have resulted from your studies have been very useful to us. I feel sure that they will be of even greater use when the day for reconstruction comes at the end of hostilities."[71] In the same vein, Joseph Grew, a noted member of the so-called "Japan crowd" and the deputy secretary of the State Department, praised the WPS by remarking that "the program [the WPS] will be useful to the Department in its work and will contribute materially to the formation of informed and enlightened public opinion on the extremely important problems involved."[72] These remarks clearly suggest that the WPS project was highly thought of by the State Department.

The influence of the WPS project on official policy making, however, should not be overrated, in the opinion of the present writer. First, some evidence indicates that the initiative to set the agenda of each group lay in the hands of key career officials of the State Department. In their zealous efforts to be useful to the State Department, the steering committee of the WPS continuously sought counseling from key State Department officials to make the agenda of each group of the WPS meet with the concrete needs of the State Department. In return, such key officials as Under Secretary Sumner Welles and Special Assistant to the Secretary of State Leo Pasvolsky, gave concrete advice and suggestions on the appropriate topics that each group of the WPS ought to pursue.[73] In other words, as the WPS progressed during the war, the initiative for agenda setting was gradually placed in the hands of the key career officials of the State Department. Viewed this way, as Inderjeet Parmer has argued, the State's power had the upper hand over the CFR: The former used the latter for its own needs.[74]

Second, it can be observed that as the postwar planning entered the final stage in which actual policies were formulated, there took place an incremental reduction in the participation of nonofficial members in the key planning apparatus of the U.S. government. For instance, few WPS participants became members of the State-War-Navy Coordinating Committee (established in November 1944) whose subcommittee for the Far East issued the basic instruments and directives on Japan at the last stage of the Second World War.[75] This development was inevitable for the sake of maintaining secrecy, but it suggested that at the final stage of postwar planning, career officials in governmental agencies came to prevail over private citizens.[76]

In spite of the limits on the extent to which the WPS project influenced practical governmental policy making as described, there is no denying that the CFR members through the WPS project enjoyed intimate and privileged relationships with the State Department. Indeed, it can be observed that no other private foreign affairs organizations, including the IPR, enjoyed access to the state apparatus concerned with making postwar planning. As a result, it can be concluded that the WPS project helped establish the framework of analysis of, as well as acting as intellectual catalyst for, important postwar issues,[77] by providing scholarly, knowledgeable memoranda in a timely manner.[78]

CONCLUSION

In the last few years before the end of the Second World War, the IPR and CFR boldly took on the arduous task of analyzing major issues regarding peace settlements with Japan as the military collapse of the Axis nation drew closer in sight. Indeed, the experts and intellectuals who gathered around the activities of both organizations—the IPR and CFR—dealt with major problems in security and control measures regarding Japan. In doing so, they made utmost efforts to utilize their expertise to provide a scholarly analysis by attempting to engage in rational discussion divorced from emotionalism and propaganda. Indeed, what characterized the activities of these American intellectuals and experts during these years was that their diagnosis and prognosis for Japan contained an integrated historical and structural analysis that carefully investigated the causes of Japan's aggressive behavior and thoughtfully recommended solutions for the introduction of reforms in a defeated Japan. Their activities focused on current, hot, and controversial issues of immediate public interest and great policy relevance.

On a broad general level, there are certain similarities in the views of the treatment of a defeated Japan between the American IPR and the CFR. Both the American delegation to the Hot Springs Conference and the members of the CFR stressed the need for the total demilitarization and democratization of Japan so that the country would not pose a security threat again. Both organizations supported the idea that Japan would need a spiritual demilitarization, thereby transforming itself into a peace-loving democracy. To achieve these ends, it was deemed necessary for the United Nations to foster conditions for the growth of democratic forces within Japan.

On the other hand, in terms of the general tenor and specific contents of the discussion, there existed, depending on the issue, subtle and marked differences of opinion about key issues regarding the treatment of a defeated Japan between the American IPR and the CFR. First, they differed in their view of the extent to which the United Nations would take the initiative to create a stable democracy. The IPR delegation at the Hot Springs Conference subscribed to the belief that the Allied Nations should rigorously pursue the course of reforming Japanese social and industrial institutions in fundamental ways. To achieve these objectives, they argued, the United Nations should manifest a strong guiding hand, and the resultant economic plight and social chaos accompanied by drastic reforms were necessary evils. In contrast, although opinions were not unanimous, the majority opinion of the foreign policy experts and intellectuals who participated in the CFR's WPS project did not support the idea of drastic fundamental changes of the existing social and industrial setup of Japan under the forceful guidance of United Nations authority. Because a stable political and economic structure was a precondition for the growth of a stable democracy, they reasoned, too much interference by the Allied powers in the existing industrial and social institutions of Japan would not be desirable.

Nowhere can this divergence of opinion regarding peace settlements with Japan be more clearly seen than the treatment of the Emperor and the Imperial institution. Indeed, the American IPR and the Armaments

Group of the CFR presented more markedly contrasting views on the treatment of the Emperor and the Imperial system than on any other issue. By emphasizing the close ties between the Emperor system and Japanese militarism, members of the American IPR favored the idea of abolishing the institution although they stopped short of advocating a violent overthrow. On the other hand, the Armaments Group of the CFR refrained from advocating any fundamental transformation in the nature of Emperor worship. Rather, they envisaged that the Imperial system would likely provide the locus of stability, and they believed in a democracy with the Imperial institution as its figurehead.[79]

What accounts, then, for the difference in their views on the treatment of a defeated Japan? At the general cognitive level, these contrasting views between the American IPR and the CFR reflect a fundamental difference over what social change should be in regard to a defeated Japan— evolutionary change versus revolutionary change and immediate transformation versus gradual transformation. They also disagreed over whether or not such a change should be brought about with the strong interference of outside authorities. Furthermore, in explaining the differences, we need to take into account the considerable differences in terms of organizational structure and intellectual process between the IPR and the CFR.

Although the American IPR was an American branch of the international IPR, the CFR has been an exclusively American nongovernmental organization. Whereas the American IPR had to take pains to maintain good working relationships with other national councils, at the same time, it opted to assert its *raison d'être* by adopting a progressive political stance on controversial foreign policy issues. The intellectual rivalry and tensions between the American IPR and Chatham House over concrete issues bearing on the postwar international order also played a significant role.[80] On the other hand, the CFR could discuss foreign policy issues from the American perspective and express American national interests more straightforwardly than the American IPR.[81] In addition, in terms of the style and operating codes of leadership, although the American IPR oriented itself toward providing a forum for enlightened discussion among private citizens, the CFR consciously sought direct access to the government and tried to influence governmental policy making. And there is no denying that the American IPR was staffed with Asian specialists of liberal and left-wing persuasions who tended to have an idealist belief in the universal applicability and appeal of democratic values.[82] In contrast, the foreign policy experts of the CFR were more or less realists more prone to adopt geopolitical perspectives to suit American strategic interests.

In spite of these differences in the visions of reforming a militaristic Japan into a peace-loving nation, however, those foreign policy experts who took part in the activities of the IPR and the CFR shared the same characteristics and qualities. Even though the two organizations have been viewed as polar opposites in terms of their ideological orientation,[83] it is important to pay attention to their similarities in terms of intellectual cast.[84] On the whole, these people were clearly motivated by their desire to be socially useful in time of war, putting a premium on intelligent analysis and interpretation with a sense of obligation and responsibility, thereby building an intellectual foundation on which forward-looking, positive foreign policy would be forged. Indeed, those who participated in the wartime activities of the American IPR and the CFR sought to bridge the gap between specialized, expert knowledge and public needs for informed discussion on important foreign policy issues. In doing so, they tried to be critically objective yet socially involved, speculative yet practical, and ethical but cooperative, in order to make their expertise relevant to contemporary foreign policy issues. Thus, at a more general level, these intellectuals can be called service intellectuals rather than servant of powers, or subversive leftists, as critics of the American IPR and the CFR have often charged.[85] In the opinion of the present writer, the fact that the United States government was able to enlist the direct and indirect support of these two organizations capable of presenting divergent views on the peace settlements with Japan was a great asset in a democratic formulation of foreign policies in a time of war.

NOTES

1. *Asahi Shimbun*, July 25, 2005. Dower's article was originally published in the October 27 issue of *The New York Times*, which was subsequently reprinted in the January 2003 issue of *Sekai* [the World], the leading opinion journal published in Japan. John Dower, *Embracing Defeat: Japan in the Wake of World War II* (New York: W. W. Norton, 2000).

2. Ibid. In his essay, Dower issues a strong warning against the tendency among some high-ranking officials in Washington to use the Japanese case as a model for the American occupation of Iraq, dismissing it as a gross misuse of history, or worse, as propaganda. Dower points out that none of the conditions that had made the American occupation of Japan successful exist in the case of

the American occupation of Iraq. Those conditions include the acceptance of the American occupation by the general Japanese public, the tradition of prewar civil society in Japan, the meticulous planning for the occupation, and the existence of a charismatic leader in the person of General MacArthur.

3. The scholarly works dealing with the occupation of Japan and its aftermath are too numerous to cite. However, major works include Iokibe Makoto, *Beikoku no Nihon Senryō Seisaku* [*The American Occupation Policy Toward Japan*] , 2 vols. (Tokyo: Chū ō kōron-sha, 1985); Michael Schaller, *The American Occupation of Japan: The Origins of the Cold War in Asia* (New York: Oxford University Press, 1985); Sakamoto Yoshikazu and R. E. Ward, eds., *Nihon Senryō no Kenkyū* [Democratizing Japan: The Allied Occupation] (Tokyo: University of Tokyo Press, 1987); Nakamura Masanori, et al. *Sengo Nihon Senryō to Sengo Kaikaku: Senryō to Kaikaku* [The Postwar Japan—Occupation and Postwar Reform, vol. 2: Occupation and Reform] (Tokyo: Iwanami Shoten, 2005). Takeshi Matsuda, *Soft Power and Its Perils: US Cultural Policy in Early Postwar Japan and Permanent Dependency* (Washington, D.C. and Stanford, California: Woodrow Wilson Center Press and Stanford University Press, 2007).

4. For representative works that take this line of argument, see Yui Daizaburo, *Mikan no Senryō Kaikaku: Amerika Chishikijin to Suterareta Nihonminshyuka- kōsō* [Unfinished Occupation Reforms: American Intellectuals and the Abandoned Idea of Democratization of Japan] (Tokyo: University of Tokyo Press, 1989); Takemae Eiji, *Sneryo Sengo-shi* [*A History of the Postwar Occupation*] (Tokyo: Iwanami Shoten, 1992).

5. The IPR was founded in Hawaii by a group of prominent businessmen, educators, and YMCA leaders and representatives from China, Canada, Australia, New Zealand, the Philippines, Korea, and the United States in 1925. For the English language literature on some aspects of the history of the IPR, see John N. Thomas, *The Institute of Pacific Relations: Asian Scholars and American Politics* (Seattle: The University of Washington Press, 1973); Allan Raucher, "The First Foreign Think Tanks," *American Quarterly* 30 (Fall 1978): 493–513; Paul H. Hooper, *Elusive Destiny: The Internationalist Movement in Modern Hawaii* (Honolulu: University of Hawaii Press, 1980), 107–117; also "The Institute of Pacific Relations and the Origins of Asian and Pacific Studies," by Paul H. Hooper, *Pacific Affairs* 61(1) (Spring 1988): 98–121; Lawrence T. Woods, *Asia-Pacific Diplomacy: Nongovernmental Organization and International Relations* (Vancouver, British Columbia, Canada: University of British Columbia Press, 1993), 29–40; Tomoko Akami, *Internationalizing the Pacific: The United States, Japan and the Institute of Pacific Relations in War and Peace, 1919–45* (London: Routledge, 2002).

6. I have discussed in detail the activities of the IPR after the outbreak of the Sino–Japanese War in my dissertation. See Yutaka Sasaki, "The Struggle for Scholarly Objectivity: The Institute of Pacific Relations and Unofficial Diplomacy from the Sino–Japanese War to the McCarthy Era" (PhD diss., Rutgers University, 2005).

7. Ray Lyman Wilbur, "The American Council and the War," Philip C. Jessup Papers, Library of Congress, Box 127.

8. On the Mont Tremblant Conference and its aftermath, see Christopher Thorne, "Chatham House, Whitehall, and Far Eastern Issues: 1941–45," *International Affairs* (January 1978): 17–24; see also Sasaki, "The Struggle for Scholarly Objectivity," chap. 3.

9. For the brief discussion of the Hot Spring Conference, see Christopher Thorne, *Allies of a Kind: The United States, Britain, and the War Against Japan, 1941–1945* (New York: Oxford University Press, 1978), 540–42. It should be noted that in early January 1944, approximately one year before the Hot Springs Conference, a small-scale interim conference of the Pacific Council, the Institute's governing body, was held in Atlantic City, New Jersey, at which the future of Japan became one of the main subjects. For a detailed analysis of this interim conference, see my dissertation, chap. 4.

10. *Security in the Pacific: A Preliminary Report of the Ninth Conference of the Institute of Pacific Relations, Hot Springs, Virginia, January 6–17* (New York: International Secretariat of the IPR, 1945), 155–60.

11. Ibid., 149–53.

12. Raymond Dennett, "Report on the Ninth International Conference of the Institute of Pacific Relations," (n.d.), Philip C. Jessup Papers, Box 128, p. 2.

13. Robert Fearey and Knight Biggerstaff, "Minutes of the Hot Springs Conference," in U.S. Congress, Senate, Committee on the Judiciary, Subcommittee on Internal Security. *The Amerasia Papers: A Clue to the Catastrophe of China*, vol. 2., 91st Cong., 1st sess., 1970, 1277 (hereafter "Minutes of the Hot Springs Conference," in *The Amerasia Papers*).

14. William C. Johnstone, "The Hot Springs Conference," *Far Eastern Survey*, XIV(2) (January 31, 1945): 16–17.

15. Dennett, "Report on the Ninth International Conference of the Institute of Pacific Relations," 2; "Minutes of the Hot Springs Conference," in *The Amerasia Papers*, 1274–75.

16. *Security in the Pacific*, 41, 42; "Minutes of the Hot Springs Conference," in *The Amerasia Papers*, 1298. Chatham House developed this line of argument elaborately in its data paper to the Conference. See "Japan in Defeat: A Report by

a Chatham House Study Group," United Kingdom Paper No. 4, IPR Papers, Rare Book and Manuscript Library, Columbia University, Box 469. The data paper was later published in book form as *Japan in Defeat: A Report by a Chatham House Study Group* (London: Oxford University Press, 1945).

17. "Minutes of the Hot Springs Conference," in *The Amerasia Papers*, 1275.

18. *Security in the Pacific*, 25, 43; Johnstone, "The Hot Springs Conference," 17; Dennett, 2. On this, Dower has argued that "left-wing publications" of the IPR, including *Amerasia*, *Far Eastern Survey*, and *Pacific Affairs*, draw attention to "the existence of a genuine potential for democratization from below." See Dower, *Embracing Defeat*, 221.

19. "Minutes of the Hot Springs Conference" in *The Amerasia Papers*, 1276.

20. Ibid., 1277.

21. Ibid., 1281; *Security in the Pacific*, 47–48.

22. Ibid., 36.

23. Ibid., 48–49; Johnstone, "The Hot Springs Conference," 17.

24. "Minutes of the Hot Springs Conference," in *The Amerasia Papers*, 1281; *Security in the Pacific*, 49.

25. Ibid., 39, 40.

26. "Japan in Defeat: A Report by a Chatham House Study Group," 11, 119.

27. *Security in the Pacific*, 40.

28. William C. Johnstone, "The Future of Japan," American Council Paper No. 5, IPR Papers, Box 469, 18. It should be noted that Johnstone presented his arguments against any support for the Imperial Throne after the war in a more stark way in his own monograph on Japan. He stated, "For the United Nations to support the Imperial Throne in Japan after the war, either actively or by their official silence on the subject, is to strengthen an institution subversive of all the principles and aims for which this war is being fought. The ultimate goal of a transformed Japan, willing to live at peace with her neighbors, must not be compromised by attempts to gain the short-term advantage of a temporary stability, which will prevent the Japanese people from freeing themselves at the earliest possible moment form the shackles of an extreme nationalism of which the Imperial Throne is the key." See Johnstone *The Future of Japan* (New York: Oxford University Press, 1945), 100. For a relatively recent English language work that analyzes the power and responsibility during the war of the Showa Emperor, see Herbert P. Bix, *Hirohito and the Making of Modern Japan* (New York: HarperCollins, 2000).

29. "Minutes of the Hot Springs Conference," in *The Amerasia Papers*, 1294.

30. Ibid., 1295–96.

31. The essentially same view as that of Lattimore was expressed by some other prominent participants of the Hot Springs Conference, including E. H. Norman, the leading Japan expert at the Conference. Norman argued, "The program which appears to me wisest . . . would be for military government to set up a regency, either a single man or a regency council, quietly taking Hirohito [the Emperor] out of picture to some place like Hayama [a resort town in the countryside] where he would be known to be safe, making no statements about his future disposition or status." Ibid., 1295.

32. *Security in the Pacific*, 40–41.

33. Philip C. Jessup, "Confidential Memorandum to the President," January 18, 1945, Philip C. Jessup Papers, Box 127.

34. Dower, *Embracing Defeat*, 221–23.

35. On this point, see Iokibe, *Beikoku no Nihon Senryō Seisaku*, vol. 2, 52–69.

36. "Minutes of the Hot Springs Conference," in *The Amerasia Papers*, 1277.

37. On an insightful analysis of Armstrong's career, see Priscilla Roberts, "'The Council has been your Creation': Hamilton Fish Armstrong, Paradigm of the American Foreign Policy Establishment?" *Journal of American Studies*, 35(I) (2001): 65–94.

38. CFR, *The War and Peace Studies of the Council on Foreign Relations, 1939–1945* (New York: The Council on Foreign Relations, 1946), 2–3; Memorandum of Conversation from G. S. Messersmith to the Secretary, The Under Secretary, September 12, 1939, 1–3. Hamilton Fish Armstrong Papers, Seeley G. Mudd Manuscript Library, Princeton University, Box 75 (hereafter cited as Armstrong Papers). This project was funded by the Rockefeller Foundation throughout its operation.

39. The original members of the Steering Committee were Norman Davis (chairman), Hamilton Fish Armstrong (vice chairman), Walter H. Mallory (secretary), Paul F. Johnes (administrative secretary), Isaiah Bowman, Allen W. Dulles, Alvin H. Hansen, Whitney H. Sheperdson, and Jacob Viner. Walter H. Mallory, "Progress Report of the Secretary, War and Peace Studies Project, CFR, December 15, 1939–July 1, 1940," Armstrong Papers, Box 75.

40. After individual members prepared a draft memorandum, it was subjected to thorough discussion by the members of each group. In the wake of such discussion, the memorandum was put into final form for transmission for use by the appropriate officials of the State Department and other departments. In the end, a total of 682 documents were prepared and sent to the State Department. CFR, *The War and Peace Studies of the Council on Foreign Relations, 1939–1945*, 4, 11.

41. It is to be noted that the CFR organized a Far Eastern study group composed of Far Eastern experts immediately before and after the outbreak of the Pacific War. The overall theme of the study group was "Do bases [sic] for a real peace exist between the United States and Japan?" under which the group met six times between November 1941 and April 1942. On the analysis of the discussions of this study group, see Iokibe, *Beikoku no Nihon Senryō Seisaku*, vol. 1, 201–11.

42. The original members of the Armaments Group at the start of the work in January 1940 included nine members: Allen W. Dulles (rapporteur), William M. Franklin (research decretary), Hanson Baldwin, Major General Frank R. McCoy (ret.), Brigadier General Thomas J. Betts, Admiral William H. Standley (ret.), Stacy May, Major General George V. Strong, and Edward P. Warner. Mallory, "Progress Report of the Secretary." The members were somewhat altered as the work of the group expanded.

43. Previous scholarly works that analyzed the WPS are Lawrence Shoup and William Minter, *Imperial Brain Trust* (New York: Monthly Review Press, 1977), 117–87;

Robert D. Schulzinger, *The Wise Men of Foreign Affairs: The History of the Council on Foreign Relations* (New York: Columbia University Press, 1984), chaps. 3–4; Michael Wala, *The Council on Foreign Relations and American Foreign Policy in the Early Cold War* (New York: Berghahn Books, 1994), 30–46; Carlo Maria Santoro, *Diffidence and Ambition: The Intellectual Sources of U.S. Foreign Policy* (Oxford: Westview Press, 1992), passim; Inderjeet Parmer, "The Issue of State Power: The Council on Foreign Relations as a Case Study," *Journal of American Studies* 29 (1995): 73–95; also, *Think Tanks and Power in Foreign Policy: A Comparative Study of the Role and Influence of the Council on Foreign Relations and the Royal Institute of International Affairs, 1939–1945*, by Inderjeet Parmer (New York: Palgrave McMillan, 2004), chap. 5. While there are brief discussions of the treatment of Japan in the WPS project in these works, they are largely based on rather brief analysis of some of the memoranda dealing with Japan and its postwar treatment. Furthermore, digests of discussions directly concerned with each memorandum have not been utilized in these works. I have analyzed memoranda and discussions on peace settlements toward Japan in CFR's War and Peace Studies in a more detailed fashion in a recent article. See Sasaki, "Gaikō- mondai Hyōgikai 'Sensō to Heiwa no Kenkyū ' ni-okeru Tainichi Sengo-shori Kōsō" [Postwar Settlements vis-a-vis Japan in the Council on Foreign Relations' War and Peace Studies], in Sugita Yoneyuki, ed., *Amerika Gaikō no Bunseki: Rekishiteki Tenkai to Genjō Bunseki* [An Analysis of American Diplomacy: Historical Development and the Current State of Affairs] (Okayama: Daigaku Kyōiku Publishing Company, 2008), 117–67.

44. The Thirty-Ninth Meeting of the Armaments Group (A–A 39), November 2, 1943, 7–8, WPS; The Fortieth Meeting of the Armaments Group (A–A 40), November 29, 1943, 6–9, WPS; Records of Groups, CFR Archives, New York. Hereafter, in making reference to the primary sources of the WPS, the following abbreviation will be used. That is to say, the first letter in the citation indicates the group where the material originated, where the letter A following the dash is used for digests of discussion and the letter B following the dash is used for group memoranda. Thus, "A–A 39" indicates the digest of discussion of the 39th meeting of the Armaments Group, whereas "A–B 97" means the 97th memorandum issued by the Armament Group.

45. A–A 40, November 29, 1943, 5–7, 8–9. WPS.

46. Hanson W. Baldwin, "Security Policy Vis-à-vis Japan," November 29, 1943, A–B 97, 1–2. WPS.

47. Ibid., 4–5. WPS.

48. This statement is especially noteworthy in that Baldwin was conscious of a possible accusation that the present war was a race war in which Western powers were ready to impose severe punishments against a non-Western power. Ibid., 6–7. WPS.

49. A–A 43, April 4, 1944, 6. WPS.

50. A–A 44, May 1, 1944, 9–10. WPS.

51. Major George Fielding Eliot, "The Disarmament of Japan," May 1, 1944, A–B 106, 1–2. WPS.

52. Ibid., 3. WPS.

53. Elizabeth Schumpeter, "The Postwar Treatment of Japan," December 16, 1944, E–C 15, 1–12. WPS.

54. E–A 61, December 16, 1944, 6–8. WPS.

55. During World War I, Japan gained control over the former German islands north of the equator by military occupation. They were the Marianas, the Carolines, and the Marshalls. After the Paris conference, the Japanese mandate over these three island groups was confirmed by the League of the Nations in 1920.

56. A–A 39, November 2, 1943, 2–4. WPS.

57. Grayson Kirk, "Pacific Security and the Japanese Mandated Islands," November 2, 1943. A–B 96, 2–4. WPS.

58. P–A 47, May 22, 1944, 14. WPS.

59. P–A 48, June 26, 1944, 6. WPS.

60. Political Group, "The Disposition of the Japanese Mandated Islands," July 5, 1944, P–B 85, 1–3. WPS.

61. Henry M. Wriston, "The Case for Annexation of Micronesia by the United States," September 25, 1944. P–B 88, 1–3. WPS.

62. A–A 43, April 4, 1944, 8–9. WPS. Armstrong argued that a lenient treatment of the Japanese Emperor by the Allied Nations might have the undesirable effect of reinforcing the Japanese belief in his supernatural character; ibid., 9. WPS.

63. Julius W. Pratt, "The Treatment of the Japanese Emperor," April 4, 1944, A–B 107, 1–2. WPS.

64. Ibid., 3–4. WPS.

65. Ibid., 4–5. WPS. In making reference to the question of the personal inclination of the present Emperor, Pratt sided with the view of an American journalist who argued that Hirohito was essentially a man of peace. Pratt also cited Sir George Sansom, the noted authority on Japan, who avowed his disbelief that the Emperor was responsible for the present war; ibid., 5–6. WPS.

66. Ibid., 6–7. WPS.

67. Peter Grosse, *Continuing Inquiry: The Council on Foreign Relations from 1921 to 1996* (New York: The Council on Foreign Relations, 1996), 23.

68. Harry Notter, *Postwar Foreign Policy Preparation, 1939–1945* (Washington, D.C.: U.S. Government Printing Office, 1949), 82, 106, 131.

69. Ibid., 81–82, 152, 155, 209–10. For detailed information about the mobilization of CFR members to these committees, see CFR, 5–7.

70. This episode was documented and recounted by Minter and Shoup. See *Imperial Brain Trust*, 158–60.

71. Cordell Hull to Norman H. Davis, November 12, 1940, Armstrong Papers, Box 75.

72. Joseph C. Grew to Russell C. Leffingwell, February 14, 1945, CFR Records MC 104 1918–2004 Series 3: Studies Department, Seeley G. Mudd Manuscript Library, Princeton University, Box 298.

73. "Report on a visit of the Messrs. Franklin, Langsam, and Upgren to Mr. Hugh Wilson in Washington, Friday, July 12, 1940," CFR Records MC 104 1918–2004 Series 3: Studies Department Box 300; "Minutes of the Steering Committee of the War and Peace Studies Project," Oct. 30, 1942; ibid., Hamilton F. Armstrong to Leo Pasvolsky, October 5, 1943.

74. Parmer, "The Issue of State Power," 92–93.

75. The only exception is Army General George Strong, who was a member of the Security and Armaments Group.

76. For a perceptive analysis of the logic of officialdom to exclude private citizens from actual decision making, see Iokibe, *Beikoku no Nihon Senryō Seisaku*, vol. 2, 6–7.

77. One example illustrates this point. In a meeting of the Committee on Post-War Programs held in April 1944, the memorandum on the treatment of the Emperor by Julius Pratt was introduced by Joseph C. Green, a member of the Armaments Group, to buttress the position of those members who maintained the necessity of preserving it for the sake of political stability of Japan. Iokibe, *Beikoku no Nihon Senryō Seisaku*, vol. 2, 64.

78. For an elaborate discussion of this point, see Parmer, *Think Tanks and Power in Foreign Policy*, 116–19, 126–29.

79. It should be noted that this view held by the CFR on the role of the Emperor and the Imperial institution in creating a stable democracy in the postwar Japan bore a close resemblance to that of Chatham House group at the Hot Springs Conference.

80. Indeed, there took place considerable discussions and resultant disagreements over the decolonization of the British Empire between the American IPR and Chatham House. On this, see Sasaki, "The Struggle for Scholarly Objectivity," chap. 4.

81. On an analysis of the differences in outlook and orientation between the IPR and the CFR, see Yui, *Mikan no Senryō Kaikaku*, 69–70.

82. On the discussion of the possibility of a democratic revolution held by Japan experts, see Dower, *Embracing Defeat*, 217–22.

83. Critics of both organizations have charged that the IPR was a "pro-Communist organization" promoting the interests of international Communism and that the CFR was an "Imperial brain trust" bent on equipping the United States for an imperial role on the world stage.

84. On this, it is to be noted that there was some personnel overlap between the IPR and the CFR during the wartime. Grayson Kirk and Major General McCoy, both of whom were members of the Armaments Group, joined the American delegation at the Hot Springs Conference. In addition, Owen Lattimore, one of the most outspoken delegates of the IPR conference, was also an active member of the Territorial group of the WPS project.

85. Raucher has specifically applied the term "service intellectuals" to staff members of the American IPR (Raucher, "The First Foreign Affairs Think Tanks," 497). For historical treatment of "service intellectuals," see Richard S. Kirkendall, "Franklin D. Roosevelt and the Service Intellectual," *Mississippi Valley Historical Review* XLIX (June 1962–March 1963): 456–71.

chapter eleven

HIROSHIMA AND THE U.S. PEACE MOVEMENT: COMMEMORATION OF AUGUST 6, 1948–1960

Rieko Asai

For more than 60 years, Americans have showed remarkable ambiguity concerning the use of the atomic bomb during World War II. In the immediate postwar years, there emerged triumphal narratives, which maintained that the atomic attack on Japan ended the ferocious war and saved numerous American lives that would have been lost in the event of a U.S. invasion. Although a majority of Americans accepted this discourse, concerned minorities expressed grave antagonism and publicly criticized the use of atomic weapons as a moral wrong and a strategic mistake. Later, during the 1960s, diplomatic historians challenged the mainstream narrative through their analysis of historical circumstances surrounding the decision to use the bomb in 1945. Although many disapproved of the so-called leftist historians, the debate between the orthodox and revisionist camps is one of the few scholarly debates that the general public pays attention to.[1] The *Enola Gay* controversy in 1995 highlighted the fierce rivalry between the competing narratives.[2]

This chapter attempts to examine the role that the U.S. peace movement played in shaping the public memory of the atomic bombing of Hiroshima. Peace protestors led the dissent against U.S. nuclear weapons policies, and these protestors clearly used the memory of Hiroshima to strengthen their position. Although there are many studies on the public memory of Hiroshima, the views of antinuclear activists have not been fully explored by scholars. Researchers such as Lifton, Mitchell, and Boyer argue that while activists strongly challenged the nuclear arms race and invoked Hiroshima as a symbol of the nuclear threat, they avoided criticizing the use of the bomb in 1945.[3] In general, scholars who specialize in the history of the nuclear disarmament movement have not paid close attention to antinuclear activists' views on the decision to use the bomb against Japan.[4]

Taking these scholarly works into consideration, this chapter deals with the public commemoration of August 6, known as Hiroshima Day. The date has offered an excellent opportunity for Americans to remember that tragic event in 1945. Since the end of the war, peace activists as well as peace-minded people have held observances every year on August 6 to mark the anniversary of the atomic bombing of Hiroshima. Especially in the early 1960s and early 1980s when the anti-nuclear weapons movement flourished, many peace groups and individuals conducted demonstrations, rallies, vigils, and so on. These commemorations succinctly show how the U.S. peace movement formulated the collective memory of the atomic bombing of Hiroshima. This chapter particularly pays attention to public commemorations held from the late 1940s through the early 1960s, when the nuclear disarmament movement experienced great ebbs and flows. Closely examining the style of commemoration as well as its content, the chapter shows how peace activists marked this anniversary and memorialize the Hiroshima bombing, as well as what kind of messages they intended to convey to other Americans. Yoneyama argues that possessing and showing each person's own memories is inseparably linked to "questions of power and autonomy."[5] How did peace activists present Hiroshima while resisting the dominant discourse? This study also explores how international and domestic issues affected how peace groups commemorated the anniversary of the bombing. Furthermore, it examines the media's role in shaping the commemorations by investigating how media bias influenced the way in which activists observed the anniversary.[6] This work demonstrates that meanings other than that of a symbol of nuclear dangers have been attached to Hiroshima since the late 1940s, but Hiroshima as a symbol of nuclear menace came to dominate activists' rhetoric in the early 1960s. The chapter concludes by following the process of the dehistoricization of Hiroshima up to the 1980s and contemplating its meaning in relation to the formation of the public memory of Hiroshima.

The essential part of the public memory of the atomic bombing of Hiroshima was largely formulated in the very early phase of the Cold War and has been generally uncontested. Most researchers point out that the official narrative given by American political leaders was decisive in forming the public memory of Hiroshima. The first influential official narrative was President Harry S. Truman's official announcement of the dropping of the bomb on Hiroshima on August 6, 1945. In this speech, Truman justified the use of the bomb as righteous revenge for Pearl Harbor, underlined that Hiroshima contained a major military base, and glorified the scientific achievement that produced the bomb. The second critical document was Henry Stimson's article published in *Harper's Magazine* in early 1947, which established the justification for dropping the bomb.[7] In this highly influential document, he stated that the planned invasion of Japan would "cost over a million casualties, to American forces alone," which were avoided by the use of the bombs.[8] Their statements have been repeated and even overstated by influential individuals and groups, including presidents, the scientists who had been involved in the production of the bomb, the pilots and crewmen who carried out the atomic bombing of Japan, the veterans of World War II, and the national media. Echoed in both official and unofficial narratives, these two documents have continued to be dominant in the public memory of the Hiroshima bombing in American society.

In the immediate aftermath of World War II, a concerned minority, greatly shocked by the unprecedented destructiveness of A-bombs, began to criticize the decision to use them on ethical grounds and eventually launched campaigns to prevent their use in future wars. The movement consisted primarily of three groups: atomic scientists, world federalists, and pacifists. The first group, atomic scientists, formed the Federation of Atomic Scientists in November 1945, which in 1946 was renamed the Federation of American Scientists (FAS). Driven by an urgent sense of responsibility, they sought to educate the public about atomic power and work for the establishment of the international control of atomic energy.

The second group, world federalists, supported the idea of bestowing sovereignty on a supranational structure in the world community. The shock of the atomic bombing convinced many diverse groups that the establishment of such a government was necessary to avoid a nuclear war.

The idea of world government drew support from a variety of prominent individuals and groups, and Norman Cousins emerged as the most effective speaker for the cause. Helped by the increasing popularity of the idea among Americans, new organizations sprang up, presenting the diversity of their proposals for the structure and functions of world government.[9]

The last group opposing nuclear weapons were pacifists. Compared with the other two groups, their position had less appeal to the American people. During World War II, approximately 6,000 pacifists went to jail; and 12,000 served unpaid work in Civilian Public Service camps, owing to their refusal to be drafted. Their influence continued to be weak after the war. The pacifists' core were the established pacifist organizations such as the Fellowship of Reconciliation (FOR); War Resisters League (WRL); Women's International League for Peace and Freedom (WILPF); and religious organizations, including the Catholic Worker Movement, Quakers, Mennonites, and Brethrens. Unlike atomic scientists and world federalists, pacifists did not generally perceive the advent of the atomic bomb as a revolutionary phenomenon or as a watershed in human history. Because their ultimate goal was to abolish war, they avoided giving the bomb a special status. However, they strongly recognized the threat of nuclear weapons to human survival, and their discourse gradually became similar to those of the other two groups. As a result, these three groups conveyed the sense of urgency and demanded that A-bombs never be used again.[10]

Commemoration of the Hiroshima bombing did not originate with atomic scientists, prominent world federalists, or established pacifist organizations. Instead, it was started by an obscure European immigrant named Alfred Parker, who lived in Oakland, California, and spread his idea to churches across the country. Although their activities rarely caught the interest of national media, evidence shows that hundreds of thousands of Christians participated in memorial services to mark the first use of the atomic bomb. More importantly, this commemoration was made in accordance with the international movement that originated in Hiroshima, designating August 6 as World Peace Day. Parker played a crucial role in promoting the movement both in the United States and the world.

The initiative for the World Peace Day movement came from Hiroshima, where since 1946, citizens had actively campaigned for such a day of commemoration. The 1946 and 1947 events and ceremonies were more like peace festivals that celebrated and facilitated economic rehabilitation, not solemn observances. Unsatisfied with the nature of these ceremonies,

Kiyoshi Tanimoto, a Methodist minister and survivor of the bomb who became famous as the hero of John Hersey's *Hiroshima*, launched a campaign in the fall of 1947 to make August 6 World Peace Day and commemorate the day worldwide in a more religious, solemn way. After deciding to hold a religious conference for peace in Hiroshima on August 6, 1948, he quickly set about organizing this global conference and in March 1948 news of his movement was delivered worldwide by United Press.[11]

This news drew various eager responses in the United States, but Alfred Parker's was the most enthusiastic. An Austrian émigré who had been a journalist and peace activist in Vienna, he had formed an Austrian antiwar league after World War I and took a crucial role in the peace movement in the interwar years. Having fled from the Nazis to the United States via England in 1940, he worked at various jobs as a night watchman, dishwasher, and bookkeeper to support himself and then moved to California. Working as a janitor at the Lakeshore Avenue Baptist Church in Oakland, he started international humanitarian relief work on his own after World War II. With the assistance of Lakeshore's minister, Harold Geistweit, Parker sent 3,000 parcels of food and clothing to 17 war-damaged countries in Europe and Asia.[12]

Strongly sympathizing with Tanimoto's movement, Parker immediately began organizing the movement in America. Naming his movement "No More Hiroshimas," he formed an international committee for World Peace Day in Oakland in April 1948 to facilitate the observance of the day throughout the world. Thanks to Parker's international network of peace activists, the committee secured nearly 80 sponsors all over the world, including well-known figures such as Pierre van Paassen of the United States, Nnamdi Azikiwe of Nigeria (who was called the African Gandhi), and Johannes Ude, the Austrian university professor, along with Tanimoto and Hiroshima Mayor Shinzo Hamai. The committee conceived that World Peace Day was to bear two meanings. First, it was to be a memorial to the A-bomb victims of Hiroshima and to all other victims of wars. Second, August 6 would be a warning to all countries to abolish war lest the tragedy of Hiroshima be repeated. In a 1948 World Peace Day flier, Parker explained the significance of August 6 to world peace:

> Why celebrate Hiroshima Day as World Peace Day? Because, beyond time and space, Hiroshima is the symbol of what war means in the atomic age. No other day gives a better resonance for thoughts and

sentiments of peace all over the world. All nations are guilty that war still prevails and that atomic bombs are used. All nations face the most horrible destruction, if we do not do all we can to bring nearer the fulfillment of the dreams of the best of all nations and ages: PEACE FOREVER.[13]

The aim of global World Peace Day was simply to coordinate and unite all efforts for world peace. Regarding the World Peace Day movement as a people's movement, Parker expected that the day would become an occasion for stimulating the desire for peace at the grassroots level throughout the world.[14]

Another important aspect of World Peace Day was that many Christians perceived August 6 as a day of repentance. Upon the first anniversary of the atomic bombing, Christians in Hiroshima met in the devastated ruins of their church and expressed penitence: They felt that they had not done enough to prevent the war. Geistweit, minister of Lakeshore Avenue Baptist Church, conceived that Americans had committed a sin by dropping the atomic bombs on Japan. He wrote in the bulletin for his church members that more Americans were beginning to think that the atomic bombing of Hiroshima was "going down in history as one of the blackest days and spots on American history."[15] His understanding was shared by countless other Americans. Four thousand delegates to the Northern Baptist Convention, at which Geistweit served as chairman of the board of finance and promotion, met in Milwaukee and adopted a resolution committing the Convention to the observance of August 6 as a day of repentance and prayer. This resolution was to be recommended at 7,000 churches in 36 states consisting of 1.6 million members. The Brethren adopted a similar resolution.[16]

On August 6, 1948, people in 26 countries commemorated the atomic bombing of Hiroshima by holding public meetings, conferences, and church services. In Hiroshima, a formal peace ceremony was held at the newly erected Hiroshima Memorial Tower of Peace, where a large sign reading "No More Hiroshimas"—the basic theme of the peace ceremony—stood. Mayor Hamai delivered an address titled "Peace Declaration" to 15,000 people. In this plea to prevent a recurrence of the Hiroshima tragedy, the Mayor urged the abolition of war itself and had his address sent off to 160 cities in 68 countries. In Salisbury, England, members from 30 countries and 50 local chapters in Great Britain of War Resisters' International met, declared "No More Hiroshimas," and discussed new ways to prevent war. In New Delhi, another international group, the Indian branch of the Caravan of East and West, held a World Peace Day observance and high government officials participated in it. In the United States, the Northern Baptist Convention and the Brethren committed their church members to observe the day. Parker also reported that hundreds of supporting letters from 32 countries were sent to him.[17]

In the next year, ceremonies and observances multiplied both in size and number throughout the world. In Hiroshima, 30,000 people gathered to commemorate the fourth anniversary of the atomic bombing of the city, making it the largest ceremony to that time. In Berlin, the permanent fire was lit in a park for victims of the A-bombing; in New Delhi, messages from 18 ambassadors were read; in Budapest, a women's conference met to adopt a resolution facilitating their cooperation for the No More Wars movement; mass meetings were held in Budapest, Hamburg, Munich, and London. In other countries, including Sweden, the Philippines, Nigeria, Australia, and New Zealand, people held observances, public meetings, demonstrations, and religious ceremonies. Many advocates of world government, too, availed themselves of the anniversary to promote their cause. Thus the campaign to set aside August 6 as World Peace Day spread worldwide, especially in Europe. In war-devastated nations, August 6 seemed to offer an appropriate opportunity to express a strong longing for peace.[18]

In the United States, however, the World Peace Day movement did not arouse public interest beyond religious bodies. Nor did the mass media pay attention to it, so the movement remained invisible on the national scene. Parker remained virtually unknown in America although his name was widely known in Japan.[19] Frustrated with his meager success in the United States, he once complained to Tanimoto, "I am only a janitor and have no social status. So, no one in the US pays attentions to my movement, but people in foreign countries offer their cooperation one after another. A janitor's peace movement. Isn't it ridiculous?"[20] Notwithstanding public apathy, Parker did not lose his zeal for the No More Hiroshimas movement.

Starting in late 1949, heightened Cold War tension hit the World Peace Day movement severely. The Soviet Union's first nuclear test in late August 1949, combined with the establishment of Communist China in the fall of that year, stiffened the U.S. government's attitude toward Communism. In January 1950, Truman authorized the development of the hydrogen bomb, and the Korean War broke out in June. Moreover, the emerging pro-Soviet peace movement complicated the position of peace seekers in non-Communist nations. In March 1950, a leading Communist-led peace organization met in Stockholm and adopted a resolution, later known as the Stockholm Peace Appeal, which demanded the prohibition of atomic bombs. Using the Appeal as a petition, the organization soon launched a massive international campaign to muster signatures and gained substantial success. In this international climate, conducting observances on the anniversary of the Hiroshima bombing would leave an organization open to charges that it was Communist controlled. Thus, no formal observances or major ceremonies occurred anywhere in the world in 1950, the fifth anniversary of the A-bombing of Hiroshima. Even in Hiroshima, the planned peace ceremony and related programs were all cancelled abruptly four days before the anniversary. The committee responsible for the ceremony explained that the cancellation was a result of negotiations with the police department. The Hiroshima City Police had distributed fliers in the city labeling peace meetings planned by certain groups as anti-Japanese and asked people to not join them. The World Peace Day movement suffered a grave setback in 1950 and never regained its momentum in subsequent years.[21]

Despite his efforts to keep the World Peace Day movement alive, Parker could not shield his work from the Cold War's deleterious effect. In 1950, his International World Peace Day Committee sought to link the observance to the movement for world government. Alarmed by intensifying international tensions, the committee contended that the fifth anniversary of Hiroshima was the best opportunity to highlight the crisis in international affairs. Referring to the development of a hydrogen bomb, it insisted that federal world government was the only way to avoid a third world war. Parker hoped that the anniversary would mobilize support for the "people's world convention," which was one of the major proposals for the establishment of world government and which was especially popular in Europe. The idea originated from Henry Usborne, member of the British Parliament. According to Usborne, delegates chosen in direct popular election in as many countries as possible were supposed to gather at the first session to discuss the establishment of the World Constitution, thus marking the first step to establish a Federal World Government. But this convention ended in failure, lacking enough official delegates. In subsequent years, Parker continued the movement for World Peace Day, but it never regained the worldwide popularity it had once enjoyed.[22]

Another attempt to observe August 6 took place within established American pacifist groups in 1950, which shifted the context and settings of Hiroshima observances. The three major American pacifist organizations and groups—the FOR, the WRL, and Peacemakers—set up an ad hoc group named the Hiroshima 1950 Committee, under the strong leadership of A. J. Muste, the executive secretary of the FOR. Unlike the World Peace Day movement, pacifists' commemorations took place only on American soil, and therefore both the participants and the audience were Americans. This shift of context significantly affected the content of the commemoration: Messages conveyed on the anniversary were straightforwardly directed to the U.S. government and its people. Strongly reflecting Christian pacifism, they contained moral revulsion for dropping the atomic bombs and appealed to Americans to repent their sins and spearhead the movement to eliminate nuclear weapons.[23]

To facilitate preparations for the observance at the grassroots level, the committee made various efforts. The Hiroshima 1950 Committee prepared a draft entitled "Call to Observe Hiroshima Day—August 6" to enlist pacifist leaders. Noting that neither national governments nor major religious bodies were arranging observances of the day, the "Call" urged individual Americans, churches, and other local groups to observe the day. Offering materials that local groups could consult when organizing their observances, the "Call" also provided a range of suggestions for groups and individuals. Initially, the "Call" suggested holding religious services at atomic installations or research centers around the time when the atomic bomb was dropped on Hiroshima to show "repentance for the sin of launching atomic war on the earth and [to make] a call to break with the war method." The "Call" also recommended conducting demonstrations and holding observances for those who were not interested in religious meetings.[24]

Organizing materials in the "Call" clearly represented the position of the Committee. The aid packet included excerpts from two books written by high officials during World War II, which, respectively, criticized the dropping of the bombs on Japan from a strategic and an ethical point of view. One excerpt contained the assertion that Japan would have surrendered even if the U.S. government had not resorted to the use of atomic bombs. The other excerpt emphasized Americans' responsibility for ushering in the Atomic Age and urged them to take action to abolish nuclear weapons. The packet also included a summary of the affirmation and appeal adopted at a major religious conference held in May 1950. The affirmation requested churches all over the world to abandon war, and it called on individual Christians to "refuse to make or to use weapons of destruction" and use instead "the methods of reconciliation and nonviolent action." The themes of the "Call"—criticism of the use of the bombs, Americans' responsibility, and the search for nonviolent solutions to war—crammed the aid packets. The Committee hoped local organizers would incorporate these stances and ideas.[25]

On the fifth anniversary of the atomic bombing of Hiroshima, local observances took place across the country. Thanks to the efforts of the Committee to publicize planned commemorative activities, some observances caught the attention of the media. For example, *The New York Times* announced beforehand that churches in the New York area were arranging special prayers or public gatherings on August 6, and gave an account of the one conducted under the auspices of the New York branch of the FOR.[26] Muste confidently reported that August 6 was observed in "several hundred communities and churches" across the country, adding that gatherings were generally bigger and "the interest deeper than had been expected."[27] Although it is hard to speculate actually how widely August 6 was observed, it is certain that pacifists' endeavors added new meanings to the commemoration of the Hiroshima bombing.

Both the international and domestic environment rapidly changed in subsequent years, significantly affecting the conduct of Hiroshima observances as well as U.S. nuclear disarmament activism. In the early 1950s, the Cold War and McCarthyism suppressed dissent to United States foreign policy, and the American peace movement was at its nadir. There were practically no major observances that drew the attention of the national media. In 1953–1954, however, the political climate improved after the end of the Korean War, the fall of Senator Joseph McCarthy, and the improvement in U.S.–Soviet relations. Then the first H-bomb test conducted at Bikini atoll in the Marshall Islands by the U.S. government in March 1954 gave a new impetus to antinuclear activists. Along with the unexpectedly huge blast, the test produced deadly radioactive fallout that contaminated many inhabitants of the Marshall Islands and Japanese fishermen working nearby. This incident triggered deep concern all over the world about nuclear testing, and in the United States, too, old critics of nuclear weapons, such as pacifists, scientists, and advocates of world government, recommenced their resistance to nuclear weapons.[28]

Encouraged by the revival of the once-dormant antinuclear weapons activism, peace groups resumed their commemorative activities on Hiroshima Day. On August 6, 1954, the WRL, Peacemakers, and Catholic Worker Movement sent a letter to the people in Hiroshima and Nagasaki. The letter expressed their regret and repentance over the nuclear attack on Japan, the accumulation of nuclear weapons, and the development of the H-bomb.[29] In May 1955, the 25 so-called Hiroshima Maidens came to the United States to receive plastic surgery at the invitation of Norman Cousins (editor of *The Saturday Review*) and Reverend Kiyoshi Tanimoto. This project lasted for a year and a half, was publicized widely, obtained favorable support from Americans, and might well have encouraged renewed commemoration activities.[30]

In 1955, the FOR once again conducted Hiroshima observances. Although their message had not changed since the 1950 observance, they were more successful in terms of scale and visibility on the national scene. First, they succeeded in conveying their message to the public effectively through mass media. On August 1 and 3, *The New York Times* carried their statement criticizing the use of the bomb, appealing to Americans to designate August 6 as a day of repentance, and urging the abolition of war itself. Second, the FOR did better than in 1950 in encouraging local branches to hold observances in their communities. By 1955, a variety of Japanese resources revealing the human effect of the atomic bomb had become available in the United States. Recommending the use of such material as survivors' narratives, pictures, and films, the national office helped local groups to organize observances from the standpoint of bomb victims and survivors. As a result, those in Chicago and New York held impressive commemorations of the atomic bombing of Hiroshima that drew the attention of local media. FOR's success demonstrated that it was possible to resist the dominant view on the Hiroshima bombing and disseminate alternative views.[31]

The FOR and its pacifist cohorts continued to express their critical views on the Hiroshima bombing the following year. On August 6, 1956, the FOR, the WRL, and the Catholic Workers initiated a poster walk before the Japanese Consulate in New York City. Nine protestors, including A. J. Muste of the FOR and Dorothy Day of the Catholic Workers, marched in the rain and delivered a letter to the consulate. It expressed their "sorrow that the United States had destroyed Japanese cities with atomic bombs" and urged the Japanese people to join them in opposing not only nuclear weapons testing but war itself.[32] Like the commemorative activities of pacifist groups in previous years, this demonstration reiterated the belief that the atomic bombing of Hiroshima and Nagasaki was wrong and that the United States had a special moral obligation to promote peace and disarmament because it had ushered in the nuclear arms race by dropping the bombs on Japan. The FOR also made an appeal to the governments of the United States and the Soviet Union on the eleventh anniversary of the atomic attacks when the organization's national chairman, Charles Lawrence, appealed for a halt to all nuclear tests. There was a conspicuous difference between the length and contents of those appeals: President Dwight D. Eisenhower received a letter of more than three pages, but a cable to Premier Nikolai Bulganin consisted of only a few lines. Also, in Eisenhower's lengthy letter, the FOR fiercely attacked U.S. nuclear weapons policy on various grounds. It was clear that the FOR criticized the U.S. government more strongly than it did the Soviet government.[33]

The FOR reserved its most bitter criticism for the U.S. government for several reasons. First, it decried the passive attitude of the U.S. government regarding nuclear weapons tests. The letter mentioned that whereas Great Britain and the Soviet Union had agreed to the Japanese Diet's call for a moratorium on nuclear testing, the United States had not. Their letter insisted that the U.S. government should announce its readiness to halt nuclear weapons tests. More importantly, the FOR outlined the link between U.S. nuclear weapons policy and racial discrimination. The letter maintained that both the atomic attacks on Japan and nuclear weapons tests in the Pacific derived from the U.S. government's discrimination against Asians. It demanded that the government stop nuclear weapons testing there or in any other areas "outside the limits of continental United States." If nuclear tests continued, the appeal contended, they had to be held within the borders of the country carrying out the tests. In this way, all risks would be shouldered by the testing nation. Furthermore, the appeal argued, continued nuclear weapons testing in the Pacific was not only "morally revolting" but also a grave political mistake. Such tests would enrage millions of Asian people and convince them "that America holds Asian lives very cheap." Consequently, the appeal warned, Asians would consider Communism more attractive than the Christianity that the United States professed. Given that the FOR had been involved in promoting racial equality since the early 1940s, it is understandable that they focused so intently on the issue of racial justice. In addition, with the civil rights movement growing in the South, the FOR might have thought that this topical criticism would appeal to racial and ethnic minorities in the United States.[34]

International as well as domestic events strengthened the antinuclear climate among Americans during 1957. While the United States and the Soviet Union continued their nuclear weapons testing, the British government, too, announced in early 1957 that it was planning to test its first H-bomb on Christmas Island in the Pacific in May. This announcement heightened worldwide antagonism against nuclear tests and prompted prominent world figures began to speak out. Among them was Dr. Albert Schweitzer, who made the most impressive plea to halt nuclear testing. A world-renowned musician, physician, and humanitarian, Schweitzer delivered his message through Norwegian radio on April 23, 1957. In the message, he emphasized the danger of radioactive fallout on human beings and called for the people of the world to end nuclear weapons testing. His appeal had an immediate impact all over the world. In the United States, the well-known chemist Linus Pauling was so impressed by Schweitzer's appeal that he set out to mobilize American scientists for the test ban cause. He drafted a petition calling for an international agreement to end nuclear weapons tests and secured approximately 2,000 signatures, including those of leading scientists. This petition was endorsed by scientists in other countries, and eventually it contained more than 11,000 signatures from 49 countries.[35]

Along with the international, elite-led antinuclear weapons movement, ordinary Americans also began gradually to oppose U.S. policy in myriad ways. On June 15, 1955, for example, radical pacifists assailed a massive civil defense drill, code-named Operation Alert, in New York City. The protesters challenged the government's assertion that the country could survive a nuclear strike utilizing civil defense shelters. Opposing all wars, radical pacifists considered militant nonviolent direct action, including civil disobedience, as a crucial tool for bringing about major societal change. Manifesting their opposition, 28 members of the WRL, the FOR,

Peacemakers, and the Catholic Workers Movement refused to take a shelter during this nationwide civil defense drill and were consequently arrested. This incident marked the first act of civil disobedience undertaken by major peace organizations since 1945 and was repeated by the core members of the group every year until 1961. Significantly, the number of protesters involved grew year by year. Sympathetic media treatment produced publicity for the pacifist critique of civil defense drills, and the participation and support of prominent New Yorkers, as well as of ordinary mothers and students, expanded the scale of the demonstrations. For the 1960 protest, 1,000 dissenters gathered at City Hall Park, and half of them refused to take shelter during the drill. The 1961 protest was even larger, and in 1962, the civil defense drills were canceled in New York State. Thus radical pacifists' civil defense protests eventually gained broad public support and paved the way for popular action on nuclear arms policy.[36]

As the popular outcry against nuclear testing swelled, the revitalization of the antinuclear movement finally occurred. In the spring of 1957, two new antinuclear groups were formed: Non-Violent Action Against Nuclear Weapons (NVAANW), which would later be renamed the Committee for Non-Violent Action (CNVA), and the National Committee for a Sane Nuclear Policy, which was later called simply SANE. The person who was responsible for their inauguration was Lawrence Scott, a member of WRL and the peace education secretary of the American Friends Service Committee (AFSC). Alarmed by the escalation of nuclear testing, Scott came to believe that traditional political action and peace education alone were not enough. Encouraged by the recent success of the Montgomery bus boycott and the protests against the civil defense drills in New York, he was convinced that the time was ripe for taking nonviolent direct action. He persuaded leaders of major peace groups to launch a new anti-nuclear campaign, and a meeting was held in Philadelphia on April 22, 1957. At this meeting, organizers decided that the new antinuclear movement would have three wings: an ad hoc radical pacifist organization, which would become NVAANW; an ad hoc liberal, nonpacifist organization that would later be called SANE; and the older, established peace organizations, such as the FOR, AFSC, and the WILPF, which would assist the two ad hoc committees.[37]

NVAANW professed radical pacifism and supported dramatic nonviolent direct action as a method to protest nuclear weapons. Radical pacifism arose from the nonviolent struggles of conscientious objectors who, with the introduction of the draft in 1940, were interned in Civilian Public Service camps or in federal prisons. In the postwar years, a small circle of radical pacifists developed and used nonviolent action in the struggle against militarism and in the promotion of racial justice. After going through the setbacks brought on by the Korean War and McCarthyism, radical pacifism restored its vigor in the mid-1950s. While the nonviolent action of radical pacifists began to gain support, the older peace organizations, such as the FOR and the AFSC, hesitated to champion them out of fear of losing support among their constituency. Therefore, radical pacifists welcomed Scott's call for a meeting in Philadelphia to reorganize the peace movement. One month later at the Philadelphia meeting, pacifist organizations supporting Scott's idea met again and established an ad hoc committee that advocated Gandhian techniques of nonviolent direct action and civil disobedience.[38]

SANE, which was formally created around the same time as NVAANW, grew out of a June 1957 meeting organized by Lawrence Scott, Clarence Pickett (executive secretary emeritus of the AFSC), and Norman Cousins and attended by 27 leading church leaders and liberals. Pickett set the agenda. "Something should be done," he stated, "to bring out the latent sensitivity of the American people to the poisoning effect of nuclear bombs on international relations and on humanity." Participants agreed that the group should emphasize public education and arousing nationwide debate about nuclear testing. Incorporating the idea of Erich Fromm, the famous psychoanalyst and advocate of a test ban, that people needed to bring back sanity, the group adopted their name: the National Committee for a Sane Nuclear Policy.[39]

SANE's dramatic progress in November roused a mass movement against nuclear weapons. On November 15, it ran a full-page advertisement in *The New York Times* under the heading, "We Are Facing a Danger Unlike Any Danger That Has Ever Existed." Largely written by Cousins and signed by 48 eminent public figures, the statement called on all countries to immediately suspend nuclear testing and to place "a higher loyalty—loyalty by man to the human community" above national interests. The impact of the advertisement was immense: some 2,500 letters poured into SANE's office within six months; 32 different newspapers reprinted the original ad; and donations to the organization grew to more than $12,000 by January. Responding to grassroots concern, SANE decided to change from a steering committee to a national membership organization.

By the summer of 1958, SANE had grown rapidly and contained approximately 130 chapters and 25,000 members. Focusing on arousing people's interest in nuclear testing through publications and the media, SANE became the largest and most influential antinuclear organization in the United States.[40]

SANE's style and philosophy were strikingly different from that of NVAANW. SANE was an organization that consisted of nuclear pacifists, who believed that nuclear war was always unacceptable because of the special destructive power of nuclear weapons and therefore opposed their development and deployment. Unlike pacifists who opposed all wars, nuclear pacifists generally regarded conventional war as justifiable under certain circumstances. Nuclear pacifism was centered among the traditional internationalist groups comprising scientists, intellectuals, writers, and other professionals who had opposed World War II. SANE was mainly composed of two groups of nuclear pacifists: supporters of world government and atomic scientists. They believed that the U.S. government had an aptitude and willingness to change and that its policies could be put right through effective discussion and communication. They therefore considered public opinion and political advocacy essential in favorably affecting policy makers. Taking a pragmatic stance toward specific issues like nuclear testing, they relied on conventional methods such as public education and lobbying.[41]

HIROSHIMA AS CONTESTED TERRAIN

The rebirth of the American peace movement in the spring of 1957 also influenced how peace advocates observed Hiroshima Day that year. More peace groups than ever before joined in the commemoration, and their messages conveyed the movement's growing diversity. In New York, peace groups conducted their commemorative protest and invoked Hiroshima in many ways. A group of demonstrators marched in front of the headquarters of the United States and Soviet delegations to the United Nations to signal their opposition to each country's ongoing nuclear testing. Organized by the FOR, the Catholic Worker Movement, the WRL, and the Jewish Peace Fellowship, 15 protestors demonstrated outside each office for about an hour and a half. Wearing black sashes or armbands, they walked holding placards that read, "We walk to mourn the dead and save the living" and "We mourn the past and future victims of radioactive fall-out."[42] Meanwhile, another antinuclear group, the New York Committee Against Testing Nuclear Weapons, held a meeting, and approximately 1,000 people attended. The Socialist leader Norman Thomas spoke at the meeting and advocated the end of nuclear weapons tests as the first step toward nuclear disarmament. Thomas warned that the escalating nuclear arms race was making Hiroshima and Nagasaki "comparatively small examples." He invoked these Japanese cities to underscore the destructive power of new H-bombs. This tactic appeared frequently in the rhetoric of test ban campaigners in subsequent years: They repeatedly stressed that the hydrogen bomb was "a thousand times more powerful" than one dropped on Hiroshima.[43]

The U.S. section of the WILPF, one of the oldest pacifist groups in the United States, also began to challenge the dominant view of the Hiroshima bombing. WILPF had been active in opposing nuclear weapons since the H-bomb test in 1954. It ran advertisements in national papers in 1956 condemning the tests and organized petition campaigns the next year, calling for a halt to nuclear weapons tests. Then the organization joined in the 1957 Hiroshima observance. Its national office may have judged that Hiroshima Day would furnish an excellent opportunity to express their opposition to the use of the bomb in 1945.[44]

On August 6, 1957, a five-member delegation from the WILPF visited the Japanese embassy in Washington, D.C., to present a statement that explicitly put forward the organization's views on nuclear weapons. The statement was based on a belief that citizens of a country could not dissociate themselves from their government's actions. According to their statement, WILPF members paid a visit to the Japanese embassy "as citizens of that country which first used the atomic bomb." Their statement also noted their responsibility for shaping America's nuclear weapons policy as well as the country's various shortcomings. They further acknowledged that the use of the bomb was a mistake, confessing that "the weight of the guilt for the death and desolation of Hiroshima rests heavily on us." Unlike the FOR, which criticized the nuclear attack on Japan in religious terms, the WILPF based their criticism on secular grounds, stressing the political responsibilities of the citizens of the United States. Then the statement added that although they did not always support its actions, they had loyalty and affection toward their country. Their penance was followed by a pledge to work for an end to nuclear testing, which the organization regarded "as a first step in a universal, enforceable disarmament agreement." Finally, based on its organizational goals, the statement pledged to continue to work for "those conditions which guarantee peace, freedom, and justice."[45]

The WILPF's actions were not generally well received by Japanese officials. The Japanese embassy was unenthusiastic about the women's visit from the beginning, and when the organization sent a letter to the Japanese ambassador in advance to inform him of their intention to call on him on the anniversary, the first thing the embassy did was to investigate the WILPF's intentions. After an exchange of letters, which allowed the WILPF to clarify its position, the ambassador's secretary informed the WILPF that because the ambassador was scheduled to be out of town on that day the minister plenipotentiary would receive the delegation.[46] On August 6, the embassy continued to distance itself from the WILPF. Responding to the delegation's expression of "deep regret" over the use of the atomic bomb against Japan, the Japanese minister Takezo Shimoda told the WILPF women, "don't mention your regret." He said that Japan was not blaming the United States for dropping the bomb and that it was no use to argue about past events. Neither was he sympathetic with their plea to halt nuclear weapons tests. Supporting nuclear deterrence, he stated that because Western countries faced the threat of Communism, they should not stop nuclear testing immediately. Furthermore, the minister, repeating the question he had asked in previous correspondence with the organization, again asked about the character and purposes of the WILPF and wanted to know whether they had anything to do with Communism. When the delegation assured the minister that they were not a front organization, he explained that Communists in Japan sometimes made use of annual anniversary ceremonies in Hiroshima to further their political aims. In general, the embassy treated the delegation with suspicion throughout the meeting, which prevented both sides from reaching an agreement.[47]

The Japanese embassy's official attitude toward the visit of the WILPF delegation might not be surprising given Japanese–U.S. diplomacy. Relations between the two countries were generally good at that time. The Eisenhower administration had welcomed Nobusuke Kishi as the new prime minister because of his anti-Communist, pro-American stance. Although the good relationship was shaken by the case of Sergeant William S. Girard, who killed a Japanese woman collecting brass shells on an

American base in January 1957, Kishi's visit to the United States that June had repaired the strain. Therefore, the Japanese embassy was understandably very sensitive to anything that would impair the good relationship between Japan and the United States.[48]

The visit to the Japanese embassy disappointed the WILPF women. Frustrated with how the Japanese minister treated the delegation, one member commented afterward that the minister was aware of the presence of the press and simply reiterated the official statement of the Japanese government on the Hiroshima bombing, which did not criticize the U.S. decision to use the bomb. Even worse, their visit considerably hurt their reputation. The *Washington Post* quoted the Japanese minister when he expressed his suspicions about the organization's Communist connections, thus tarnishing the organization's image nationwide. As a result of this bitter experience, the national office of the WILPF seemed to cease to express their regret over Hiroshima formally upon the anniversary thereafter. There has been no evidence that shows their commemoration of August 6 until 1960.[49]

Probably the most impressive of the 1957 Hiroshima observances was the one that took place in Nevada. Incorporating nonviolent civil disobedience, this commemorative action dramatically invoked Hiroshima as a symbol of the antinuclear weapons movement. The project was initiated by the newly formed antinuclear group, NVAANW. In their formative meeting, the group named Lawrence Scott coordinator and decided to target the Atomic Energy Commission's (AEC) August 6 nuclear test in the Nevada desert for their first act of civil disobedience.[50]

NVAANW leaders enunciated their position against nuclear weapons and described their action as a moral protest to nuclear weapons. Prior to their action in Nevada, they issued "A Call to Non-Violent Action Against Nuclear Weapons," which was signed by 76 ministers, educators, scientists, and writers and which was sent to peace groups and pacifists across the country. The "Call" admitted that scientists differed as to the extent and effects of radioactive fallout but declared that they were against nuclear testing as long as there was "any question of danger to life anywhere." Thus, NVAANW opposed "the production, testing, and use of nuclear weapons by any and all governments." Moreover, the "Call" condemned the policies of military containment and nuclear deterrence as a way of bringing about peace, calling these policies an expression of "moral insensitivity." To confront the nuclear arsenals, the "Call" expressed its determination to confront the world's growing nuclear arsenals and stated, "we will take our risk on the side of life and of all humanity."[51]

NVAANW articulated the meaning of civil disobedience as part of their Nevada protest. The planned act of civil disobedience was unlawful, but NVAANW members argued that these laws contradicted the moral law of God, which prohibited any nation from contaminating other peoples' air and soil. Quoting Gandhi's words, they proclaimed that "the moral law of God transcends the law of any nation" and that moral men and women should disengage themselves from "immoral and irrational" laws. To be sure, this belief did not mean that they had no respect for the law. Instead, they put a great deal of faith in democracy and the political process, so they were ready to willingly accept their punishment. Civil disobedience, members claimed, should be conducted "not in the spirit of rebellion or vindictiveness but with good will and genuine humility and knowledge and acceptance of consequences." They hoped that their actions would speak to "the deepest element of good in all." Believing that an individual's conscience was a vanguard of democracy, they sought to appeal to individual Americans through self-sacrifice.[52]

After careful preparation, the workshop on the nonviolent direct action was opened in Las Vegas on August 3, and more than 30 members of NVAANW and its supporters gathered. NVAANW started their antinuclear weapons campaign by distributing leaflets that carried factual information on radioactive fallout in towns near the test site. Additionally, they picketed the AEC headquarters in Las Vegas and held a Prayer Conscience Vigil at the entrance to Camp Mercury to commemorate the twelfth anniversary of the atomic bombing of Hiroshima. Finally, on August 6, 11 members left the vigil and entered the test site in an act of civil disobedience. Because the group had announced their intention to the AEC, state police, and the press, approximately 100 people, including representatives of the major networks, watched the demonstration. Anticipating a possible riot, some 50 armed men, consisting of AEC security guards, the sheriff and his deputies, and state police, stood around the gateway to the test site. The long planned project ended in a few minutes with the immediate arrest of the trespassers, but the event was well publicized by radio networks, TV, and the major newspapers.[53]

Consequently, the Nevada action helped dehistoricize the bombing of Hiroshima. NVAANW's incorporation of civil disobedience and their protest at the actual test site dramatized their direct confrontation with the

U.S. government's current nuclear policies rather than focusing on past events. To be sure, group members often expressed their sympathy for the victims and survivors of the bomb. For instance, when the leaders of NVAANW held a press conference and delivered the names of participants in the planned action, they called attention to the fact that the AEC had announced that the bomb to be tested on August 6 was very similar in size and type to the ones dropped on Hiroshima and Nagasaki, and they accused the AEC of "insensitivity to the dead and the living who suffered in Japan." Also, when the test took place, some protesters looked directly at the blast despite AEC's warning not to do so because they wanted "to be a little closer to realizing how the people of Hiroshima had felt."[54]

However, on the whole, NVAANW did not confront the decision to drop the bombs in 1945. Their concern was more about human sufferings brought by the bomb rather than the decision itself. Such an interpretation of Hiroshima, along with the image of the group, was widely imparted through media reports. Many newspapers carried their story although on inside pages, and, unlike the case of the WILPF, they did not label the group as Communist-related. Such media treatment enabled their new protest style to be accepted in American society and most likely encouraged the group to continue their unique protest style thereafter. The symbolic invocation of Hiroshima on the anniversary of the bombing became a regular practice among antinuclear activists: NVAANW continued its civil disobedience at atomic installations in Nebraska after 1957 on Hiroshima Days, very often drawing the attention of local and national media. Thus, as the criticism of the actual bombing of Hiroshima gave way to confrontations between activists and authorities, the dehistoricization of Hiroshima further prevailed in the U.S. peace movement.[55]

The dehistoricization of the Hiroshima bombing accelerated the following year when SANE, which had grown to the largest antinuclear organization in the United States, held a ceremony in New York to commemorate the thirteenth anniversary of the atomic bombing of Hiroshima. Held under the auspices of the Greater New York chapter, this was SANE's first effort at commemorating the Hiroshima attack. Unlike NVAANW's commemorations, SANE's was more conciliatory and peaceful, and it succeeded in conveying new Hiroshima symbolism through its wide publicity. The ceremony was particularly remarkable because it underlined the growing friendship between the United States and Japan and further sought to promote a sense of unity among countries through the idea of world citizenship. SANE arranged to bring a survivor of the Hiroshima bombing to the ceremony. Shigeko Nimoto, 26, was one of the 25 Hiroshima Maidens who had come to the United States to receive plastic surgery. Among others, she particularly had become close to Cousins and stayed at his house for more than one year, attending a nursing school in order to start a new life in the United States. Her presence at the ceremony literally invoked the tragedy of Hiroshima, but her speech instead showed American benevolence and the growing friendship between the United States and Japan at that time. Moreover, through her words, SANE further sought to promote a sense of unity among countries through the idea of world citizenship.[56]

The whole ceremony went well. Gathering at Bryant Park behind the New York Public Library, SANE members walked toward United Nations Plaza, bearing flowers for Nimoto. A man held a poster that read, "On This Hiroshima Day, a Tribute of Flowers." When the marchers arrived at the plaza where Nimoto awaited them, they presented flowers to her one by one. The executive director of the Protestant Council of New York delivered an invocation, and then a 3-year-old girl presented a bouquet of yellow chrysanthemums to Nimoto. The highlight of the ceremony was Nimoto's speech. While she was wearing white gloves to cover her disfigured hands, scars still remained on her face despite the plastic surgery she had undergone. Disregarding her disfigurement, she started by expressing her gratitude for the tribute. Then she told the crowd that she had been adopted by an American family and thus she belonged to two countries:

> People ask me "Aren't you confused to belong to two families?" And I answer that I am not confused. I feel enough love for both. It is the same with countries. I was born in Japan and have love for Japan. Now I belong to an American family and have love for the United States.[57]

In her conclusion, Nimoto appealed to the audience to cultivate the sense of being world citizens. Drawing on her own experiences, she claimed that love for Japan and the United States was not enough:

> Now I must be a citizen of the world. And many times I have thought all people must belong to each other. Maybe they will feel happy and free only when they all become citizens of the world. No one has to give up his love for his country. But the love for country becomes important and bigger when we become citizens of the world.[58]

Covering the event in its entirety, SANE's New York chapter described the ceremony as "a moving event."

The ceremony sought to convey two main messages: reconciliation between Japan and the United States and a plea to forge world federalism. Several important symbols were employed to convey these messages. First of all, Nimoto's presence itself personified the main message of the ceremony because she embodied both American benevolence and postwar U.S. efforts to lessen lingering Japanese animosity over the atomic bombing of Hiroshima and Nagasaki. Telling the crowd that she had love for both Japan and the United States, Nimoto presented herself as a bridge between the two countries. The fact that she hardly touched on the atomic bombing of Hiroshima implicitly shows that the organizers of the ceremony intended to focus on contemporary issues rather than on past events.

Another important message of the ceremony, promoting world federalism, was clearly evident in SANE's choice of the United Nations Plaza, across from the building of United Nations, as the site for the observance. SANE supported a stronger United Nation, and, as Nimoto's speech demonstrated, the ceremony emphasized the importance of thinking in global rather than in national terms. Through Nimoto's words, the organizers of the ceremony sought to convey the view that nourishing the sense of world citizenship was crucial for world peace. As such, the whole ceremony was filled with concerns for contemporary issues and hope for the future. Avoiding a direct confrontation with the decision to use the atomic bomb, Hiroshima Day symbolically functioned as a bridge between the past, the present, and the future.[59]

The media's coverage of SANE's first Hiroshima observance was so successful that it set the course for the organization's future Hiroshima Day commemorations. SANE's newsletter boasted that more than 20 representatives of the press, television, and radio came to the ceremony to report on it, adding that "there was coverage by the wire services, major newspapers, CBS radio and NBC radio and television."[60] *The New York Times* carried a picture of the gathering at the United Nations Plaza, along with its account on the ceremony, and also ran a separate column about Nimoto, who recounted her experience of the atomic bombing of Hiroshima. Such favorable treatment by the media encouraged the organization to continue their style of commemoration the next year, when the Greater New York chapter of SANE held a similar commemoration on

August 6. About 60 people conducted a peace walk, distributing leaflets that opposed New York City's nuclear shelter program, and gathered at the United Nations Plaza, just like in the previous year. Reflecting the ongoing annual protest to the city's civil defense drills, marchers included young mothers and children. Filled with hope, their concerns were more about current and future issues rather than with the past. As in the previous year, *The New York Times* carried the picture of marchers along with the story, helping publicize their message.[61]

By the early 1960s, presenting Hiroshima as a symbol of the nuclear menace became a regular practice for the peace movement. In their public speeches, antinuclear and peace groups removed Hiroshima from its historical context. On August 6, 1960, for example, many peace and antinuclear groups, as well as other civic bodies, cosponsored Hiroshima Day activities in major cities across the country, thus mobilizing a much larger number of participants than ever before. Posters, leaflets peace rallies, and other activities, all stressed "No More Hiroshimas" as a main slogan, mirroring Alfred Parker's decade-old plea for peace. In all these activities, peace and antinuclear groups continued to avoid confronting the decision to use the bomb in 1945.[62] To speculate about the reasons for this is not easy, but the words of a leader in the antinuclear campaign might shed light on their thinking. Donald Keys, SANE's first full-time executive director, sent local SANE groups instructions in 1961 and 1962 on how to observe Hiroshima Day. In his instructions, he summarizes Americans' feelings about atomic bombing of Japanese cities and the meanings of Hiroshima observances:

> Americans in general *do* feel badly about the A-bombings, even if they convince themselves it was necessary. For this reason there is little use in protest activity. People don't like to have their noses rubbed in their mistakes. There is, however, a general acceptance of the date of August 6th as a memorial, and as an appropriate occasion upon which to express the wish that the world will find peace before humanity again turns atomic bombs loose.[63]

Keys maintains that Americans remember the A-bombings with a guilty conscience in their heart. Therefore, he believes, criticizing the bomb publicly would be of no use and would only rub Americans the wrong way. This might indicate SANE's political expediency and pragmatic approach, but at the same time, his words might come from his realization of Americans' complicated feelings about Hiroshima.

CONCLUSION

In retrospect, August 6 was contested terrain even within the U.S. peace movement. Various groups and individuals observed the anniversary of the Hiroshima bombing, and, consciously or unconsciously, they presented their divergent views on peace, the world, their country, and the American people. In the late 1940s, a worldwide movement to designate August 6 as World Peace Day flourished, and people like Alfred Parker enthusiastically promoted the movement, believing that the tragedy of Hiroshima would unite people all over the world for the making of a warless world. As the context of Hiroshima observances shifted from the international arena to the United States in the early 1950s, organizers increasingly came to craft messages directly aimed at the U.S. government and its people. For example, the FOR and other religious pacifists publicly condemned the use of the bomb and called for Americans to repent for this sin. On the other hand, the main secular pacifist organization, the WILPF, declared that citizens of a country bore a responsibility for even the past conduct of their government, thus stressing the political nature of human beings. Meanwhile, Hiroshima Day offered the appropriate opportunity for newly established antinuclear weapons groups to demonstrate their political legitimacy and ideological authenticity. Putting a great faith in the individual conscience, the radical pacifist group NVAANW argued that moral men and women should dissociate themselves from immoral and irrational laws. SANE, another influential antinuclear group, presented the reconciliation between the United States and Japan, and it exhibited the ideal American as a world citizen. Thus the anniversary of the atomic bombing of Hiroshima became more an opportunity for competing views to claim their own rights than a day for remembering that historical event.

The years 1957 and 1958 were the turning point in terms of commemorating the atomic attack on Hiroshima in that activists increasingly presented Hiroshima as a symbol of the antinuclear cause. More importantly, this fact was intrinsically linked with the rebirth of the U.S. peace movement in the mid-1950s. Leaders of the peace movement restructured their organizations, setting up ad hoc committees for radical pacifists and nuclear pacifists respectively, which would spawn NVAANW and SANE.

Soon after the reorganization, NVAANW conducted a unique, symbolic commemoration, and SANE followed the next year. Thereafter, Hiroshima Day increasingly served more as an opportunity for criticizing current nuclear policy rather than as an opportunity to reflect on Hiroshima's tragic past. This trend grew in tandem with the test ban movement.

There may be several reasons for this. First, August 6 seemed to be the most suitable occasion for activists to highlight their anti-nuclear cause. More fundamentally, as the case of the WILPF shows, raising historical argument on the use of the bomb often risked being called a Communist. Such discourse not only damaged the reputation of individual groups, but also could ruin the movement as a whole. McCarthyism was not truly over in the late 1950s, and SANE's voluntary expulsion of alleged Communists in 1960, in response to the Dodd committee's accusations, illustrates the problematic relations between the Communist issue and the peace movement. Therefore, organizers of the commemorations might have sacrificed condemning the A-bombing to safeguard their credentials and gain public support for a test ban movement. Still, as Donald Keys summed up, Americans' complicated attitude toward Hiroshima also helped remove Hiroshima from its historical context.

As antinuclear activism went through ups and downs, observances of Hiroshima Day also experienced ebbs and flows after 1946. The first surge of the antinuclear campaign crested with the ratification of the Limited Nuclear Test Ban Treaty in 1963, and the practice of holding Hiroshima observances declined. Not until the early 1980s did Hiroshima observances regain their lost vigor. This second antinuclear surge in the United States emerged in the late 1970s. The product of mounting concerns about nuclear power and fueled by antinuclear activism in Europe against the incorporation of Pershing missiles, the movement was also a response to President Ronald Reagan's administration's aggressive policy and rhetoric toward the Soviet Union, which aroused among Americans the fear of nuclear war. The movement to freeze the development and deployment of nuclear weapons heightened during 1982 and 1983; and, reflecting this strong antinuclear sentiment, many groups and individuals participated across the country in local commemorations of the Hiroshima bombing.

Compared with the 1950s, the commemorations during the 1980s were both larger and far more diverse. The number of participants in commemorations grew dramatically as, in addition to established peace organizations, many newly formed grassroots groups participated in these efforts.

Directing their opposition to particular nuclear weapons facilities in their area, these protestors held commemorative resistance at many atomic weapons sites and research institutions. Also, spurred by the nuclear accident at Three Mile Island in 1979, opponents of nuclear power held their own Hiroshima observances. In contrast to the 1950s, protesters came to commemorate both Hiroshima and Nagasaki Days. Participants employed a variety of means to convey their antinuclear messages: vigils, candlelight marches, demonstrations, mass die-ins, the floating of paper lanterns on the Mississippi and other rivers, street theater, shadow paintings on the sidewalks, and encircling the Pentagon with peace ribbon were but a few methods. These tactics appealed to the media, and protesters succeeded in conveying their antinuclear message across the country.[64]

On the other hand, participants in commemorations during the 1980s in most cases did not openly criticize the decision to use the bomb. Like other critics in U.S. society, commemorators in the 1980s were much more focused on the Reagan administration's aggressive foreign policy. Overall, American commemorations of the Hiroshima and Nagasaki bombings in the 1980s had much less to do with Japan than with the current American attitudes toward nuclear weapons or nuclear power plants. Thus paradoxically the symbolism of the Hiroshima-Nagasaki bombings seems to have grown more powerful in the United States over time, even as the events become more distant in the past. In other words, the symbols have become more useful to activist protesters as we get further away from them. Such discourse surely constitutes the important part of the public memory of Hiroshima in the United States.

NOTES

1. See, for example, Michael Hogan, ed., *Hiroshima in History and Memory* (Cambridge, United Kingdom: Cambridge University Press, 1996).

2. The American public memory of the atomic attack on Japan has neglected Nagasaki. It is often pointed out that whereas Hiroshima is justified on the grounds that it led the Japanese government to surrender, the bombing of Nagasaki is difficult to justify because the bombing of Nagasaki was carried out only three days later, without giving the Japanese government the time to inspect the effect of the first bomb and decide how they would act. Thus, as John Dower writes, "the American narrative almost invariably ends with Hiroshima as the fixation of the Enola Gay reveals." John Dower, "Three Narratives of Our Humanity," in *History Wars: The Enola Gay Controversy and Other Battles for the American*

Past, ed. Edward T. Linenthal and Thomas Engelhardt, (New York: Metropolitan Books, 1996), 78. Even in the discourse of counternarratives and scholarly works, Hiroshima has received much more attention than Nagasaki.

3. Robert J. Lifton and Greg Mitchell, *Hiroshima in America: A Half Century of Denial* (New York: Avon Books, 1995), 252–53, 261–63; Paul Boyer, "Exotic Resonances: Hiroshima in American Memory," in Hogan, 145, 148–51.

4. Historians have analyzed the nuclear disarmament movement from various perspectives. For example, Lawrence S. Wittner examines it as a global movement from the late 1940s up to the present in his trilogy. Lawrence S. Wittner, *The Struggle Against the Bomb*, 2 vols. (Stanford, Calif.: Stanford University Press, 1993–1997); *Toward Nuclear Abolition: A History of the World Nuclear Disarmament Movement, 1971–Present* (Stanford, Calif.: Stanford University Press, 2003). Other historians are more likely to focus either on a test ban campaign in the late 1950s and early 1960s or on the nuclear freeze movement in the early 1980s. For example, Robert Divine's work is representative of the studies on the test ban controversy in the late 1950s. Robert Divine, *Blowing on the Wind: The Nuclear Test Ban Debate, 1954–1960* (New York: Oxford University Press, 1978). Still others chronicle the organizational history of specific groups. For example, see Milton Katz, *Ban the Bomb: A History of SANE, The Committee for a Sane Nuclear Policy, 1957–1985* (Westport, Conn.: Greenwood Press, 1986).

5. Lisa Yoneyama, *Hiroshima Traces: Time, Space, and the Dialectics of Memory* (Berkeley: University of California Press, 1999), 151.

6. Emily Rosenberg maintains that media has played a crucial role in the process of formulating collective memory in modern America. Emily Rosenberg, *A Date Which Will Live: Pearl Harbor in American Memory* (Durham, N.C.: Duke University Press, 2003). In this chapter, I base much of my media coverage on a careful reading of *The New York Times*.

7. See, for example, Lifton and Mitchell, 3–7, 93–114; Laura Hein and Mark Selden, eds., *Living with the Bomb: American and Japanese Cultural Conflicts in the Nuclear Age* (Armonk, N.Y.: M. E. Sharpe, 1997), 4–5.

8. Henry Stimson, "The Decision to Use the Atomic Bomb," in *Hiroshima's Shadow*, ed. Kai Bird and Lawrence Lifschultz, (Stony Creek, Conn.: Pamphleteer's Press, 1998), 197–210.

9. Paul Boyer, *By the Bomb's Early Light: American Thought and Culture at the Dawn of the Atomic Age* (Chapel Hill, N.C.: University of North Carolina Press, 1985), 49–106, 196–210; Lawrence S. Wittner, *One World or None: A History of the World Nuclear Disarmament Movement Through 1953* (Stanford, Calif.: Stanford University Press, 1993), 66–71.

10. Ibid., 71–73; Scott H. Bennett, *Radical Pacifism: The War Resisters League and Gandhian Nonviolence in America, 1915–1963* (Syracuse, N.Y.: Syracuse University Press, 2003), 136.

11. For the commemorations of the atomic bombing of Hiroshima held by the city to date, see Satoru Ubuki, *Heiwa kinen shikiten no ayumi* [The Development of Peace Ceremonies] (Hiroshima: Hiroshima Peace Culture Foundation, 1992). For the early peace ceremonies in 1947 and 1948, see also Shinzo Hamai, *Gembaku shicho—Hiroshima to tomoni niju nen* [The Mayor of the A-Bombed City: 20 Years with Hiroshima] (Tokyo: Asahi Shimbun, 1967), 102–14; Kiyoshi Tanimoto, "Susume No Moa Hiroshimazu [Keep Going, No More Hiroshimas]," *Chugoku Shimbun*, August 1, 1948, 4; "No Moa Hiroshimazu undo [No More Hiroshimas Movement]," *Chugoku Shimbun*, August 2, 1948, 1. *Chugoku Shimbun* is one of influential local newspaper publishing companies located in Hiroshima.

12. Kiyoshi Tanimoto, *Hiroshima no jujika o daite* [Bearing the Cross of Hiroshima] (Tokyo: Kodansha, 1950), 184–86; Eugene Relgis, trans., Oliver Szilagyi, "Austrian Serves Humanity," *The American Vegetarian*, March 1948, 5, International World Peace Day Committee Records, Swarthmore College Peace Collection [hereafter cited as SCPC].

13. Alfred Parker, "Join the March of Peace on World Peace Day 1948 (August 6th)," June 6, 1948, International World Peace Day Committee Records, SCPC.

14. Alfred Parker, "World Peace Day Committee—No More Hiroshima Movement," n.d., probably December 1948, International World Peace Day Committee Records, SCPC.

15. Quoted in Henry Topping and Helen F. Topping, "World Peace and World Government Day 1949 (August 6th)," n.d., World Peace Day Records, SCPC.

16. Parker, "Join the March of Peace on World Peace Day 1948 (August 6th)"; Tanimoto, 186–87.

17. Ubuki, 14–16; Wittner, *One World or None*, 49; "No Moa Hiroshimazu [No More Hiroshimas]," *Chugoku Shimbun*, August 7, 1948, 1; Parker, "World Peace Day Committee—No More Hiroshima Movement."

18. Wittner, *One World or None*, 49; Ubuki, 18–19; Tanimoto, 187–88; *Chugoku Shimbun*, August 7, 1949, 2.

19. Parker's name was frequently mentioned in *Chugoku Shimbun* as the promoter of the World Peace Day movement. *Chugoku Shimbun*, August 2, 1948, 1; August 6, 1949, 1; August 18, 1949, 1. *Chugoku Shimbun* of July 31, 1949 carries a column introducing his personal history with a title "A Light for Humanity and Peace" and a photograph of his face; Toyobumi Ogura, "Jindo heiwa no hi—no

moa hiroshimazu no shudosha paka-shi sugao," *Chugoku Shimbun*, July 31, 1949, 4.

20. Quoted in Tanimoto, 189–90. Translated by the author.

21. Robbie Lieberman, *The Strangest Dream: Communism, Anticommunism, and the U.S. Peace Movement, 1945–1963* (Syracuse, N.Y.: Syracuse University Press, 2000), 88–92; Wittner, *One World or None*, 182–83; Ubuki, 19–23.

22. Henry Usborne, "The Crusade for World Government," *Bulletin of the Atomic Scientists* 3 (December 1947): 359–60; Wesley T. Wooley, *Alternatives to Anarchy: American Supranationalism Since World War II* (Bloomington: Indiana University Press, 1988), 53–54; Alfred Parker, "5th Anniversary of Hiroshima," n.d., Series B-10, Records of War Resisters League [hereafter cited as WRL], SCPC; Alfred Parker, "World Constituent Assembly (People's World Convention) December 30, 1950," 15 November 1950, Series B-10, Records of WRL, SCPC; "A Call to Be Read Out and Published on Hiroshima Day," 1950, Series B-10, Records of WRL, SCPC. *Chugoku Shimbun* of August 6, 1952 carries Parker's message to Hiroshima citizens, along with Pearl Buck, Norman Cousins, and other Americans who helped Hiroshima's rehabilitation; *Chugoku Shimbun*, August 6, 1952, 2.

23. As for the detailed account of commemoration of the Hiroshima bombing conducted by those pacifists, see Rieko Asai, "Commemoration of Hiroshima Day in the Antinuclear Weapons Movement in the United States, 1950–1955: The Case of the Fellowship of Reconciliation," *The Tsuda Review* 46 (November 2001): 1–26.

24. Hiroshima 1950 Committee, "Call to Observe Hiroshima Day—August 6," June 1950, Series B-10, Records of WRL, SCPC.

25. Ibid.

26. Hiroshima 1950 Committee, "For Immediate Release—Religious Observances, Demonstrations to Mark Hiroshima Day," 6 August 1950, Subseries A-4, Box 3, Records of Fellowship of Reconciliation [hereafter cited as FOR], SCPC; Preston King Sheldon, "Prayers Will Note Bomb Anniversary," *The New York Times*, August 5, 1950, 16; "Group Here Marks Date of Hiroshima," *The New York Times*, August 7, 1950, 17.

27. Letter from A. J. Muste to the members of the FOR, September 5, 1950, Subseries A-4, Box 3, Records of FOR, SCPC.

28. Lawrence S. Wittner, *Resisting the Bomb: A History of the World Nuclear Disarmament Movement, 1954–1970* (Stanford, Calif.: Stanford University Press, 1997), 1–3.

29. Bennett, 190–91.

30. Rodney Baker, *The Hiroshima Maidens: The Story of Twenty-Five Remarkable Women and Their Heroic Journey to America* (New York: Viking Penguin, 1985).

31. "Hiroshima Bomb Condemned by 40," *The New York Times*, August 1, 1955, 9; "Use of A-Bomb Condemned; Group Notes Tenth Anniversary of Bombing of Hiroshima," *The New York Times*, August 3, 1955, 22; "Nation's Repentance For Hiroshima Asked," *Fellowship*, September 1955, 23; "Hiroshima Day," June 1955, Subseries A-4, Box 3, Records of FOR, SCPC; Pamphlet, "If She Were YOUR Little Girl," 1954, Subseries A-5, Box 3, Records of FOR, SCPC;" FOR-AFSC Cosponsor Hiroshima Service," *Fellowship*, November 1955, 24; "Urey, Tugwell Make Pleas for Peace at Atomic Site," *Chicago Daily News*, August 6, 1955, 4; "A-War Would Imperil World, Urey Says in Hiroshima Rite," *Chicago Sun-Times*, August 7, 1955, 12; "Open Letter to Hiroshima Sent by New York FOR," *Fellowship*, October 1955, 24; "F.O.R. Gets Unique Japanese Movie," *Fellowship*, February 1955, 21. For the detailed account of the public meeting held by Chicago FOR, see Rieko Asai, "*Semegiau Hiroshima no kioku: 1955 nen Shikago ni okeru Hiroshima gembaku toka bi no kinen shukai to sono shimbun hodo o meguru ichi-kosatsu* [Contesting Memories of Hiroshima: The Commemoration of the 10th Anniversary of the Hiroshima Bombing in Chicago and Its News Coverage]," *Rikkyo American Studies* 26 (March 2004): 111–28.

32. Roy Finch to members of the WRL, August 1956, Series BIII, Box B3, Records of WRL, SCPC; "A-Bomb is Protested: Pacifists Picket in Rain and Commiserate with Japanese," *The New York Times*, August 7, 1956, 5.

33. Charles R. Lawrence, "Letter to President Eisenhower," August 1, 1956, Subseries A-4, Box 3, Records of FOR, SCPC; FOR, "Cable to Premier Nikolai Bulganin," August 3, 1956, Subseries A-4, Box 3, Records of FOR, SCPC; A. J. Muste, "Anniversary of Hiroshima-Nagasaki," a circulation among members of the organization, July 1956, Subseries A-4, Box 3, Records of FOR, SCPC; FOR, News Release "Stop H-Tests in Pacific, U.S. Peace Leader Urges Ike. Also Cables Bulganin on H-Tests," August 5, 1956, Subseries A-4, Box 3, Records of FOR, SCPC.

34. Lawrence.

35. Divine, 120–29; Wittner, *Resisting the Bomb*, 37–39.

36. Bennett, 207–16; Maurice Isserman, *If I Had a Hammer . . . : The Death of Old Left and the Birth of New Left* (New York: Basic Books, 1987), 144–45; Dee Garrison, "'Our Skirts Gave them Courage': The Civil Defense Protest Movement in New York City, 1955–1961," in *Not June Cleaver: Women and Gender in Postwar America, 1945–1960*, ed. Joanne Meyerowitz, (Philadelphia: Temple University Press, 1994), 201–10.

37. Bennett, 226–27; Neil H. Katz, "Radical Pacifism and the Contemporary American Peace Movement: The Committee for Non-Violent Action, 1957–1967," (PhD diss., University of Maryland, 1974), 36–37; Milton S. Katz and Neil H. Katz, "Pragmatists and Visionaries in the Post-World War II American Peace Movement: SANE and CNVA," in Solomon Wanks, ed., *Doves and Diplomats: Foreign Offices and Peace Movements in Europe and America in the Twentieth Century* (Westport, Conn.: Greenwood, 1978), 267.

38. Ibid., 275–77.

39. Milton Katz, 21–25.

40. Ibid., 26–29; Wittner, *Resisting the Bomb*, 52–53.

41. Katz and Katz, 265–66.

42. "Pickets Here Seek Nuclear Test Halt," *The New York Times*, August 7, 1957, 24.

43. *The New York Times*, August 7, 1957, 4; Boyer "Exotic Resonances," 150.

44. Wittner, *Resisting the Bomb*, 10; "Petition Urge End of Bomb Tests," *Washington Post*, July 26, 1957, C19.

45. WILPF, News Release to *The New York Times*, August 6, 1957, Sec. II, Series A6, Box 3, Records of Women's International League for Peace and Freedom, U.S. Section [hereafter cited as WILPF], SCPC.

46. Letter from Annalee Stewart to the Ambassador of the Japanese Embassy, July 10, 1957, Section II, Series A6, Box 3, Records of WILPF, SCPC; Letter from Stewart to Yoshio Hatano, July 12, 1957, Section II, Series A6, Box 3, Records of WILPF, SCPC; Letter from Hatano to Stewart, July 23, 1957, Section II, Series A6, Box 3, Records of WILPF, SCPC; Letter from Stewart to Hatano, July 30, 1957, Section II, Series A6, Box 3, Records of WILPF, SCPC.

47. Eileen Summers, "Japanese Envoy Tells Women Don't Voice Regret for Hiroshima Bombing," *Washington Post*, August 7, 1957, D3.

48. Michael Shaller, *Altered States: The United States and Japan Since the Occupation* (New York: Oxford University Press, 1997), 127–33.

49. *Four Lights*, 17: 4 (October 1957). Local chapters of the WILPF often held observance in their communities upon Hiroshima Day.

50. Bennett, 226–27.

51. NVAANW, "A Call to Non-Violent Action Against Nuclear Weapons," 1957, Series VI, Box 11, Records of the Committee for Nonviolent Action [hereafter cited as CNVA], SCPC.

52. Ibid.; NVAANW, "A Statement to Those Who Share Our Concern," 1957, Series VI, Box 11, Records of CNVA, SCPC; Lawrence Scott, "Reason and Morality: Requisites for Human Civilization," n.d., Series VI, Box 11, Records of CNVA, SCPC.

53. Bennett, 227; "Atom Site Guarded Against Protesters," *The New York Times*, August 6, 1957, 2; Gladwin Hill, "11 Pacifists Held in Atom Protest: Group Opposed to Testing of Nuclear Weapons Tries to Enter A.E.C. Grounds," *The New York Times*, August 7, 1957.

54. Neil Katz, "The Committee for Non-Violent Action," 42–43; Bennett, 228.

55. Isserman, 150; *Capital* (Madison) *Times*, August 6, 1957; *Journal* (Neb.), August 6, 1957; Katz and Katz, 278.

56. *Newsletter of SANE-Greater New York*, August 1958, Series I, Box 2, Records of SANE, SCPC; Baker, 160–65, 192–94.

57. Nimoto quoted in *Newsletter of SANE-Greater New York*, 2.

58. Ibid.

59. Ibid.

60. Ibid.

61. "Marchers Honor A-Bomb Survivor: Floral Tribute to Hiroshima Woman Here Protests Nuclear Weapons," *The New York Times*, August 7, 1958, 2; Meyer Berger, "About New York: a Young Woman Who Was a Schoolgirl in Hiroshima Tells of Aug. 6, 1945," *The New York Times*, August 6, 1958, 51; "Hiroshima Anniversary Is Marked," *The New York Times*, August 7, 1959, 2.

62. Hiroshima Day Coordinating Committee, Greater New York Committee of the National Committee for A Sane Nuclear Policy, "Project Memo," July 11, 1960, Box B-13, Records of WRL, SCPC; Greater New York Committee of the National Committee for A Sane Nuclear Policy, "For release Thursday, July 28, 1960—SANE Release No. 3," July 24, 1960, Box B-13, Records of WRL, SCPC.

63. Donald Keys, "Hiroshima Day 1961," 1961, Series B-5, Box 40, Records of SANE, SCPC; Donald Keys, "Hiroshima Day, 1962," 1962, Series B-5, Box 40, Records of SANE, SCPC.

64. As for the detailed account of commemoration of the Hiroshima and Nagasaki bombings in the 1980s, see Rieko Asai, "Commemoration of Hiroshima and Nagasaki Days in the United States: A Preliminary Comparison, 1980 and 1985," *Theory of Information Culture* 7 (December 2006): 74–90.

CONTRIBUTORS

Rieko Asai is an associate professor at Kokugakuin University, Tokyo, Japan, where she mainly teaches English language. She works primarily on the history of the American peace movement in the twentieth century. Her writings include *"Semegiau hiroshima no kioku: 1955 nenn shikago ni okeru Hiroshima gennbaku touka bi no kinenn shuukai to sono shinnbunn houdou wo meguru ichi kousatsu* [Contesting Memories of Hiroshima: The Commemoration of the 10th Anniversary of the Hiroshima Bombing in Chicago and Its News Coverage]" [Rikkyo American Studies 26 (2004)]; "Commemoration of Hiroshima and Nagasaki Days in the United States: A Preliminary Comparison, 1980 and 1985" [Theory of Information Culture 7 (2006)]; and *"Gennbaku to amerika no hannkaku undo: 8 gatsu 6 ka no kinenn katsudo wo chuushinn ni* [The Bomb and the U.S. Antinuclear Movement; Commemoration of August 6th]" [Kokugakuin Zasshi CVII, 12 (2006)].

Scott H. Bennett is an associate professor of history at Georgian Court University in Lakewood, New Jersey. He holds a Ph.D. from Rutgers University. At Georgian Court, he teaches courses on modern American history, peace history, and nonviolent social movements. He has published and spoken widely on peace history, radical pacifism, nonviolent social movements, and World War II conscientious objectors. He has written *Radical Pacifism: The War Resisters League and Gandhian Nonviolence in America, 1915–1923* (Syracuse, N.Y.: Syracuse Studies on Peace and Conflict Resolution [Syracuse University Press], 2003) and edited *Army GI, Pacifist CO: The World War II Letters of Frank and Albert Dietrich* (New York: Fordham University Press, 2005). He is completing a book manuscript on the lives and World War II prison letters of radical pacifist siblings Igal and Vivien Roodenko. He is president of the Peace History Society.

J. **Garry Clifford** is a professor of political science at the University of Connecticut and director of its graduate program. He earned his B.A. from Williams College (1964) and his Ph.D. from Indiana University. He has also taught at the University of Tennessee and Dartmouth College. For his book *The Citizen Soldiers* (Lexington: University Press of Kentucky, 1972), he won the Frederick Jackson Turner Award of the Organization of American Historians. With Norman Cousins, he has edited *Memoirs of a Man: Grenville Clark* (New York: W. W. Norton, 1975); and with Samuel R. Spencer, Jr., he has written *The First Peacetime Draft* (Lawrence: University Press of Kansas, 1986). With Thomas G. Paterson, Kenneth J. Hagan, Deborah Kisatsky, and Shane Maddock, he coauthored *American Foreign Relations: A History* (Boston: Houghton Mifflin, 7th. ed., 2009). With Theodore A. Wilson, he edited *Presidents, Diplomats, and Other Mortals: Essays in Honor of Robert H. Ferrell* (Columbia: University of Missouri Press, 2007). His essays have also appeared in Gordon Martel, ed., *American Foreign Relations Reconsidered* (New York: Routledge, 1994); Michael J. Hogan and Thomas G. Paterson, eds., *Explaining the History of American Foreign Relations* (New York: Cambridge University Press, 1991 and 2004); and Arnold A. Offner and Theodore A. Wilson, eds., *Victory in Europe, 1945* (Lawrence: University Press of Kansas, 2000). He has served on the editorial board of *Diplomatic History* as well as on the editorial board of the Modern War Series of the University Press of Kansas.

A graduate of Bowling Green University and veteran of World War II, **Robert H. Ferrell** received his M.A. and Ph.D. from Yale University under the direction of Samuel Flagg Bemis. From 1953 until his retirement in 1988 he taught U.S. diplomatic history at Indiana University, where he mentored more than thirty-five Ph.D. students of his own. Beginning with *Peace in Their Time* (1952), which won the George Louis Beer Prize of the American Historical Association, Ferrell has published more than sixty books, most notably *American Diplomacy in the Great Depression* (1957), *The Teaching of American History in the High Schools* (1964), *Dear Bess* (1983), *Woodrow Wilson and World War I* (1985), *Harry S. Truman: A Life* (1995), *The Dying President* (1998), and *America's Deadliest Battle: The Meuse-Argonne, 1918* (2007). He has served as president of the Society for Historians of American Foreign Relations. He currently lives in Ann Arbor, Michigan.

Justin Hart is an assistant professor of history at Texas Tech University. He earned a Ph.D. in history at Rutgers University under the direction of Lloyd Gardner. He is the author of "Archibald MacLeish Rediscovered: The Poetry of U.S. Foreign Policy" [*Historically Speaking* (January/February 2007)] and "Making Democracy Safe for the World: Race, Propaganda, and the Transformation of U.S. Foreign Policy During World War II" [*Pacific Historical Review* (February 2004)]. He is the winner of the W. Turrentine Jackson Prize from the Pacific Coast Branch of the American Historical Association and the James Madison Prize from the Society for History in the Federal Government. He is presently completing a book manuscript entitled *Empire of Ideas: Propaganda, Culture, and Image in U.S. Foreign Policy, 1936–1953*.

Nicholas D. Molnar is a doctoral student in history at Rutgers University, New Brunswick, New Jersey, and a staff member of the Rutgers Oral History Archives of World War II. He graduated from Rutgers College in 2005 with a bachelor's degree, magna cum laude, and highest honors in history, and received the sole Bevier Award Fellowship granted by Rutgers University that year. His chapter originated as a Henry Rutgers Senior Honors Thesis under the direction of Professor John Whiteclay Chambers II.

Sidney Pash is an assistant professor of history at Fayetteville State University, where he teaches courses in U.S., world, and East Asian history. He earned his Ph.D. in 2001 from Rutgers University, where he specialized in interwar U.S.–Japanese diplomatic relations. His most recent works have appeared in the *Journal of the North Carolina Association of Historians, The New England Journal of History*, and in José de Arimatéia da Cruz, Becky K. da Cruz, and Andrew J. Dowdle, eds., *American Politics: Transformation and Change* (Upper Saddle River, N.J.: Pearson, 2004).

Ann Pfau is a research associate at the New York State Museum. Her book *Miss Yourlovin: GIs, Gender, and Domesticity During World War II* was published by Columbia University Press (New York) in 2008 and is available online at www.gutenberg-e.org/pfau.

G. Kurt Piehler is author of *Remembering War the American Way* (Smithsonian Institution Press, 1995; reprint ed., 2004), author of *World War II* (American Soldiers' Lives Series, Westport, Conn.: Greenwood Press,

2007), and co-editor of *Major Problems in American Military History* (Boston: Houghton Mifflin, 1999). He is consulting editor for the *Oxford Companion to American Military History* (New York: Oxford University Press, 1999) and associate editor of *Americans at War: Society, Culture, and the Homefront* (New York: Macmillan Reference/Gale, 2005). His articles have appeared in the *History of Education Quarterly, Journal of the Rutgers University Libraries,* and the anthology *Commemorations: The Politics of National Identity* (Princeton, N.J.: Princeton University Press, 1994). As founding director (1994–98) of the Rutgers Oral History Archives of World War II, Piehler conducted more than 200 interviews with veterans of this conflict.

Yutaka Sasaki is a professor of American history at Soai University, Osaka, Japan. He studied at Keio University, Tokyo (A.B. 1983, M.A. 1985), at Brown University (M.A., 1989), and at Rutgers University (Ph.D., 2005). His dissertation, "The Struggle for Scholarly Objectivity: Unofficial Diplomacy and The Institute of Pacific Relations from the Sino–Japanese War to the McCarthy Era," was written under the guidance of Professor John W. Chambers. His previous publications include "U.S.–Japan Nonprofit Exchanges as Cultural Interaction: The Emerging Role of Nonprofit Organizations as Agents of Cultural Transmission and Transformation," in Takeshi Matsuda, ed., *The Age of Creolization in the Pacific: In Search of Emerging Cultures and Shared Values in the Japan–America Borderlands* (Hiroshima: Keisuisha, 2001); "The Rockefeller Foundation and the Institute of Pacific Relations: An Analysis of Their Entangled Relationships in the Early Cold War Years," *American Review* 37 (2003) [in Japanese]; and "Post-War Settlements Vis-à-vis Japan in the Council on Foreign Relations' War and Peace Studies," in Sugita Yoneyuki, ed., *An Analysis of American Diplomacy: Historical Development and the Current State of Affairs* (Okayama: Daigaku-kyoiku Publishing Co., 2008) [in Japanese].

Mark A. Snell is an associate professor of history and director of The George Tyler Moore Center for the Study of the Civil War at Shepherd University in Shepherdstown, West Virginia. He is a retired army officer who also taught U.S. history at West Point. Dr. Snell is the author or editor of four books, the most recent of which is *Unknown Soldiers: The American Expeditionary Forces in Memory and Remembrance* (Kent, Ohio: Kent State University Press, 2008). He holds a Ph.D. in history and public administration from the University of Missouri, Kansas City. In 2008 he was the visiting senior lecturer of War Studies at the Royal Military Academy, Sandhurst.

Barbara Brooks Tomblin received a B.A. from Scripps College in Claremont, California, and her M.A. and Ph.D. in American history from Rutgers University. She taught history at Middlesex County College, Morris County College, and the College of St. Elizabeth's weekend school in New Jersey and was a lecturer in American military history at Rutgers University in New Brunswick, New Jersey. She is the author of *G.I. Nightingales: The Army Nurse Corps in World War II* (Lexington: University Press of Kentucky, 1996) and *With Utmost Spirit: Allied Naval Operations in the Mediterranean 1942–45* (Lexington: University Press of Kentucky, 2004) and the forthcoming *Bluejackets and Contrabands: African Americans and the Union Navy* (Lexington: University Press of Kentucky).

INDEX

Civil Rights Movement, 263–64, 267, 345; conscientious objectors protest segregation, 273–77, 282

Civil War, U.S., 144, 217–18, 220–21

Civilian Conservation Corps, 268

Civilian Public Service Camps (CPS), 6, 101, 260, 268–74, 336, 347; at Big Flats, New York, 290n20; conscientious objectors disillusionment with, 265; divisions within, 268; peace churches support, 266

Clancy, Jerry, 160

Clark, Bennett C., 22

Clark, D. Worth, 22

Clark, Grenville, 18, 23

Clark, Miriam, 22

Clarke, A. W., 297

Clink, The (newspaper), 275

clothing, 226, 253, 337

Coe, Frank, 297

Coast Guard, U.S., 5, 6, 236

Coast Guard (book), 6

Coast Guard Academy, U.S., 238–39, 254

Coast Guard Receiving Center, 254

Coffman, Edward M., 224

Cold War: and commemoration of atomic bombing of Hiroshima, 8, 335, 339–40, 342; diplomatic engagement during, 46; impact of Japanese–U.S. relations, 294; impact of nuclear weapons on course of, 53; impact on U.S. policy toward decolonization and desegregation, 95–96n30; integration of military during, 228; propaganda campaigns during, 3, 69, 82; writing military history during, 217

Cole, Hugh M., 222

Cole, William B., 251, 254

Collier's (magazine), 130

Collins, Lawton, 151, 152

Columbia University, 224, 297, 314, 315

Commerce Department, 44

Committee for Amnesty, 280–81

Committee to Defend America by Aiding the Allies, 18, 19

Committee for Non-Violent Action (CNVA), 346

Compass, The (magazine), 271

Congress, U.S.: approves 18-month extension of service, 25–26; approves National Defense Act, 44–45; attitude toward economic warfare, 43–44; characterized, 28; and civilian and military authority over CPS camps, 272; and convoys in Atlantic, 2, 18, 30; cuts OWI budget, 90; Elmer Davis appears before, 78–79; and FDR's actions in 1941, 29–30; FDR's lack of mastery of, 13, 23; holds hearing on increasing dependency allowances, 99, 102; information not provided by FDR, 10; investigates attack on Pearl Harbor, 59–60; isolationist members in, 17, 24; lobbied on conscription issue, 262; opponents of convoys in Atlantic, 21–22; passes Starnes Amendment, 270–71; provides more liberal provisions for conscientious objectors, 265, 281; submits statement to, 96n32

Congress of Racial Equality (CORE), 6, 264, 282

Connally, Tom, 24

Connecticut State Hospital, 282

Conolly, Richard, 180, 184, 211n53

Conscientious Objector (journal), 264

conscription: FOR and WRL stage simulated draft board tribunals, 263;

Dulles, Allen W., 328n39, 329n42
Duluth, Minnesota, 125n42
Dumas, Alexander, 107
Durgin, E. R., 182
Dutch East Indies: defense of, 52; supports American embargo of Japan, 46
Dykstra, Clarence, 266

E-boat, 5, 150, 173, 189, 196–97, 210–11n50, 214n70, 244
Eagle (Coast Guard training vessel), 254
East Indies, 60
Eastern Naval Task Force, 243
Easton, Jane, 106
Eaton, Jean, 115
Eaton, Walter, 114, 115–17
Eberle (destroyer), 176
Edison (destroyer), 185
Egypt, 12
Eighth Air Force (8th), 163
Eighty-Second Airborne Division (82), 240
Eisenhower Center, 224
Eisenhower, Dwight D., 86, 172, 344, 350; appoints Forrest Pogue as historian of SHAEF, 223; detailed to American Battle Monuments Commission, 218; planning for Operation Overlord, 207n34, 207n35
Eisenhower, Milton, 86
Elder, Glen H., Jr., 111, 118
Eliot, George F., 311, 312
Embracing Defeat (book), 7, 293
Emerson, Ruppert, 297
Emmet, Robert, 177, 209n42
Emmons, USS, 159, 160, 161, 169, 171, 203n17, 206n31
Empire Javelin (LSI), 164, 165
engineers, army, 247

England: U.S. Coast Guard deployment to, 241; wounded ferried to, 252
English Channel, 159, 190, 242
Enola Gay (airplane), controversy surrounding, 333, 359
Enterprise, HMS, 151, 152
environmental movement, 282
Erebus, HMS, 151, 202n13
ESPN (cable television network), 144, 149n80
Essary, Helen, 32n16
Ethiopia, 53, 89
Everson, William, 271

Falmouth, 242
Family Guy (television show), 144, 149n74
Far Eastern Survey (journal), 297
Farmer, James, 264
Farmer, Victor, 297
Farquharson, Mary, 263, 264
Farrar, Arthur, 239, 241, 242
Fearey, Robert, 298, 299, 307, 326n13
Federal Bureau of Investigation (FBI), 24, 264
Federation of Atomic Scientists, 335
Feis, Hebert, 44
Fellows, Taylor, 165
Fellowship (journal), 264
Fellowship of Reconciliation (FOR), 336; absolute pacifist position of, 262; advocates nonviolent methods, 261; commemoration of Hiroshima bombing, 8, 341, 343; encourages peace action, 263; members often absolutist conscientious objectors, 268, 271–72; protests civil defense drill, 345–46; protests organized by, 348–49; role in World War II, 6
Field, Frederick V., 297

fatigue, 230; quality of troops defending Utah Beach, 202*n*14; records regarding Rommel, 225; U.S. troops compared with soldiers from, 141

German Navy, sinks LSTs off Slapton Sands, 241

Germany: alliance with Japan, 48–49, 54, 56; behavior of American troops in, 109; declares war against U.S., 260; defenses at Normandy, 5, 246–47; defenses at Utah Beach, 152; deports German Jews to East, 29; effort by U.S. to encourage defection of ambassador, 74; efforts to deny raw materials to, 44; firing first shot, 20; gains in 1941, 12; infantry officer stationed in, 106; portrayed in *Why We Fight* documentary, 230–31; prisoners of war from, 217; propaganda regarding race, 83; state of relations with Japan, 46; treatment of shell shock in World War I, 229; Versailles Treaty imposed on, 262; war against Soviet Union, 2, 24, 28, 30, 40, 45, 49–50, 60

Gerow, Leonard T., 56, 164, 171

Gibbons, Joseph H., 166, 204–5*n*23

Gibraltar, 6, 188, 213*n*68, 240

Giguerre, Robert, 205*n*26

Gilbert, H. N., 100

Girard, William S., 350–51

Gislason, Gene R., 244, 249–50, 253

Glasgow (HMS), 151, 159, 160, 206*n*32

Glendora, California, 265

Glennon, 197, 201*n*11, 211*n*51

Gneisenau (German cruiser), 27

Goebbels, Josef, 81

Goodrich, Carter, 315

Gottschalk, Louis, 224

Great Britain: assessment of chances of war against Japan, 60; and the Battle of the Atlantic, 11; and control over Japanese Mandate Islands, 315; differs with U.S. on economic future for Japan, 303; ends alliance with Japan, 40; executes soldiers for desertion in World War I, 229; fights Germany alone, 48; future U.S. ambassador to, 25; impact of German–Soviet War on, 49–50; military situation of, 58–59; more conservative on planning for postwar Japan, 307; naval forces participating in Operation Neptune, 199*n*2; and nuclear testing, 344–45; Pogue interviews military leaders from, 223; position on retention of Japanese Imperial institutions, 304–5; possible German invasion of, 2; represented at Hot Springs conference, 7, 296, 297, 299, 300–1; Senator Tobey's position on aid to, 21; setbacks in 1941, 12; supports economic measures against Japan, 46; treatment of soldiers during Napoleonic wars, 220; U.S. commitments to, 28–30; and U.S. propaganda, 84; U.S. provides Lend-Lease to, 10; war hawks in FDR cabinet seek greater support for, 18

Great Depression, 43, 117, 259

Greece, 12

Green, Jimmy, 164, 165, 169, 204*n*22

Green, Joseph C., 310, 311, 317, 332*n*77

Greenland, 11, 16, 19

Greer, USS, 28

Grew, Joseph: praises work of WPS group, 320; response to Japanese seizure of Manchuria, 41; supports

efforts by U.S. Army to document, 216–19, 221–24; Roosevelt's view of, 27, 36n83; of Sherman tank, 129, 142–43; views of American propaganda efforts, 66

Hitler, Adolf, 19, 53, 153, 225; actions prod Japanese to occupy French Indochina, 11; blames Jews for war, 37n92; compared to Japanese Emperor, 318; implications of victory by, 88; invades Soviet Union, 28; invasion of Russia, 19; orders transport of German Jews east, 29; pacifist attitudes toward, 261–62; plot to assassinate, 74; quest for world domination, 10; refuses to allow laying of pressure mines, 191, 214n70; Sieg Heil salute, 15; unlikely to retaliate immediately, 30

Hoffman, George Dewey, 154–55, 200–1n8

Holocaust, 29, 230

Hoover, Herbert, 20, 41, 43, 52

Hopi Indians, 267

Hopkins, Harry, 15, 17, 18

Hornbeck, Stanley: assessment of Japanese intentions, 49; doubts effectiveness of Japanese–American diplomacy, 52; minimizes threat of war, 58; reports to Hull on German reactions to negotiations with Japan, 51; seeks to draw out negotiations with Japan, 48; seeks tougher stance in negotiations with Japan, 50; sees U.S. prepared for war in Pacific, 55; and U.S. role in Sino–Japanese relations 41–42, 47

Hoshino, Naoki, 45

hospitals, 269, 282

Hot Springs, Virginia, 296

Hot Springs Conference, 7, 296–307, 322, 326n9, 328n31

House Appropriations Committee, 90

House Foreign Affairs Committee, 23

House Naval Affairs Committee, 43

House of Representatives, U.S., 25

Houser, George, 264

Howes, Davis C., 161, 169

Hu, Shih, 306

Huebner, C. R., 159, 215n75

Hughan, Jessie Wallace, 260

Hull, Cordell: assessment of Japanese actions, 40; attends war cabinet meeting, 17; attitudes toward OWI, 68–69, 92–93n3; character of, 25; clashes with OWI, 89; compliments work of WPS Group, 320; fears naval clashes in Atlantic, 12; influence of Hornbeck on, 42; movement of fleet from Pearl Harbor, 18; negotiations with Nomura, 28, 48–49, 50–51, 57–60; and proposal of Harry Dexter White, 56; and repeal of Neutrality Act, 26; role in shaping public opinion, 3n97; seeks to avoid negotiations with Japan, 41, 46–47, 55, 65n26; speech on naval patrols, 14; supports internationalism, 81; views on convoy policy, 16

humanitarian relief, overseas, 270–71

Hurley, Anne, 110

Hurley, Patrick, 25

Husky, Operation, 174, 178–79, 181–82, 186, 189, 192, 194, 195, 197, 209–10n45, 213n68, 240

Hussein, Saddam, 236

Huston, John, 230

Hutchinson, George, 251–52, 253

Hyde Park, New York, 12

hydrogen bomb, 339, 340, 342, 345, 349

Johnstone, William C., 297, 298–99, 305

Joint Chiefs of Staff, 77

Joseph T. Dickman (USS), 243

Juggler, The (book), 2

Justice Department, 267

juvenile delinquency, 100

Kampelman, Max, 291*n*24

Kapp Putsch, 261

Kawada, Isao, 45

Keegan, John, 229

Keeler, Owen F., 170

Keen, Grace, 107

Keenleyside, H. L., 298

Kelly, Monroe, 178

Kennan, George, 71

Kennedy, David M., 11

Kentucky, 275

Kepler, Roy, 290*n*21

Kesselring, Albert, 187

Key West, Florida, 239

Keys, Donald, 356

Kimball, Warren F., 2

Kimmel, Husband E., 14

King, Ernest J., 151

King, Fred, 152, 153–54, 200*n*7, 202*n*12

King, Martin Luther, Jr., 264

King, W. L. Mackenzie, 27

Kirk, Alan G., 172–73, 203*n*18, 206–7*n*33, 242–43

Kirk, Grayson, 297, 314–15, 332*n*84

Kishi, Nobusuke, 350–51

Knox, Frank: characterized as secondary leader to FDR, 37*n*97; and the convoy question, 17–19, 21–22; favors hard line with Japan, 56; meets with FDR, 59; seeks to enlist support of Alf Landon, 10–11; serves in FDR's cabinet, 15, 25

Konoe, Fumimaro, 46, 48–51, 54, 60, 65*n*26

Korea, 325*n*5

Korean War, 223, 342, 347

Kramer, Milton, 275

Kramer, Saul, 106

Kramer et al. v. U.S. (1945), 272

Kreider, Robert, 270

Krock, Arthur, 89–90

Kroner, Hayes, 52

Kunzru, H. N., 298

Kupper, Herbert, 107–8

Kurusu, Saburo, 57

Kwajalein, 207*n*219

Ladies Home Journal (magazine), 107, 108

Lafollette, Robert, Jr., 22

Lakeshore Avenue Baptist Church (Oakland, California), 337, 338

Lamont, Thomas W., 16

Landing Craft, Vehicle and Personnel (LCVP), 237, 246, 254

Landing Craft Assault (LCA), 237

Landing Craft Infantry (LCI), 6, 237, 238, 239, 240, 241, 244, 245, 246; commander of, 249–50

Landing Ship Tank (LST), 238, 244; launch tanks on D-Day, 246; in Mediterranean armed with 40mm Bofors guns, 196; modification of bow doors, 241

Landon, Alfred, 10–11, 19

Langdon, Walter, 55

LaRoche, Chester J., 81

Las Vegas, Nevada, 352

Lattimore, Owen, 297, 305–6, 328*n*31, 332*n*84

Laub, 192

Lawrence, Charles, 344

Lazarus, Frieda, 280

McCloy, John J., 23, 218, 289–90n18, 329n42
McCook (destroyer), 160, 161, 169, 171, 172
McCoy, Frank R., 297, 311–12, 329n42, 332n84
McCreery, R., 182
McFadyean, Andrew, 297
McIntyre, Marvin, 23
McNary, Charles, 24
Maddox (destroyer), 180, 210n48
Mainz, Germany, 133
Makin, Battle of, 219, 221
malaria, 270
Malaya, 45, 52, 58, 60
Mallory, Walter H., 308, 328n39
Malta, 185, 210–11n50, 213n68
Manchester, William, 228
Manchuria, 40–41, 42, 56
March on Washington Movement (MOWM), 264, 282
Marianas Islands, 33n55
Mariano, John, 113
Marines, Royal, 179
Marines, U.S., 116; psychiatrist, 107; use of oral history, 223
marriage, 13; fears of unfaithful wives, 99–103; impact of returning GIs on, 108–18
Marriage in War and Peace (book), 107
Marshall, George C.: believes air power can secure Philippines, 55; biography of, 224; informs FDR on places of likely Japanese attack, 58; meets with Hull, 59; opinion surveys of American troops, 225–26; persuasive witness on Capitol Hill, 23; and possible occupation of Azores, 17; receives assessment of situation in China and Philippines, 52; sends Cortlett to advise Eisenhower and

Bradley, 207n34; supports army history, 5, 218, 219
Marshall, S. L. A.: biography of, 219; methodology and influence of, 221–23; pioneering work as combat historian, 5, 216–17
Marshall Islands, 144, 330n55, 342, 343
Martin, Joseph, 25, 36n78
Maryland, 273
Massachusetts, USS, 208–9n41, 209n44
Matsuoka, Yosuke, 12, 48
Mauldin, Bill, 221
May, Stacy, 314, 329n42
Mayers, Albert, 105
Mayo (destroyer), 187, 190
Mayrant (USS), 208–9n41
medals and decorations (U.S.), 252, 253, 279; creation of Combat Infantryman's Badge, 227; double amputee holds Silver and Bronze Star, 102
Medical Corps, Army, 279, 281
medical research, 269–70, 281
Mediterranean Theater: amphibious landings in, 174; fire support during amphibious landings, 178, 182, 193–94; lack of experience with prelanding bombardment, 191–92; lack of minesweepers, 213n68; lessons learned from, 150, 151, 157–58, 164, 170, 172–73, 175, 176, 187–88, 190, 197–99, 208n39; naval attacks against tanks, 185; naval landings in, 4–5; naval vessels lost, 189–90; outlook for British, 12; problem of air coverage, 188–89; reluctance of army commanders to agree to daylight naval bombardment, 203n16; and role of Coast Guard Flotilla 4, 240; role of smaller vessels in amphibious landings, 196; use of naval

learned from, 151, 172, 175, 193, 198–99n1; lessons ignored by Eisenhower and Bradley, 207n34; need for U.S. minesweepers in, 191; use of atabrine tablets by troops serving in, 226; writing battle histories in, 219, 222

Pacifica Radio, 282

pacifists, 259–83, 341

Page, Kirby, 261

Palomares, 189

Pan-African Congress, 95–96n30

Panama, 226

Panama Canal, 253

Pandit, L. V., 298

Park Forest, Illinois, 118

Parker, Alfred, 8, 336–40, 357

Parmer, Inderjeet, 321

Partridge (tug), 197

Pasvolsky, Leo, 320

Patterson, Robert P., 25

Patton, George S., 129, 130–35, 136–45

Patton: A Genius for War (book), 4

Pauling, Linus, 345

Pavalko, Eliza K., 111

PC-533, 196

PC-568, 161

PC-1261, 155, 159, 201–2n11

peace movement, U.S., 6, 7–8, 33, 259–83, 333–59; in Austria, 337

Peacemakers, 341; protest civil defense drill, 346

Pearce, Hap, 185

Pearl Harbor Congressional Committee, 59

Pearl Harbor, Hawaii: attack on, end "hegemonic interregnum," 93n4; deployment of fleet to, 18, 28; and impact of attack on American politics, 10; pacifist response to attack of, 6, 260–61; supports war effort

after Pearl Harbor, 296; War Advertising Council established before Japanese attack on, 81

Peck, Jim, 270, 275, 276, 277

Pellecchia, James, 102

Penelope, HMS (cruiser), 186

Pennsylvania, 275

Peoria, Illinois, 125n42

Perret, Marvin, 237

Pershing, John J., 218

Persian Gulf War, 223

Philadelphia, USS (cruiser), 174, 180, 182, 194; collides with *Laub*, 192; fires at German land targets, 212n60; fires on a group of German tanks, 185; guided through mine field, 183; participates in Operation Torch, 194

Philadelphia, Pennsylvania: establishment of CPS camp in, 270; peace movement meeting in, 346, 347

Philippines: commemoration of Hiroshima bombing, 339; defense of, 52, 55; deployment of B-17 to, 27; and plans for postwar Japan, 300; potential of Japanese attack, 60; sacrificed early in the war, 316; U.S. forces strengthened in, 45; and White proposal, 56

photography, at D-Day, 249

Pickett, Charles, 347

Piersen, Dwight, 180

Piper Cub, 196

Pittsburgh, Pennsylvania, 125n42

Plymouth, England, 164, 206n31

pneumonia, 270

Pogue, Forrest: influence of, 5, 216, 231; interviews men later killed, 222; on Omaha Beach, 222; prepares for D-Day invasion, 224; on reliability of oral history, 224–25; writes *Supreme Command*, 223

Pointe de la Percee, 161, 206*n*29

Pointe du Hoc, 157, 161, 168, 200*n*5, 206*n*29, 224

Poland, 46, 243

Popular Science (magazine), 130

Port Arthur, 39

Port en Bassin, 171

Port Lyautey, 240

Portent (minesweeper), 189

Portugal, 37*n*91

postage stamps, 144, 149*n*76

Powell, Robert E., 154, 201*n*9

Powellsville, Maryland, 271, 273

Pratt, Julius, 317–19, 331*n*65, 332*n*77

Price, Paton, 278

Prince Charles, HMS, 164

Pringle, Henry, 86

prison, federal, 6, 274–78, 280–81, 347

prisoners of war, 112, 217

Psychiatric Primer for the Veteran's Family and Friends (book), 107

psychiatry, military, 105, 228–30

public opinion, 81, 120*n*7; and the convey question, 2; efforts by FDR to gauge, 13–14; favors firm stand against Japan, 53; isolationists seek to influence, 17; surveying American soldiers, 227–28; use of Gallup and Roper polls to measure it, 97*n*34

Puerto Rico, 267

Pulitzer Prize, 74, 86

Pyle, Ernie, 221

Quakers, 260, 263, 264, 336; contribute support to CPS, 266; countering Nazi propaganda, 83; proposals for occupation of Japan, 302, 330*n*48; serve in army and navy, 262

Queens College, Oxford, 77

Quincy, USS, 151, 152–53, 155, 157, 199*n*4, 200*n*5, 200*n*6, 200*n*7, 200–1*n*8, 202*n*12

radar, 160, 162–63, 181, 188, 189, 200*n*5, 208*n*39, 208–9*n*41, 209–10*n*45, 217

Ramsay, Bertram H., 172, 173, 190–91, 193, 207*n*34, 207–8*n*35, 214*n*70, 242

Randolph, A. Philip, 264

Ranger, USS (aircraft carrier), 188

Rangers, U.S. Army, 157, 161, 210*n*49, 245

Rankin, Jeannette, 17

Reagan, Ronald, 23, 358, 359

Reardon, Carol, 218

reconnaissance, aerial, 150

Red Army, 49, 59

Red Sea, 11, 20

refugees, 337

religion: FDR's possible prejudices, 21; motivation for conscientious objection, 274–75; overseas relief efforts of peace churches, 270; parish priest comments on behavior of war widows, 104–5; peace churches compromise on opposition to Jim Crow, 273–74; peace churches and conscription, 265–67; "second mile" principle for Christians, 271; and the treatment of postwar Japan, 317–18; vessels fire at church steeple, 171

Research Branch, 226

Reynolds, David, 27

Reynolds, Robert R., 22, 24

Rhine River, 135

Rich (destroyer), 197, 215*n*77

Richards, Alfred, 183, 213*n*68

Ridder, James E., 16

Riley, Francis Xavier, 252

Robin Moor (American freighter), 20, 28

Rockefeller Foundation, 314

Rockefeller, Nelson, 71

rockets, 152, 159, 162, 163, 174, 175, 179, 182, 184, 186–87, 195; destroy beach land mines, 212n62; inflict little damage, 203–4n19; landing craft fitted for, 210n47, 211n56; role in silencing German defenses at Omaha Beach, 197; refusal to use, 214n72; smoke from, 206–7n33; use ordered at Salerno, 221n56

Rockwell, Dean L., 163–64, 204n21

Roe (destroyer), 181, 176, 192, 210–11n50

Roma, 230

Roman Catholics, 267

Rome, Italy, 10, 175

Rommel, Erwin, 12, 59, 131, 225

Roodenko, Igal, 275, 281, 290n22

Roodenko, Vivien, 280

Roodenko et al. v. U.S. (1944), 272

Roosevelt, Belle, 19

Roosevelt, Eleanor, 13, 32n16, 271, 289–90n18

Roosevelt, Franklin: appoints Elmer Davis, 77; attends meeting on Japanese policy, 60; and Badoglio government, 89–90; and the Battle of the Atlantic, 11; biography of, 87; caution of, 12–20; concerns about anti-pacifist sentiment, 268; creates COI at urging of William Donovan, 74; creates Office of War Information, 68, 76; diplomacy of, 2; escalates U.S. involvement in war, 28–30; holds press conference, 31n7, absent from White House, 32n16, assessment of convoy speech, 32n22; informed by Ambassador Johnson, 47; issues Executive Order 9066, 263; lack of candor, 10; leadership of, 91, 92, 97, issues directive on preserving historical record, 218; and negotiations with Japan, 59; opposes the Starnes Amendment, 289–90n18; political support of Southern Congressman, 88; press applauds actions against Japan, 53; pressured by A. Phillip Randolph, 264; proposed Japanese–American summit, 46, 50; public pronouncements on reasons to fight, 230; receives personal message from Konoe, 51; receives report on Hot Springs conference, 7; receives report written by Philip Jessup, 307; relationship with Congress, 21–27; sent telegraph, 260; Stimson offers views to, 56; transfer Coast Guard to Navy Department, 237

Roosevelt, Franklin, administration: creates several propaganda agencies, 70–71; criticism of OWI within, 85; policy of containment against Japan, 41; naval buildup, 43; pursues strategy of global activism, 93n4; response to Second Sino–Japanese War, 39

Roosevelt, Kermit, 19

Roosevelt, Sara, 13

Roosevelt, Theodore, 41

Roosevelt, Theodore, Jr., 156, 157

Roper, Elmo, 81

Roper Poll, 97n34

Rosenberg, Anna, 13

Rosenberg, Emily, 360n4

Rosenman, Samuel, 76

Rowan (destroyer), 185

Rozier, Charles P., 158

Ruhr Valley, 261

WORLD WAR II:
THE GLOBAL, HUMAN, AND ETHICAL DIMENSION
G. Kurt Piehler, *series editor*